BOTANY IN A DAY APG

The Patterns Method of Plant Identification
An Herbal Field Guide to Plant Families of North America
6th Edition

Dedicated to Dad
Thank you for showing me
my first edible wild plants.

HOPS Press, LLC
12 Quartz Street
Pony, Montana 59747-0697
www.hopspress.com
www.wildflowers-and-weeds.com

clasping pepperweed
Lepidium perfoliatum
Mustard Family

Botany in a Day ^{APG}
The Patterns Method of Plant Identification
An Herbal Field Guide to Plant Families of North America

Copyright: 1st Edition. Comb bound. 1996. 25 copies printed.
Revised & Expanded 2nd Edition. Comb bound. 1997. 500 copies printed.
Revised & Expanded 3rd Edition. First paperback edition. 1998. 2,000 copies printed.
Revised & Expanded 4th Edition. 2000, 2001. 12,500 copies printed.
Revised & Expanded 5th Edition. Expanded tutorial. 2004, 2006, 2008, 2010, 2012. 42,500 copies printed.
Revised & Expanded 6th Edition. APG + Color. May 2013.
ISBN: 978-1-892784-35-3

Help refine this book! Please e-mail your suggested additions, corrections, and comments to us via the current address posted on our web site at **www.hopspress.com**. I will do my best to incorporate your input into future editions.

Permissions Note: There are several pages in the book that may be freely copied for classroom or personal use, and they are marked as such. *Please do not copy any other pages.* I have worked very hard to bring you this text. If you need multiple copies, please inquire about our generous **wholesale discounts** through HOPS Press at **www.hopspress.com**.

About the Artwork: Most illustrations in this book were adapted from public domain sources listed in the bibliography. A few were drawn by the author. All edits, revisions, and arrangements of public domain images by the author are subject to copyright law. Please inquire before you use. Thanks!

Legal Note: There is a big difference between knowing the properties of plants and knowing how to apply them to the body. This guide is intended for the identification of plants and their properties only. It is *not* a field guide to the human body or how to prescribe or prepare herbal medicines. The author is not responsible for your accidents. Also keep in mind that every plant book has errors, and every person who uses a plant book makes errors. It is very important that you crosscheck the identification *and* the uses of these plants with other sources.

Publisher's Cataloging-in-Publication Data
Elpel, Thomas J. 1967-
    Botany in a Day ^{APG}: The Patterns Method of Plant Identification / Thomas J. Elpel. —6th ed.

    Includes bibliographical references and index.
    ISBN: 978-1-892784-35-3 $30.00 Pbk. (alk. paper)
    1. Plants—Identification. 2. Botany—North America. 3. Medicinal Plants. 4. Edible Plants.
    I. Elpel, Thomas J. II. Title.
    QK110.E46 2000 581.023 99-068343

Botany in a Day is printed in the USA with soy-based inks on recycled paper with 100% post-consumer waste.

Remember to recycle your papers!

HOPS Press, LLC
12 Quartz Street
Pony, MT 59747-0697
www.hopspress.com
www.wildflowers-and-weeds.com

Table of Contents

Foreword: Path of Discovery i

Region Covered ii

Part I—Botany in a Day: The Patterns Method of Plant Identification

Botany in a Day Tutorial: How to Proceed 1

Plant Names and Classification 2

Evolution of Plants 5

    A Puzzle Without all the Pieces 5

    Life Begins 6

    The Land Plants 8

        Spore Plants without a Vascular System 8

        Spore Plants with a Vascular System 9

        Naked Seeds 10

        Flowering Plants 11

        Monocots, Dicots, and Eudicots 15

        Specialized Flowers 17

        Composite Flowers: Aster Family 17

Learning Plants by Families 19

Problems in Taxonomic Paradise 22

How to Use the Keys 23

Profile Your Flower 24

    Key to Regular Dicot Flowers with Numerous Petals 25

    Key to Irregular Dicot Flowers 26

    Key to Regular Dicot Flowers with 0, 3 or 6 Petals 27

    Key to Regular Dicot Flowers with 4 Petals 28

    Key to Regular Dicot Flowers with 5 United Petals 29

    Key to Regular Dicot Flowers with 5 Separate Petals 30

    Key to Dicot Trees and Shrubs by Their Fruits 32

    Key to Monocot Flowers 34

Part II—Reference Guide: An Herbal Field Guide to Plant Families

Clubmoss Clade 38

Fern Clade 40

Naked Seed Clade 46

Flowering Plants Clade 50

    Water Lily Clade 50

    Magnolia Clade 51

    Hornwort Clade 54

    Eudicots Clade 55

        Eudicots / Rosids Clade 62

        Core Eudicots Clade 112

        Eudicots / Asterids Clade 124

    Monocots Clade 182

Medicinal Properties of Plants 210

Bibliography 223

Index of Plants by Genus 226

Index of Plants by Common Names 230

Index of Plant Families and Subfamilies by Botanical Names 234

Index of Plant Families and Subfamilies by Common Names 235

In Memory of Frank Cook
1963 - 2009

Photo by Zen Southerland.

I "knew" Frank Cook for seven or eight years via extensive email correspondence. Frank helped edit the fifth edition of *Botany in a Day*, and he used it as a guide in his plant classes around the world. Every time he would place an order for the book he would provide a new address "in care of" someone on the East coast, the West coast, or occasionally overseas.

Frank also led online discussion groups using *Botany in a Day*. I enjoyed reading his emails about getting to know the plants, and I was constantly amazed to hear about his adventures as he wandered all over the world discovering new plants and meeting new people. Frank used my book more than I have and clearly knew more about plants than I ever will. Although I never met Frank, nor spoke with him on the phone, I came to think of him as a friend.

Frank was like a grapevine, reaching out this way and that with his tendrils, making connections with people all over the world. I was one of those connections, and I felt connected through him to other people he met in his travels, as well as the plant people he discovered along the way. I also connected with his globe-trotting wanderlust in a vicarious way via his letters. My own life is very rooted in place with projects and family commitments, and I somehow felt freer just knowing that Frank was out there, exploring the world and getting to know the plant people. I will greatly miss Frank's presence, his correspondence, and his wandering spirit.

—Thomas J. Elpel

Looking for an online community of plant enthusiasts?
The Frank Cook tradition is being continued by Marc Williams:
www.botanyeveryday.com | www.plantsandhealers.org

yellowbells
Fritillaria pudica
Lily Family

Path of Discovery

Grandma Josie loved to walk her dogs in the meadows, following cow trails through the willow thickets and junipers along the creek. I loved to walk with her, and together we collected wild herbs for teas, including yarrow, blue violets, peppermint, red clover, and strawberry leaves. We drank herbal tea every day. When I was sick she gave me yarrow tea with honey in it, plus she buried cloves of garlic in cheese to help me get them down. Grandma kindled my passion for plants. She taught me the plants she knew, and then I wanted to learn about all the rest.

We collected unfamiliar flowers on our walks and paged through books of color pictures to identify them. It was not a fast process, but I was a kid and had the luxury of time. If I could not find the name of a specimen in our books, then I brought it to the herbarium at the university and asked for help. Botanists keyed out the plant and gave me a botanical name for it. At home I researched the name through all of my books to learn anything I could about the uses for that species.

There are hundreds of thousands of species of plants in the world, and I approached them one-by-one, as if each one had nothing to do with any others. It seemed like there should be some rationale to the plant world, but I did not find it in my library of plant books. Nevertheless, I learned most of the significant plants of southwest Montana before graduating from high school, or so I thought.

Years later, married and with our house half built, I launched a nature education school and hosted an herbal class at our place. I thought I "knew" most of the plants discussed in the class, but the herbalist, Robyn Klein, used an approach I had never seen before. We found several members of the Rose family, and Robyn pointed out the patterns—that the flowers had five petals and typically numerous stamens, plus each of them contained tannic acid and were useful as astringents, to help tighten up tissues. An astringent herb, she told us, would help close a wound, tighten up inflammations, dry up digestive secretions (an aid for diarrhea) and about twenty other things, as you will learn through the pages of this book. In a few short words she outlined the identification and uses for the majority of plants in this one family. On this walk she went on to summarize several other families of plants in a similar way. She cracked open a door to a whole new way of looking at plants.

Some of my books listed family names for the plants, but never suggested how that information could be useful. I realized that while I knew many plants by name, I never actually stopped to look at any of them! This may sound alarming, but it is surprisingly easy to match a plant to a picture without studying it to count the flower parts or notice how they are positioned in relation to each other. In short, Robyn's class changed everything I ever knew about plants. From there I had to relearn all the plants in a whole new way. I set out to study patterns among related species, learning to identify plants and their uses together as groups and families.

avens
Geum elatum
Rose Family

I wrote this book not merely because I wanted to share what I knew about patterns in plants, but also because I wanted to use it myself. One principle I have learned while writing and teaching is that the ease or difficulty of learning a subject is not so much a factor of the complexity or volume of the information, but rather of its packaging. Even the most complex mathematical concepts can be simple to understand if they are packaged and presented well. Similarly, learning a thousand different plants and many of their uses can be a snap when presented with the right packaging. The only way I could really learn plant patterns was to gather all the information I could find into one place and see what patterns were revealed.

This book is designed to shortcut the study of botany and herbology. The beginning naturalist will quickly have a foundation for the future. The more experienced may find their knowledge suddenly snapped into focus with a new and solid foundation under that which is already known.

Thomas J. Elpel
Pony, Montana

Region Covered

Botany in a Day is intended to give the reader the big picture of botany and medicinal plant properties. It deals more with patterns among related plants than with the details of specific plants. Because the book content is broad, the coverage is also broad. *Botany in a Day* covers most plants you are likely to encounter from coast to coast across the northern latitudes of North America, with extensive coverage throughout southern states as well.

In addition, many species in North America are identical or very similar to those of Europe and other countries of similar latitude. Unique plants exist in every locality, yet the majority of plants where you live are likely to be the same or similar to those covered in this text. Basically, any place that has real winters with hard freezes will have a great number of plants in common with this book. The vegetation does not radically change until you travel far enough south and low enough in elevation to drop below the frost belt.

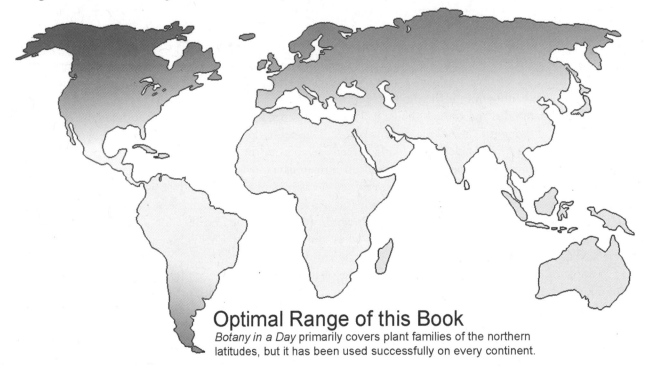

Optimal Range of this Book
Botany in a Day primarily covers plant families of the northern latitudes, but it has been used successfully on every continent.

pink turtlehead
Chelone obliqua
Plantain Family

Below the frost-belt you will continue to find many of the same and similar plants, but you will also find whole new plant families not found in the North. With each revision of the book I have added new plant families and worked to expand coverage across the southern states.

The biggest challenge with any plant book is in trying to identify a specimen that is not included in the text. There is a human tendency to make a plant fit the available description, even when it is not related to anything in the book. From that standpoint, *Botany in a Day* is most useful in the frost belt of North America where coverage is most complete and slightly less useful as you move farther south. However, readers have successfully used this book all over the world, and many people written to share their experiences and observations.

Readers have provided helpful tips about the identification and uses of related plants from their part of the world. This feedback is incorporated into this ever-evolving book to the greatest extent possible without compromising book quality for North American readers.

In this text, "North America" refers to the United States and Canada—everything north of our border with Mexico. Thus, a plant that is "Native to all of North America." may or may not be found south of the border.

Part I:
Botany in a Day
The Patterns Method of Plant Identification

pinnate
prairie coneflower
Ratibida pinnata
Aster Family

Botany in a Day Tutorial: How to Proceed

1. The study of botany is the study of patterns in plants. Find a comfortable, quiet place to read for a while. You will need to read through the tutorial on *Plant Names and Classification* and *The Evolution of Plants* to understand the big picture of how plants are related to each other and how botanists have sorted them into a filing system based on their relationships. This background is essential for understanding how and why plants are placed in certain groups. Did you know, for instance, that grasses are considered "flowering" plants? After you read these chapters you will be ready to learn some useful patterns for identifying common plants.

2. Read the next section in the tutorial, *Learning Plants by Families,* and learn to recognize some of the most common family patterns found throughout the world. Read about these families to learn their characteristics, then go for a walk and look for plants—wild or domestic—that fit the patterns. The eight families described here (Mint, Mustard, Parsley, Pea, Lily, Grass, Rose, and Aster) include more than 45,000 species of plants worldwide. Learn the basic patterns and you will know something about these plants wherever you encounter them. Do not concern yourself with individual plant names at first; just concentrate on learning the patterns of the families. You will be farther ahead in the long run, and you may be surprised to discover how much you can know about a new plant without even knowing its name. See how many plants you can find in each of the families you are studying. Now you are doing botany!

3. As you become comfortable with the patterns of the plant families from the tutorial, then you can begin studying new family patterns. I've highlighted the most common and easy-to-learn plant families in **bold** in the *Index of Plant Families and Subfamilies by Common Names*. Practice identifying these families until you are comfortable with most or all of them before you start learning the rest. I also recommend reading through *The Medicinal Properties of Plants* section in the back of the book. A basic understanding of plant properties will often aid you in identifying a plant. Please wait on utilizing any plants until you build up confidence in your identification skills.

There are many places to look for patterns in plants. Look at wildflowers and weeds and study the flowers in your yard. Look at pictures in other plant guides and notice those plants that fit the patterns of the families you are studying. Floral shops, greenhouses, nurseries, and botanic gardens are other good places to study plant patterns. Some gardens have living displays of plants from all around the world. There you will recognize plants from other continents that belong to the families you know!

If you are on a nature trail or in a nursery—any place where plants are labeled with their botanical names—you can look up their names in the *Index of Plants by Genus*. Read about the family characteristics and look for those patterns in the specimen before you. You may use the key included in this book at any time, although it is no substitute for learning the patterns of the families. Start with showy, distinctive flowers first—and simply match them against the patterns in the key.

4. As you become confident with a few family patterns then you might start identifying individual plants. The easy method is to search through the drawings and photos of plants *within the proper family*. Instead of randomly searching through hundreds or thousands of pictures, you can narrow it down to a single family. Some illustrations are provided for that purpose in this text, but you should also use this book in conjunction with other picture books.

Many plant guides are organized alphabetically or by the color of the flower; these books can ultimately hinder your progress in learning plants. Look for books that are organized according to plant families. At the very least, make sure the book includes the family name with each plant. A few of my favorite field guides, plus access to hundreds of my own wildflower photos, are available through our web site at **www.wildflowers-and-weeds.com**.

Plant Names and Classification

The Name Game

On picnics with my grandmother, we often picked teaberries, which grew in dense profusion beneath the canopy of lodgepole pine trees. The berries were delicious and infinitely abundant, yet so small that a person could starve to death while gorging on them. Strangely, I couldn't find a plant called "teaberry" in my library of plant books. That's the problem with common names; they vary from place to place and person to person. Even if there was a consensus on a plant name throughout a country or within one language, one would naturally expect different names in different languages. Moreover, unrelated plants might share the same common name, making it impossible to know which plant is the subject of discussion or study. That can become a serious problem when trying to determine the edible or medicinal uses of a plant.

I didn't know what a teaberry was until I successfully identified the plant myself in a book, listed under the name "grouse whortleberry," so named because grouse eat the berries. But it wasn't the new common name that mattered so much as having the plant's botanical name, *Vaccinium scoparium*.

Every plant has a unique two-part botanical name or binomial nomenclature, based on a system established by Carl Linnaeus in his 1753 book *Species Plantarum*. Botanical names are primarily formed from Latin and classical Greek roots, as well as Latinized names and phrases from other languages. The first name is the **genus** name (plural: **genera**), and the first letter is always capitalized. The second part is the **species** name, and it is always lowercased. Both are always italicized, as in *Vaccinium scoparium*. I may not know how to pronounce this botanical name, but this one name is used in every book, and by every author on every continent and in every language.

Herbalist Robyn Klein points out that these two-part names are much like our system of first and last names. For example, I belong to the genus *Elpel*, and my species name is *Thomas*. Other "species" of the Elpel genus include: *Cherie, Nick, Alan, Marc,* and *Jeanne*. Species names are meaningless on their own, because many people have the same names around the world. But the names *Cherie Elpel* or *Jeanne Elpel* are quite unique.

common bilberry
Vaccinium myrtillus
Heath Family

Similarly, there are about 450 species of *Vaccinium* in the world, including more than 40 species in North America and 7 species in my home state of Montana. Fortunately you do not have to write out *Vaccinium* for each species. You can abbreviate the genus after the first time you have used it. For instance, other species of huckleberries in Montana include *V. cespitosum, V. membranaceum, V. myrtilloides, V. myrtillus, V. ovalifolium,* and *V. uliginosum*. If you want to talk about the whole group at once then you just write out "*Vaccinium* spp." This abbreviation means **species plural**.

It is not necessary to memorize botanical names; you only need to refer to them when communicating about a plant to another person, or if you want to research that plant in other books. But you may be surprised at how many names you memorize just by looking them up in the indexes of other books.

Botanical names are especially useful for emphasizing relationships among plants. For example, *Vaccinium* is the genus name for huckleberries, blueberries, and bilberries. Knowing that instantly redefines what a grouse whortleberry really is. And if you learn a few huckleberries and blueberries, then you will likely recognize any new ones you encounter as well, even if you don't know their individual names. You could be hiking in the middle of Siberia and find a berry bush you have never seen or heard of before, but because you recognize its similarity to other huckleberries, you know you can safely eat it.

2

What do the numbers and dots mean?

After each plant listed in this book you will see some numbers in parenthesis. The numbers indicate how many species from that genus are present around the world, in North America, as well as in my home state of Montana. For example, *"Rosa—*rose (100/54/6)" indicates that there are about 100 different species of rose in the world, 54 native and/or introduced species in North America, and 6 species just in Montana. Your state may have more or less than this number. Most species within a genus will have similar properties and uses. For example, all 100 species of roses likely produce edible rosehips, or at least it is highly improbable that any of them are seriously poisonous.

The dot "•" after many of the names is my personal checklist of recognized genera. You are encouraged to mark the plants that you learn as well. You might use a high-lighter on the names, and you may want to make a note of the location to help jog your memory the next time you come across the name in the book. You can also highlight the names in the index.

I've been building a gallery of color photos on our web site at **www.wildflowers-and-weeds.com**. If there is a "•" after a name, then there is a good chance we have one or more color photos from that genus posted on our web site. New photos are added each year.

In other words, sometimes it is more important to recognize a plant as a relative of other plants you know, rather than to know its individual name. For that reason, I don't refer to *V. scoparium* as grouse whortleberry or teaberry. Instead, I call it dwarf huckleberry, which succinctly describes what the plant is, how it compares in size to other huckleberries, and the fact that it is edible and delicious. In this sense, standardized common names can be as useful as botanical names for conveying information about plants and their uses. Interestingly, common names are becoming increasingly standardized, at least within the English language, as they are used online in a shared global dialogue. Unfortunately, the opposite is true with formal botanical names, which are multiplying at an alarming rate as botanists attempt to clarify genetic relationships between plants.

Classification Schemes

If you had a few hundred thousand files to organize in a filing cabinet, how would you do it? How would you organize all the information so that you, or anyone else on the planet, could quickly and efficiently find any one file out of the whole bunch? And what if you had a file in hand, but didn't know what it was called or where it fit into the filing system? How would you ever figure it out? In botany, the process can be surprisingly easy, because plants are grouped according to patterns of similarity. Learn the patterns, and you can start with an unknown specimen and track it down through the filing system to learn its identity.

At its most basic level, plant patterns are often quite simple. Suppose you had two different species of wild rose. They clearly look like different plants, and yet, both plants look like roses, so you call one the prickly rose (*Rosa acicularis*) and the other the climbing rose (*R. setigera*). Binomial nomenclature is fairly instinctive in this regard.

Grouping closely related species together into genera like this is the first step in building a filing system. But, let's say you ripped every living plant from the earth and sorted them all into piles by genera. That would still leave thousands of separate piles, with no clear means to organize them. So the next step is to compare genera and lump similar genera together into bigger piles, which we call the **family**. Family patterns are not nearly as close as the patterns within any one genus, but still similar enough that one can learn to recognize many such patterns at a glance.

If a family is especially large, or its members sufficiently distinct from one another, then there may be subgroupings within a family, called the **subfamily** and **tribe**. For example, pears belong to the Apple tribe of the Almond subfamily within the Rose family. This indicates that pears are more closely related to apples and loquats than to raspberries, which are of the Rose subfamily of the Rose family. By grouping plants according to family patterns, we reduce the total number of piles to a few hundred, which is far better than thousands, but still too many piles to make an efficient filing system.

rosehip

prickly rose
Rosa acicularis
Rose Family

A higher level of classification, above the species, genus, and family, is the **order**. For the purposes of field identification, orders are sufficiently different from one another that there are few useful patterns to work with. But that doesn't stop botanists from trying to classify them. For example, based on careful scrutiny, the Saxifrage, Gooseberry, Hydrangea, Pea, and many other families were previously classified as part of the Rose order. However, genetic analysis refuted those associations and instead revealed that the Rose order should include families such as the Hemp, Oleaster, Mulberry, Buckthorn, Elm, and Stinging Nettle—none of which share any obvious resemblance with the Rose family.

Above the level of order, there are (or were) additional levels of classification, some with useful characteristics for identification, and some without. Imagine the entire plant kingdom as a filing cabinet in which botanists identified distinct divisions, classes, subclasses, orders, families, subfamilies, tribes, genera, and species, as outlined here, along with each appropriate suffix:

Division (*-phyta*)
Class (*-eae, opsida*)
Subclass (*-ae*)
Order (*-ales*)
Family (*-aceae*)
Subfamily (*-oideae*)
Tribe (*-eae*)
Genus
Species

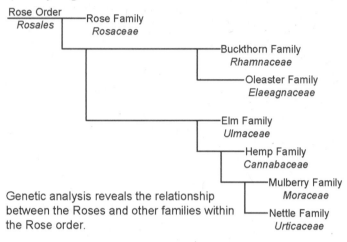

Phylogenetic Tree of the Rose Order

Rose Order
Rosales
— Rose Family
Rosaceae
— Buckthorn Family
Rhamnaceae
— Oleaster Family
Elaeagnaceae
— Elm Family
Ulmaceae
— Hemp Family
Cannabaceae
— Mulberry Family
Moraceae
— Nettle Family
Urticaceae

Genetic analysis reveals the relationship between the Roses and other families within the Rose order.

Many different classification schemes have been proposed, adopted, utilized, and ultimately rejected as more accurate information becomes available. The latest effort (and hopefully the last) is based on genetic research coordinated by a worldwide team of taxonomists known as the Angiosperm Phylogeny Group (APG). Taxonomists sequence a small part of the genome from a species and map out how closely it is related to other species, producing detailed branching *phylogenetic* trees, as shown above for families of the Rose order. The APG approach is theoretically more accurate, because taxonomists are compiling objective data about genetic relationships, rather than just looking at each species and guessing its relationship to other species.

The APG system recognizes orders, families, subfamilies, and so forth, but doesn't (yet) categorize anything above orders, except as *monophyletic* groups known as *clades*. Monophyletic translates to "one branch," meaning that any group of organisms should include only the genetic descendants (all of them) going back to a particular ancestor.

For example, Genghis Khan fathered several hundred, if not thousands of children, and his sons were also prolific, leading to an estimated 16 million descendents today, nearly 800 years later. Selecting Khan as an arbitrary branching point, a monophyletic group or clade would include all of his descendants.

If any of Khan's brothers' descendants were accidentally included, it would be considered a *polyphyletic* group. On the other hand, if any of Khan's descendants were accidentally classified as descendants of either of his brothers, it would be considered a *paraphyletic* group. But don't panic. These terms are not used elsewhere in this book. Only *phylogenetic tree* and *clade* are used in the text.

A Clade of Khans
Selecting Genghis Khan as an arbitrary branching point, a monophyletic group or clade would include his descendants (all of them), but none from his siblings.

Evolution of Plants

A Puzzle Without All the Pieces

Piecing together the story of evolution is challenging, since 99.9 percent of everything that ever lived is now extinct. Trying to understand evolution through living species of plants and animals is like trying to interpret a novel from the last paragraph. You can see the outcome, but do not know how the story unfolded.

The plot lies hidden in fossil records where plants and animals have been buried and turned to stone over thousands of millenia. Although this story is conveniently laid down in the linear sequence of geologic time, it is unfortunately a very fragmented tale. At best, fossil records are the equivalent of finding a few scattered words and phrases to the story. Most living organisms rot away without leaving a trace. Fossilized specimens are the exception rather than the rule, and evolutionary links connecting one species to another are even more scarce.

Scientists once assumed that the entire gene pool of each species continually underwent gradual change. But mutant genes tend to get diluted away in large populations and fail to spread. And fossil records typically reveal sudden, dramatic changes from one layer to the next, not gradual changes. Researchers now understand that gradual changes and new species evolve "on the margin."

"The fossil record is the equivalent of finding a few scattered words and phrases to the story. Most living organisms rot away without leaving a trace."

Imagine a valley hundreds of miles across, surrounded by mountains on all sides. Suppose that only one type of grass seed were deposited into this valley. Coincidentally, the whole expanse of the valley is the ideal habitat for this particular type of grass. The valley fills up and evolution stalls. There are always mutations, but the grass is already optimized for the environment so the mutations fail to spread. However, there is greater habitat diversity around the perimeter of the valley. Individual microclimates might be warmer or colder or more wet or dry than the valley itself. There could also be different soil chemistry. The valley grass might survive in each of these areas, but it wouldn't prosper. Gradual mutations would occur over time, and some abnormalities would be more optimized to conditions on the margin. Given enough time, distinct new species could evolve.

"Evolution proceeds both gradually and suddenly. It is revealed in the fossil record as long periods of stability with periodic jumps to completely new species."

Then a sudden disturbance comes to the valley. Perhaps the climate changes, causing the valley to become slightly warmer and wetter. The valley becomes more favorable to a grass species from the margin, resulting in an apparent "jump" in evolution from one species to another. The previously dominant species is limited back to habitat on the margin or completely eliminated while the new species suddenly invades the habitat. Thus evolution proceeds both gradually and suddenly. It is revealed in the fossil record as long periods of stability with periodic jumps to completely new species. For example, scientists researching trilobites, an extinct marine arthropod, found a jump in the fossil record from those with seventeen pairs of eyes to those with eighteen pairs of eyes. It took years of searching to find the margin where both types were present.

Similarly, it could be said that stable, balanced ecosystems tend to limit innovations, while major life-killing disturbances—such as meteor impacts—tend to favor them. Eliminating competition greatly increases the odds for all kinds of mutations to survive and fill the void. New species emerge, optimize to fit specific ecological niches, and evolution stalls again. In the fossil record we see it as long periods of stability with sudden jumps to completely new life forms. The geologically brief periods of significant mutant activity are much less likely to be recorded or found in the fossil record.

Era	Period	Mil Years	Evolutionary Event
Cenozoic	Quarternary	0-1.65	Modern humans.
	Tert./Neogene	1.65-23	Human ancestors, horses, dogs, asters, pinks.
	Tert./Paleogene	23-65	Primates, deer, grasses, lilies, roses, peas, grapes.
Mesozoic	Cretaceous	65-143	Flowering plants spread. Broad-leaf trees, palms.
	Jurassic	143-213	First flowering plants. First birds.
	Triassic	213-248	First dinosaurs and mammals.
Paleozoic	Permian	248-290	Modern insects like dragonflies and beetles appear.
	Pennsylvanian	290-323	Coal age— First cycads, ginkos, primitive conifers.
	Mississippian	323-362	Coal age— First winged insects. Reptiles.
	Devonian	362-408	Ferns, horsetails, club mosses. First amphibians.
	Silurian	408-440	Vascular plants, first millipedes. Fish with jaws.
	Ordovician	440-510	First fish. Plant/fungus symbiosis begins on land.
	Cambrian	510-570	Marine life: invertebrates, shells, predators.
Neo-Proterozoic		570-900	First multi-celled life, and first herbivores.
Meso-Proterozoic		900-1,600	Atmosphere oxygenated. First bisexual reproduction.
Paleo-Proterozoic		1,600-2,500	First Eukaryotic cells with nucleus and organelles.
Archean Eon		2,500-3,800	First simple bacteria & blue-green algae cells.
Hadean Eon		3,800-4,500	Earth's Crust and Oceans Form. No Life.

Life Begins

Life started in the oceans an estimated 3.6 to 3.8 billion years ago as simple, single-celled organisms called *prokaryotes*, which lacked a nucleus, mitochondria, or other membrane-bound organelles. There are two distinct groups of prokaryotes, known as bacteria and archaea. These organisms reproduce asexually, each splitting in half to form two exact copies of the original. For example, blue-green algae (also known as cyanobacteria) uses energy from sunlight to convert resources into living tissue. The algae grew, multiplied, and populated the oceans. Each cell divided into exact duplicates of itself, so mutations were few and far between. That was about it for life on Earth until approximately 2 to 2.5 billion years ago, when cells developed specialized parts.

Complex cells with a nucleus apparently originated when prokaryote cells absorbed other species, forming symbiotic relationships. Previously independent archaea and bacteria became specialized organelles for storing DNA, digesting nutrients, burning sugars for energy, or copying DNA into new proteins. These new *eukaryotic* cells became the foundation for more complex life forms, and sped up the process of evolution, but just barely.

It wasn't until about 1.5 billion years ago that the next significant evolutionary event occurred: bisexual reproduction. Bisexual reproduction allowed slightly different versions of genetic knowledge to be combined into new, living products. This accelerated the evolutionary process and led to the development of the first multicellular organisms 900 million years ago, including tiny animals, worms, sponges, and large forms of algae. The first herbivores (plant-eaters) evolved a few hundred million years later, and may have triggered the Cambrian explosion of new species that started about 570 million years ago.

Herbivores were the first "predators." Until they came along, early multicellular organisms lived in peaceful coexistence. Herbivores upset the balance and wiped out many primitive, defenseless organisms. Evolution favored mutants, and oceans of habitat awaited any organisms capable of escaping, hiding, or defending themselves against predators. This, in turn, encouraged the evolution of more advanced predators, in a feedback cycle that quickly filled the oceans with all kinds of life, such as jel-

Phylogenetic Tree of Life

We are all descended from common ancestry. This illustration depicts inferred evolutionary relationships between all lifeforms on earth.

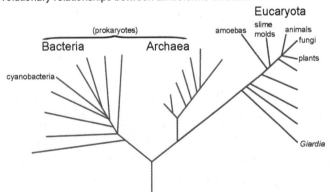

lyfish, shelled animals, and arthropods. (Arthropods became the ancestors of later insects, spiders, and crustaceans.) Evolution of the herbivores may have also helped initiate the rapid colonization of land a mere 60 million years later, starting in the Ordovician period. Any primitive plant that could adapt to the shoreline of an estuary, river, or lake would have the added advantage of living beyond the reach of herbivores in the ocean. However, there was one major obstacle in the effort to colonize land.

Life in the ocean was sustained solely by the external flow of nutrients. Plant life in the ocean survived by absorbing nutrients from the water. These nutrients reached plants through disturbances at sea. Upwellings brought minerals up from the bottom while ocean currents brought minerals out from shore. Plants survived in these paths of disturbance and animals survived by eating the plants. Otherwise, the ocean was (and still is) largely a desert because the minerals are not equally distributed.

To make the transition to land, plants had to evolve from floating in the nutrient stream to carrying the nutrient stream inside. Paleontologists Mark and Dianna McMenamin theorize that this evolutionary jump was accomplished by plants forming a symbiotic relationship with fungus.

Fungus is neither plant nor animal. It is a third type of life that produces enzymes capable of breaking down dead organic matter, living tissue, and even rock. It is speculated that somewhere along a shoreline, a defective proto-fungus attacked a proto-plant, but failed to kill it. Instead the fungus inadvertently began feeding the plant with minerals from the soil, while simultaneously extracting carbohydrates back from the plant.

Today, 90 percent of all plants associate with fungus in the soil, and 80 percent could not survive without their fungal partners. In many cases, fungi live in the core of the plant. Some simple plants like the club mosses lack a complete vascular system for circulating water and nutrients, but their fungal partners live inside the stems and provide that function.

The McMenamins researched the fossil record for signs of symbiosis between plants and fungi, and found evidence of a link among the earliest fossils. They examined slices of cells from high-quality fossils and found fungal hyphae inside the plant cells. The plant-fungus association internalized the nutrient stream and gave the proto-plant independence from the ocean currents to grow and evolve along the shore and ultimately on land. The force of evaporation served as a pump to move nutrients up from the soil through the plants.

The symbiotic relationship between plants and fungi set the stage for yet another explosion of new life forms. Within 100 million years life on land had become more diverse than in the oceans. In the remaining 350 million years since then, life on land seems to have evolved at an ever-increasing speed. Today there are twice as many species on land as in the ocean. Although the surface of the planet is one-third land and two-thirds water, the land area produces a whopping fifty times as much biomass (organic matter) as the oceans.

Living Partnerships

Most plants form symbiotic relationships with fungi in the soil. The fungi help extend the reach of the plant roots to obtain water and nutrients that might not be available otherwise. In return, the plants manufacture sugars through photosynthesis to feed the fungi. Ninety percent of all plants associate with fungi this way. Eighty percent of all plants, including this orchid, could not survive without their fungal partners.

Lichens form as a symbiotic relationship between algae and fungi. The algae use chlorophyll to photosynthesize sugars from sunlight, water, and air. The fungus provides a protective structure and feeds off sugars produced by the algae.

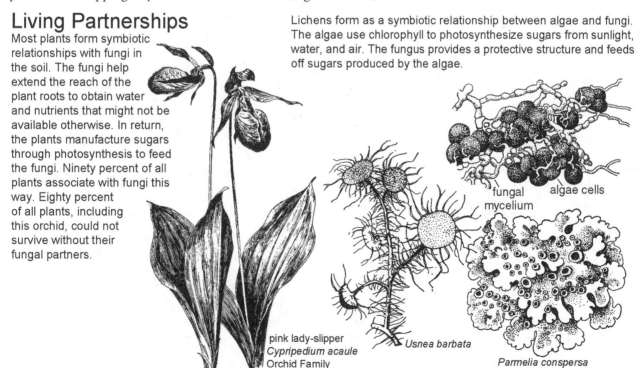

pink lady-slipper
Cypripedium acaule
Orchid Family

Usnea barbata

fungal mycelium   algae cells

Parmelia conspersa

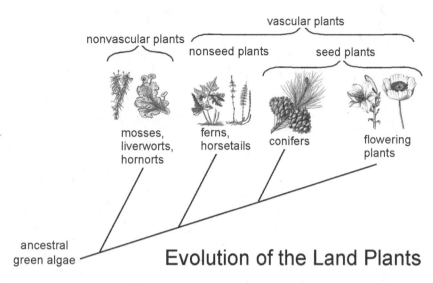

nonvascular plants

vascular plants

nonseed plants

seed plants

mosses, liverworts, hornorts

ferns, horsetails

conifers

flowering plants

ancestral green algae

Evolution of the Land Plants

The Land Plants

Few fossil links have been found in the from the development of modern plants, but the available living and fossilized plants, in addition to genetic evidence, suggests a logical progression from simple to complex vegetation. The following list provides a generalized outline of the evolutionary process:

- **Spore Plants without a Vascular System**
- **Spore Plants with a Vascular System**
- **Naked Seeds**
- **Flowering plants**
- **Monocots, Dicots, and Eudicots**
- **Specialized Flowers**
- **Composite Flowers**

Note that **lichens** evolved independently from true plants as an association between fungi and algae. The algae are a layer of single-celled plants near the surface, just below a gelatinized layer of fungal hyphae. Algae absorb nutrients through the surface and provide energy through photosynthesis, while the fungi absorbs moisture and provides a protective structure for the algae. This habit gives lichens the adaptability to live almost anywhere, even on rocks, trees or buildings. On the other hand, lichens are highly susceptible to airborne pollutants, which they absorb in toxic concentrations. The fungi and algae are otherwise independent organisms capable of surviving without each other, and they only form lichens when both are present.

Varied and often bright lichen colors come from acid crystals stored in their tissues. The acid is used to etch holes in wood, rock, buildings, and other surfaces to give the lichens something to grab. The lichens then insert thread-like appendages as anchors. Most of the so-called "mosses," especially those found hanging from tree branches, are actually lichens. True mosses are distinctively green like other plants. Lichens are now considered part of the Fungi kingdom, and are not included in this book.

Spore Plants without a Vascular system

The most simple land plants reproduce with spores and have no vascular system (internal plumbing). These plants—the true mosses, hornworts, and liverworts—are limited in size because they lack internal plumbing to transport water and nutrients. Mosses and liverworts live in many environments, but are especially common on rocks along babbling brooks where they are above the water, but constantly damp. These soft-bodied plants leave little trace in the fossil record, but seem to have arisen early in the lineage of the land plants.

Specific information about the medicinal properties of mosses and liverworts is hard to come by, but *Sphagnum* and other mosses are typically highly acidic and antibiotic. *Sphagnum* moss has been used to dress wounds, with better results than ordinary sterilized pads. Corpses of people that drowned in peat bogs long ago were nicely preserved by the acidic water. Beyond this introduction, spore plants without a vascular system are not covered in this book.

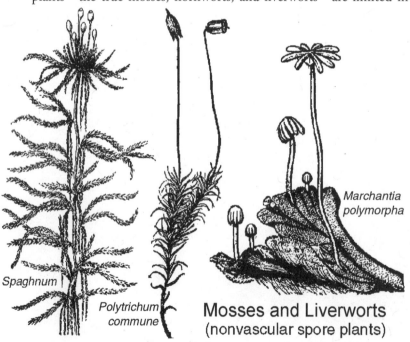

Spaghnum

Polytrichum commune

Marchantia polymorpha

Mosses and Liverworts
(nonvascular spore plants)

Spore Plants with a Vascular System

The first plants with a vascular system apparently developed through an association between plants and fungi, where the fungi provided mineral nutrients and the plants provided energy through photosynthesis. This association helped internalize the nutrient stream so that water and nutrients could be transported through the vegetation. Given that water molecules are naturally drawn to each other like weak magnets, evaporation through the leaves (a.k.a. "transpiration") effectively serves as a pump to pull an unbroken chain of water molecules up from the soil.

The relationship between plants and fungi has likely led to genetic exchanges over time. There is a tremendous evolutionary advantage in being able to share genetic information between wholly unrelated species. Just imagine if you exchanged DNA with a bird, an apple, or a mushroom. Many such exchanges could lead to fatal defects, but any successful exchange would tend to accelerate the evolutionary process much more than simply exchanging genes with a member of your own species. Much of the human genome is believed to be bits of DNA acquired from viruses.

The development of the vascular system allowed plants to stand upright and reach for the sky, a distinct evolutionary advantage over the lowly mosses and liverworts. Our first forests were comprised of these spore-producers with vascular systems—the ferns, clubmosses, and horsetails. In this first forest, the clubmosses and horsetails grew into giant trees, often over a 100 feet tall. These plants thrived at a time when the earth's climate was moderated by ocean currents circulating warm equatorial waters up around the poles. The spore plants flourished in the tropical climate for millions of years and laid down the organic matter that eventually became our coal deposits.

Primitive plants like clubmosses, horsetails, and ferns reproduce with spores. The spores drop to the ground and grow into a minute vegetative part called the "thallus." This term is used to describe a vegetative structure that is not differentiated into leaves or a stem. The thallus produces sexual organs, including female egg cells and male swimming sperms to fertilize them. After fertilization the thallus grows into a new plant, as illustrated above. Read more about spore plants with a vascular system on pages 38 to 45.

Reproduction with Spores

Spores drop to the ground and develop into a thallus with male and female organs. The male organs have swimming sperms to find and fertilize the egg cells. After fertilization, the thallus grows into a new plant.

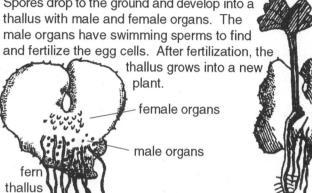

female organs

male organs

fern thallus

new plant

Ferns and their Allies
(vascular spore plants)

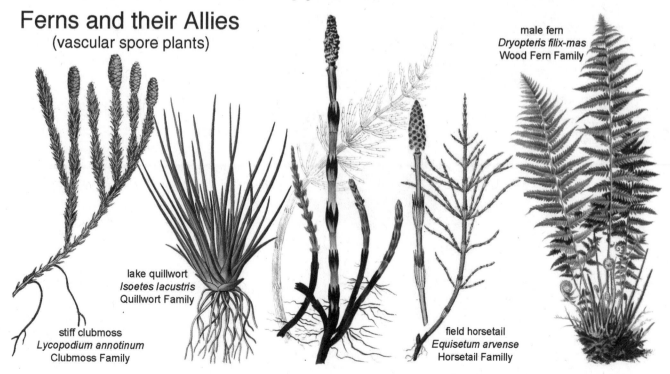

stiff clubmoss
Lycopodium annotinum
Clubmoss Family

lake quillwort
Isoetes lacustris
Quillwort Family

field horsetail
Equisetum arvense
Horsetail Familly

male fern
Dryopteris filix-mas
Wood Fern Family

Naked Seeds

Evolution eventually led to fertilization occurring on the mother plant, rather than on the ground. Seed ferns, now extinct, were the first seed producers, followed by cycads and ginkos, and later conifers and flowering plants.

Conifers, for example, produce two sizes of cones from modified clusters of leaves with spore sacks at the base of each "leaf." Large cones produce big spores, which develop into a thallus-like structure and produce egg cells, called ovules, within the cones. The smaller cones produce tiny spores, which also develop into a thallus-like structure, but they produce the male sperm cells called pollen. Instead of tails to swim, the sperm or pollen is encased in a tough coat to resist drying. The cones open and release the pollen to the wind to find and fertilize the egg cells.

Pollen reaches the egg cells and fertilizes them within the protective structure of the plant. The fertilized cells begin to develop into a new plant, but then the growth is stopped, and the new plant is shed as a **seed**. In favorable conditions the seed absorbs moisture, swells, and resumes growth. This gives the baby plants a considerable advantage over those that are borne from spores.

whitebark pine
Pinus albicaulis
Pine Family

pine embryo

pine seedling

Naked Seeds

The first plants to evolve beyond spores to produce true seeds were the gymnosperms (literally "naked seeds"). They are considered naked because their egg cells are exposed to the air and fertilized when pollen lands directly on them.

In a crude analogy, imagine that spore plants are like the reptiles that lay their eggs and leave, whereas seed plants are more like mammals that gestate the eggs internally and give birth to a partially developed being. It is a tactical advantage for the seed plants as they are developmentally ahead of the spore plants when they reach the soil. In addition, the seed provides a means of storing starch. The seedling relies on this energy reserve for rapid growth while it establishes itself among the competition.

The *gymnosperms* (literally "naked seeds") first appear in the fossil record about 360 million years ago. These were the first plants to evolve beyond spores and produce true seeds. They are referred to as naked seeds because the egg cells are slightly exposed to the air and fertilized by the pollen landing directly on the surface.

Among conifers, for example, the female cones become elongated for a short time when the male cones are releasing pollen. This exposes the egg cells or ovules to the pollen in the wind. The shape of the cones causes air currents to swirl around them to help catch this pollen. The shape of the pollen and the shape of the cones are aerodynamically matched to each other, so each species captures its own pollen. After pollination the scales grow rapidly and cover the ovules, allowing them to mature into seeds. Read more about naked seed plants of North America on pages 46 to 49.

maidenhair tree
Ginkgo biloba
Ginkgo Family

Ginkgo, a native of China, is considered a "living fossil," similar to fossil specimens from 270 million years ago. It has no close living relatives.

Flowering Plants

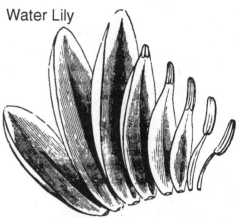

Water Lily

It is difficult to imagine a world of greenery without colorful flowers. But flowers first appear in the fossil record only about 130 million years ago and didn't become widespread until about 100 million years ago. Flowers co-evolved with insects, presumably as primitive insects tracked pollen from the male sporangia over to female egg cells on the same or separate plants. Eventually the plants developed nectaries and showy petals to attract and feed the insects, and the insects developed wings to move from flower to flower.

Like many gymnosperms, ancestral flowers typically developed reproductive parts on cone-like receptacles. There were multiple, overlapping layers of sepals and petals, or "tepals" if one could not be distinguished from the other. Male stamens and female carpels or pistils were also numerous and variable in number.

sepals-to-petals-to-stamens transition

These floral parts evolved as modifications of the leaves. Today, sepals are green and leaf-like on most plants, but in some species they are colored like petals. In the water lily there is a visible transition from sepals on the outside to petals and then stamens on the inside. Thus, petals are modifications of the sepals, and stamens are modifications of petals. Plant breeders often manipulate these features of the flowers. For example, most plants of the Rose family have five petals, including wild roses. The extra petals in many domestic rose varieties were bred from stamens.

A defining step in the evolution of flowering plants was to enclose the developing seeds deeper inside the parent plant. While gymnosperms expose their ovules to open air for pollination, flowering plants, or *angiosperms*, wrap the ovules entirely inside the ovary or pistil, which, in its most simple form, consists of a single carpel. Pollen lands on the tip of the pistil and grows a sort of "root" down into the ovary to reach the ovule. The pollen has two nuclei: the first nucleus controls growth through the pistil, while the second carries genetic information and passes it along to the ovule. Chemicals used by the pollen to burrow through the pistil are identical to some that are produced by fungi, so it is suspected that plants acquired genes to do this through their intimate relationship with fungi.

Evolution of the Pistil

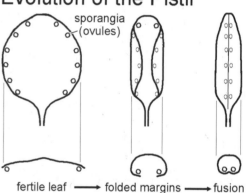

sporangia (ovules)

fertile leaf ⟶ folded margins ⟶ fusion

The enclosed ovary of the flowering plants likely evolved through modification of fertile leaves. Plants with folded leaves better protected the ovules, leading to more successful offspring. As the trend continued over time, the leaf margins completely fused together, forming an individual carpel or simple pistil.

The enclosed ovary became a flexible means of creating many new dispersal systems. For instance, berries and other fruits are usually swollen ovaries, designed to be eaten and later defecated as a means to transport and plant the seeds. The ovaries around maple seeds develop into wings to disperse the seeds on the wind. The ovaries of some plants develop into spring-like systems to propel the seeds away. The evolution of mammals is closely linked to development of the plant ovary and its fleshy fruits, nuts, and grains.

You might be surprised that grass and many other non-showy plants are considered flowering plants. They also produce stamens and pistils and develop seeds in an enclosed ovary. They have merely adapted to wind pollination and lack a need for showy petals to attract insects. (See the *Quick Guide to Flower Terms* inside the front cover for

It is helpful to anthropomorphize botany for a better grasp of the reproductive process, much as it was described by Peter Tompkins and Christopher Bird in their book *The Secret Life of Plants*:

"School children might have been fascinated to learn that each corn kernel on a cob in summer is a separate ovule, that each strand on the pubic corn silk tufted around the cob is an individual vagina ready to suck up the pollen sperm brought to it on the wind, that it may wriggle the entire length of the stylized vagina to impregnate each kernel on the cob, that every single seed produced on the plant is the result of a separate impregnation. Instead of struggling with archaic nomenclature, teenagers might be interested to learn that each pollen grain impregnates but one womb, which contains but one seed, that a capsule of tobacco contains on average 2,500 seeds which require 2,500 impregnations, all of which must be effected within a period of 24 hours in a space less than one-sixteenth of an inch in diameter."

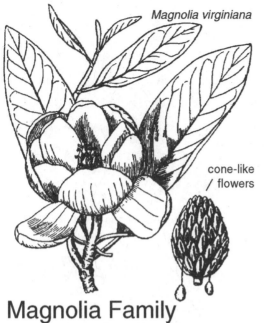

Magnolia virginiana

cone-like / flowers

Magnolia Family

more details on floral parts.) Despite being recently evolved (geologically speaking), flowering plants now dominate the planet with the most species and most widespread abundance. Remnants of evolutionary progression can still be seen in modern flowering plants, particularly of the Water Lily, Magnolia, and Buttercup families (pages 50 - 57). In particular, trees of the Magnolia family bear seeds in a large cone-like structure at the center of the flowers. To a lesser degree the plants of the Buttercup family produce similar flowers.

Counterintuitively, big trees and small plants with flowers are often closely related. For example, strawberries and apples are both in the Rose family. The flower pattern matters more than the vegetation. To understand why, imagine a dandelion growing in shade and another growing in full sun. The one in the shade is going to appear lush, with leaves up to a foot long, while the dandelion in the sun will be a much smaller, more compact plant. An amateur naturalist might not even recognize them as the same plant. Yet the flowers on both plants are identical. The shape of leaves and stems are very flexible and easily adapt to new and different conditions. Overall, there is more evolutionary pressure on the vegetation than on the flowers, so a group of related plants can have vastly different vegetation, but similar blossoms.

Another development in flowering plants was deciduous vegetation, possibly the result of climate change. The world climate was moderated 300 million years ago during the Coal Age by warm ocean currents flowing from the equator up over the North Pole. The climate today is much harsher. Flowering trees adapted to the climate by dropping their leaves and becoming dormant in the winter. They shed old, worn-out leaves to enrich their own soil while also safeguarding against potential damage from heavy snows. In the spring they burst forth with vigorous new leaves. In a similar way, perennial flowers can be thought of as deciduous too. They store excess energy in their roots during the growing season, then die off above ground for the winter. The energy stored in the roots allows the plants to re-emerge in the spring.

Illustrations on the next two pages summarize everything we have covered so far, followed by the next step in this evolutionary progression—monocots, dicots, and the newly defined eudicots.

The Flowering Plants

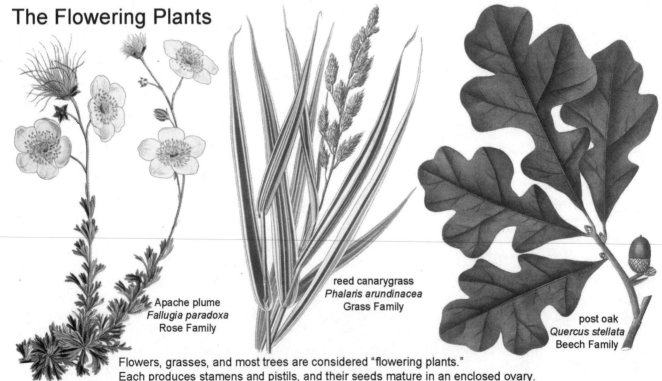

Apache plume
Fallugia paradoxa
Rose Family

reed canarygrass
Phalaris arundinacea
Grass Family

post oak
Quercus stellata
Beech Family

Flowers, grasses, and most trees are considered "flowering plants."
Each produces stamens and pistils, and their seeds mature in an enclosed ovary.

Three Domains and Six Kingdoms

Early classification systems had just two **kingdoms**: Plants and Animals. In 1894, Ernst Haeckel added a third kingdom for one-celled life, called the Protists. In 1969, Robert Whittaker separated the bacteria (cells without a nuclei) from the Protists into a new kingdom called the Monera. He also split the Fungi out from the Plants, for a total of five kingdoms. In 1977, Carl Woese replaced the Monera kingdom with two distinct kingdoms of bacteria: the Archaeabacteria and the Eubacteria, for a total of six kingdoms. However, research showed that the Plant, Animal, and Fungus kingdoms shared the same cell-structure as the Protists, and all belonged in one group. Therefore, in 1990 Woese originated the concept of **domains** that superceded the kingdoms. He grouped the Plants, Animals, Fungi, and Protists into the new Eukarya domain. The two kingdoms of bacteria were both elevated to domain status. This illustration depicts the three domains and all six kingdoms. Time and research will bring more revisions.

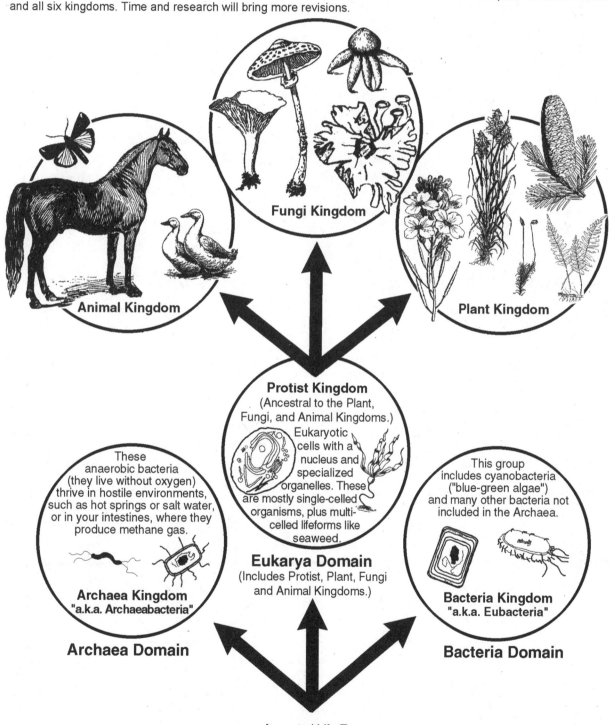

Fungi Kingdom

Animal Kingdom

Plant Kingdom

Protist Kingdom
(Ancestral to the Plant, Fungi, and Animal Kingdoms.) Eukaryotic cells with a nucleus and specialized organelles. These are mostly single-celled organisms, plus multi-celled lifeforms like seaweed.

Eukarya Domain
(Includes Protist, Plant, Fungi and Animal Kingdoms.)

These anaerobic bacteria (they live without oxygen) thrive in hostile environments, such as hot springs or salt water, or in your intestines, where they produce methane gas.

Archaea Kingdom
"a.k.a. Archaeabacteria"

Archaea Domain

This group includes cyanobacteria ("blue-green algae") and many other bacteria not included in the Archaea.

Bacteria Kingdom
"a.k.a. Eubacteria"

Bacteria Domain

Ancestral Life Forms
3.6 – 3.8 Billion Years Ago

Variation in the Plant Kingdom

Nonvascular Spore Plants: The most simple members of the Plant Kingdom are the mosses, hornworts, and liverworts. These plants reproduce with spores, and they are limited in size because they lack a vascular system (internal plumbing) for transporting water and nutrients.

Vascular Spore Plants: Moving clockwise around the graph, the plants become increasingly complex. Clubmosses, horsetails, and ferns also reproduce with spores, but they do have a vascular system for transporting water and nutrients, so they can grow much larger.

Naked Seeds: Cycads, ginko, conifers, and gnetums also have a vascular system, but reproduce with seeds instead of spores. They are called gymnosperms or "naked seeds" because the ovule (female egg cell) is exposed to the open air during pollination.

Flowering Plants: Angiosperms or flowering plants dominate the world today. In these plants, ovules are completely contained within the ovary of the flower. Pollen has to penetrate the ovary to fertilize the ovules.

Numbers below reflect the approximate number of known species worldwide. There may be as many more species yet undiscovered.

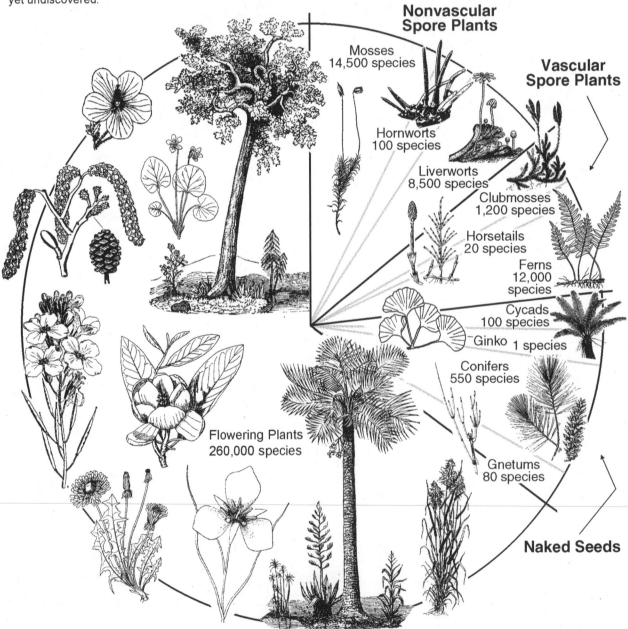

Nonvascular Spore Plants

Mosses
14,500 species

Vascular Spore Plants

Hornworts
100 species

Liverworts
8,500 species

Clubmosses
1,200 species

Horsetails
20 species

Ferns
12,000 species

Cycads
100 species

Ginko 1 species

Conifers
550 species

Flowering Plants
260,000 species

Gnetums
80 species

Naked Seeds

Seeds totally enclosed inside the ovary

Monocots, Dicots, and Eudicots

All flowering plants were previously classified as one of two major groups: monocotyledons or dicotyledons, depending on whether the seeds have one seed leaf or two. Breaking it down, *mono* means one, *di* means two, and *cotyle-don* translates to "seed-leaf." Corn is a **monocot** because it has only one seed leaf. A bean, on the other hand, is a **dicot** because their are two seed leaves. Soak a bean in wet paper towels until it sprouts and you can see the two seed leaves, one from each half of the bean. (Note that *non-flowering* plants, such as pine trees, can have variable numbers of cotyledons. See the pine seedling on page 10.)

There are some striking differences between monocots and dicot plants. Most monocot plants have leaves with *parallel veins*, like grass, while most dicot plants have *net-veined* leaves. Even dicots that initially seem to have parallel venation, such as plantain (*Plantago*), actually have a smaller net-like pattern between the larger veins. There are always exceptions, but leaf venation is a good starting point. In addition, most (not all) dicot plants have floral parts in fours and fives. On the other hand, most monocot plants (not all) have floral parts in threes. If a plant has both parallel veins in the leaves *and* floral parts in multiples of three then it is definitely a monocot.

If there is still any doubt, then take a look at the branches or roots. Monocots are typically simple and some-what symmetrical, like a palm tree, but only rarely that big. Underground, their roots radiate from the central stalk or spread under the soil surface like grass roots. Dicots, on the other hand, often have complicated, asymmetrical branching patterns, much like an oak tree or rose bush. Underground, they often have a woody taproot. It is easy to pick out the differences between monocots and dicots. Go out and look at plants for fifteen to twenty minutes and you will get the idea.

A newer term, *eudicots*, meaning "true dicots" is more relevant to classification than identification. Monocots and dicots were previously considered two equal classes. However, it has been determined that monocots arose from early dicot ancestors, as illustrated in the phylogenetic tree on the following page. That insight effectively split the dicots into two separate groups: the basal dicots (also known as "pre-dicots") before the split, and the eudicots after the split. Fortunately, there is no need to distinguish between basal dicots and eudicots to identify a plant using the keys in this book. For our purposes, there are only monocots and dicots.

Is your Flowering Plant a Dicot / Eudicot or a Monocot?

Dicots / Eudicots
-two seed leaves
-netted veins in the leaves
-usually tap-rooted
-usually complex branching
-floral parts mostly in 4's and 5's

Monocots
-one seed leaf
-parallel veins in the leaves
-horizontal rootstalks
-usually simple branching
-floral parts mostly in 3's

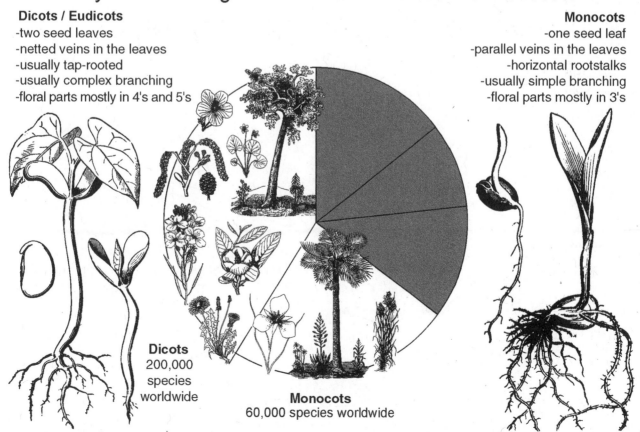

Dicots
200,000 species worldwide

Monocots
60,000 species worldwide

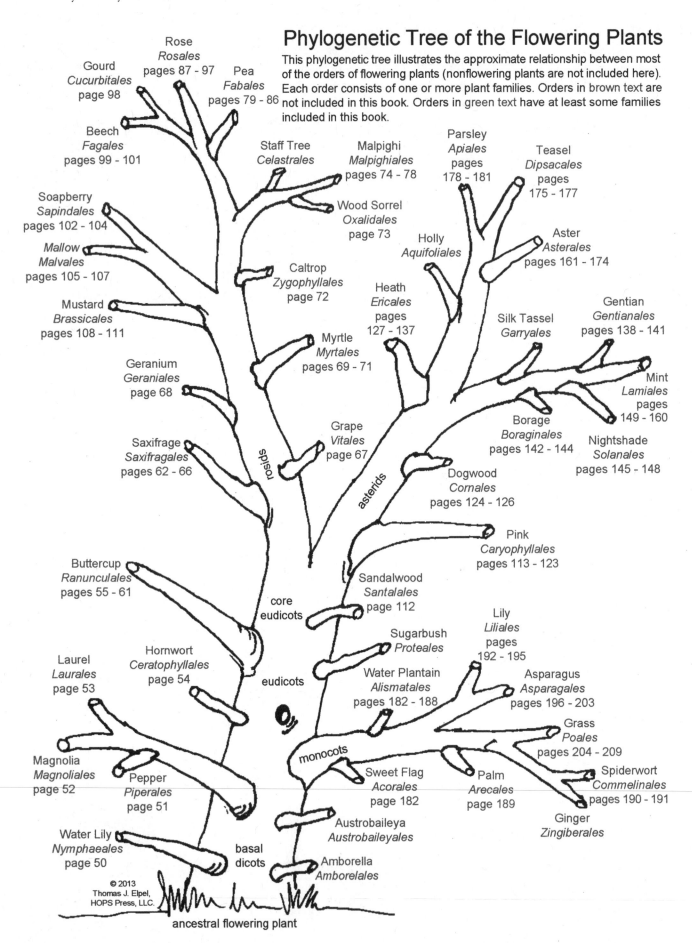

Phylogenetic Tree of the Flowering Plants

This phylogenetic tree illustrates the approximate relationship between most of the orders of flowering plants (nonflowering plants are not included here). Each order consists of one or more plant families. Orders in brown text are not included in this book. Orders in green text have at least some families included in this book.

Gourd
Cucurbitales
page 98

Rose
Rosales
pages 87 - 97

Pea
Fabales
pages 79 - 86

Beech
Fagales
pages 99 - 101

Staff Tree
Celastrales

Malpighi
Malpighiales
pages 74 - 78

Parsley
Apiales
pages
178 - 181

Teasel
Dipsacales
pages
175 - 177

Soapberry
Sapindales
pages 102 - 104

Wood Sorrel
Oxalidales
page 73

Holly
Aquifoliales

Aster
Asterales
pages 161 - 174

Mallow
Malvales
pages 105 - 107

Caltrop
Zygophyllales
page 72

Heath
Ericales
pages
127 - 137

Silk Tassel
Garryales

Gentian
Gentianales
pages 138 - 141

Mustard
Brassicales
pages 108 - 111

Myrtle
Myrtales
pages 69 - 71

Mint
Lamiales
pages
149 - 160

Geranium
Geraniales
page 68

Borage
Boraginales
pages 142 - 144

Nightshade
Solanales
pages 145 - 148

Saxifrage
Saxifragales
pages 62 - 66

Grape
Vitales
page 67

rosids

asterids

Dogwood
Cornales
pages 124 - 126

Buttercup
Ranunculales
pages 55 - 61

Pink
Caryophyllales
pages 113 - 123

core
eudicots

Sandalwood
Santalales
page 112

Lily
Liliales
pages
192 - 195

Laurel
Laurales
page 53

Hornwort
Ceratophyllales
page 54

eudicots

Sugarbush
Proteales

Water Plantain
Alismatales
pages 182 - 188

Asparagus
Asparagales
pages 196 - 203

Grass
Poales
pages 204 - 209

Magnolia
Magnoliales
page 52

Pepper
Piperales
page 51

monocots

Sweet Flag
Acorales
page 182

Palm
Arecales
page 189

Spiderwort
Commelinales
pages 190 - 191

Water Lily
Nymphaeales
page 50

basal
dicots

Austrobaileya
Austrobaileyales

Ginger
Zingiberales

Amborella
Amborelales

© 2013
Thomas J. Elpel,
HOPS Press, LLC.

ancestral flowering plant

From Simple to Specialized Flowers

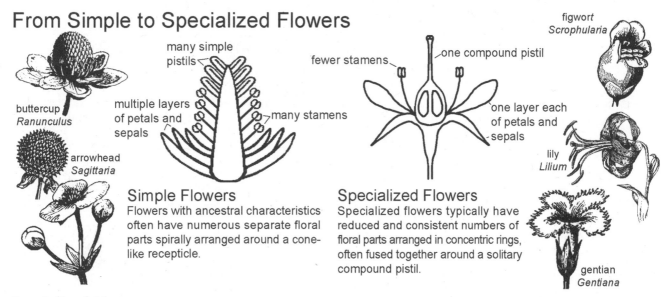

buttercup
Ranunculus

arrowhead
Sagittaria

many simple pistils

multiple layers of petals and sepals

many stamens

fewer stamens

one compound pistil

one layer each of petals and sepals

figwort
Scrophularia

lily
Lilium

gentian
Gentiana

Simple Flowers
Flowers with ancestral characteristics often have numerous separate floral parts spirally arranged around a cone-like recepticle.

Specialized Flowers
Specialized flowers typically have reduced and consistent numbers of floral parts arranged in concentric rings, often fused together around a solitary compound pistil.

Specialized Flowers

Continued evolution of flowering plants led from simple flowers with numerous separate parts to specialized flowers with fewer, often fused parts. Simple or "primitive" flowers usually have numerous sepals, petals, stamens, and pistils, while more specialized flowers typically have reduced numbers of each, and the parts are often fused together. Modern plants evolved from now-extinct species, but some plants retained many ancestral characteristics, as illustrated above. Notice how the arrowhead (*Sagittaria*) and buttercup (*Ranunculus*) are similar in appearance, even though one is a monocot and the other is a dicot.

There are many variations in the continuum between simple and specialized flowers. Go outside and look at a flower now. Are the sepals separate from one another or partially or wholly fused together? How about the petals? Are there numerous stamens or only a few? Are they fused to each other or to the petals? Need a refresher on floral terms? Turn to the inside front cover for a *Quick Guide to Flower Terms*.

Now look at the center of the flower. Are there multiple pistils or just one? If only one pistil, does it look like several carpels that have fused together to make a compound pistil? Not sure? Turn the page and read about *Progressive Fusion of the Pistils*. Some plants have become so specialized that each flower produces only one seed, as is the case with the Aster family.

Composite Flowers: Aster Family

Asters may seem like simple flowers with numerous parts, but in fact they are highly specialized plants. Most families of plants have floral parts in a similar order: a ring of sepals on the outside, then a ring of petals, a ring of stamens, and the pistil or pistils in the middle. Some parts may be missing, but the basic order is always the same. The Aster family is a bit different. The "sepals" are really bracts (modified leaves), and they often appear in multiple layers. The "petals" make it look like one big flower, but peek inside and you will discover a *composite* head of many very small flowers—dozens or even hundreds of them. In the sunflower, for example, every seed is produced by one small flower within the larger head. These itsy-bitsy flowers each have tiny sepals and petals—although these have been modified enough that they have their own terminology. In fact, each of the main "petals" is a flower too, often with stamens and a pistil. Read more about the Aster family on page 163.

Jerusalem artichoke
Helianthus tuberosus
Aster Family

In the Aster family, each tiny flower produces a single seed.

Progressive Fusion of the Pistils

Making sense of **carpels**, **chambers**, **partition walls** and **placentation**.

Most of the information on this page is *not* required to identify plants with *Botany in a Day*, but it is helpful for making sense of why flowers look like they do, and it provides useful a useful background for reading other botanical texts.

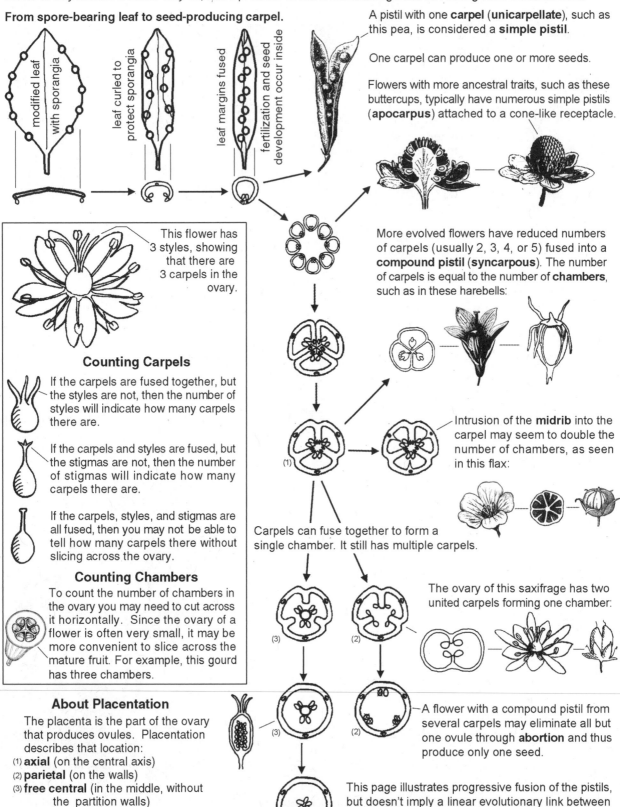

From spore-bearing leaf to seed-producing carpel.

modified leaf with sporangia

leaf curled to protect sporangia

leaf margins fused

fertilization and seed development occur inside

A pistil with one **carpel** (**unicarpellate**), such as this pea, is considered a **simple pistil**.

One carpel can produce one or more seeds.

Flowers with more ancestral traits, such as these buttercups, typically have numerous simple pistils (**apocarpus**) attached to a cone-like receptacle.

This flower has 3 styles, showing that there are 3 carpels in the ovary.

More evolved flowers have reduced numbers of carpels (usually 2, 3, 4, or 5) fused into a **compound pistil** (**syncarpous**). The number of carpels is equal to the number of **chambers**, such as in these harebells:

Counting Carpels

If the carpels are fused together, but the styles are not, then the number of styles will indicate how many carpels there are.

If the carpels and styles are fused, but the stigmas are not, then the number of stigmas will indicate how many carpels there are.

If the carpels, styles, and stigmas are all fused, then you may not be able to tell how many carpels there without slicing across the ovary.

Intrusion of the **midrib** into the carpel may seem to double the number of chambers, as seen in this flax:

Counting Chambers

To count the number of chambers in the ovary you may need to cut across it horizontally. Since the ovary of a flower is often very small, it may be more convenient to slice across the mature fruit. For example, this gourd has three chambers.

Carpels can fuse together to form a single chamber. It still has multiple carpels.

The ovary of this saxifrage has two united carpels forming one chamber:

About Placentation

The placenta is the part of the ovary that produces ovules. Placentation describes that location:

(1) **axial** (on the central axis)
(2) **parietal** (on the walls)
(3) **free central** (in the middle, without the partition walls)
(4) **basal** (attached to the base)

A flower with a compound pistil from several carpels may eliminate all but one ovule through **abortion** and thus produce only one seed.

This page illustrates progressive fusion of the pistils, but doesn't imply a linear evolutionary link between the sample flowers.

Learning Plants by Families

Plant identification is all about patterns. Related plants usually have similar characteristics for identification, and often similar uses. Learn a few common patterns, and you have a powerful tool for exploring the world of plants. Instead of being clueless when you encounter a new species, you may recognize its family pattern. You may not know its name, but recognizing the family pattern narrows down the range of possibilities when searching for an identity. Moreover, you may know something about the plant's edible or medicinal properties, just by recognizing which family it belongs to.

Start by learning patterns for the Mint, Parsley, Mustard, Pea, Lily, Grass, Rose, and Aster families. Knowing these few basic patterns enables you to recognize the correct family for more than 45,000 species of plants worldwide. Learn these patterns well, and you will have a good foundation for learning additional plant family patterns.

These eight families are the same ones I usually cover when I lead students on a beginning plant walk. The names of the plants are irrelevant at this stage. A more essential goal is to recognize family patterns. When we come to a new plant, I don't tell my students what the plant is. I ask them. With minimal instruction, students can correctly identify the family for a great number of the plants we encounter.

I incorporated the same eight core families into a metaphorical story for the children's book, *Shanleya's Quest: A Botany Adventure for Kids Ages 9 to 99*, which I often use in adult classes. In addition, I created the *Patterns in Plants Card Game*, which also covers these families. In its briefest form, I can introduce all eight family patterns to adults or kids in about two minutes. Then we start playing card games, including *Memory*, *Slap Flower*, *Crazy Flowers*, *Wildflower Rummy*, and *Shanleya's Harvest*, a game based on the story. Interestingly, kids who miss the introduction can watch the game and quickly grasp the family patterns and game rules without any instruction whatsoever. Our species naturally excels at pattern recognition!

Thirty-two of the fifty-two cards in the *Patterns in Plants Card Game* are reproduced on the next two pages, accompanied by a brief description of each family pattern. You can learn the patterns entirely from the text in this book, or pick up a copy of the game (**www.hopspress.com**), if you want to practice pattern recognition at a more intuitive level. Learn these eight families really well first. You will then be properly prepared to learn additional plant family patterns, or to key out an entirely unknown plant to learn its identity.

Identifying the Unknown

Family patterns are amazing tools for plant identification—right up until you encounter a plant that doesn't match any of the patterns you already know. If you are comfortable with the core family patterns discussed above, then you may proceed to the next step and identify new plants using the keys included in this book.

The keys will help you determine the correct family. Turn to that family in the book, and read the description to make sure it is correct. Look for possible matches in the included artwork. Space is limited, so you will likely need to turn to another book for more pictures. Look for a local field guide that is organized according to families, or check out our website for suggested companion books for your area.

If you need to positively identify a plant down to the species level, then pick up a local flora and use the book *Plant Identification Terminology* by James and Melinda Harris to help guide you through the botanical key from the family or genus down to the species. It is amazingly easy to key out flowers by using all of these books together, compared to trying to do it using only a botanical key. Recommended books and hundreds of wildflower photos are available through our web site at **www.wildflowers-and-weeds.com**.

Mint Family

The pattern for this family is *square stalks, opposite leaves, and usually aromatic*. The stem is visibly four-sided. The leaves come out of the stem opposite from each other (just as your arms do), rather than alternating up the stem. These characteristics may be found in a few non-Mint plants as well, but crush a leaf and smell it. Does it smell aromatic, maybe even a little bit minty? Most Mints are spicy but edible. Learn more about the Mint family on page 157.

Parsley Family

The distinctive pattern for this family is *compound umbels*. Notice how the individual stems of the flowerhead branch out from a single point, much like the spokes of an umbrella. This is called an umbel. In the Parsley family there is also a smaller umbel at the end of each main spoke. That makes it a compound umbel.

The Parsley family includes some good edibles, but also the most poisonous plants in North America, so precise identification is required. Learn more about the Parsley family on page 179.

Mustard Family

The unique pattern for this family is *4 petals with 6 stamens—4 tall and 2 short*. If you find a four-petaled flower, look inside. Do you see four tall stamens and two short stamens? If so, then you have a member of the Mustard family, which are all edible—at least to the degree that they are palatable.

You can also learn to recognize patterns in the arrangement of the seed pods and the mustard-like smell of the vegetation. Learn more about the Mustards on page 109.

Pea Family

Take another look at the Mustard family. See how the flowers are symmetrical? This is a *regular* flower. Pea flowers, on the other hand, are asymmetrical or *irregular*.

There are many families with irregular flowers (including the Mints above), but the Pea family has distinctive *banner, wings, and keel* petals that are not found in other flowers. The big upper petal is the banner, much like a big sign. The two petals on the sides are the wings, much like the wings on a bird. This is technically a five-petaled flower, with the last two petals usually fused together to make the keel, much like the keel of a boat. Learn more about the Pea family on page 79.

Lily Family and its Allies

The key pattern for the Lily family and its allies is *3 sepals and 3 petals, usually identical in size and color.*

When investigating any flower, always count from the outside towards the middle: sepals, petals, stamens, pistil(s). A flower may be missing parts, but they are never out of order. Starting on the outside of a Lily, you will notice two distinct layers: three colored sepals, and three colored petals. Learn more about the Lily family and its allies starting on page 192.

Lily Family
showy monocot flowers

6 stamens

3-parted pistil

3 sepals and 3 petals (same size and color)

Lilies are showy "monocot" flowers (look for parallel veins in the leaves) with floral parts in multiples of three.

Grass Family

The Lily and Grass families are monocots, while all the other families featured on these two pages are dicots. Turn back to page 15 for a refresher on monocots versus dicots.

We don't normally think of grasses as being "flowers," but they do have stamens and a pistil like other flowers, and they form seeds enclosed within the ovary. They just don't look like flowers because they are wind-pollinated and thus have no need for showy sepals or petals.

Grass family plants have *hollow flower stems with knee-like nodes or joints* that help to distinguish them from other grass-like plants. Learn more about the Grass family on page 207.

Grass Family
wind-pollinated flowers

pistil

3 stamens

bract

bract

A bract is a modified leaf.

Grasses are petalless, wind-pollinated monocot flowers with the stamens and/or a pistil enclosed in bracts.

Rose Family

The pattern for this family is *5 petals and numerous stamens, often with oval, serrated leaves.* There are many other families of plants with five-petaled flowers as well, some with separate petals and some with their petals fused together. Each five-petaled family has a unique pattern that distinguishes it from all other families with five-petaled flowers.

In the Rose family, the petals are separate, and the numerous stamens are distinctive. At the center of the flower you will often see a fuzzy center consisting of partially fused pistils. This family includes many edible fruits. Learn more about the Rose family on page 91.

Rose Family
5 petals, lots of stamens

numerous stamens

5 petals

5 sepals

Roses have 5 petals, typically with numerous stamens and a fuzzy center made of many partially fused pistils.

Aster Family

Plants of the Aster family have unique *composite* flowerheads. One flowerhead is made up of many smaller flowers, each attached to a pitted disk, like flowers planted in a garden. In a sunflower, for example, each sunflower seed is produced by an individual flower within the larger flowerhead.

The flowers in the middle are called *disk flowers*, while the big "petals" around the outside are also considered individual flowers, known as *ray flowers*. A flowerhead may include disk flowers and/or ray flowers. Learn more about the Aster family on page 163.

Aster Family
composite flowers

ray flowers

disk flowers

pistil

stamens

5 fused petals

pitted disc

Asters have "composite" flowerheads with multiple small flowers attached to a pitted disc.

Problems in Taxonomic Paradise

The benefit to using botanical names versus common names is that each plant theoretically has only one botanical name, which is used worldwide in every country and language, while common names can vary tremendously from region to region. However, as taxonomists wrangle over the relationships between plants they frequently rename a species or an entire genus, tribe, subfamily, family, or order. And with new evidence, they may even abandon a new name and revert to a historic name. The end result is a more accurate classification system, but at the cost of muddying up the literature with old and new names that don't obviously connect with one another.

For example, the old Lily family was a catch-all for similar flowers that botanists knew were not closely related, but couldn't devise a clear-cut system to accurately split them into more appropriate families. Many different families have been proposed in the past, breaking the Lily family into as many as seventy new families. These families are put into circulation, listed in books, and referenced by authors. Lily family plants have been shuffled back and forth between different proposed families so many times that a reader might find a plant listed in five different families in five different books! The APG system clarifies these old relationships by providing yet another classification scheme, which retains some previously proposed families, rejects others, and redefines what goes into each family.

The same process happens at the genus level as well. For example, there were once about twenty species of death camas classified as *Zigadenus* of the Lily family. However, based on new evidence, all but *Z. glaberrimus* have been shuffled to other genera, spread out across *Amianthium*, *Anticlea*, *Stenanthium*, and *Toxicoscordion*. Meanwhile, other plants in these genera were shuffled around as well, rototilling each genera so thoroughly that it can be nearly impossible to sort it all out when researching a particular plant. And all of the above genera have been segregated from the Lily family into the Bunchflower Family.

The meadow death camas, common in the West, is presently known as *Toxicoscordion venenosum*. But it has also been known as *T. arenicola*, *T. salinum*, *Zigadenus diegoensis*, *Z. salinus*, and *Z. venenosus*. Strangely, I've been writing, teaching, and talking about several different species of *Zigadenus* my entire life, only to discover that, due to taxonomic slight-of-hand, *Zigadenus* no longer exists in Montana and I've never even seen one! To find a true *Zigadenus*, I would have to travel to the southeast and look for the sandbog death camas, *Z. glaberrimus*.

This name game has been in play ever since Linnaeus established the binomial system. Historically, the changes came along slow enough that people could adapt, just as people adapted to Saint Petersburg in Russia being renamed Petrograd in 1914, Leningrad in 1924, and back to Saint Petersburg in 1991. But it could lead to confusion if you thought these were three separate cities, or if you tried to find Petrograd on a modern map after reading a 1920 book about Russia.

For taxonomists, the ultimate goal is to classify every plant according to clean monophyletic clades, in which each group contains all the descendents from an arbitrary common ancestor and none from parallel lines. As a result, taxonomists are reclassifying and renaming thousands of plants all at the same time. Some plants have cycled through as many as ten different botanical names. The end product may be more taxonomically accurate, but at the risk of making botanical names so confusing as to render them obsolete. One can only hope that researchers will ultimately arrive at a final consensus for all life on earth, so that future generations won't be faced with different names in every reference guide!

sandbog deathcamas
Zigadenus glaberrimus
Bunchflower Family

How to Use the Keys

1. What major group does your specimen belong to?

The *Botany in a Day Tutorial* provided an overview of the major groupings within the plant kingdom, including: nonvascular spore plants, vascular spore plants, naked seeds, and flowering plants. (For review, turn to the illustration on page 14.) After reading the tutorial, you should be able to pick up virtually any plant and make an educated guess as to which of these groups it belongs. Coverage of nonvascular spore plants is limited to the text on page 8. For more information on vascular spore plants, such as ferns and horsetails, turn to pages 38 to 45. And for naked seeds, such as the Pine family, see pages 46 to 49. If your sample is a flowering plant then you will need to continue through the keys to narrow down the choices.

2. Is your plant a monocot or a dicot?

If your sample is a flowering plant, then you need to determine whether it is a monocot or a dicot/eudicot. Remember, monocot plants usually have parallel-veined leaves and flower parts mostly in threes. Dicot plants mostly have net-veined leaves and parts in fours and fives. For a refresher on the differences between monocots and dicots, or if you have an unusual specimen about which you are uncertain, then return to page 15 for review.

If your plant is a monocot, then turn to the *Key to Monocot Flowers* on page 34. Monocot plants with showy flowers are covered in the top section. Monocots with grassy flowers are in the bottom section. If you are uncertain which section yours belongs to, then try both. It never hurts to come up with more than one answer. Turn to the family descriptions in the book and read about each one in greater detail to determine which family is the best match. On the other hand, if your plant is a dicot then continue reading here.

3. Is your dicot plant a member of the Aster family?

The Aster family is the largest family of flowering plants in the northern latitudes. As a matter of probability, it makes sense to determine whether or not your sample is a member of the Aster family before checking any others. But more than that, Asters can be misleading with their composite flowers. Aster flowers superficially seem to have numerous sepals or numerous petals, but they are really composed of many smaller flowers with parts in fives. You must sort out all members of the Aster family before proceeding through the dicot keys. For a thorough refresher on the Aster family, see page 163. Also familiarize yourself with the similar-looking Teasel family. If your plant is definitely *not* a member of the Aster family, then continue reading here.

4. Profile your dicot flower and key it out.

If your dicot flower is not a member of the Aster family then turn the page and work up a complete profile on your flower to help guide you through the dicot keys that follow. You may not be able to fill in every blank on the form, but do the best you can. Then key out your flower to determine which family it belongs to.

The keys in this book are, to the greatest extent possible, based on field characteristics that can be observed without a razor blade to dissect the flowers or a microscope to see the parts. Most of the required features can be seen entirely with the unaided eye, or with regular reading glasses. However, a hand lens or "loupe" will be required for keying out some of the smaller flowers. Loupes and recommended companion books are available through **www.wildflowers-and-weeds.com**.

Profile your flower Before you use the Keys

Practice keying out the large flowers first, then try smaller and smaller samples.

Start at the bottom of the page and work your way up, filling in the blanks. Skip sections that do not apply, or that you do not know how to answer. Remember to look at the individual flower. A clover blossom, for example, is a cluster of dozens of small, irregular flowers.

Always start on the outside of a flower and work inward. The first layer will be the sepals (do not confuse them with bracts that are present in some species.), then the petals, stamens, and pistil(s). Some parts may be missing, but all parts that are present will be in that order. If you find a flower without green sepals, then look close and you may find two overlapping rings of "petals." The outer ring consists of colored sepals that look like petals. If there is only one ring then you have a flower with sepals, but no petals, even if the sepals are colored like petals. (There are a few exceptions, but these rules work most of the time.) These are important distinctions for properly using the keys. A flower with 4 colored sepals and no actual petals would be found in the Key to Regular Dicot Flowers with 0, 3, or 6 petals, and not in the other keys.

Be sure to turn to the inside front and back covers for additional help on flower and leaf terms.

Always count parts from the outside to the inside: sepals, petals, stamens and pistil.

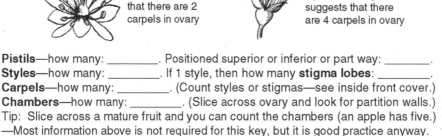

2 styles suggest that there are 2 carpels in ovary

style with 4 stigmas suggests that there are 4 carpels in ovary

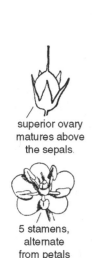

superior ovary matures above the sepals

Pistils—how many: _____. Positioned superior or inferior or part way: _____.
Styles—how many: _____. If 1 style, then how many **stigma lobes**: _____.
Carpels—how many: _____. (Count styles or stigmas—see inside front cover.)
Chambers—how many: _____. (Slice across ovary and look for partition walls.)
Tip: Slice across a mature fruit and you can count the chambers (an apple has five.)
—Most information above is not required for this key, but it is good practice anyway.

inferior ovary matures below the sepals

5 stamens, alternate from petals

Stamens—Separate or fused to each other or to the petals or pistil: _____.
How many: _____. When there are 11 or more stamens, enter "numerous".
Are they alternate or opposite from the petals: _____. (May not apply.)
Some stamens may be confusing to recognize if they have lost their anthers.

5 stamens, fused with petals (and alternate)

separate petals

Petals—separate or united: _____. How many: _____. Color: _____.
Petals may be united only at the base (try lifting them out together) or absent.
Caution: some flowers have colored petal-like sepals.

united petals

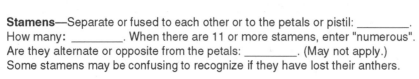

Sepals—separate or united: _____. How many: _____. Color: _____.
Sepals may be united only at the base, or difficult to determine, or absent.
Caution: green or colored bracts (modified leaves) may be mistaken for sepals.
Also, some flowers lose their sepals upon opening.

separate sepals

united sepals

regular flower

Regular or **irregular** flowers: _____. **Bisexual** or **unisexual**: _____.

—Start at the bottom and work up the page.—

irregular flower

bisexual flower has stamens and pistil

unisexual flowers
staminate flower
pistilate flower

Choose the Correct Dicot Key

Once you have profiled your dicot flower in detail, then identify it through the following keys. These keys incorporate the primary patterns for each family in this book. Color illustrations are intentionally excluded from these keys to help you focus on the flower details without being falsely swayed by flowers of a simliar hue. With these keys you can successfully identify thousands of plants across North America and around the world, at least down to the family level.

Keep in mind, however, that there are always exceptions. For example, almost all 2,000 species of the Pink family have 5 petals. But there are a few anomalies with only 4 petals, which are not covered in the keys. Some families have almost no exceptions, while others have numerous exceptions. It is impractical to include all exceptions in a key like this, although I have included as many as practical. Several families are included in more than one key. If you know a family well, then there is a good chance you will recognize an anomaly or exception from that family when you encounter it. The vegetation and flowers may share similarities with other plants of the family, even if the flower configuration doesn't fit the rules.

This text covers *most* plant families across the frost belt of North America and the *majority* of families farther south. That leaves a few exceptions in the North and more in the South that are not included in the book or keys.

Now turn to the appropriate key on the next few pages and search the text and illustrations for the closest match you can find. Not every species is illustrated in the keys, while other families include a number of illustrations to show the range of possibilities. Your flower may not exactly match the samples shown, but pick the family that seems like the closest match. Turn to the page indicated and carefully read the family description to see if your flower fits in that family. Always double-check your conclusions. You may need to go back to the key and pick another family with similar characteristics. It is easy to make a plant "fit" into a family when trying to identity it.

Note that shrubs and trees without showy flowers (sepals and petals are absent, or small and green) are included only in the *Key to Dicot Trees and Shrubs by Their Fruits*.

After identifying the correct family, check the illustrations on the family page to look for a possible match. You can also cross-reference with other plant identification books organized by families to help narrow the identity down to the correct genus and species. In addition, try looking up botanical names in a Google image search to check your work.

Key to Regular Dicot Flowers with Numerous Petals
(Numerous means 11 or more.)

Cactus Family

Miner's Lettuce Family

Buttercup Family

Water Lily Family

Caution: Aster family plants are not included here. See instructions on page 23.

Trees with large, showy flowers. Numerous stamens and pistils. Large flowers with cone-like fruits. .... Magnolia: 52

Numerous sepals, petals, and stamens. Succulent plants with spines. Desert habitats. .... Cactus: 123

2 sepals. Numerous petals and stamens. Succulent plants, often in intense sunlight. *Lewisia.* .... Miner's Lettuce: 120

3 to 15 sepals. 0 to 23 petals. Numerous stamens. 3+ simple pistils, often with hooked tips. .... Buttercup: 55

4 or 5 sepals. Numerous petals and stamens. Aquatic plants, usually with broad, floating leaves. .... Water Lily: 50

30 sepals. 30 petals. 30 or 60 stamens. Succulent plants, usually in grainy soil. .... Stonecrop: 64

Note: Many cultivated plants with numerous petals were bred from species that originally had 5 separate petals, particularly from the Buttercup, Rose, Pink, Geranium, Mallow, and Miner's Lettuce families. If you have a cultivated plant with numerous separate petals, try keying it out as a five-petaled flower.

Key to Irregular Dicot Flowers
(Including regular flowers with spurs.)

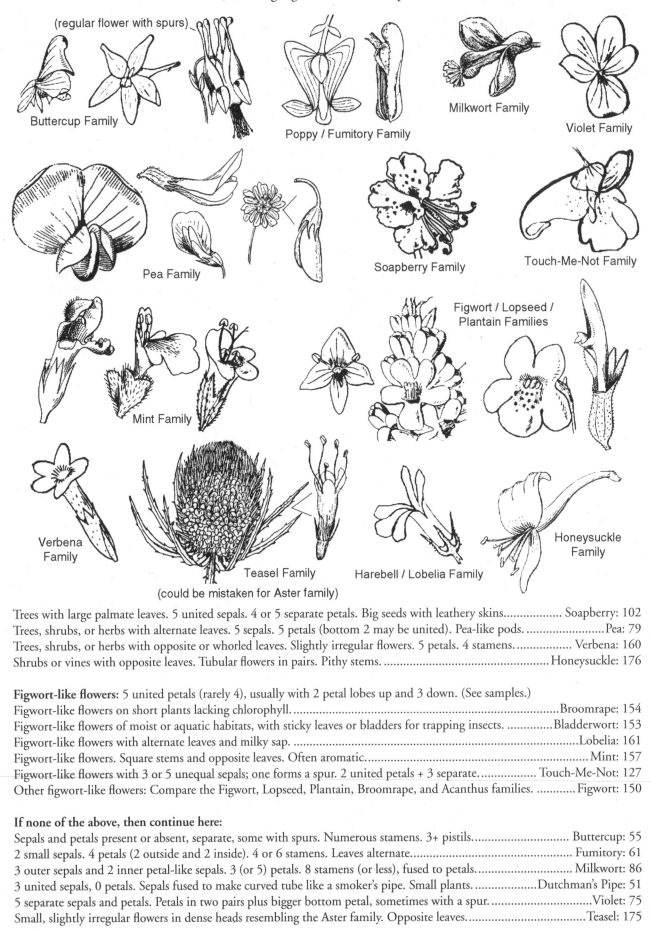

(regular flower with spurs)

Buttercup Family

Poppy / Fumitory Family

Milkwort Family

Violet Family

Pea Family

Soapberry Family

Touch-Me-Not Family

Figwort / Lopseed / Plantain Families

Mint Family

Verbena Family

Teasel Family
(could be mistaken for Aster family)

Harebell / Lobelia Family

Honeysuckle Family

Trees with large palmate leaves. 5 united sepals. 4 or 5 separate petals. Big seeds with leathery skins.................Soapberry: 102
Trees, shrubs, or herbs with alternate leaves. 5 sepals. 5 petals (bottom 2 may be united). Pea-like pods. ....Pea: 79
Trees, shrubs, or herbs with opposite or whorled leaves. Slightly irregular flowers. 5 petals. 4 stamens.................Verbena: 160
Shrubs or vines with opposite leaves. Tubular flowers in pairs. Pithy stems. ....Honeysuckle: 176

Figwort-like flowers: 5 united petals (rarely 4), usually with 2 petal lobes up and 3 down. (See samples.)
Figwort-like flowers on short plants lacking chlorophyll. ....Broomrape: 154
Figwort-like flowers of moist or aquatic habitats, with sticky leaves or bladders for trapping insects. ....Bladderwort: 153
Figwort-like flowers with alternate leaves and milky sap. ....Lobelia: 161
Figwort-like flowers. Square stems and opposite leaves. Often aromatic.. Mint: 157
Figwort-like flowers with 3 or 5 unequal sepals; one forms a spur. 2 united petals + 3 separate.................Touch-Me-Not: 127
Other figwort-like flowers: Compare the Figwort, Lopseed, Plantain, Broomrape, and Acanthus families. ....Figwort: 150

If none of the above, then continue here:
Sepals and petals present or absent, separate, some with spurs. Numerous stamens. 3+ pistils.............................. Buttercup: 55
2 small sepals. 4 petals (2 outside and 2 inside). 4 or 6 stamens. Leaves alternate... Fumitory: 61
3 outer sepals and 2 inner petal-like sepals. 3 (or 5) petals. 8 stamens (or less), fused to petals.............................Milkwort: 86
3 united sepals, 0 petals. Sepals fused to make curved tube like a smoker's pipe. Small plants...................Dutchman's Pipe: 51
5 separate sepals and petals. Petals in two pairs plus bigger bottom petal, sometimes with a spur. ....Violet: 75
Small, slightly irregular flowers in dense heads resembling the Aster family. Opposite leaves...................................Teasel: 175

Key to Regular Dicot Flowers with 0, 3, or 6 Petals
(Some have colored bracts or sepals that look like petals.)

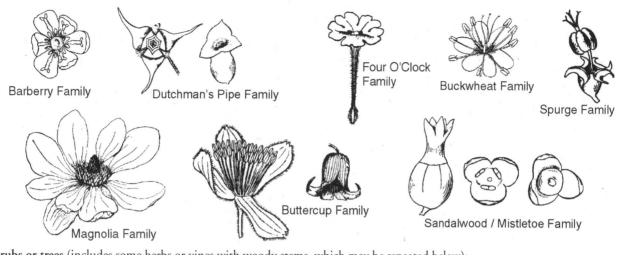

Barberry Family

Dutchman's Pipe Family

Four O'Clock Family

Buckwheat Family

Spurge Family

Magnolia Family

Buttercup Family

Sandalwood / Mistletoe Family

Shrubs or trees (includes some herbs or vines with woody stems, which may be repeated below):

Leaves opposite (rarely alternate). Petal-like bracts beneath clusters of small flowers. Fruit is a drupe.................Dogwood: 124

Leaves opposite or alternate. Sometimes thorny. Small flowers, often showy clusters. 3-celled fruit.................... Buckthorn: 96

Leaves opposite or alternate. Usually silvery. Sometimes thorny. 5 colored sepals. 0 petals. Fruit is a drupe. .... Oleaster: 97

Leaves alternate. 3 sepals. 3+ petals. Numerous stamens and pistils. Large flowers with cone-like fruits............... Magnolia: 52

Leaves alternate and aromatic. 6 (rarely 4) sepals: greenish yellow, yellow, or white. 0 petals.................................... Laurel: 53

Leaves alternate and sometimes pinnate. Evergreen. Sepals and petals in layers of 3, often as 3 + 3 + 3 + 3............Barberry: 58

Leaves alternate and often trifoliate or pinnate. 3 sepals. 0 or 3 petals. Fruit is a drupe. ....Cashew: 104

Leaves alternate and needle-like. Often evergreen. 3 bracts. 3 sepals. 3 petals. Fruit is a drupe or berry .... Crowberry: 133

Note: Shrubs and trees without showy flowers (sepals and petals are absent, or small and green) are included only in the *Key to Dicot Trees and Shrubs by Their Fruits.*)

Herbs with 3 or 6 petals:

Aquatic herbs with large floating leaves. 3 sepals. 3 petals. 3, 6, 12, or 18 stamens. .... Fanwort: 50

Herbs without chlorophyll. 2-6 sepals. 3-6 petals (separate or united). 6-12 stamens..............................Indian Pipe: 137

Succulent herbs. Often in grainy soil. 2 sepals. 4-6 petals and 1x or 2x as many stamens. ....Miner's Lettuce/Purslane: 120

Leaves alternate. Sap often milky. 2-3 sepals (may fall early). 6 petals (usually 4, 8, or 12)... Poppy: 60

Leaves alternate or basal. Sepals and petals in layers of 3, often as 3 + 3 + 3 + 3 ....Barberry: 58

Leaves alternate (rarely opposite). 3-15 sepals. 0-23 petals. Numerous stamens. 3+ simple pistils. .... Buttercup: 55

Leaves opposite or whorled. 4, 6, or 8 sepals and petals and 2x as many stamens in 2 sets, short and tall........... Loosestrife: 69

Herbs with colored bracts and 0 petals:

Colored bracts beneath flowers. 0 or 5 sepals. Milky juice. Mostly found in warm climates....................................... Spurge: 77

Dense flower clusters. Each flower enclosed by 3 green or colored, often pointy bracts. 4-5 sepals...................... Amaranth: 117

Herbs with colored sepals and 0 petals:

3 united sepals, tubular. 12 stamens (rarely 6 to 36). 6-celled ovary. Often in moist forests. ....Dutchman's Pipe: 51

3-5 separate or united sepals with an equal number of stamens, aligned with the sepals. Small plants............ Sandalwood: 112

3-6 separate sepals, sometimes as 3+3. 3 to 9 stamens. Seeds 3-sided or lens-shaped..Buckwheat: 113

3 to 15 sepals. Numerous stamens. 3+ simple pistils, often with hooked tips. .... Buttercup: 55

4 separate sepals. 2-12 stamens. 1-3 simple pistils. Small, white flowers. *Sanguisorba*...Rose: 91

5 united sepals (rarely 3 to 10). Tubular flowers. May have colored bracts. Mostly desert habitats. ....Four-O'Clock: 122

Herbs or vines with greenish flowers and 0 petals:

Aquatic plants with finely divided leaves in the water, but entire or whole leaves above water. ....Water Milfoil: 63

Aquatic plants, often erect, with whorled leaves. Only 1 stamen and one pistil. *Hippuris*. .... Water Starwort: 152

Submerged aquatic plants with whorled leaves. Numerous stamens. Flowers surrounded by bracts. .... Hornwort: 54

Plants parasitic on tree branches. Fruit is a berry .... Sandalwood: 112

Palmate or pinnate leaves. Coarse, somewhat aromatic vegetation. Separate male and female flowers. .... Hemp: 89

Squarish stalks and opposite leaves, usually with stinging hairs.. Stinging Nettle: 90

Usually disturbed or alkaline soils. Flowers globular or pointy. .... Amaranth: 117

Key to Regular Dicot Flowers with 4 Petals
(Includes some flowers with 6, 8, or 12 petals.)

Poppy Family · **Mustard Family** · **Loosestrife Family** · **Beeplant Family** · **Evening Primrose Family** · **Hydrangea Family** · **Madder Family** · **Gentian Family** · **Harebell Family** · **Olive Family** · **Plantain Family** · **Heath Family**

Shrubs or trees (includes some herbs or vines with woody stems, which may be repeated below):

Leaves opposite and rarely pinnate. Sometimes squarish stems. United petals. Usually 2 stamens. ....Olive: 149

Leaves opposite and palmate or rarely pinnate. Separate petals. Fruit is a pair of winged seeds. *Acer*. .... Soapberry: 103

Leaves opposite. Often pithy stems. Separate petals. 4+ stamens. Fruit a capsule. ....Hydrangea: 125

Leaves opposite (rarely alternate). Often showy bracts. Petals separate. Fruit a berry-like drupe. ....Dogwood: 124

Leaves opposite. United petals, often with pointy tips. 4-5 stamens. 2- or 4-chambered ovary. ....Madder: 138

Leaves opposite or alternate. Sometimes thorny. Small flowers, often in showy clusters. 3-celled fruit................ Buckthorn: 96

Leaves alternate and palmate. Sometimes thorny. 4 sepals. 4 petals. 5 stamens. Fruit is a berry. ....Gooseberry: 65

Leaves alternate or basal. Evergreen. 4-5 sepals. 4-5 petals. 2x as many stamens. Fruit is a capsule. ....Pyrola: 136

Leaves alternate. Often evergreen. Mostly bell-shaped flowers, petals united. Fruit a capsule or berry. .... Heath: 132

Leaves alternate. Separate petals, often ribbon-like. 4 stamens. Woody capsules with bony seeds. .... Witch Hazel: 62

Herbs with distinctive vegetative features:

Forest plants without chlorophyll. ....Indian Pipe: 137

Aquatic plants with finely divided leaves under water, but whole leaves above water. ....Water Milfoil: 63

Vining plants with alternate leaves, tendrils, and clusters of berries. Petals may be fused at tips and fall away............. Grape: 67

Bristly, hairy, or sticky plants. Numerous stamens. Fruit a capsule. Arid or warm habitats. .... Loasa: 126

Continue here if none of the above fit your sample:

Herbs that have flowers with 4 united petals:

Leaves opposite. Sepals united or separate. Flowers in dense heads resembling the Aster family. ....Teasel: 175

Leaves opposite or whorled. Stamens fused to the petals. Bell- or dish-shaped flowers. .... Gentian: 139

Leaves opposite or whorled. 4-5 sepals. Petals often pointy tips. 4-5 stamens. 2- or 4-chambered ovary.................Madder: 138

Leaves opposite or alternate. Sepals united. Flowers tubular with dish-shaped faces. .... Phlox: 128

Leaves alternate. May have milky juice. Sepals separate. *Triodanis spp.* (not common). ....Harebell: 161

Leaves alternate, basal or whorled. Stamens aligned opposite petals. Fruit is a capsule. Moist habitats. .... Primrose: 130

Leaves are basal with parallel-like veins. Sepals united. Small greenish flowers on slender spike.............................Plantain: 150

Herbs that have flowers with 4 separate petals:

Leaves opposite. 4 sepals. 4 petals. 10+ stamens. Usually yellow petals, often with red-orange spots. .... Saint Johnswort: 74

Leaves opposite or whorled. 4, 6, or 8 sepals and petals and 2x as many stamens in 2 sets, short and tall........... Loosestrife: 69

Leaves opposite or alternate. Succulent. 2 sepals. 4-6 petals and 1x or 2x as many stamens.........Miner's Lettuce/Purslane: 120

Leaves opposite or alternate. Succulent. 4 sepals. 4 petals and 1x or 2x as many stamens. 3+ pistils. .... Stonecrop: 64

Leaves opposite, alternate, or basal. 4 sepals and petals. 4 or 8 stamens. Often a 4-parted stigma.............Evening Primrose: 70

Leaves alternate. Bristly, hairy, or sticky plants. Numerous stamens. Fruit a capsule. Arid habitats............................Loasa: 126

Leaves alternate. Milky sap. 2-3 sepals (may fall early). 4-12 petals. Numerous stamens. Arid habitats. .... Poppy: 60

Leaves alternate. Often weedy annual plants. 4 sepals. 4 petals. 6 stamens: 4 tall and 2 short. ....Mustard: 109

Leaves alternate and 3-parted or palmately divided. 4 sepals. 4 petals. 4+ stamens. Pea-like pods.........................Beeplant: 108

Leaves alternate. 8-10 sepals. 8-10 petals. Numerous stamens and pistils. *Dryas.* ....Rose: 91

Leaves alternate, basal, or whorled. Stamens aligned opposite petals. Fruit is a capsule. Moist habitats. .... Primrose: 130

Leaves alternate or basal. Evergreen. 4-5 sepals. 4-5 petals. 2x as many stamens. Fruit is a capsule..........................Pyrola: 136

Key to Regular Dicot Flowers with 5 United Petals
(Includes some flowers with 10 petals.)

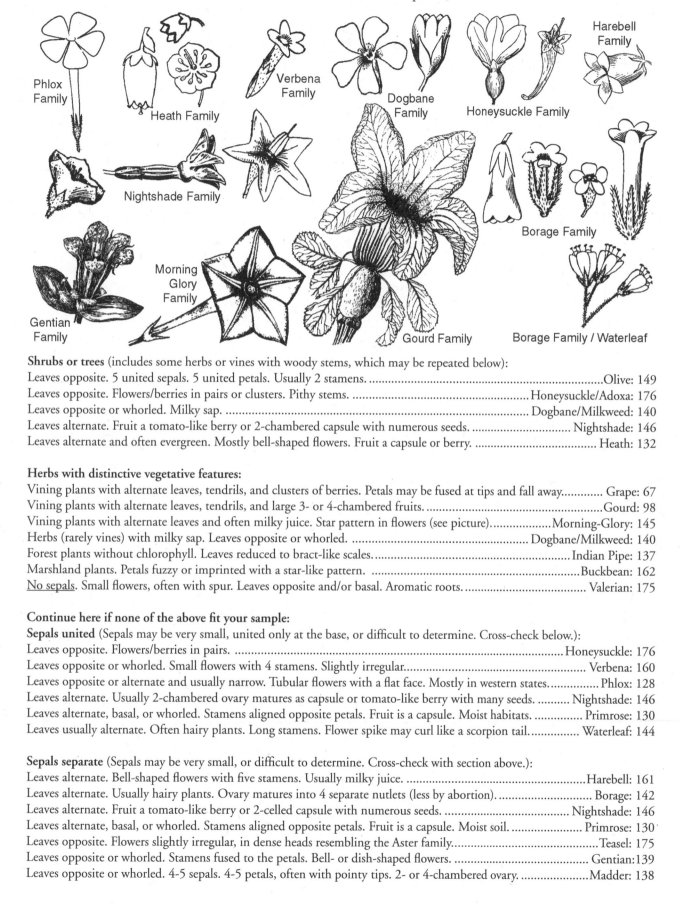

Phlox Family

Heath Family

Verbena Family

Dogbane Family

Honeysuckle Family

Harebell Family

Nightshade Family

Borage Family

Gentian Family

Morning Glory Family

Gourd Family

Borage Family / Waterleaf

Shrubs or trees (includes some herbs or vines with woody stems, which may be repeated below):

Leaves opposite. 5 united sepals. 5 united petals. Usually 2 stamens. ....Olive: 149

Leaves opposite. Flowers/berries in pairs or clusters. Pithy stems. ....Honeysuckle/Adoxa: 176

Leaves opposite or whorled. Milky sap. .... Dogbane/Milkweed: 140

Leaves alternate. Fruit a tomato-like berry or 2-chambered capsule with numerous seeds. .... Nightshade: 146

Leaves alternate and often evergreen. Mostly bell-shaped flowers. Fruit a capsule or berry. .... Heath: 132

Herbs with distinctive vegetative features:

Vining plants with alternate leaves, tendrils, and clusters of berries. Petals may be fused at tips and fall away............. Grape: 67

Vining plants with alternate leaves, tendrils, and large 3- or 4-chambered fruits. ....Gourd: 98

Vining plants with alternate leaves and often milky juice. Star pattern in flowers (see picture)...................Morning-Glory: 145

Herbs (rarely vines) with milky sap. Leaves opposite or whorled. .... Dogbane/Milkweed: 140

Forest plants without chlorophyll. Leaves reduced to bract-like scales...Indian Pipe: 137

Marshland plants. Petals fuzzy or imprinted with a star-like pattern. ....Buckbean: 162

No sepals. Small flowers, often with spur. Leaves opposite and/or basal. Aromatic roots..................... Valerian: 175

Continue here if none of the above fit your sample:

Sepals united (Sepals may be very small, united only at the base, or difficult to determine. Cross-check below.):

Leaves opposite. Flowers/berries in pairs. ....Honeysuckle: 176

Leaves opposite or whorled. Small flowers with 4 stamens. Slightly irregular...................................... Verbena: 160

Leaves opposite or alternate and usually narrow. Tubular flowers with a flat face. Mostly in western states...............Phlox: 128

Leaves alternate. Usually 2-chambered ovary matures as capsule or tomato-like berry with many seeds. .... Nightshade: 146

Leaves alternate, basal, or whorled. Stamens aligned opposite petals. Fruit is a capsule. Moist habitats. ....Primrose: 130

Leaves usually alternate. Often hairy plants. Long stamens. Flower spike may curl like a scorpion tail...............Waterleaf: 144

Sepals separate (Sepals may be very small, or difficult to determine. Cross-check with section above.):

Leaves alternate. Bell-shaped flowers with five stamens. Usually milky juice. ....Harebell: 161

Leaves alternate. Usually hairy plants. Ovary matures into 4 separate nutlets (less by abortion). .... Borage: 142

Leaves alternate. Fruit a tomato-like berry or 2-celled capsule with numerous seeds. .... Nightshade: 146

Leaves alternate, basal, or whorled. Stamens aligned opposite petals. Fruit is a capsule. Moist soil. .... Primrose: 130

Leaves opposite. Flowers slightly irregular, in dense heads resembling the Aster family...Teasel: 175

Leaves opposite or whorled. Stamens fused to the petals. Bell- or dish-shaped flowers. Gentian:139

Leaves opposite or whorled. 4-5 sepals. 4-5 petals, often with pointy tips. 2- or 4-chambered ovary. ....Madder: 138

Key to Regular Dicot Flowers with 5 Separate Petals

(Includes some flowers with 10 petals.)

Shrubs or trees (includes some herbs or vines with woody stems, which may be repeated below):
—A mature fruit may be required. Try looking for the remains of last year's fruits on branches or on the ground.
Leaves opposite. Often pithy stems. 5 or 10 united sepals. 5 or 10 separate petals. Fruit a capsule. .... Hydrangea: 125
Leaves opposite (rarely alternate). Small sepals. Often large showy bracts. Fruit is a berry-like drupe. .... Dogwood: 124
Leaves opposite and pinnate. 5 sepals. 5 petals. 5, 10, or 15 stamens. 5-chambered ovary. Warm climates. .... Caltrop: 72
Leaves opposite and palmate or rarely pinnate. Fruit is a pair of winged seeds. *Acer.* .... Soapberry: 102
Leaves opposite or alternate. Sometimes thorny. Small flowers, often in showy clusters. 3-celled fruit. .... Buckthorn: 96
Leaves alternate and palmately lobed. Ovary inferior. Fruit is a berry with vertical lines. .... Gooseberry: 65
Leaves alternate and often palmately lobed. Slimy juice. Numerous stamens fused in a column. .... Mallow: 105
Leaves alternate and palmately or pinnately divided. Ovary inferior. Berries in umbels, heads, or spikes. .... Ginseng: 178
Leaves alternate and trifoliate or pinnately divided. Ovary superior. Fruit is a drupe, often in clusters. .... Cashew: 104
Leaves alternate, sometimes pinnately divided (rarely palmately lobed or divided) and often oval and serrated.
     5, 10, or 15+ stamens. 1 to numerous pistils. Fruits extremely variable. .... Rose: 91
Leaves alternate or basal. Evergreen. 4-5 sepals. 4-5 petals. 2x as many stamens. Fruit is a capsule. .... Pyrola: 136
Leaves alternate. Flower cluster attached to slender bract. 5 sepals. 5 petals. Numerous stamens. .... Basswood: 107
Leaves alternate. Large flowers with cone-like fruits. 3 sepals. 3+ petals. Numerous stamens and pistils. .... Magnolia: 52
Leaves alternate. Usually small flowers in dense clusters. 10+ stamens. Fruit is a pea-like pod. .... Mimosa: 80
Leaves alternate. Fruit a woody capsule with bony seeds. 5 basally united sepals. 5 narrow petals. .... Witch Hazel: 62
     —Be sure to read up on the Rose family, since it is challenging to write an adequate description here.—

Plants with distinctive vegetative features:
Aquatic plants with broad, floating leaves. 4 or 5 sepals, 5, 15 or more petals. Numerous stamens. .... Water Lily: 50
Colored bracts beneath flowers. Milky juice. Mostly found in warm climates. .... Spurge: 77
Vining plants with alternate leaves, tendrils, forming clusters of berries. Petals may fall upon opening. .... Grape: 67
Succulent plants. 5 sepals. 5 petals. 5 or 10 stamens. 3 or more simple pistils. Usually in grainy soil. .... Stonecrop: 64
Succulent plants. 2 sepals. 4-6 petals and 1 or 2x as many stamens. .... Miner's Lettuce/Purslane: 120
Bristly, hairy, or sticky plants. 5 sepals. 5 or 10 petals. Numerous stamens. Fruit a capsule. Arid habitats. .... Loasa: 126
3-parted shamrock leaf. 5 sepals. 5 petals. 10 stamens. 5-celled ovary. Favors moist soils. .... Woodsorrel: 73
Leaves tubular and vase-like to trap and drown insects. 4-5 sepals. 5 petals. Numerous stamens .... Pitcher Plant: 129
Leaves basal and sticky to trap insects. Moist forests. 4-5 sepals. 4-5 petals. 5 or 10-20 stamens. .... Sundew: 116

Continue here if none of the above fit your sample:
Leaves opposite and pinnately divided. Warm climates. 5 sepals. 5 petals. 5, 10, or 15 stamens. .... Caltrop: 72
Leaves opposite. 5 sepals, united or separate. 5 petals. 5 or 10 stamens. 2-5 styles. Petal ends are usually split. .... Pink: 114
Leaves opposite. 5 sepals. 5 petals. 10+ stamens. Usually yellow petals, often with red-orange spots. .... St. John's Wort: 74
Leaves opposite or alternate. 5 sepals. 5 petals. 5 or 10 stamens. Capsule splits like the sections of an orange. .... Flax: 78
Leaves opposite or alternate and palmately lobed or pinnately divided. Needle-like pistil. .... Geranium: 68
Leaves opposite, alternate, or basal. 5 sepals. 5 or 10 stamens. 5-parted stigma. Ovary inferior. .... Evening Primrose: 70
Leaves alternate or basal. Evergreen. 5 sepals. 5 petals. 10 stamens. Mostly bell-shaped flowers. .... Pyrola: 136
Leaves alternate or basal. 5 leathery sepals. 5 petals (up to 10). Numerous stamens. 3 to 5 simple pistils. .... Peony: 63
Leaves alternate, basal, or whorled. Stamens aligned opposite petals. Fruit is a capsule. Moist soil. .... Primrose: 130
Leaves alternate or basal. Usually an oblong ovary with 2 styles. Small flowers. Usually in mountains. .... Saxifrage: 66
Leaves alternate and often palmately lobed. Slimy juice. Numerous stamens fused in a column. .... Mallow: 105
Leaves alternate and often palmately lobed. Slimy juice. 5, 10, or numerous stamens. .... Cacao: 107
Leaves alternate. 3-15 sepals. 0-15 petals. Numerous stamens. 3+ simple pistils often with hooked tips. .... Buttercup: 55
Leaves alternate. 5 sepals. 5 petals. 5 stamens. Hollow stalks and compound umbels. .... Parsley: 179
Leaves alternate, sometimes pinnately divided (rarely palmately lobed or divided) and often oval and serrated.
     (continued) 5, 10, 15+ stamens. 1 to numerous pistils. Fruits extremely variable. .... Rose: 91
     —Be sure to read up on the Rose family, since it is challenging to write an adequate description here.—

Key to Regular Dicot Flowers with 5 Separate Petals

(Includes some flowers with 10 petals.)

Gooseberry Family

Heath Family / Pyrola

Hydrangea Family

Grape Family

Sundew Family

Pitcher Plant Family

Ginseng Family

Parsley Family

Buttercup Family

Caltrop Family

Geranium Family

Flax Family

Miner's Lettuce / Purslane Families

Mallow / Basswood Family

Rose Family

Saint John's Wort Family

Stonecrop Family

Saxifrage Family

Loasa Family

Pink Family

Primrose Family

Woodsorrel Family

Key to Dicot Trees and Shrubs by Their Fruits
(Species with showy flowers are also included in the flower keys)

Start here:

Leaves alternate. Fruits clustered in catkins. Individual fruits are small capsules, often with silky hairs. ....Willow: 76

Leaves alternate. Milky sap. Fruits spiny. *Maclura*. .... Mulberry: 88

Leaves alternate and usually pinnate. Fruit is a pea-like pod. ....Pea: 79

Leaves alternate and simple. Fruits clustered in usually large, cone-like structures. Big flowers............................Magnolia: 52

Leaves alternate and serrated. Fruits in cone-like catkins. Individual fruits are nuts or winged seeds. ....Birch: 101

Leaves alternate and serrated, often oval. Fruits are dry seeds or follicles. 5 persistent sepals...Rose: 91

Continue here if none of the above fit your sample:

Fruit is a winged seed (not including seeds from catkins):

Leaves opposite and palmate or rarely pinnate. Winged seeds develop in pairs. *Acer*. .... Soapberry: 102

Leaves opposite and pinnate. Winged seeds in loose clusters. *Fraxinus*. ....Olive: 149

Leaves alternate, often asymmetrical. Seed positioned in middle of wing. *Ulmus*. ....Elm: 87

Fruit is a nut or nut-like (walnut, acorn, etc.):

Leaves opposite and palmate. Large, nut-like seed wrapped in leathery or spiny skin...................................... Soapberry: 102

Leaves alternate and pinnate. Hard-shelled nuts in husks. Inside looks like walnuts or pecans. Aromatic................ Walnut: 99

Leaves alternate. Mostly acorn-like nuts, usually attached to a cap. Cap may have spines....................................Beech: 100

Leaves alternate. Nuts with attached bracts...Hazelnut: 101

Fruit is a capsule:

Leaves opposite. 3- to 6-chambered capsule with numerous seeds. Showy flowers. .... Hydrangea: 125

Leaves opposite and simple. 2-chambered capsule with 2 seeds per cell. ....Olive: 149

Leaves opposite and pinnate. 5 sepals. 5 petals. 5, 10, 15 stamens. 5-chambered ovary. Desert habitats.................. Caltrop: 72

Leaves opposite or alternate. 3-chambered capsule (sometimes 2 or 4). May have thorns................................... Buckthorn: 96

Leaves alternate. 2-chambered woody or leathery capsule with 1 or 2 bony seeds per chamber. .... Witch Hazel: 62

Leaves alternate and simple. Often evergreen. 4-5 (up to 10) chambers with numerous seeds................................ Heath: 132

Leaves alternate and serrated. 2-5 chambered capsule. 5 persistent sepals...Rose: 91

Fleshy fruits that are not true berries:

Leaves alternate, usually serrated. Pulpy fruit with sepals still attached on the bottom, forming a "star." ....Rose: 91

Leaves alternate and serrated. Aggregate fruit, like a raspberry. Bushes or brambles. *Rubus spp*...................................Rose: 91

Leaves alternate. Milky sap. Aggregate fruit. *Morus*. .... Mulberry: 88

Leaves alternate. Milky sap. Fig-like fruit. Tropical. *Ficus*.. Mulberry: 88

Continue here if none of the above fit your sample:

Fruit is a berry with several to numerous small seeds (Cross-check with the section below.):

Leaves opposite and simple, pinnate, or palmate. Fruits in pairs or clusters. Pithy stems.....................Honeysuckle/Adoxa: 176

Leaves alternate. Berry translucent with lines running end to end. Sepals remaining. Shrubs.......................... Gooseberry: 65

Leaves alternate. Often evergreen. Mostly small shrubs. Circular indentation or star at end of berry....................... Heath: 132

Leaves alternate or opposite. May have thorns. 3-chambered berry (sometimes 2 or 4)..................................... Buckthorn: 96

Leaves alternate and palmate or pinnate. Berries form in umbels, dense heads, or elongated spikes...................... Ginseng: 178

Fruit is a drupe—a fleshy fruit with a stony pit. (Cross-check with the section above.):

Leaves opposite. Flowers with 4-5 sepals, 4-5 petals, 2 stamens. Fruit is a purple drupe or berry..............................Olive: 149

Leaves opposite or sometimes alternate or whorled. Flowers often with showy, colored bracts. ....Dogwood: 124

Leaves opposite and simple, pinnate, or palmate. Fruits in pairs or clusters. Pithy stems.....................Honeysuckle/Adoxa: 176

Leaves opposite and pinnate. 5 sepals. 5 petals. 5, 10, or 15 stamens. 5-celled ovary. Desert habitats......................Caltrop: 72

Leaves opposite or alternate, usually silvery in color or with orange dots underneath. May have thorns................. Oleaster: 97

Leaves alternate. Highly aromatic. Deciduous in the North, but evergreen in the South.. Laurel: 53

Leaves alternate. Fruit with a "seam" down one side like a cherry. *Prunus*. ....Rose: 91

Leaves alternate. Loose cluster of dry fruits from a single stem attached to the middle of a bract. Trees. ....Basswood: 107

Leaves alternate, often asymmetrical. Trees or shrubs. *Celtis*..Elm: 87

Leaves alternate and either trifoliate or pinnate. Shrubs. Red or white berries......................................Cashew: 104

Leaves alternate and simple or pinnate, with spines on margin. Evergreen. Bright yellow inner bark. ....Barberry: 58

Leaves alternate and pinnate. Nut-like seed wrapped in translucent, fleshy skin... Soapberry: 102

Key to Dicot Trees and Shrubs by Their Fruits
(Species with showy flowers are also included in the flower keys)

Flowers are often very consistent across a family, while fruits tend to be much more variable. The Rose family, for instance, includes many plants with dry seeds or one-celled capsules, but also fleshy fruits as varied as strawberries, apples, and cherries. Nevertheless, it is helpful to have a *Key to Trees and Shrubs by their Fruits* because the fruits are often much more visible than the flowers. Readers may not notice a tree in bloom if the flowers are inconspicious and have no petals. Therefore, such families are not included in the flower keys. But readers may be drawn to a tree or shrub during the fruiting stage, so it is necessary to include the key here. Note that trees and shrubs *with* showy flowers are included in both this key as well as the flower keys.

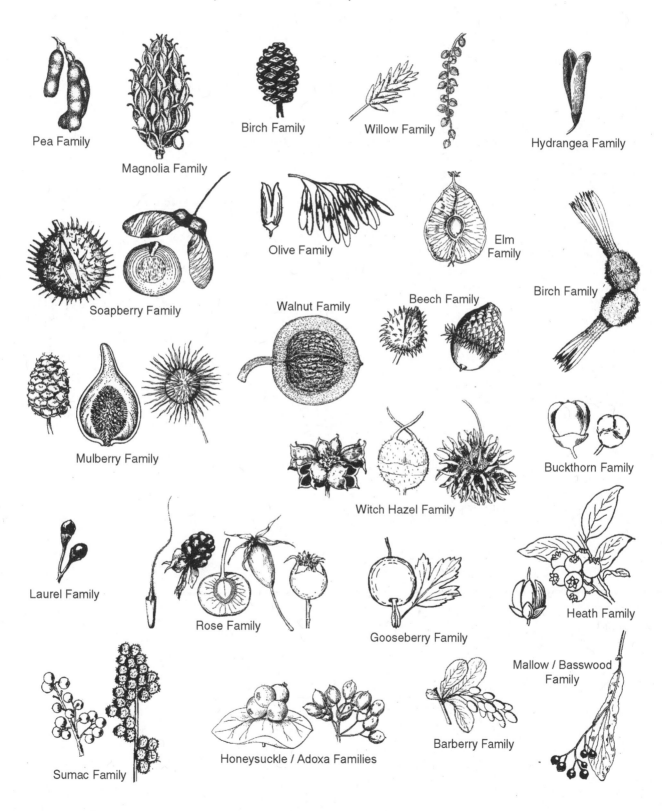

Pea Family

Magnolia Family

Birch Family

Willow Family

Hydrangea Family

Soapberry Family

Olive Family

Walnut Family

Elm Family

Beech Family

Birch Family

Mulberry Family

Witch Hazel Family

Buckthorn Family

Laurel Family

Rose Family

Gooseberry Family

Heath Family

Sumac Family

Honeysuckle / Adoxa Families

Barberry Family

Mallow / Basswood Family

Key to Monocot Flowers

(Excluding Trees. See the Palm Family, page: 189)

Monocots with Showy Flowers

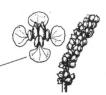

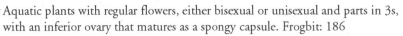

Aquatic plants with flower parts in 3s and 6 to numerous simple pistils, usually on a cone-like head. Water Plantain: 183

Aquatic plants of fresh or saltwater with flower parts in 4s and 1-4 simple pistils. Pondweed (also listed below): 188

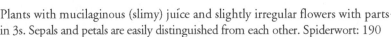

Aquatic plants with regular flowers, either bisexual or unisexual and parts in 3s, with an inferior ovary that matures as a spongy capsule. Frogbit: 186

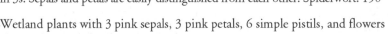

Plants with mucilaginous (slimy) juice and slightly irregular flowers with parts in 3s. Sepals and petals are easily distinguished from each other. Spiderwort: 190

Wetland plants with 3 pink sepals, 3 pink petals, 6 simple pistils, and flowers clustered in umbels. Flowering Rush: 182

Flowers densely clustered in a showy spike, often wrapped in a large green or white modified leaf called a "spathe." (Individual flowers are small and non-showy.) Fruit is a berry. Arum: 184 (Lacking a spathe: Sweet Flag: 182)

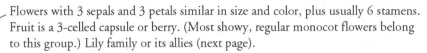

Flowers with 3 sepals and 3 petals similar in size and color, plus usually 6 stamens. Fruit is a 3-celled capsule or berry. (Most showy, regular monocot flowers belong to this group.) Lily family or its allies (next page).

Aquatic plants with lily-like flowers and spongy stems. Pickerelweed: 191

Lily-like flowers, but only 3 stamens. Leaves usually arise from base of the plant in a flat plane. Iris: 201

Distinctly irregular monocot flowers (sometimes not showy). Inferior ovary swells to become seed capsule. Orchid: 202

Monocots with Non-Showy Flowers

Vining plants with or without tendrils. Flowers/berries clustered in umbels. Greenbrier: 195

Aquatic plants with long, narrow leaves. Minute flowers clustered in spikes or balls with male flowers above and female flowers below. Cattail: 204

Aquatic, grassy plants with 6 green tepals, 6 stamens, and 3 simple pistils. Rannoch-Rush: 187

Aquatic plants (often in damp meadows) with grassy leaves. Flower parts in 3s with 3 to 6 simple pistils (sometimes basally united). Arrowgrass: 187

Submerged aquatic plants with narrow, serrated leaves. Submerged unisexual flowers with a single stamen enclosed by a bract, or a single pistil, sometimes enclosed by a bract. Water Nymph: 186

Aquatic plants of fresh or salt water with flower parts mostly in 4s and 1-4 simple pistils (also listed above). Pondweed: 188

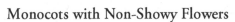

Grassy plants with knee-like joins (nodes) present on the main flower stem. Grass: 207

Grass like plants with triangular flower stems and no nodes. (Some have round, pithy stems.) Sedge: 206

Grass-like plants with small, green, lily-like flowers and parts in 3s. Rush: 205

Minute aquatic plants floating in the water, without noticeable stems or flowers. Duckweed: 184

Key to Lily-Like Monocot Flowers
(Flowers with 3 sepals and 3 petals usually identical in size and color.)

Refined Taxonomy

Aside from the Pickerelweed family, all the families and subfamilies below were previously lumped together as the conglomerate Lily family. These are monocot plants with 3 sepals and 3 petals that are usually identical in size and color, as well as 6 stamens, and a 3-parted pistil. Taxonomists recognized that many of these plants were not closely related to each other, but their proper relationships were difficult to discern from appearances alone. Many different schemes were proposed, with up to seventy different possible families or subfamilies split out of the original family. However, there were always contradictory plants that didn't fit neatly within one grouping or seemed to overlap with another one.

Recently, taxonomists have turned to molecular and genetic studies to tease out the proper relationships between these plants, segregating the old Lily family into a number of families and subfamilies that are presumably more accurate than those proposed in the past. Unfortunately, many of these new families lack obvious patterns for simple memorization and identification, and there is still a great deal of overlap between the families.

If your flower has lily-like characteristics, you can use this key to help narrow down the identification to the proper family. However, when cross-referencing with other sources, such as keying out a flower in another book, keep in mind that any plant from the following families or subfamilies might be listed as part of either the Lily family, or several other possible families previously proposed by taxonomists.

lady tulip
Tulipa clusiana
Lily Family

Lily-like flowers, but with distinct sepals and petals:
3 large, leaf-like green bracts. 3 green sepals. 3 showy white to pink or red petals. *Trillium* .... Bunchflower: 194
Slender leaves. 3 green or colored sepals. 3 petals, often hairy-feathery, accented near base. ....Sego Lily: 192

Lily-like flowers with similar sepals and petals:
Aquatic plants with spongy stems. ....Pickerelweed: 191
Leaves fern-like, feathery. Small flowers. Fruit a red or greenish berry. *Asparagus* .... Asparagus: 197
Leaves whorled. Flowers small and greenish. Fruit a berry. *Medeola* .... Indian Cucumber: 192
Leaves whorled or alternate. Flowers showy, often with spots on the petals. Fruit is a capsule. *Lilium* .... Lily: 192
Leaves alternate. Stem zigzags from leaf to leaf:
    Flower solitary beneath each leaf. Fruit an orange or red berry. *Streptopus* .... Sego Lily: 192
    Flowers one to several beneath each leaf. Fruit a red to purple berry. *Polygonatum* .... Beargrass: 198
    Flowers at end of stem, often in pairs. Fruit a lumpy or pointed red berry, often fuzzy. *Prosartes* .... Sego Lily: 192
    Flowers at end of stem, numerous. Fruit a spotted or striped berry. *Smilacina / Maianthemum*...................... Nolina: 198
    Flowers at end of stem. Fruit a capsule. *Uvularia* .... Autumn Crocus: 195
Leaves alternate or basal. Bunches of white or green flowers in spike or raceme. Pistil with 3 styles. .... Bunchflower: 194
Leaves alternate or basal. Flowers arranged in a spike. Starchy bulb layered similar to an onion. ....Agave: 199
Leaves alternate or basal. Flowers in umbels or solitary, emerging from spathe-like bract (wrapped in a modified leaf).
    Petals separate. Bulb layered like an onion. (May or may not have onion smell.) .... Amaryllis: 196
    Petals united. Bulb is a starchy corm without layers. .... Brodiaea: 197
Leaves basal. White or yellow flowers. Fruit is a purple berry. *Clintonia* .... Indian Cucumber: 192
Leaves basal. Flowers large and lily-like. Long, tuberous roots. *Hemerocallis* .... Day Lily: 200
Leaves basal. Flowers white with united petals. Fruit a red berry. *Convallaria* .... Nolina: 198
Leaves basal, usually fibrous. Rugged desert plants with a tall central flower spike. .... Beargrass or Agave: 198/199
Leaves basal, filled with mucilaginous (slimy) juice. Desert-like plants. Tubular flowers. *Aloe* .... Asphodel: 200
Leaves basal. Showy flowers. If none of the above fit, it is probably a true member of the Lily family. ....Lily: 192

Part II:

Reference Guide
An Herbal Field Guide
to Plant Families of North America

broadleaf plantain
Plantago major
Plantain Family

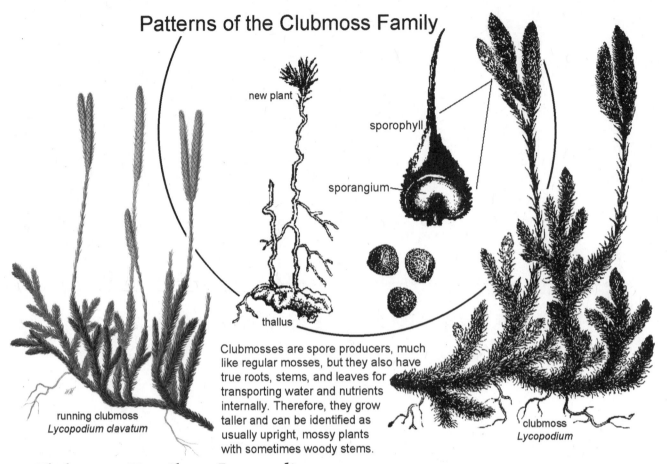

Patterns of the Clubmoss Family

new plant

sporophyll

sporangium

thallus

running clubmoss
Lycopodium clavatum

clubmoss
Lycopodium

Clubmosses are spore producers, much like regular mosses, but they also have true roots, stems, and leaves for transporting water and nutrients internally. Therefore, they grow taller and can be identified as usually upright, mossy plants with sometimes woody stems.

Clubmoss Family—*Lycopodiaceae*

The northern hemisphere was covered with vast, swampy forests from about 200 to 250 million years ago. These forests included now-extinct species of the Clubmoss family that grew to more than one hundred feet high! Note that peat moss (*Sphagnum*) is not a Clubmoss since it has no vascular system. (See page 8.)

The Clubmosses have horizontal branching stems, either above or below ground. These send up erect shoots ranging in size from a half inch to over a foot tall in some species. The clubmosses produce spores in a cone-like structure at the end of a stalk. They are "homosporous," meaning they produce spores that are neither male nor female. The spores are shed, then germinate to become a minute "thallus," meaning a plant part that is not differentiated into leaves or a stem. The thallus produces male sperm cells and female egg cells. Upon fertilization, the egg cells develop into new plants. The reproductive cycle is exceedingly slow in the club mosses. Twenty years or more can pass between the dropping of the spores and the final germination of the new plant.

Worldwide, there are about 13 genera and 400 species, most of which were formely lumped together within *Lycopodium*. Due to segregation, there are potentially 7 genera in North America, including *Diphasiastrum, Lycopodiella, Palhinhaea, Pseudolycopodiella, Huperzia*, and *Phlegmariurus*. Some taxonomists propose segregating the latter two genera into a new family, *Huperziaceae*.

Huperzia—firmoss (15/11/1) Firmosses grow in clumps. Some northern species superficially resemble fir trees (*Abies*).

Lycopodium—clubmoss (25/14/7) • Clubmoss spores have been used as a homeostatic for nosebleed or other hemorrhaging and to absorb fluids from damaged tissues (Lust). The spores were once used as flash powder for stage performances (Smith). Picking and drying the moss will cause it to produce a large, final crop of spores.

Staghorn clubmoss (*L. clavatum*) reportedly contains toxic alkaloids (Schauenberg), but Native Americans used the tea as an analgesic to relieve pain after childbirth (Willard). The whole plant can be applied to relieve muscle cramps (Treben). Chinese used the pollen as a dusting powder to coat suppositories and to keep pills from sticking together. Today clubmoss spores are sold as "vegetable sulphur;" the powder is dusted onto diaper rashes, bed sores, and herpes eruptions. The spores contain a waxy substance that is soothing on the skin, and it repels water. Reportedly you can dip a spore-coated hand in water and remain completely dry. The spores were formerly used as a dusting powder for condoms. The roots were used as a mordant to set dyes (Rogers).

Spike Moss Family—*Selaginellaceae*

Members of the Spike Moss family have small leaves arranged in four rows along the stems. Each leaf has a small, scale-like appendage at the base of the upper surface, which helps distinguish them from the Clubmoss family. This is believed to be an ancestral hold-over with no function in the living species.

Spike Mosses are heterosporous, meaning that they produce both male and female spores on the plant. In an intermediate step on the way to producing seeds, the female spores develop into a thallus on the plant and are fertilized before being shed. Worldwide, there is 1 genus and some 750 species.

Selaginella—spike moss, resurrection plant (700/37/4) In times of drought, the resurrection plant (*S. lepidophylla*) of the desert soutwest rolls its leaves into a tight dry ball. Upon exposure to moisture it immediately uncurls and continues growing. It is often cultivated as a curiosity. Note that another resurrection plant, called *Anastatica,* belongs to the Mustard family (Asch). There is also a resurrection fern in the Polypody family. Medicinally, spike moss can be mashed and simmered in milk, used internally or externally for snake or spider bites (Rogers).

Spike Moss Family

club spike moss
Selaginella selaginoides

meadow spike moss
Selaginella apoda

female spore

male spores

These are short, upright or spreading plants with branching stems. They produce both male and female spores.

Quillwort Family—*Isoetaceae*

If you raise fish in an aquarium, then you may already be familiar with the Quillwort family. The Quillworts are small plants, typically found growing on the bottom of fresh-water ponds and lakes. They have hollow quill-like leaves, with a spore sack (sporangia) at the base of each leaf. They are heterosporous, meaning that they produce both male and female spores. The outer leaves produce the male spore sacks, while the inner leaves produce the female spore sacks.

Worldwide, there are 2 genera and 77 species. Only *Isoetes* is found in North America. *Stylites* is only found in the Peruvian Andes.

Isoetes—quillwort (75/45/5) Various species are native to states and provinces throughout North America. Quillwort is often planted in aquariums. Turn to page 9 for an illustration of lake quillwort (*I. lacustris*)

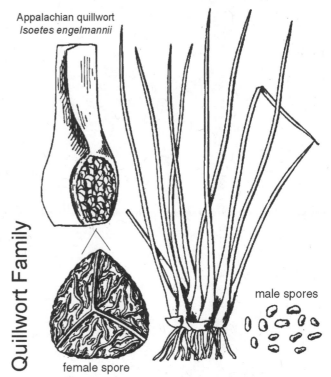

Appalachian quillwort
Isoetes engelmannii

Quillwort Family

female spore

male spores

These are short, aquatic, grass-like plants with quill-like (hollow) leaves that produce both male and female spores.

Adder's Tongue Family—*Ophioglossaceae*

The Adder's Tongue or Grape-fern family is more primitive than the other ferns. The sporangia form as globe-shaped sacks on a stalk or at the base, unlike most other ferns with sporangia on the underside of the leaves. They are homosporous, meaning the spores are neither male nor female. Males and females are produced on a thallus on the ground, where fertilization takes place. World-wide, there are 4 genera and 70 species. North American genera are listed below.

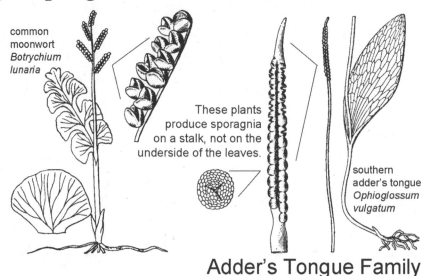

These plants produce sporagnia on a stalk, not on the underside of the leaves.

common moonwort
Botrychium lunaria

southern adder's tongue
Ophioglossum vulgatum

Adder's Tongue Family

Botrychium—grape fern, moon-wort (40/33/10) One species is known to be boiled and eaten in the Himalayas and New Zealand (Sturtevant). A tea of the root has emetic, expectorant, and diaphoretic properties (Fern). The tea induces a gentle, warm sweat while soothing the nervous system. It is also mildly diuretic (Rogers).

Ophioglossum—adder's tongue (30/10/1) The botanical name is Greek for "snake tongue," which the spore-bearing stalk resembles. Other ferns unroll their new leaves, but the grape ferns open them laterally. The leaves of at least one species are edible. Medicinally, the juice of the leaves is taken for internal bleeding and bruises (Fern).

rattlesnake fern
Botrychium virginianum

Common Terminology for Ferns

Fern leaves are similar to other types of leaves, but have a unique terminology. The whole leaf is often called a *frond*. Young fern fronds are often coiled up as *fiddleheads*. The stem or petiole is known as a *stipe*, while the leafy part is known as the *blade*. The stem may extend through the blade as the midrib, known as a *rachis*. In a few species, the blade may be *simple* like the adder's tongue above, or sometimes lobed or deeply lobed or *pinnatifid*. Most often, the blade is divided to form a *pinnate* leaf. Each segment of the pinnate leaf is known as a *pinna* (plural: *pinnae*). These pinnae may also be divided, forming a *bipinnate* frond, where the smaller segments are known as *pinnules*. In rare cases, these pinnules may also be divided, forming a *tripinnate* frond.

A frond may be either *sterile* or *fertile*. The spore cases or *sporangia* are typically clustered into a *sorus* (plural: *sori*), typically found on the underside of a fertile frond. The shape and position of these sori are often helpful aids for identification. In many species, the sorus is covered by a thin membrane, known as an *indusium* (plural: *indusia*), which may wither away as the frond matures. The presence or absence and shape of an indusium is also utilized in fern identification.

Horsetail Family—*Equisetaceae*

Horsetail produces two different stalks in some species. One is the fertile "jointgrass," the other is the sterile "horsetail." The fertile stalk produces a cone-like structure at the top, which is covered with spore-producing scales. The spores are wrapped with small bands. These bands unwrap in dry weather to function as a parachute to carry the spores on the wind. On the ground, the spores produce a thallus, cross-fertilize, then develop into a new plant. There is 1 genus and 23 species worldwide.

Ancestral Horsetails were abundant during the Carbiniferous period, 360 to 299 million years ago. Many species grew into giant trees. These ancient plants became a significant portion of our coal deposits. Today, the tallest living species is the giant Mexican horsetail (*E. myriochaetum*), which often grows more than fifteen feet tall. Horsetails have an abrasive quality to them because they absorb silica from the soil, giving strength to the plant structure.

Equisetum—horsetail, joint grass, scouring rush (23/16/8) • The horsetail contains significant quantities (5–8%) of silica and silicic acids plus saponins (Tyler), which makes it an excellent abrasive pad for cleaning camp cookware. This silica content is beneficial for the hair and fingernails (Bigfoot). The roots of some species are starchy and edible (Sturtevant). Medicinally, a tea of the plant is mildly diuretic and astringent, useful for urinary tract infections, intestinal bleeding, excess menstruation, or external bleeding. Horsetails are also rich in calcium and other constituents believed beneficial for mending fractured bones and connective tissues.

The fresh plant contains thiaminase, an enzyme that destroys vitamin B1 stored in the body. Cooking renders it safe. However, the silica content can irritate the urinary tract and kidneys with excessive use. The plants are known to accumulate heavy metals and chemicals from polluted soil. (Tilford).

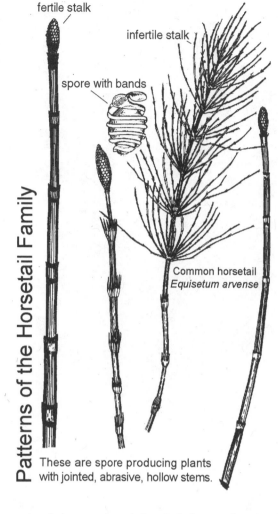

fertile stalk

infertile stalk

spore with bands

Common horsetail
Equisetum arvense

Patterns of the Horsetail Family

These are spore producing plants with jointed, abrasive, hollow stems.

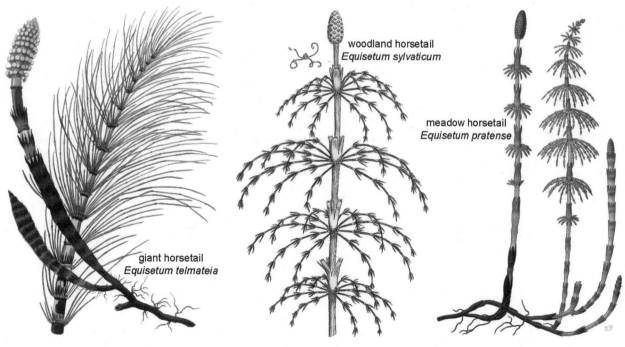

giant horsetail
Equisetum telmateia

woodland horsetail
Equisetum sylvaticum

meadow horsetail
Equisetum pratense

Sporangia form on a frond without chlorophyll, which matures as a distinctive golden-brown spike.

royal fern
Osmunda regalis

Royal Fern Family *(vertical label)*

Royal Fern Family—*Osmundaceae*

If you have ever encountered ferns with a spike of golden-brown "flowers," then you know the Royal Fern family. Often found in swampy ground, these large ferns have heavy rootstocks with dense masses of wiry roots. The ferns sometimes develop extensive colonies of clones as new ferns sprout up from the roots. In North American genera, the sporangia form on a frond without chlorophyll, which matures as a distinctive golden-brown spike that may be mistaken as flowers. This ancient lineage dates back to the Upper Permian period. Worldwide, there are 4 genera and 15 to 25 species. Our native genera, found in the eastern half of the country, are listed below. *Todea* and *Leptopteris* grow in the southern hemisphere.

Osmunda—flowering ferns (10/3/0)
Osmundastrum—cinnamon fern (2/1/1) The North American species is the cinnamon fern (*O. cinnamomeum*), formerly included in *Osmunda*. It is considered a living fossil, because it can be traced back through the fossil record to at least 75 million years old.

Water Fern Family—*Salviniaceae*

The Water Ferns are small, floating ferns. The leaves may appear in pairs or rows, grouped in twos or threes. The Water Ferns may be confused with members of the unrelated Duckweed subfamily of the Arum family. Note the submerged sporangia on the illustration here. If the sporangia are present then it is definitely a Water Fern.

Worldwide, there are 2 genera and 16 species. *Salvinia* may be found in Florida and other southern states. *Azolla* is found across the continent.

Azolla—mosquito fern (6/6/0) *Azolla* associates with cyanobacteria (blue-green algae) to "fix" nitrogen from the atmosphere in a form that is usable for plants, providing a tremendous source of fertilizer for rice paddies in southeast Asia. The ferns form such a dense mat on the water that mosquito larvae cannot come up for air, hence the common name "mosquito fern." Azolla was previously segregated into its own family, *Azollaceae*.
Salvinia—water fern (10/10/0) Water Ferns are sometimes grown in aquariums, and they grow fast if there is adequate nutrition and light. They help prevent algae growth by shading parts of the aquarium and consuming the nutrients in the water. One African species introduced to a lake created a mat covering 77 square miles in just eleven months.

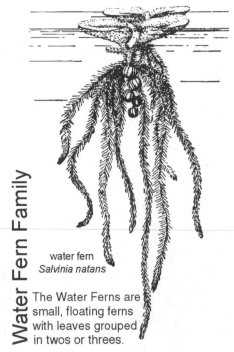

water fern
Salvinia natans

Water Fern Family *(vertical label)*

The Water Ferns are small, floating ferns with leaves grouped in twos or threes.

Bracken Fern Family—*Dennstaedtiaceae*

Ferns of this family typically have large, highly divided leaves with hairy or sometimes scaly stems. In other ferns, the sori that contain the sporangia typically form towards the center of the frond. But members of the Bracken Fern family develop sori near the edge or margin of the frond. The sori may be either round with a cup-shaped membrane (indusia), such as in *Dennstaedtia* or linear with a false indusium formed from the curled edge of the leaf, such as in *Pteridium*. Worldwide there are about 11 genera and 175 species. North American genera are listed below.

Dennstaedtia—hay-scented fern (45/4/0) *D. punctilobula* is common in Appalachia, where it often forms colonies of clones. When the light source comes from one side, such as under a tree, the leaves tend to align with each other facing the light. The crushed vegetation smells like fresh hay.

Hypolepis—bramble fern (140/1/0) *H. repens* grows in Florida.

Odontosoria—wedgelet fern (22/1/0) *O. clavata* grows in southern Florida.

Pteridium—bracken fern (10/2/1) The common name comes from the Swedish word bräken, meaning fern. Brackens are found worldwide in all environments except deserts. This genus was formerly considered as single species, *P. aquilinum*, but the different varities are now being treated as individual species. The leaves or fronds grow individually from an underground rhizome. The immature fronds, known as fiddleheads, are edible raw or cooked, with a long history of use around the world. However, raw bracken contains the enzyme thiaminase, which breaks down thiamine (Vitamin B1) in the body, leading to symptoms of beriberi with excess consumption. Bracken is also known to contain carcinogens that can lead to cancer, and consumption is now discouraged (Bell). The root contains saponin (Fern).

Bracken Fern Family

bracken fern
Pteridium aquilinum

Polypod Family—*Polypodiaceae*

Polypod ferns grow in soil, on rocks, or as epiphytes—plants that grow on other plants but are not parasitic. Leaves are variously shaped and divided with spores forming in rows of receptacles, called sori, on each side of the midrib on the underside of the leaf. The sori lack a membrane covering (indusium). Worldwide there are about 40 genera and 500 species. North American genera are listed below.

Campyloneurum—strap fern (50/4/0) Native to Florida.

Microgramma—snake fern (20/1/0) Native to Florida.

Neurodium—ribbon fern (1/1/0) Native to Florida.

Pecluma—rockcap fern (30/3/0) Native to Florida. Formerly included in *Polypodium*.

Phlebodium—golden polypody (2/2/0) Native to Florida. Formerly included in *Polypodium*.

Pleopeltis—resurrection fern (20/5/0) Grows from Texas to Florida, as far north as New York.

Polypodium—polypody (100/18/1) The root contains a resinous, bitter substance, volatile oils, and a sugary mucilage (Schauenberg). A strong tea of the root of the licorice fern (*P. glycyrrhiza*) is useful as an anti-inflammatory, especially as a mild alternative to antihistamines (Moore). *P. vulgare* contains osladin, which is 300 times sweeter than sugar (Rogers).

The resurrection fern shrivels when dry, but quickly unfurls when wet. It is commonly found on the trunks of oaks and elms in the southern states.

resurrection fern
Pleopeltis squalida

Polypod Family

Maidenhair Fern Family—*Pteridaceae*

Members of the Maidenhair Fern family typically grow in soil or on rocks with pinnately divided leaves. Sporangia-bearing sori typically form along the veins and often grow together with age, forming a continuous band or dense covering. The sori lack a true indusium (protective membrane), typically protected instead by a false indusium formed from the recurved edge of the leaf.

Classification of the ferns remains uncertain and hotly contested among botanists. Each authoritative source adopts a different classification scheme, with some splitting *Pteridaceae* into as many as eighteen smaller families. The larger and more accepted families include the Bracken Fern, Polypod, Wood Fern, and Spleenwort families, which have been separated out in the text. The leftover ferns remain lumped together here. The family was also known as *Adiantaceae* for awhile.

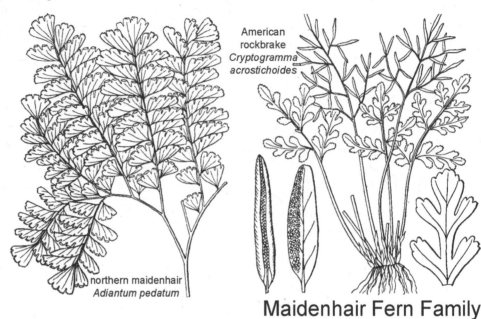

American rockbrake
Cryptogramma acrostichoides

northern maidenhair
Adiantum pedatum

Maidenhair Fern Family

Acrostichum—leather fern (3/2/0) Native to Florida.

Adiantum—maidenhair (200/12/1) Various species grow from coast to coast. A tea of the leaves is an expectorant and refrigerant, used for coughs and colds (Lust). A tea of the leaves or root is used as a menstrual stimulant (Moore), or as a hair rinse to add shine and body (Tilford).

heartleaf cliffbrake
Pellaea cordifolia

Argyrochosma—false cloak fern (20/6/0) New genus derived from species formerly in *Notholaena* and *Pellaea*. Various species are native from California to Wyoming, Texas, and Illinois.

Aspidotis—lace fern (4/3/1) Mostly native to slopes, ridges, and rocky outcroppings, from British Columbia to Montana to Mexico.

Astrolepis—cloak fern (8/4/0) New genus derived from species formerly in *Cheilanthes* and *Notholaena*. Native to the southern states from California to Georgia.

Ceratopteris—water fern (3/3/0) Aquatic and semi-aquatic fern found in California and from Texas to Florida.

Cheilanthes—lip fern (150/28/2) Lip ferns are adapted to mostly dry conditions, often found on rocks, growing from coast to coast.

Cryptogramma—rock brake (8/4/3) The regular fronds look much like parsely leaves, while the fertile, spore-bearing leaves have long, narrow, bumpy segments covered thickly on the underside with sporangia. The ferns often grow in crevices and cracks of rocks.

Notholaena—cloak fern (25/10/0) Cloak ferns are common in coarse, gravelly soils of mountain ranges in warm, semiarid regions from California to Texas.

Pteris—brake fern (280/5/0) Introduced to subtropical climates from California to Florida, north to Maryland. "Brake" is an old English term for "fern."

Pellaea—cliff brake (40/15/2) Various species are found from coast to coast, mostly in moist, rocky habitats. A tea of the plant can be taken for tuberculosis and other lung infections (Bigfoot).

Pityrogramma—gold fern (15/2/0) Native to Florida.

Vittaria—shoestring fern (50/3/0) Native east of the Mississippi River.

Wood Fern Family—*Dryopteridaceae*

The Wood Fern family was segregated from the Maidenhair Fern family and has become widely accepted as its own family, but not yet well defined. Various genera included here are sometimes segregated into several smaller families. As yet, the family remains too varied to offer any obvious patterns for convenient field identification.

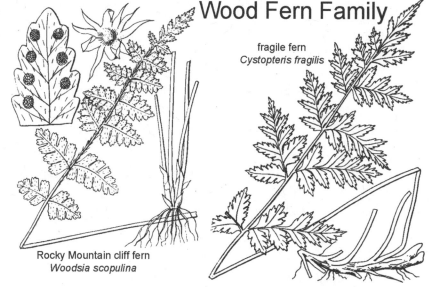

Wood Fern Family

fragile fern
Cystopteris fragilis

Rocky Mountain cliff fern
Woodsia scopulina

Athyrium—lady fern (150/2/2) It contains a constituent like filicic acid (Densmore).

Arachniodes—holly fern (50/1/0) Holly fern is a non-native plant now growing in South Carolina.

Ctenitis—lace fern (150/2/0) Native to Louisiana and Florida.

Cyrtomium—netvein hollyfern (15/2/0) *C. caryotideum* is native from Louisiana to Alabama. The Japanese *C. falcatum* has become naturalized in coast states from Oregon to Texas to New York.

Cystopteris—bladder fern (18/11/2)

Deparia—false spleenwort (50/2/0) Grows east of the Mississippi River.

Diplazium—twinsorus fern (400/3/0) Grows east of the Mississippi River.

Dryopteris—shield fern (225/30/4) The plant contains potent acids. A tea of the root is used to expel worms, but must be followed by a purgative shortly afterwards to keep from poisoning the body. It should never be mixed with alcohol. The tea is also used as a foot bath for varicose veins (Lust). A poultice of the fresh, grated root is helpful for inflammation of the lymphatic glands. (Rogers).

Gymnocarpium—oak fern (9/9/3) Various species are found across the northern latitudes and south throughout the Rockies.

Lomariopsis—fringed fern (45/1/0) *L. kunzeana* is a native of Florida.

Matteuccia—ostrich fern (3/1/0) *M. struthiopteris.* The young fiddleheads are edible in moderation, but fresh they contain thiaminase, which destroys vitamin B1 in the body, so they must be cooked. Native Americans in Canada roasted the roots, then peeled away the outside and ate the cores.

Nephrolepis—sword fern (25/6/0) Various species grow from Arizona to Florida.

Onoclea—sensitive fern (1/1/0) *O. sensibilis* is found from Texas north to Manitoba, east to the Atlantic.

Phanerophlebia—vein fern (8/2/0) Grows from Arizona to Texas.

Polystichum—holly fern, sword fern (260/15/5) The roasted roots are edible (Sturtevant). The fronds were used to line steam pits for cooking (Turner).

Tectaria—Halberd fern (200/5/0) Various species grow in Texas and Florida.

Woodsia—cliff fern (30/16/2) Grows throughout North America. *Woodsia* is sometimes split out into its own family, *Woodsiaceae*.

Spleenwort Family–*Aspleniaceae*

Ferns of the Spleenwort family all have linear sori near the edge of the frond, with a flap-like indusium (membrane) arising along one side. Worldwide, there is only 1 genus and about 700 species.

Asplenium (including *Camptosorus*)—spleenwort (700/28/2) A tea of the plant is used to remove obstructions from the liver and spleen, and gravel from the bladder (Kadans).

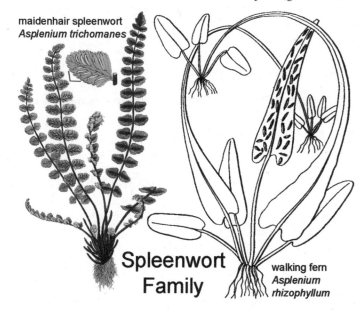

maidenhair spleenwort
Asplenium trichomanes

Spleenwort Family

walking fern
Asplenium rhizophyllum

Clade: Naked Seed > Order: Pine > Family: Pine

Pine Family—*Pinaceae*

The Pine family is as familiar as Christmas. Pines are mostly evergreen trees and shrubs with spirally arranged, linear, needle-like leaves. Male cones are small and fall soon after dispersing their pollen to the wind. Female cones briefly become elongated, exposing ovules to pollen in the air. These cones are aerodynamically shaped to create swirling wind currents to help catch the pollen. The pollen and cones are aerodynamically matched to each other, so that each species captures its own pollen. After pollination, the scales grow rapidly and again cover the ovules, allowing them to mature into seeds. Lightweight, winged seeds are primarily dispersed by wind. Heavier seeds are disperesed by squirrels and birds. The sprouting seeds are multi-cotyledonous, with 3 to 24 seed leaves.

Primitive conifers first came into being about 300 million years ago, but most or all are extinct now. The Pine family as we know it originated about 100 million years ago. Worldwide there are 11 genera and 220 species. Our native genera are listed below. Between 35 and 40 million trees from multiple genera are cut and sold each year in the United States as Christmas trees. Amber is the fossilized pitch from this family.

The Pine family produces edible seeds that are rich in oils, although they are small and difficult to gather from most species. The needles may be used in tea as a beverage, or medicinally for a diuretic. The Pine family is highly resinous, useful for its expectorant properties, but over consumption may lead to kidney complications, so caution is advised. Read more about resins in the *Medicinal Properties* section of this book.

Tips for Identifying Pine Family Genera

Pines have 1 to 8 needles wrapped together at the base by a thin membrane.
Larches have bright green, deciduous needles arranged in a spiral at the branch buds.
The spruces usually have sharp, pointed needles that roll between the fingers. The cones hang down.
The firs have soft, "furry" needles that are flat and won't roll between the fingers. The cones point up.
Douglas fir cones hang down. The cones have distinctive, 3-lobed, trident-like bracts between the scales.
Hemlock trees have short, flat, blunt needles attached by a small stem.

Abies—fir (50/9/2) • Fir contains turpentine, an oleoresin made of essential oils and resin. The oleoresin is used internally as a stimulant, diuretic, and diaphoretic or externally as a rubefacient (Densmore). The needles can be used as an aromatic bath for rheumatism and nervous diseases (Klein). Steeped fir needles make one of my favorite wilderness teas.

Larix—larch, tamarack (10/5/2) • Larches are deciduous, turning yellow in the fall before dropping their needles. The trees sometimes exude a sweet, edible sap (Sturtevant). Medicinally, the needles, bark, and resin all contain varying amounts of volatile oils, essentially turpentine. Drink a tea of the needles as a carminative to expel gas, or add the tea to your bath water for inflamed joints. Excess consumption can injure the kidneys (Lust).

Picea—spruce (50/7/2) • Spruce trees like damp soil. Here in the West, they are often found along small streams in pine or Douglas fir forests. Spruces are the most effective conifer for shedding rain. On one botanical outing, I led a group of fifteen people under a big spruce tree to wait out a storm. We had a potluck picnic under the tree while the rain poured down inches away. Medicinally, a tea of the shoots is expectorant and diaphoretic, ideal for coughs and bronchitis (Lust).

Pinus—pine (100/50/5) • Pine needles are generally (not always) attached to the branches in clusters of two (red pine group), three (yellow pine group), or five (white pine group) needles per cluster. All pine nuts are edible, but many are impractical to harvest. Store-bought pine nuts typically come from Asia, or from any of several species of one- and two-needle "pinyon pines" in the southwest. In addition, five-needle pines, such as whitebark (*P. albicaulis*) and limber pine (*P. flexilis*) are pretty good alternatives. See *Participating in Nature* for instructions on harvesting and processing pine nuts.

Pines are resinous and aromatic. Medicinally, the tea is useful as an expectorant, but can irritate the kidneys. It is reported that the needles of some pines cause abortions in cattle, so caution is advised here. Externally, the resin has a disinfectant quality, like Pine-Sol®, which historically contained pine oil. The bark of some species contains powerful antioxidants.

Pseudotsuga—Douglas fir (7/2/1) • The common name "Douglas fir" doesn't fit well with the botanical name, which means "false hemlock." In damp weather, large Douglas firs often provide dry shelter for camping or waiting out a storm. Isolated trees may be at risk for lightening strikes, but those in a forest are unlikely to be hit. The seeds are edible like pine nuts, but smaller and not really worth the harvesting effort.

Tsuga—hemlock tree (15/5/2) There is no relationship between the hemlock tree and the poison hemlocks of the Parsley family. *Tsuga* is astringent, diuretic, and diaphoretic. A tea of the bark or twigs is used for a sore mouth or throat, and kidney or bladder problems. Externally it is used as a wash for sores (Lust). The inner bark was reportedly used by the Native Americans for food in the springtime (Sturtevant).

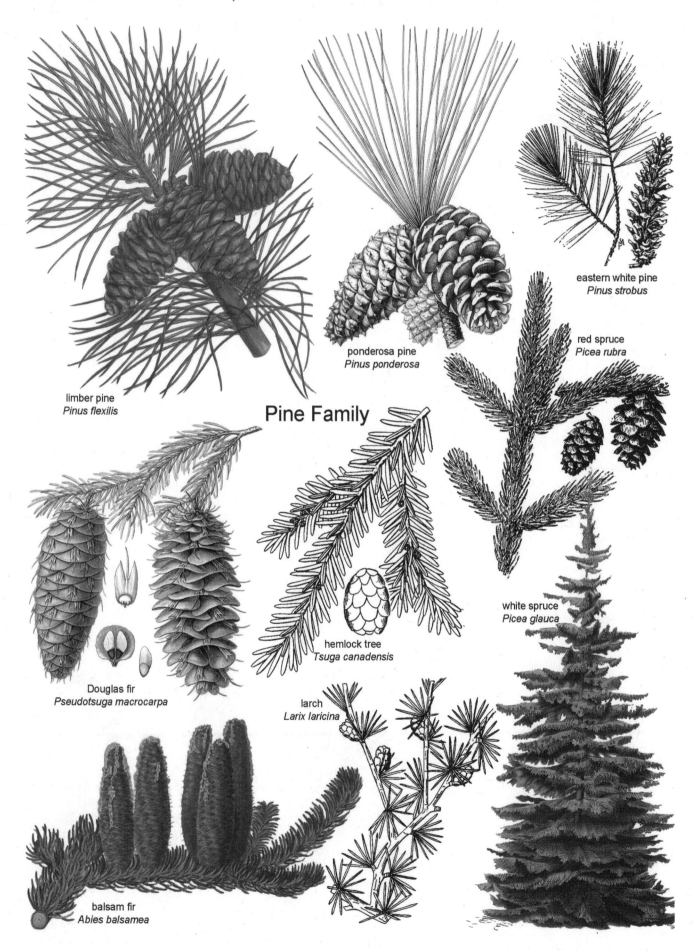

limber pine
Pinus flexilis

ponderosa pine
Pinus ponderosa

eastern white pine
Pinus strobus

red spruce
Picea rubra

Pine Family

Douglas fir
Pseudotsuga macrocarpa

hemlock tree
Tsuga canadensis

white spruce
Picea glauca

balsam fir
Abies balsamea

larch
Larix laricina

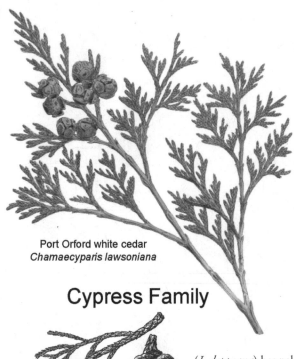

Port Orford white cedar
Chamaecyparis lawsoniana

Cypress Family

giant sequoia
Sequoiadendron giganteum

Cypress or Cedar Family—*Cupressaceae*

If you have ever smelled cedar or juniper wood, then you know the Cypress family. These are mostly evergreen trees or shrubs with small, scaly leaves and separate male and female cones, sometimes on separate trees. The seed cones are typically woody or leathery, with one to several seeds behind each scale. The juniper "berry" is actually a cone with merged, fleshy scales. Most species are richly aromatic, especially useful as incense. The wood is naturally resistant to decay, and frequently used for construction and fence posts. Worldwide, there are about 27 genera and 130 species. The former Bald Cypress family (*Taxodiaceae*) is now included within the Cypress family.

Calocedrus (Libocedrus)—incense cedar (3/1/0) *C. decurrens* is native to California, Nevada, and Oregon. A tea of the aromatic twigs can be sipped for stomach troubles or inhaled to aid a head cold (Fern).

Chamaecyparis—white cedar (7/2/0) White cedar is used in sweat lodges to ease rheumatism, arthritis, and other aches. It may also be used as a wash or bath. The tea is a powerful diuretic (Fern).

Cupressus—cypress (15/10/0) A tea of the leaves is used internally or externally to stop bleeding and for colds (Fern).

Juniperus—juniper, savine (60/15/4) • The southwestern aligator juniper (*J. deppeana*) has palatable fruits. Stronger tasting species are less edible, and excess consumption can damage the kidneys. Juniper berries contain potent volatile oils and resins. The bitter berries are used in making gin. Savine (*J. sabina*), of southern and central Europe, is considered toxic. As a rule, if it tastes like food it probably is. If it tastes like turpentine, limit your consumption.

Medicinally, the fruits are eaten as a carminative to expel gas, and the distilled oil is rubbed on painful joints. Juniper berries are not recommended for pregnant women (Lust, Tyler). Due to the germ-killing effects of the potent volatile oils, you may be able to decrease the risk of catching a virus by keeping juniper berries in the mouth while around others who are infected (Bigfoot). Similarly, try chewing the berries when drinking unclean water. Juniper needles can be added to bath water for a stimulating effect on rheumatic joint pain. Utah juniper (*J. osteosperma*) produces a thick, fibrous bark that is ideal tinder material for fire-starting.

Sequoia—redwood (1/1/0) • *S. sempervirens.* Redwoods are the tallest trees in the world, with one individual measuring 379 feet. Redwoods and sequoias shed a portion of their narrow leaves or twigs each year, so they are considered deciduous, even though they retain enough leaves to appear evergreen. The tea is aromatic and astringent. It is useful as an expectorant to help expel mucous, and as a mild disinfectant to the urinary tract for bladder infections (Moore).

Sequoiadendron—giant sequoia (1/1/0) • *S. giganteum.* Sequoias are not as tall as redwoods, but the trees can be significantly more massive. The General Sherman tree of Sequoia National Park in California is 275 feet tall and 36.5 feet in diameter, containing more than 50,000 cubic feet of wood. It is estimated to be 2,300 – 2,700 years old.

Taxodium—bald cypress (3/3/0) Bald cypress grows primarily in swampy habitats from Texas to New York. They often have aerial roots that brace the trees upright in the water. Resin from the cones is used as an analgesic. The bark can be used to make cordage (Fern).

Thuja—red cedar, arbor-vitae (5/2/1) • Cedar contains toxic volatile oils. It is used as a diaphoretic (promotes sweating), emmenagogue (promotes menstruation), and as an irritant poultice for rheumatic pains. (Lust).

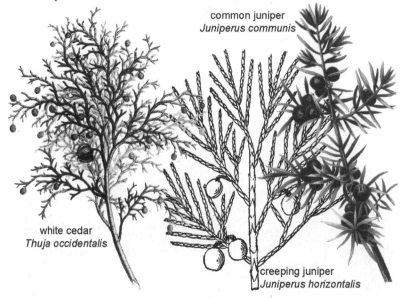

common juniper
Juniperus communis

white cedar
Thuja occidentalis

creeping juniper
Juniperus horizontalis

48

Yew Family—*Taxaceae*

If you see a shrub or tree with conifer-like branches and red or green berry-like fruits, then it is certainly a member of the Yew family. In *Taxus*, the seed cones are highly modified, each cone containing a single seed partly surrounded by a modified scale which develops into a soft, bright red berry-like structure called an aril. The fruits are eaten by thrushes, waxwings and other birds, which disperse undamaged seeds in their droppings.

Worldwide, there are 6 genera and 20 species. The genera below are native to North America. Three genera, including *Torreya*, can be considered a subfamily, or segregated as *Cephalotaxaceae*.

yew
Taxus baccata

Yew Family

Taxus—yew (10/5/1) • Yew wood is prized for making bows. The berries may be edible when ripe (Sturtevant), but all other parts of the yew tree contain poisonous alkaloids. It is listed as expectorant and purgative, but its use is not recommended without medical supervision (Lust). It also increases blood pressure (Phillips).

    A potent cancer medicine, called paclitaxel (Taxol®), can be derived from the bark of the tree, but it requires a great deal of material to make one dose. It is now produced in a laboratory.

Torreya—stinking yew, California nutmeg (6/2/0) The Florida stinking yew is *T. taxifolia*. The fruit of the California nutmeg (*T. californica*) resembles the true nutmeg (*Myristica*) in shape, but not in taste. The plants are not related. Native Americans roasted and ate the big fruits.

Mormon Tea Family—*Ephedraceae*

If you spend time hiking around the desert southwest, you are sure to encounter *Ephedra* or Mormon tea. Ephedras are leafless desert shrubs with jointed, green stems forming in whorls at nodes along the stalk. The common names comes from Mormon pioneers who drank a tea brewed from these leafless branches. The plants produce naked seeds like the pines, but they form in a colored, cup-like structure called a perianth. The male cones have 2 to 8 anthers. The female cones have bracts covering the two maturing seeds. Worldwide there is 1 genus and about 50 species.

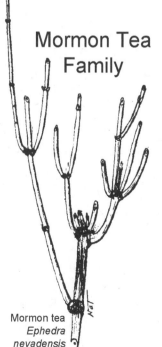

Mormon Tea Family

Ephedra—Mormon tea, joint fir, ma huang (50/15/0) • *Ephedra* is common in the desert Southwest. It is mostly used as a beverage tea. The red berry is reported to be sweet and edible (Asch).

    Medicinally, the alkaloids ephedrine and pseudoephedrine are found in most or all members of the genus. Chinese ephedra (*E. sinica*) is more potent than our native species. Ephedrine stimulates the central nervous system and is thus used as a headache medicine, much like caffeine. Over consumption can lead to nervousness, tension and insomnia. Other side effects of ephedrine include high blood pressure, reduced appetite, and reduced sexual desire (Emboden). Ephedrine has a dilating effect on the bronchials, but a constricting effect on the blood vessels. The tea is recommended for diabetes, asthma, heart ailments and syphilis (Bigfoot).

    Ephedra is often added to natural weight-loss and energy formulas. The stimulant effect is supposed to increase the burning of fats. At least fifteen people have died from over dosing on ephedrine pills. Our southwestern species contain some ephedrine, but in minute amounts compared to Chinese plants. Ephedrine is now produced synthetically for use as a decongestant in cold medications (Tyler).

Mormon tea
*Ephedra
nevadensis*

Water Lily Family—*Nymphaeaceae*

If you have ever seen a pond with lily pads then you have likely seen members of this family. These are perennial, aquatic plants with thick, horizontal rootstocks and large leaves that float on the surface of the water. They have solitary flowers on long stalks with 4 or 5 sepals, plus 5, 15, or more petals, and numerous (40 to 80) stamens. The

Water Lily Family

ovary with 5 to 25 united carpels

numerous stamens

5, 15, or more petals

4 or 5 sepals

yellow pond lily
Nuphar lutea

fragrant water lily
Nymphaea odorata

ovary is positioned superior or slightly inferior and consists of 5 to 25 united carpels, with the partition walls are present, forming an equal number of chambers. The ovary matures as a leathery, capsule-like "berry," or as a schizocarp, a fruit that breaks apart at the carpels. Worldwide, there are 6 genera and about 70 species. The lotus (*Nelumbo*) resembles the water lily and was previously placed in this family, but is now is considered a distant family of its own, *Nelumbonaceae*.

Key Words: Aquatic plants with large, floating leaves and showy flowers.

Nuphar—yellow pond lily (8/8/2) • Taxonomists debate whether all North American species are subspecies of the European *N. lutea*, pictured above. Treated separately, *N. lutea* has an edible root (Craighead), and *N. avena* of eastern America may be edible (Hall), but the common western species, *N. polysepala* is strongly medicinal. A friend and I made ourselves quite ill attempting to eat the root on a camping trip. Friends have reported similar experiences.

Pond lily seeds were eaten by Native Americans. The pods can be collected, dried, and pounded to remove the seeds. The seeds are popped like popcorn, but with mild heat, then winnowed to separate them from the hard shells and ground into meal (Hart). In my experience, the seeds have the same nauseating aroma as the roots, albeit less intense.

Nymphaea—water lily (40/13/2) The roots and seeds of several species are reported to be edible (Sturtevant). The young leaves and flower buds are edible as a potherb. The larger leaves can be used to wrap food for baking. A tea of the root or leaf is gargled for sore throat, also used as an eye wash, or as an astringent, mucilaginous lotion (Coon). Some species may contain cardiac glycosides and alkaloids (Schauenberg). Caution is advised.

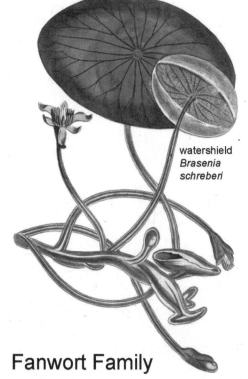

watershield
Brasenia schreberi

Fanwort Family—*Cabombaceae*

The Fanwort family is related to the Water Lily family and sometimes included within it, but the flowers typically have parts in threes, with 3 sepals, 3 petals, and 3, 6, 12, or 18 stamens. There are 3 to 18 simple pistils (apocarpous). Each pistil matures as a follicle, a dry fruit with a seam down one side.

Brasenia—water shield (1/1/1) *B. schreberi*. The starchy roots are boiled, peeled and eaten (Kirk).

Cabomba—fanwort (5/2/0) The submerged leaves are feathery. The plant is often used in aquariums.

Fanwort Family

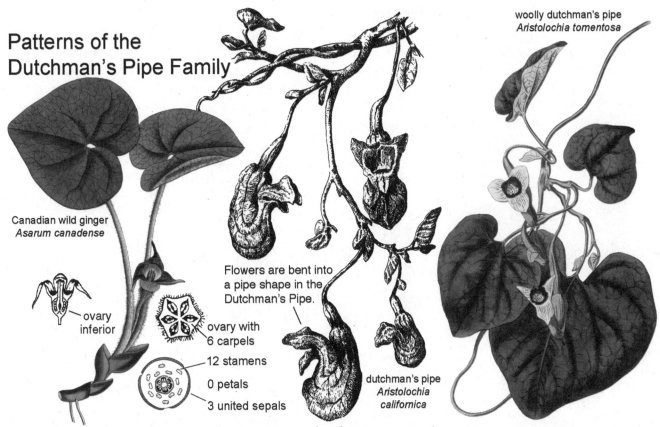

Patterns of the Dutchman's Pipe Family

woolly dutchman's pipe
Aristolochia tomentosa

Canadian wild ginger
Asarum canadense

ovary inferior

ovary with 6 carpels

12 stamens

0 petals

3 united sepals

Flowers are bent into a pipe shape in the Dutchman's Pipe.

dutchman's pipe
Aristolochia californica

Dutchman's Pipe Family—*Aristolochiaceae*

If you find a low-growing dicot-like plant with tubular flowers and parts in multiples of three, it is likely a member of the Dutchman's Pipe or Birthwort family. Our members of this family have either regular or irregular, bisexual flowers with 3 united sepals, 0 petals, and typically 12 stamens (6 to 36 possible). The ovary is positioned inferior and consists of 6 (sometimes 4) united carpels with the partition walls present, forming an equal number of chambers. It matures as a capsule with numerous seeds. Most members of this family are tropical plants. Worldwide, there are 7 genera and about 460 species. North American genera are listed below.

Plants of this family contain potent volatile oils, frequently used in herbal medicine. These spicy plants warm the body and stimulate sweating (diaphoretic), thus increasing blood flow (vasodilation) and causing increased menstruation (emmenagogue) and uterine stimulation (oxytocic), hence the name "birthwort." Read more about volatile oils in the *Medicinal Properties* section of this book. Unfortunately, many species of this family also contain toxic aristolochic acid, which can lead to permanent kidney damage or kidney failure and sometimes cancer of the urinary tract. Caution is advised.

Key Words: Dicot plants with tubular flowers and parts in threes.

Aristolochia—Dutchman's pipe, birthwort (370/8/0) • Dutchman's Pipe contains a volatile oil, an alkaloid (Weiner), and a strong, toxic acid. The tea is used for infected wounds (Schauenberg). These plants are also described as bitter, diaphoretic, and vasodilating, used to stimulate digestion, sweating, and white blood cell activity. A tea of the root is used as an oxytocic for stimulating uterine contractions during childbirth. Caution is advised in using this herb (Lust). The raw root was chewed and applied as a poultice for snake bite (Weiner).

Asarum—wild ginger (70/14/1) • Wild ginger is often common in moist forests. Thin slices can be used in oriental cooking. The powdered root (Hall) or leaves (Tilford) can be used as a spice (Hall). Medicinally, *Asarum* is a digestive stimulant, and like commercial ginger it can be used to relieve stomachaches (Coon). *A. canadense* is listed as diaphoretic, carminative, expectorant and irritant. A tea of the root was used as a contraceptive by some Native American women. A European species, *A. europaeum,* is purgative and diuretic. It is considered too dangerous for use without supervision (Lust). True ginger belongs to the Ginger family, *Zingiberaceae.*

Hexastylis—heartleaf wild ginger (10/10/0) Heartleaf wild ginger is endemic to the southeastern states, and often very rare. Plants of this genus are evergreen while the *Asarum* are deciduous. The plants share similar edible and medicinal properties, and they are sometimes treated as a single genera under *Asarum.*

Magnolia Family—*Magnoliaceae*

The trees and shrubs of the Magnolia family are distinctive with their showy flowers and "seed cones." I was fascinated by them as a young child living in California. Botanically, the flowers have 3 sepals and 3 or more petals. The sepals and petals may be difficult to distinguish from one another in some species. The flowers are bisexual with numerous stamens and numerous simple pistils. The pistils are positioned superior to the other parts. Each pistil ma-

Magnolia Family

Trees with showy flowers and numerous simple pistils forming a cone in the center of each flower.

tulip tree
Liriodendron tulipifera

southern magnolia
Magnolia grandiflora

tures into a follicle, a unicarpellate capsule with a seam down the side. In *Magnolia* the seeds sometimes fall free from the follicle to hang suspended from fine threads.

Magnolias are an ancient family, dating back more than 100 million years in the fossil record. The flowers have retained some ancestral characteristics, where the sepals, petals, stamens, and pistils are arranged in a spiral on a cone-like receptacle, rather than in concentric rings as they are in most other plant families. In addition, the stamens are not fully differentiated into filaments and anthers.

Worldwide, there are 7 genera and about 220 species in the family. The genera below are native to North America. The magnolia and tulip trees are native to eastern states, but magnolias are often planted in West Coast communities. *Michelia* is cultivated as an ornamental tree in some parts of the country.

Key Words: Broad-leaf trees with big flowers with a cone-like center.

Liriodendron—tulip tree (2/1/0) • *L. tulipifera*. The tulip tree is an important bee tree in southern Appalachia, favored for its tasty nectar (M. Williams). Some Native Americans ate the bark to expel worms and gave the seeds to children for the same purpose. The tulip tree has also been used to reduce fevers, as a diuretic, and to treat rheumatic symptoms (Weiner). The root has been used in Canada to take away the bitterness in brewing alcohol (Sturtevant).

Magnolia—magnolia (210/7/0) • The bark of the magnolia is known for its aromatic and astringent properties. A tea of the bark is used medicinally as a diaphoretic, and for indigestion or diarrhea. Reportedly, drinking the tea can help break a tobacco habit (Lust). The flowers are often very aromatic, and the wood is used for carving in Appalachia (M. Williams).

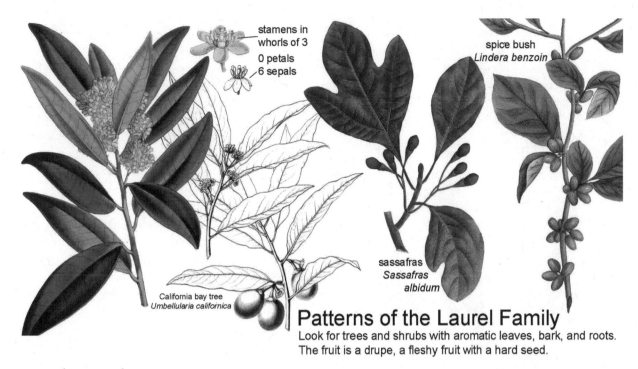

stamens in whorls of 3
0 petals
6 sepals

spice bush
Lindera benzoin

sassafras
Sassafras albidum

California bay tree
Umbellularia californica

Patterns of the Laurel Family
Look for trees and shrubs with aromatic leaves, bark, and roots.
The fruit is a drupe, a fleshy fruit with a hard seed.

Laurel Family—*Lauraceae*

If you have added bay leaves to your soup or eaten a cinnamon roll, then you know something about the Laurel family. The vegetation is usually highly aromatic in a pleasant, spicy way. These are mostly evergreen, tropical trees and shrubs, with several genera across the southern states. A few deciduous, cold-tolerant shrubs and trees are found farther north, such as *Sassafras*. Most genera have alternate leaves. Flowers are usually small, bisexual, and develop in panicles (branching clusters). There are 6 (rarely 4) sepals in two whorls, typically greenish-yellow, yellow, or white in color, and 0 petals. There are usually 9 stamens (anywhere from 3 to 12) appearing in whorls of 3. The ovary is positioned superior and consists of a single carpel. It matures as a drupe, a fleshy fruit with a stony seed. Worldwide, there are about 50 genera and 2,500 species. North America genera include pond spice (*Glabraria*), lancewood (*Nectandra* or *Ocotea*) and *Misanteca*, plus the genera below. Bay leaves come from the European bay laurel (*Laurus nobilis*), but our native genera are often used similarly.

Key Words: Highly aromatic, often evergreen trees and shrubs.

Cinnamomum—cinnamon, camphor tree (350/1/0) *C. camphora*. Introduced from the orient; the camphor tree now grows wild along the Gulf of Mexico from Texas to Florida. Cinnamon comes from bark of the cinnamon tree (*C. zeylanicum*), mostly grown in India.

Lindera—spice bush (100/3/0) The fruits can be dried, powdered, and used as spice for spice cake, frosting, and as a general "allspice" (Lincoff). A tea of the aromatic twigs and leaves can also be used as spice. Medicinally, the sap is high in benzoin, which can be made into an ointment to help heal wounds (Cook). Benzoin or benzoic acid is listed as an ingredient in many common healing ointments found in first aid kits.

Persea—red bay, swamp bay, avocado (200/3/0) The avocado, *P. americana*, is cultivated in southern California and Florida. Red bay and swamp bay grow along the East Coast.

Sassafras—sassafras (3/1/0) *S. albidum*. Unisexual flowers, with male and female flowers on separate bushes (dioecious). Sassafras root bark was the first commercial product sent to Europe by the colonists. Sassafras leaves are a key ingredient in gumbo. The leaves as well as the flowers and fruits make a nice tea. The root is recommended as a tea in traditional medicine to help people transition between seasons, but also during life changes such as a new job or moving (Cook). Sassafras contains a volatile compound called safrole, which was shown to be carcinogenic in studies with rats and mice in the 1960s, leading to a ban by the FDA on the use of sassafras as a flavoring or food additive (Tyler). Later research by James Duke debunked the earlier studies, but the ban is still in effect (Cook). Sassafras contains a compound similar to ecstasy; excess consumption can lead to similar effects (Lincoff).

Umbellularia—California bay tree, Oregon myrtle (1/1/0) *U. californica*. Native to the West Coast. It can be used as a spice like the true bay laurel, but use half the quantity. The roasted nuts are also edible. Some people get temporary headaches from inhaling too much of the aroma, but the aroma is also used as a counterirritant to cure a severe headache. The bay leaf headache typically dissipates in about ten minutes, taking the original headache along with it (Cook).

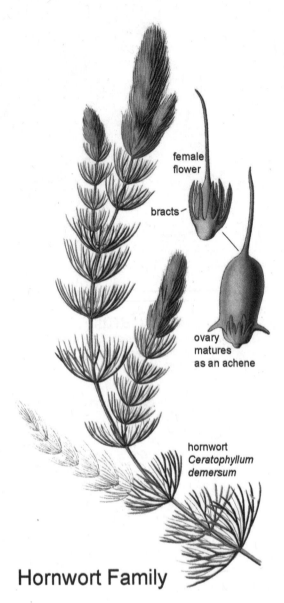

female flower

bracts

ovary matures as an achene

hornwort
Ceratophyllum demersum

Hornwort Family

Hornwort Family—*Ceratophyllaceae*

Hornworts are an ancient lineage that diverged from an evolutionary line that lead to most modern flowering plants. These are submerged or floating aquatic plants commonly found in ponds, marshes, and slow-moving streams. The plants have no roots, and may rot away on one end while growing on the other, but sometimes anchor themselves into the sediment with branches or modified, root-like leaves. The leaves are whorled around the main stem, with 3 to 10 leaves per whorl, which are often divided and become brittle with age.

The flowers are small, inconspicuous, and submerged, with the male and female flowers occurring separately on the same plant (monoecious). Pollination takes place underwater. The flowers are surrounded by 8 to 15 linear bracts (modified leaves), but there are no sepals or petals. Male flowers have 3 to 50 stamens. Female flowers have a solitary, simple pistil. It matures as a dry seed called an achene. Worldwide there is only 1 genus and 6 species, with 3 species found in North America.

Many plants develop similar characteristics in aquatic environments. Plants in other families with similar leaves include water milfoil (*Myriophyllum*), mare's tail (*Hippuris*), and the aquatic buttercup (*Ranunculus aquatilis*).

Key Words: Free-floating, submerged aquatic plants.

Ceratophyllum—hornwort (6/3/1) In the wild, the foliage and greens of hornworts are a valuable food source for migrating waterfowl (Judd). Hornworts are often introduced to aquariums and ponds to provide cover for fish. Some species excrete substances that inhibit the growth of phytoplankton and blue-green algae. *C. demersum*, native to North America, has become invasive in Australia and New Zealand.

Buttercup Family—*Ranunculaceae*

The Buttercup family is like a window back in time. While none of today's species were around 100 million years ago, the Buttercups and other primitive families have retained many ancestral characteristics. Buttercups are considered "simple" flowers because the floral parts—the sepals, petals, stamens, and pistils—are all of an indefinite number and separate from one another. Also, the stamens and pistils are spirally inserted on a cone-like receptacle (which is often small and difficult to see). In comparison, most modern plant families have reduced, specific numbers of floral parts, occurring in rings, and the parts are often fused together.

Buttercups are "simple" from an evolutionary standpoint, but the family includes some seeming complex flowers with spurred petals, such as larkspur (*Delphinium*) and columbine (*Aquilegia*). The flowers are considered "simple" because all the parts are independently attached. In addition, the family is so variable that it might seem that the only consistency is an apparent lack of a pattern. But look again. The pattern is in the pistils.

Buttercup flowers are either regular or irregular and usually, but not always bisexual. There are anywhere from 3 to 15 sepals, often colored like petals, plus 0 to 23 actual petals, and often numerous stamens. There are 3 to numerous simple pistils, which are positioned superior to the other parts. Each pistil matures as an achene (a dry seed), or a follicle (a capsule with a seam down one side), or rarely as a fleshy fruit, such as in baneberry (*Actaea*).

tall buttercup
Ranunculus acris

For the purposes of identification, look for multiple simple pistils, usually with hooked tips, at the center of the flower, as illustrated on the following page. (Flowers from most other plant families have only one pistil, a compound unit formed from the fusion of several pistils into one structure.) A flower with three or more pistils is very likely a Buttercup, but could potentially be confused with species from the Rose subfamily of the Rose family. If you see multiple pistils and hooked tips, it is likely a Buttercup. The hooked tips often persist as the ovary matures.

Worldwide, there are about 60 genera in the Buttercup family and about 2,500 species, including about twenty-five genera in North America. Cultivated plants of the Buttercup family often have extra petals. These additional petals were bred from the stamens.

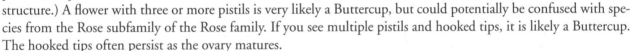

Key Words: Dicot flowers with three or more simple pistils, usually with hooked tips.

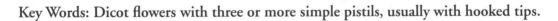

The predominant property in the plants of the Buttercup family is an acrid protoanemonin glycoside oil. Most of the species are listed as poisonous, but most are safe to *taste*. The taste is biting and acrid, stronger in some plants than others. Taste it and spit it out. The acrid properties of the Buttercups are unstable and are destroyed by drying or cooking, and very mild buttercups are edible as salad greens or potherbs. But be careful not to over do even mild plants, as the residual acrid properties may cause mild inflammation of the kidneys or liver. Mucilaginous plants can be ingested to counter-effect the acrid buttercups.

Medicinally, the acrid nature of the plants makes them great for stimulating poultices, similar to a "mustard plaster." These poultices can be used on bruises, aches, arthritis, or even mild paralysis to stimulate healing activity inside, but be careful, because the poultices can cause blistering if left in place too long. The acrid quality is also beneficial for getting rid of lice. Read more about acrid substances in the *Medicinal Properties* section of this book.

WARNING: A number of plants in this family, especially *Aconitum* and *Delphinium*, contain concentrations of toxic terpenoid alkaloids. Some of these plants can be used internally as heart and respiratory sedatives, and for nervous disorders, antispasmodics, and general sedatives, becuase the alkaloids tend to depress the central nervous system. These are toxic plants and should only be administered by a professional.

Edible and Medicinal Properties of Buttercup Family Plants

Aconitum—monkshood (275/8/1) • Water hemlock from the Parsley family may be the most poisonous plant in North America, but a species of monkshood (*A. ferrox*) from Nepal is considered the most poisonous plant in the world. Even touching or smelling the plant can cause serious poisoning (Schauenberg). North American species of monkshood are much less toxic, but still deadly poisonous (Lust). The root is the most toxic part. A tincture or liniment of the flowering plant may be used externally as an analgesic, if the skin is unbroken. It should not be used during pregnancy (Moore). Monkshood should not be used internally, except under expert supervision.

Actaea—baneberry (25/8/1) • Children have been poisoned by eating the shiny red or white berries. Otherwise, baneberry is similar to black cohosh (see *Cimicifuga* below), but apparently lacks the estrogenic compounds. A poultice or liniment of the root is useful as an anti-inflammatory and analgesic for sprains and swellings (Moore).

Adonis—pheasant's eye (26/3/2) Introduced. Contains cardiac glycosides (Geller), used for enlarged or strained heart conditions (Kadans).

Anemone—anemone (200/22/9) • The plants can be used as an acrid poultice to irritate a closed wound to stimulate healing. The tincture is used to slow and strengthen pulse and respiration (Moore). The juice in the nose can purge congestion (Culpeper). Pasque flowers were segregated from *Anemone* into *Pulsatilla*.

Aquilegia—columbine (80/23/5) • The leaves or flowers are edible in a salad or steamed (Willard), but there is a risk of toxicity (Tilford). The root, seeds and probably the leaves of some species are acrid and may be used raw for a stimulating poultice (Sweet).

Caltha—marsh marigold (20/3/1) • Marsh marigold can be eaten as a salad or potherb (Harrington). It is acrid enough to stimulate mucus flow throughout the body (Moore). *C. palustris* contains berberine (Densmore).

Cimicifuga—black cohosh, bugbane (12/5/0) This genus is now included within *Actaea* by many botanists. The root and leaves of black cohosh (different from blue cohosh of the Barberry family) are valued as peripheral vasodilators and for their anti-inflammatory, antispasmodic, and sedative properties. Black cohosh is used especially for dull aches and muscle or menstrual cramping. The root also contains estrogenic compounds useful for lessening surges of the luteinizing hormone and the related hot flashes during menopause (Moore).

Clematis—clematis, sugarbowl, virgin's bower (300/35/4) • Some species are woody vines. A tea of the plant acts as a vasoconstrictor on the brain-lining, but also as a dilator on blood vessels. It is taken for migraine headaches (Moore, Sweet). The plant is used externally as a stimulating poultice (Kloss, Moore, Willard).

Coptis—gold thread, canker root (15/4/1) • The roots of gold thread contain bitter berberine alkaloid, similar to its well known and over-harvested cousin goldenseal (see *Hydrastis* below). Gold thread has a long history of use in treating cold sores, hence its other common name.

Delphinium—larkspur, delphinium (360/67/13) • A vinegar or rubbing alcohol tincture of the plant is used for lice. However, do not apply to highly irritated skin or the toxic alkaloids may be absorbed into the body (Moore).

Enemion—false rue anemone (6/5/0) Native to the Pacific states and the eastern half of North America.

Hepatica—liverleaf (1/1/0) *H. nobilis*. Native to the eastern third of North America. The leaves have three lobes, like the liver.

Hydrastis—goldenseal (1/1/0) *H. canadensis*. Goldenseal is native to the eastern states. It contains the bitter alkaloid berberine, also found in *Coptis* (above), *Xanthorhiza* (below) and in the related Barberry family. A tea of the powdered rootstock is astringent, antiseptic, diuretic and laxative. In my experience, a tea of the powdered root is a very effective antiseptic and anti-inflammatory at the onset of a sore throat. The fresh plant is acrid. Snuffing the powder up the nose will relieve congestion (Lust). It has a vasoconstrictor effect (Kadans). Excess consumption can over stimulate the nervous system, producing nervous convulsions, miscarriage and an excessive build-up of white corpuscles in the blood. Goldenseal is threatened from overharvesting, so it is better to substitute other plants with similar properties.

Myosurus—mousetail (15/5/2) Found throughout most of North America.

Pulsatilla—pasque flower (33/2/2) • Formerly included in *Anemone*. Pasque flowers are among the first blossoms of spring. The plant has diaphoretic and diuretic properties. It contains depressant alkaloids and can be dangerous (Lust).

Ranunculus—buttercup (600/81/29) • The seeds and greens of some species of Buttercup are edible with boiling (Kirk). The edibility depends on how acrid the plants are and how well this is removed through boiling. The plants are listed as diaphoretic and antispasmodic (Lust).

Thalictrum—meadow rue (120/21/5) • The leaves of many species are edible raw or cooked. The root contains some berberine, similar to goldenseal (Willard). A tea of the root is used for colds (Murphey), and a poultice is used for rheumatism (Klein). Meadow rue is being studied as a possible cancer drug (Phillips).

Trautvetteria—false bugbane (1/1/1) *T. caroliniensis*. Native to the western and southeastern states.

Trollius—globe flower (30/2/1) • Like other members of the family, the root and plant of the globe flower have a rubefacient property when fresh, but loses the property when dry.

Xanthorhiza—yellowroot (1/1/0) *X. simplicissim*. Yellowroot has a woody stem. It is native from Texas to Maine. The yellow roots contain berberine, used medicinally much like *Hydrastis* (above). Excess consumption can be toxic. The roots were used for dye by Native Americans.

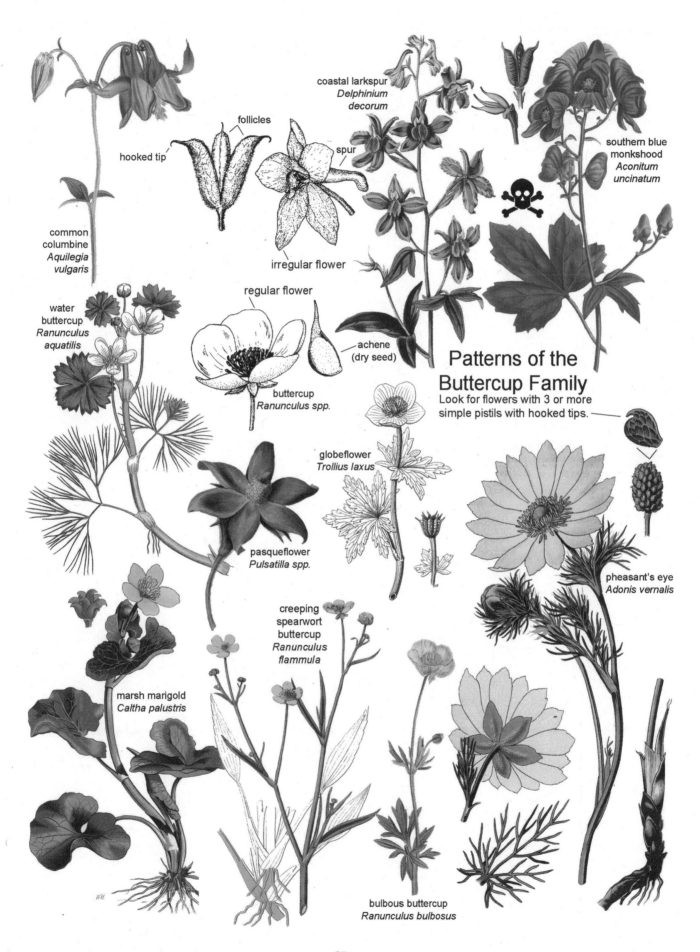

coastal larkspur
Delphinium decorum

follicles

hooked tip

spur

southern blue monkshood
Aconitum uncinatum

common columbine
Aquilegia vulgaris

irregular flower

regular flower

water buttercup
Ranunculus aquatilis

achene (dry seed)

buttercup
Ranunculus spp.

Patterns of the Buttercup Family
Look for flowers with 3 or more simple pistils with hooked tips.

globeflower
Trollius laxus

pasqueflower
Pulsatilla spp.

pheasant's eye
Adonis vernalis

creeping spearwort buttercup
Ranunculus flammula

marsh marigold
Caltha palustris

bulbous buttercup
Ranunculus bulbosus

Barberry Family—*Berberidaceae*

If you find a dicot plant or shrub with flower parts in multiples of three, then you may have a member of the Barberry family—especially if there are multiple layers of sepals and petals. The flowers are regular and bisexual and often bloom very early in spring. Some species have 2 or 3 small bracts (modified leaves) masquerading as sepals on the back of a flower. There are usually 6 true sepals (varying from 4 to 15, rarely 0) and 6 petals (up to 12, rarely 0), typically occurring in layers with 3 sepals or petals per layer. There are usually 6 or 9 stamens (up to 18, usually in multiples of 3). The ovary is positioned superior and consists of a single carpel. It matures as a berry or a follicle (a dry fruit opening along a single seam).

Worldwide, there are about 15 genera and 650 species. Taxonomists have expanded the traditional Barberry family to include the Mayapple family, *Podophyllaceae*, as included here.

Key Words:
Dicot plants or shrubs with floral parts in 3s, often with multiple layers of sepals and petals.

Achlys—deer's foot (3/2/0) No sepals or petals. Native to the Pacific states.

Berberis—barberry (600/10/1) • Generally, *Berberis* includes spiny shrubs with simple, deciduous leaves, while *Mahonia* includes evergreen plants and shrubs with pinnate leaves consisting of 5 to 15 leaflets with spines along the edges. However, neither description works for all species, and plants from the two genera are capable of hybridizing with each other. Thus, many species are shuffled back and forth between these genera and may have duplicate names, such as *Mahonia aquifolium* and *Berberis aquifolium*. In either genera the inner bark and root is a brilliant yellow, due to the presence of an intensely bitter berberine alkaloid. See *Mahonia* for properties and uses.

Caulophyllum—blue cohosh (3/2/0) Native to the eastern half of North America, but not the southernmost states. Blue cohos has a long history as a woman's herb, especially as an emmenagogue to promote the flow of blood during menstruation and to relieve cramping. The tea, taken during the last few weeks of pregnancy, can facilitate a smooth and pain-free delivery (Hutchins).

Diphylleia—umbrellaleaf (3/1/0) *D. cymosa*. Native from Alabama to Virginia.

Jeffersonia—twinleaf (2/1/0) *J. diphylla*. Native to eastern North America.

Mahonia—barberry, Oregon grape, algerita (70/11/2) • The various species of *Berberis* and *Mahonia* produce edible, but very sour berries which can be mixed with other berries to tame the flavor. With the addition of sugar, the berries are excellent in jams and jellies and provide their own pectin.

Medicinally the yellow berberine alkaloid of the roots acts as a potent bitter stimulant and antiseptic/antibacterial. As a bitter substance, berberine is stimulating to the digestive tract, promoting gastric activity, bile production, liver cleansing and acting as a laxative. By stimulating liver function it is considered a "blood purifier," useful for the venereal diseases syphilis and gonorrhea, as well as premenstrual syndrome (Hart); it calms a person by facilitating liver function. Chewing the leaves may help acne (Sweet). This is again the result of increased liver function.

Because berberine is so intensely bitter, it stimulates the entire body and not just the digestive system. It opens up the blood vessels (vasodilation) to lower blood pressure (Lust). Increased blood flow can stimulate involuntary muscles, and so the Flathead Indians used berberine to stimulate delivery of the placenta during childbirth (Hart).

Berberine is not a narcotic alkaloid, but it is reported to have a Novocaine-like effect if you chew the root prior to dental work (Bigfoot). As an antiseptic, berberine has been used externally and internally. Externally, it is a treatment for cuts and wounds. The roots are cleaned, crushed and applied to the open injuries. Berberine is also useful to lower fevers and inflammation (Moore). Any *Berberis* or *Mahonia* species are excellent substitutes for the over harvested and now endangered goldenseal (*Hydrastis*) of the Buttercup family.

Methoxyhydrocarpin or MHC, found in Colorado's Fremont barberry, has proven useful against antibiotic-resistant bacteria. MHC prevents bacteria from pumping the antibiotics, including berberine, out of the cells (Wohlberg).

Nandina—sacred bamboo (1/1/0) *N. domestica*. Introduced from Asia. Cultivated in the southern states, from Texas to Virginia. It can become invasive.

Podophyllum—mayapple (6/1/0) *P. peltatum*. Native from Texas to Ontario, east to the Atlantic. The roots, leaves, and stems are toxic, but the ripe, aromatic fruit is edible raw, cooked, or dried. It has a sweet and acid flavor. The unripe fruit is strongly laxative, and the seeds are considered inedible. Learn more about harvesting, processing, and dining on mayapples in Sam Thayer's *Nature's Garden*.

Vancouveria—insideout flower (3/3/) Native from California to British Columbia.

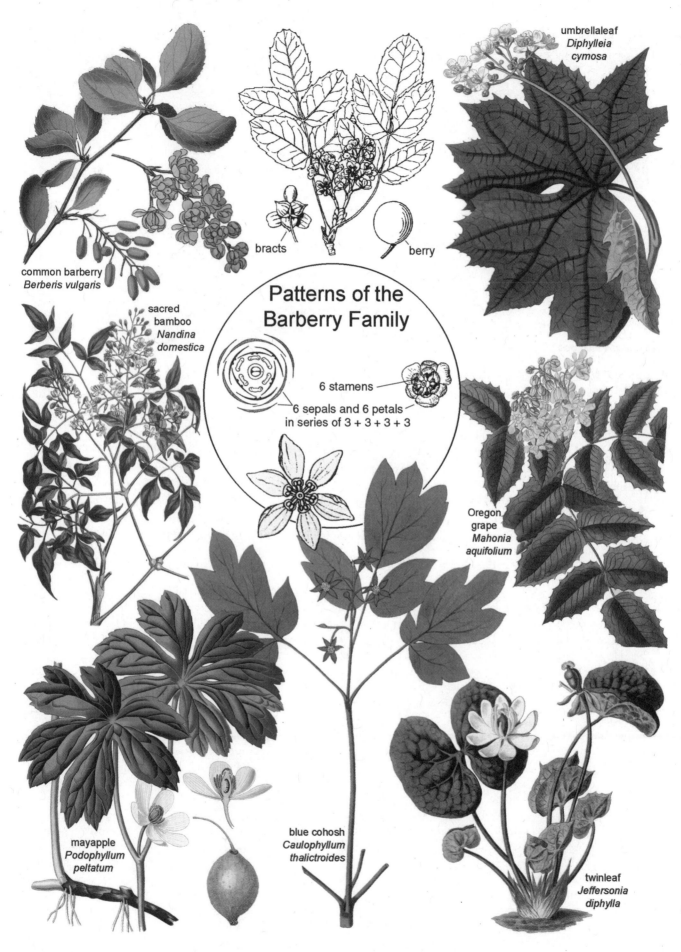

umbrellaleaf
Diphylleia cymosa

common barberry
Berberis vulgaris

bracts

berry

sacred bamboo
Nandina domestica

Patterns of the Barberry Family

6 stamens

6 sepals and 6 petals
in series of 3 + 3 + 3 + 3

Oregon grape
Mahonia aquifolium

mayapple
Podophyllum peltatum

blue cohosh
Caulophyllum thalictroides

twinleaf
Jeffersonia diphylla

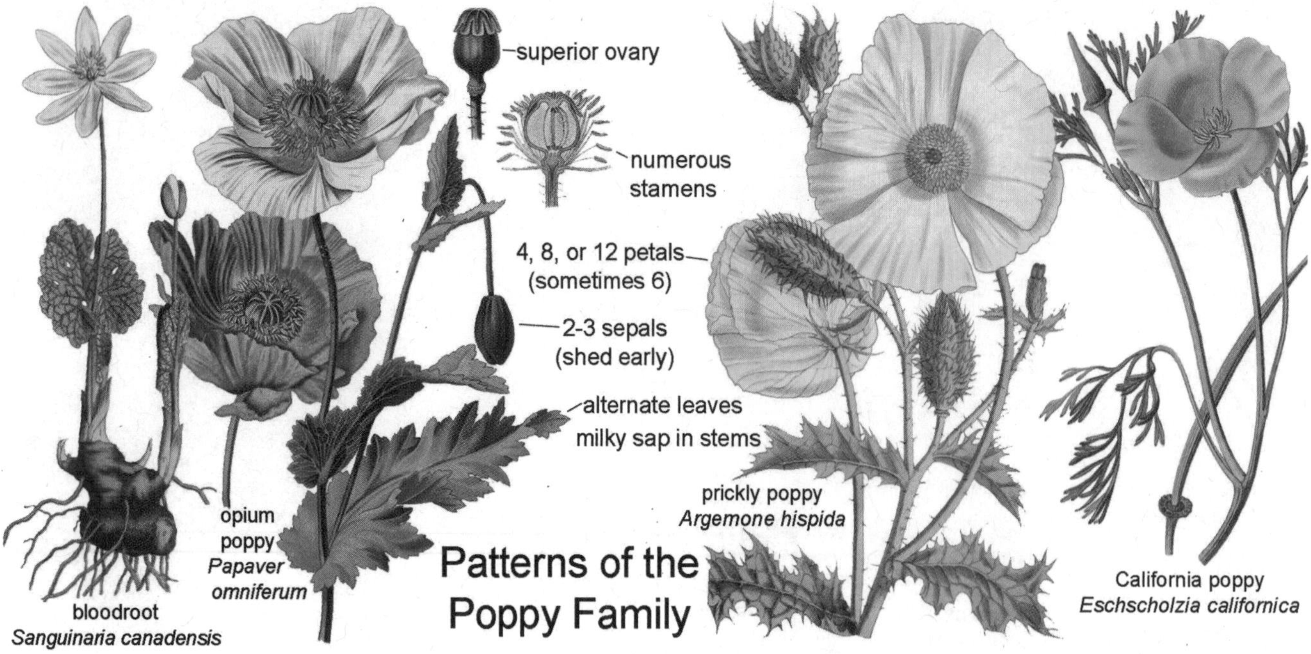

Poppy Family—*Papaveraceae*

Watch for members of the Poppy family in flower beds. The leaves are alternate and they often have milky sap in the stems. Most are herbs, but there are some shrubs and small trees in warm climates. Poppies have regular and bisexual flowers, with 2 to 3 separate sepals (united in *Eschscholzia*), which often fall away as they open. There are 4, 8, or 12 separate petals (sometimes 6), plus numerous stamens. The ovary is positioned superior and consists of at least 2 (usually more) united carpels, as indicated by the number of stigmas fused to the top of the ovary. The carpels are united to form a single chamber, which matures as a capsule containing many small seeds.

With the Fumitorys included as a subfamily, there are about 40 genera and 770 species worldwide. Many Poppies contain narcotic alkaloids and acrid latex sap. Morphine, heroin, codeine, and opium are narcotics found in *Papaver somniferum*. Read more about narcotic alkaloids in the *Medicinal Properties* section of this book.

Key Words: Petals in fours with numerous stamens and often milky sap.

Argemone—prickly poppy (30/15/1) • The seeds are edible like conventional poppy seed, but are cathartic in excess. The acrid plant juice is used for burning off warts. A tea of the leaves or seeds is mildly narcotic. It is used externally as an analgesic wash for sunburns, internally as a sedative and antispasmodic (Moore).

Chelidonium—celandine (1/1/1) *C. majus.* Native to Europe, but widely naturalized in the states. The sap contains narcotic isoquinoline alkaloids that can be used medicinally as an analgesic pain reliever. It is considered toxic in excess.

Eschscholzia—California poppy (123/10/0) • *E. californica* is the state flower of California. It contains narcotic isoquinoline alkaloids. The tea is mildly sedative and analgesic, suitable even for children. Too much can result in a hangover (Moore). The plant is said to be edible as a potherb (Sturtevant).

Glaucium—hornpoppy (25/1/1) *G. flavum.* Produces a sweet, edible oil (Sturtevant), which is also used in soap (Heywood).

Papaver—poppy (100/16/4) • The poppies include many ornamental flowers, plus *P. somniferum*, from which we derive opium, morphine and heroin (Smith). The poppies have edible seeds useful for seasoning, but minute quantities of opium are present in some species. The flower petals can be boiled into a flavorful, but medicinal syrup—it is slightly narcotic with sedative, hallucinogenic, and vasodilator effects. The latex is also narcotic and the potency varies from one species to another (Fern).

Sanguinaria—bloodroot (1/1/0) *S. canadensis.* Bloodroot is a source of red dye. Medicinally, bloodroot contains narcotic opium-like alkaloids (Fern) that depress the central nervous system; the plant or root acts as an expectorant in small doses, but it is nauseating and emetic in larger amounts (Densmore). As a narcotic, the plant is sedative in effect, but can be fatal in excess (Lust). It is used as an anesthetic and to dilate the blood vessels throughout the body, thereby improving circulation, helping the bronchioles in an infection, and stimulating menstruation. Bloodroot contains sanguinarine, which was once used as an anti-bacterial, anti-plaque agent in Viadent toothpaste. However, extended use can lead to potentially precancerous lesions in the mouth, so it was discontinued. This plant should only be administered by a qualified professional.

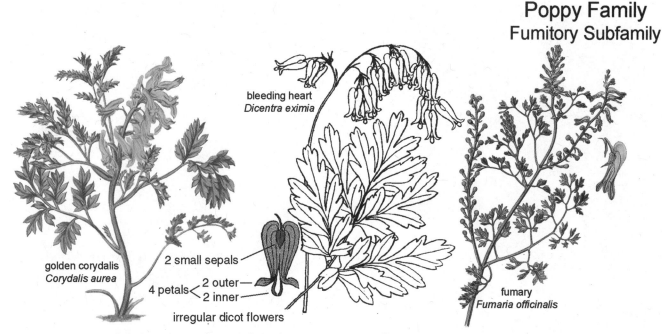

Poppy Family
Fumitory Subfamily

bleeding heart
Dicentra eximia

2 small sepals

4 petals
2 outer
2 inner

irregular dicot flowers

golden corydalis
Corydalis aurea

fumary
Fumaria officinalis

Fumitory or Bleeding Heart Subfamily—*Fumarioideae*

Taxonomists reclassified the former Fumitory or Bleeding Heart family as a subfamily of the Poppy family. By any name, the delicate flowers are always a delight to find. The flowers are irregular and bisexual with 2 scale-like sepals and 4 petals. The outer petals spread above the narrower inner petals. The flowers usually have 6 stamens in two groups of 3 on opposite sides of the pistil, but may have 4 stamens positioned opposite the petals. The ovary is positioned superior and consists of 2 united carpels forming a single chamber. It matures as a capsule or a 1-seeded nut. Worldwide, there are about 16 genera and some 450 species. North American genera are listed below. The Fumitories are rich in alkaloids, many with narcotic properties.

Key Words: Irregular dicot flowers with 2 sepals and 4 petals.

Adlumia—Allegheny vine (2/1/0) *A. fungosa.* Native from Manitoba to Tennessee, east to the Atlantic.

Corydalis—corydalis (320/13/2) • The species of *Corydalis* contain narcotic alkaloids to varying degrees, especially in the roots. The narcotic properties are used in the conventional ways for their analgesic, sedative, antispasmodic and hallucinogenic properties and to slow the pulse and dilate the bronchioles (Fern). Some species have been used to treat Parkinson's disease. These plants are potentially dangerous and should only be used by a trained professional (Lust).

Dicentra—bleeding heart, dutchman's breeches (17/9/1) • Bleeding heart contains narcotic isoquinoline alkaloids useful for nervous system disorders like paralysis and tremors and as an analgesic to relieve pains such as a toothache (Moore). A poultice of the leaves is used as a muscle rub. A tea of the root is reportedly diaphoretic and diuretic in effect. The plant may cause dermatitis in some individuals (Fern).

Fumaria—fumitory (50/7/2) Introduced. The fresh plant may be used to curdle milk. It functions as a preservative and imparts a tangy taste. Remove the plant matter after curdling (Fern). The alkaloids in fumitory are used for their bitter taste to stimulate the digestive processes (Schauenberg).

dutchman's breeches
Dicentra cucullaria

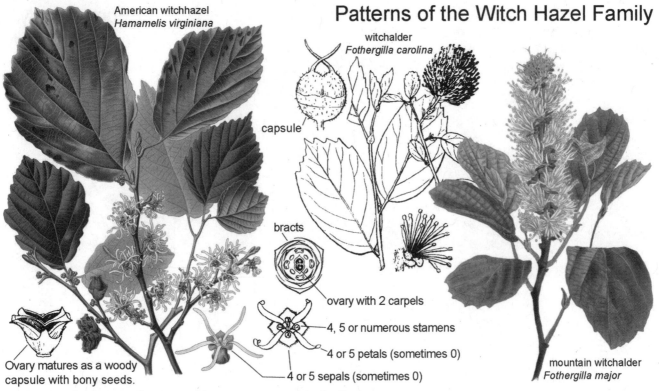

American witchhazel
Hamamelis virginiana

Patterns of the Witch Hazel Family

witchalder
Fothergilla carolina

capsule

bracts

ovary with 2 carpels

4, 5 or numerous stamens

4 or 5 petals (sometimes 0)

4 or 5 sepals (sometimes 0)

Ovary matures as a woody
capsule with bony seeds.

mountain witchalder
Fothergilla major

Witch Hazel Family—*Hamamelidaceae*

The Witch Hazel family consists of a handful of trees and shrubs with usually alternate leaves. The flowers can be either bisexual or unisexual. There are 4 or 5 (sometimes 0) sepals, fused together at the base, and 4 or 5 (sometimes 0) separate petals, which are typically narrow and ribbon-like, plus often 4 or 5 stamens (or more, up to 32). The ovary is positioned inferior or rarely superior and consists of 2 united carpels, as indicated by the number of styles. Partition walls are present, forming an equal number of chambers. It matures as a woody capsule that spreads open from the top, typically releasing 1 or 2 bony seeds from each cell. Note that two or more flowers may be clustered closely together, producing a more complex aggregation of woody capsules, such as in the sweetgum tree (*Liquidambar*). Worldwide, there are about 30 genera and 112 species in the Witch Hazel family. North American genera are listed below.

Key Words: Trees and shrubs with two-chambered woody capsules and bony seeds.

Fothergilla—witchalder (4/2/0) Grows in the southeast, from Tennessee to Florida.

Hamamelis—witch hazel (8/2/0) The seeds are reported to be edible (Weiner), but there is some question about the validity of this claim (Fern). Medicinally, the leaves and bark contain tannic acid. Witch hazel has long been used as an astringent in the typical ways, internally for sore throat and diarrhea, externally for stings, minor burns, and hemorrhoids (Lust). Native Americans used a tea of the leaves as a liniment for athletes (Weiner).

Liquidambar—sweetgum (5/1/0) *L. styraciflua*. Native from Texas to New York and east to the Atlantic. Sweetgum has distinctive tricolor leaves in the fall. The sap of the tree may be used as "chewing gum." The gum is used medicinally as a drawing poultice, also for sore throats. It is astringent and expectorant in effect (Fern, Moerman). Sweetgums are sometimes split out with other genera into a separate family, *Altingiaceae*.

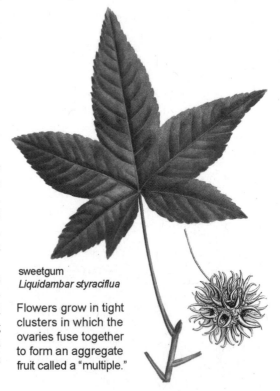

sweetgum
Liquidambar styraciflua

Flowers grow in tight clusters in which the ovaries fuse together to form an aggregate fruit called a "multiple."

Peony Family—*Paeoniaceae*

Peony Family

Do you have a peony in your yard? These perennial plants or "soft shrubs" send up fresh stems each year from their fleshy roots. Cultivated peonies are common in older neighborhoods, where homeowners have split the root clusters and shared them with others. Native, wild peonies grow in the West, found sparingly from California to Montana.

Peonies have mostly basal, typically 3-parted leaves, with each leaflet often being deeply lobed or divided yet again. Flowers are solitary or few in a cluster, forming at the end of a stem. There are typically 5 separate sepals, often leathery and sometimes unequal in size, plus separate 5 petals (sometimes up to 10). There are numerous stamens, typically 50 to 150 per flower, which are often bred to become extra petals in cultivated peonies. There are 3 to 5 separate simple pistils, positioned superior and wholly separate or united only at the base, each producing 1 dry seed. Each pistil matures as a dry capsule with a seam down one side, known as a follicle. The seeds are large and often black, typically with several seeds per follicle. Worldwide there is just the 1 genus and about 25 species.

Key Words: Large flowers with lots of stamens and 3 to 5 simple pistils.

Paeonia—peony (25/4/1) • Native species are found from the Pacific Ocean to the Rocky Mountains. Other species have been introduced to the eastern states.

Brown's Peony
Paeonia brownii

follicles

Water Milfoil Family—*Haloragaceae*

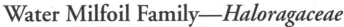

Plants of the Water Milfoil family are mostly aquatic herbs with deeply divided leaves, at least below water. The flowers are mostly unisexual with 4 separate sepals and 0 or 4 separate petals (sometimes 2 or 3 of each). The petals, when present, may also be interpreted as an extra set of sepals. There are usually 4 or 8 (sometimes less) stamens. The ovary is positioned inferior and consists of 2 to 4 united carpels with the partition walls present, forming an equal number of chambers. It matures forming one nutlet from each chamber, or sometimes drupe-like, meaning that it is fleshy with a stony seed.

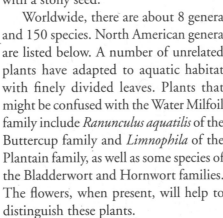

male flower

female flower

Eurasian water milfoil
Myriophyllum spicatum

Worldwide, there are about 8 genera and 150 species. North American genera are listed below. A number of unrelated plants have adapted to aquatic habitat with finely divided leaves. Plants that might be confused with the Water Milfoil family include *Ranunculus aquatilis* of the Buttercup family and *Limnophila* of the Plantain family, as well as some species of the Bladderwort and Hornwort families. The flowers, when present, will help to distinguish these plants.

Water Milfoil Family

Key Words: Aquatic plants with finely dissected, submerged leaves and greenish flowers.

Myriophyllum—water milfoil (69/13/3) Native and introduced species are found across North America. The Eurasian water milfoil (*M. spicatum*) has become invasive in many North American rivers.

Proserpinaca—mermaid weed (3/3/0) Native from Texas to Ontario, east to the Atlantic. Some species are grown as aquarium plants.

mermaid weed
Proserpinaca palustris

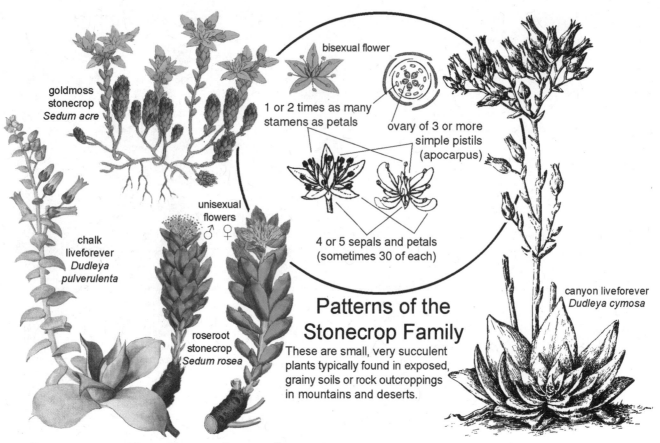

goldmoss
stonecrop
Sedum acre

chalk
liveforever
*Dudleya
pulverulenta*

roseroot
stonecrop
Sedum rosea

unisexual
flowers
♂ ♀

bisexual flower

1 or 2 times as many
stamens as petals

ovary of 3 or more
simple pistils
(apocarpus)

4 or 5 sepals and petals
(sometimes 30 of each)

Patterns of the Stonecrop Family

These are small, very succulent
plants typically found in exposed,
grainy soils or rock outcroppings
in mountains and deserts.

canyon liveforever
Dudleya cymosa

Stonecrop Family—*Crassulaceae*

If you've ever seen a hen and chicks plant (*Sempervivum*) then you have already met one member of the Stonecrop family. These are fleshy, succulent herbs with regular, bisexual flowers. There are typically 4 to 5 (sometimes 30) separate sepals and an equal number of petals, also separate. There may be as many or double the number of stamens as petals. There are 3 or more simple pistils, positioned superior and wholly separate or united only at the base, each maturing as a dry seed.

Worldwide, there are 35 genera and 1,500 species, including 9 genera in North America. Many are cultivated as ornamentals, including: *Aeonium, Cotyledon, Crassula, Dudleya, Echeveria, Kalanchoe, Sedum,* and *Sempervivum*.

Key Words: Small succulent plants with 3 or more simple pistils.

Crassula (including *Tillaea*)—jade plant, pygmyweed (195/9/2) The jade plant (*C. ovata*), and many other cultivated species from this genus are native to South Africa. North American species are primarily found in the West and South.

Diamorpha—elf orpine (1/1/0) *D. smallii*. Native from Alabama to Virginia.

Dudleya—liveforever (45/45/0) *Dudleya* is native to Arizona, California, and Baja California. The genus includes many plant formerly included in *Echeveria*.

Echeveria—desert savior (150/1/0) *E. strictiflora*. Native to Texas. Other species are native to Mexico and Central America. They are sometimes cultivated in the states. Some species resemble *Sempervivum*.

Graptopetalum—leatherpetal (19/2/0) Native to Arizona and New Mexico.

Hylotelephium—stonecrop (33/4/0) Native and introduced species, primarily in the eastern third of North America.

Lenophyllum—coastal stonecrop (7/1/0) *L. texanum*. Native to Texas.

Rhodiola—stonecrop (60/3/2) This genus is sometimes merged with *Sedum*.

Sedum—stonecrop (420/46/6) • The plants are edible as a salad green or potherb. Medicinally, the plants are mucilaginous and mildly astringent, useful for minor burns, insect bites and skin irritations (Tilford). It is a safe laxative for children (Moerman). A European species, *S. acre*, is strongly acrid and may cause blistering. It contains alkaloids and has been used medicinally for hypertension and epilepsy (Schauenberg).

hen and chicks
Sempervivum marmoreum

Gooseberry Family—*Grossulariaceae*

I remember, as a child, collecting gooseberries down in a field by my Grandmother's house. We placed tarps under the bushes and beat the berries out with a stick. At home, we floated away the leaves and made delicious gooseberry pie and jam.

Gooseberries and currants have regular, bisexual flowers, usually about 1/4-inch in diameter. The blossoms are yellow, white, greenish or sometimes red. The flowers have 5 united sepals and 5 separate petals (rarely 4 of each). There are 5 stamens, alternate with the petals. The pistil has an inferior ovary consisting of 2 carpels, as indicated by the 2 styles. The carpels are united to form a single chamber, which matures as a berry with several to numerous seeds.

As you become familiar with these shrubs, you will recognize them by their distinctive leaves alone. Note that ninebark (*Physocarpus*) of the Rose family has similar leaves. Worldwide, there is only 1 genus and about 200 species of gooseberries and currants.

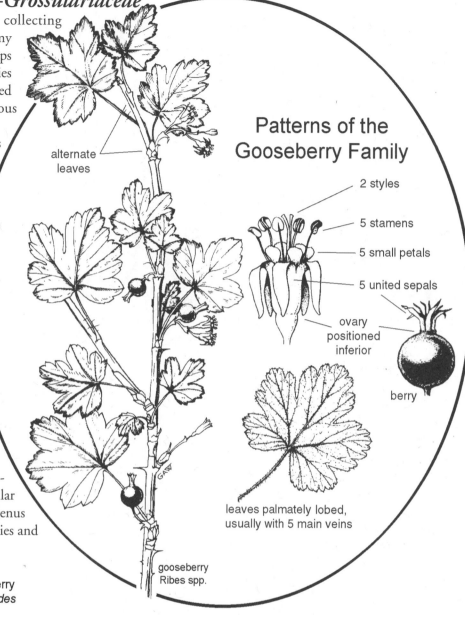

Patterns of the Gooseberry Family

alternate leaves

2 styles
5 stamens
5 small petals
5 united sepals
ovary positioned inferior
berry

leaves palmately lobed, usually with 5 main veins

gooseberry
Ribes spp.

Canadian gooseberry
Ribes oxyacanthoides

Key Words: Bushes with palmate leaves. Translucent berries with attached sepals.

Ribes (including *Grossularia*)—currants, gooseberries (150/65/11) • All currants and gooseberries have edible fruit, but some species are rank in odor and flavor. I can pick a quart of gooseberries per hour by hand or three quarts per hour by beating the berries off with a stick onto a tarp.

Medicinally, the leaves, bark, and roots are largely diaphoretic, astringent, and diuretic, often used to bring down fevers. The jelly can be used as a demulcent for sore throats or burns. A Russian study has shown that unripe gooseberries can prevent degeneration of body cells, which may stave off illness and aging. The green berries also counteract the effect of spoiled foods and help to remove toxins from the body. Black currant seeds contain omega 3 and omega 6 essential fatty acids, similar to evening primrose (*Oenothera*) (Willard, Tilford). I often find gooseberry bushes still loaded with shriveled berries in mid-winter. I crave them that time of year, and I feel their revitalizing effect on my body.

oblong pistil with 2 styles

5 or 10 stamens
5 separate petals
5 separate sepals

Many Saxifrages have palmate, basal leaves.

early saxifrage
Saxifraga virginiensis

ovary with 2 carpels

Patterns of the Saxifrage Family

starry saxifrage
Saxifraga stellaris

white mountain saxifrage
Saxifraga paniculata

miterwort
Mitella nuda

roundleaf alumroot
Heuchera cylindrica

Saxifrage Family—*Saxifragaceae*

If you spend much time in the mountains then you have probably encountered plants of the Saxifrage family. You will often find them on thin soils—pretty much growing right out of the rocks—as well as along moist, high mountain creeks. Most have rounded, variously lobed basal leaves. The flowers of the Saxifrage family are typically small, often less than 1/4 inch in diameter, with a few eye-catching individuals approaching 1/2 an inch. The flowers are regular and bisexual, with typically 5 separate sepals and 5 (rarely 0) separate petals. There are 5 or 10 stamens. The ovary is positioned superior and consists of 2 (rarely 5) carpels, as indicated by the same number of styles. Partition walls are usually present, forming an equal number of chambers. In most cases, it is an oblong-shaped ovary with 2 styles, one of the better patterns for identifying this family. It matures as a capsule with a few or numerous seeds per carpel. Worldwide, there are about 30 genera and 630 species. Twenty genera are found in North America.

Key Words: Small plants with small flowers, parts in fives, plus an oblong pistil with 2 styles.

Astilbe—astilbe, false spirea (22/3/0) Imported species of *Astilbe* are often cultivated and hybridized.

Boykinia—brookfoam (8/6/1) Drink a tea of the dried plant for lung hemorrhages or tuberculosis (Moerman).

Chrysosplenium—water carpet (57/6/1) 0 petals. The plant is edible as a salad green (Sturtevant).

Darmera—Indian rhubarb (1/1/0) *D. peltata* (a.k.a *Peltiphyllum peltatum*). Native to the southwestern states.

Heuchera—alumroot (50/40/4) • The leaves are edible as a potherb, but may be mildly astringent (Willard). Medicinally, the root contains up to 20% tannin (Tilford), for a very potent astringent, hence the common name "alumroot." For more information read the section on tannic acid in the *Medicinal Properties* section of this book.

Leptarrhena— leptarrhena (1/1/1) *L. pyrolifolia*. The tea is taken for flu. A poultice is used on wounds and sores (Moerman).

Lithophragma—woodland star (12/12/4) • The root of a California species was chewed by the Indians for colds or stomach aches (Moerman).

Mitella—miterwort (20/10/6) A tea of the plant was used medicinally by Native Americans as powerful laxative to purge the system or as an emetic to cause vomiting, or as drops for sore eyes. The crushed leaves were wrapped in cloth and placed in the ears for earaches (Moerman).

Parnassia—grass of parnassus (11/11/4) • *Parnassia* is now considered part of the mostly tropical Staff Tree family, *Celastraceae*.

Saxifraga—saxifrage (350/70/19) • Brook saxifrage is very common along streams at high elevations; it is easy to gather in quantity for use as a salad green or potherb. It is pretty much tasteless, which makes it useful for taming bitter herbs in a salad. Other species of saxifrage also appear to be edible and rich in vitamin C.

Telesonix—brookfoam (1/1/1) *T. jamesii*. Native to the Rocky Mountains.

Tiarella—false miterwort (6/5/2) Native Americans used a tea of the roots for diarrhea in children. The fresh leaves were chewed as a cough medicine (Moerman).

Patterns of the Grape Family

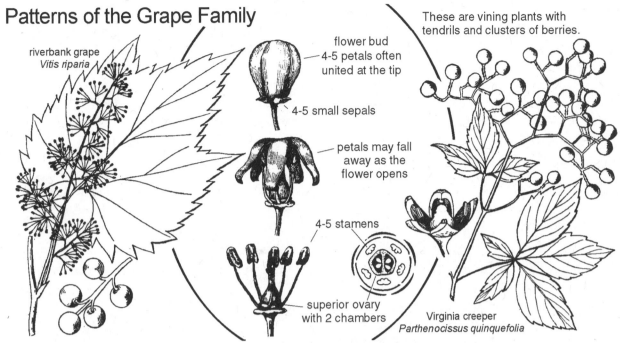

riverbank grape
Vitis riparia

These are vining plants with tendrils and clusters of berries.

flower bud
4-5 petals often united at the tip

4-5 small sepals

petals may fall away as the flower opens

4-5 stamens

superior ovary with 2 chambers

Virginia creeper
Parthenocissus quinquefolia

Grape Family—*Vitaceae*

If you can recognize a grape, then you can identify the members of the Grape family with their climbing vines and tendrils and the distinctive clusters of berries. The leaves are alternate, forming opposite from the tendrils and flowers. Flowers are regular and may be bisexual or unisexual. There are 4 or 5 small sepals, plus 4 or 5 petals, which are sometimes united at the tips, falling away as the flower opens. There are 4 or 5 stamens. The ovary is positioned superior and consists of 2 (rarely 3 to 6) united carpels. Partition walls are present, forming an equal number of chambers. It matures as a berry with 1 to 2 seeds per chamber. Worldwide, there are about 14 genera and 800 species. North America genera are listed below. Most members of the Grape family have edible leaves, stems, sap, and berries. The vegetation is often mildly astringent.

Key Words: Vining plants with tendrils and berries.

Ampelopsis—blueberry climber (20/4/0) Found from New Mexico to New Hampshire. The berries of the various species of *Ampelopsis* are reported to be edible raw or cooked, but poor in taste. The stems, leaves and leaf buds of at least one species are edible (Fern).

Cissus—sorrelvine (350/3/0) Found across the southern states from California to Florida. A tea of the plant was used by Native Americans as a liver aid for jaundice. Cordage can be made from the vines (Moerman).

Parthenocissus—Virginia creeper, woodbine (15/4/1) • Native and introduced species are found throughout North America, except western Canada and Alaska. The berries contain oxalic acid and can damage the kidneys. Excess consumption could be fatal (Tull). The bark and twigs have astringent and expectorant properties, often used as a tea for colds.

Vitis—grapes (70/19/1) • Wild grapes may be used like cultivated varieties. I grow both in the greenhouse attached to my house. The vines grow up to ten feet a year, and I have to constantly prune them back. The tender, young leaves can be added to salads or sandwiches or used as wraps for making dolmas, often stuffed with rice, chopped vegetables, and minced meats.

frost grape
Vitis vulpina

Medicinally, a tea of the leaves is helpful for the pancreas, heart, and circulation. The leaves can be used as a poultice for blisters on the feet (Bigfoot). Grape seed extract (typically from *V. vinifera*) contains powerful antioxidants called gallic esters of proanthocyanidins. Their ability to fight free radicals is reportedly twenty times stronger than vitamin C and fifty times stronger than vitamin E. The extract is also taken to maintain capillary integrity. It is especially helpful to bring increased blood flow to strained eyes from too many hours staring at a computer (Amrion, Inc.).

Geranium Family—*Geraniaceae*

Cultivated geraniums (*Pelargonium* and *Monsonia*) are common as houseplants in northern latitudes, and often grown outdoors south of the frost belt. The plants are easily propagated from cut stems inserted into moist soil. The flowers are regular and bisexual with 5 separate sepals and 5 separate petals. Some varieties have been bred to produce additional layers of petals. There are 5, 10, or 15 stamens. The styles of the pistil are fused together, but not the stigma lobes. The 5-parted stigma spreads out to form a distinctive star-like pattern amidst the stamens, but only after the stamens have lost their pollen, to avoid self-pollination. After fertilization, the pistil continues to grow and looks like a needle emerging from the center of the blossom.

The ovary is positioned superior. As indicated by the number of stigma lobes, it consists of 5 united carpels. Partition walls are present, forming an equal number of chambers. The ovary matures as a schizocarp, a dry fruit that splits apart into individual carpels (mericarps) when dry. The styles remain attached to the individual carpels and peel away together, often curling back from the bottom up. There are one or two seeds per chamber.

Worldwide, there are about 7 genera and 750 species. Members of this family contain significant quantities of tannic, ellagic, and gallic acids, making them quite astringent. The roots are especially acidic.

Key Words: Flower parts in fives with a needle-like pistil and a five-parted stigma.

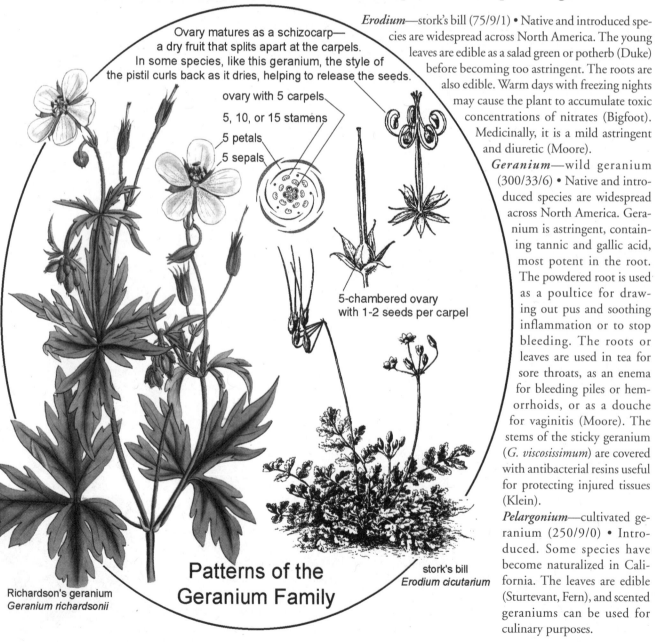

Ovary matures as a schizocarp—
a dry fruit that splits apart at the carpels.
In some species, like this geranium, the style of
the pistil curls back as it dries, helping to release the seeds.

ovary with 5 carpels

5, 10, or 15 stamens

5 petals

5 sepals

5-chambered ovary
with 1-2 seeds per carpel

Richardson's geranium
Geranium richardsonii

Patterns of the Geranium Family

stork's bill
Erodium cicutarium

Erodium—stork's bill (75/9/1) • Native and introduced species are widespread across North America. The young leaves are edible as a salad green or potherb (Duke) before becoming too astringent. The roots are also edible. Warm days with freezing nights may cause the plant to accumulate toxic concentrations of nitrates (Bigfoot). Medicinally, it is a mild astringent and diuretic (Moore).

Geranium—wild geranium (300/33/6) • Native and introduced species are widespread across North America. Geranium is astringent, containing tannic and gallic acid, most potent in the root. The powdered root is used as a poultice for drawing out pus and soothing inflammation or to stop bleeding. The roots or leaves are used in tea for sore throats, as an enema for bleeding piles or hemorrhoids, or as a douche for vaginitis (Moore). The stems of the sticky geranium (*G. viscosissimum*) are covered with antibacterial resins useful for protecting injured tissues (Klein).

Pelargonium—cultivated geranium (250/9/0) • Introduced. Some species have become naturalized in California. The leaves are edible (Sturtevant, Fern), and scented geraniums can be used for culinary purposes.

Loosestrife Family—*Lythraceae*

If you have seen a marshland of tall, skinny plants with lots of pink-purple flowers, then you have likely met a prominent member of the Loosestrife family. Purple loosestrife (*Lythrum salicaria*) was introduced as an ornamental plant from Europe in the late 1800s. Its square stems and opposite leaves may mislead you to think that it is a member of the Mint family, until you examine the flowers. Purple loosestrife propagates quickly via spreading roots and prolific seed production. It has taken over swamps from coast to coast, altering ecology and reducing habitat for native species. Any small or isolated patches should be reported to the landowner or public agency in charge of the land.

In northern latitudes, members of the Loosestrife family are herbs, while some tropical species are trees. These plants have opposite or whorled leaves. They have regular, bisexual flowers with 4, 6, or 8 sepals and the same number of petals (sometimes absent). There are typically twice as many stamens as petals, forming two circles of different lengths.

The pistil is misleading at first, because it seems to have an inferior ovary. However, it is an illusion due to the deep floral cup. Sepals and petals attach below the ovary, so it is positioned superior (or halfway in between in some species). The ovary consists of 2 to 6 carpels with the partition walls present, forming an equal number of chambers. It matures as a capsule with several to numerous seeds. Most plants in this family are adapted to damp soils.

Worldwide, there are about 300 genera and 600 species. The henna tree (*Lawsonia*) is the source of red-orange dyes often used for temporary hair color and body art. Crepe myrtle (*Lagerstroemia*) is cultivated for its long lasting flowers. Tannins and alkaloids are common in this family (Zomlefer). North American genera are listed below.

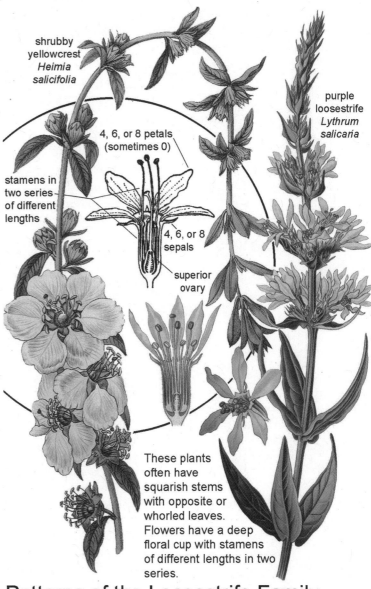

Patterns of the Loosestrife Family

Key Words: Twice the number of stamens as petals, in two series—short and tall.

Ammannia—redstem (25/4/1) Native throughout the U.S. The seeds are edible (Moerman).

Cuphea—cigar flower (275/7/0) Cigar flower is found in the southern and eastern states.

Decodon—swamp loosestrife (1/1/0) *D. verticillatus*. Native to wetlands in the eastern third of the continent.

Heimia—shrubby yellowcrest (3/1/0) *H. salicifolia*. Shrubby yellowcrest is native to Texas.

Lythrum—loosestrife (35/11/2) • The cooked leaves are edible and rich in calcium. Medicinally, the plant is highly astringent. A tea of the plant is used internally for diarrhea, excessive menstruation and internal bleeding. Externally, the tea is used as a wash for wounds. The dried, powdered plant is used to stop bleeding (Fern, Lust). Note that there are other plants called "loosestrife" in the Primrose family.

Punica—pomegranate (2/1/0) • *P. granatum*. Pomegranates were originally native to Iran, but are now cultivated in warm climates around the world. They were formerly segregated into their own family, *Punicaceae*.

Rotala—rotala (45/3/1) Native throughout most of the U.S., plus eastern and western Canada.

Trapa—water caltrop (3/1/0) Introduced. Invasive in northeastern waterways.

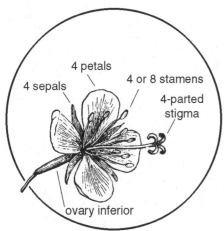

**Patterns of the
Evening Primrose Family**

Evening Primrose Family—*Onagraceae*

The delicate flowers of this family have mostly regular, bisexual flowers with 4 separate sepals (sometimes colored like petals) and 4 separate petals (rarely 2, 3, or 5 of each). There are an equal number or twice as many stamens as petals. It has a compound pistil with styles fused together, but not the stigma lobes. Note the distinctive 4-parted stigma in the illustration, an essential pattern for recognizing this family.

The styles of the pistil are fused together, but not the stigma lobes. As indicated by the number of stigma lobes, the ovary consists of 4 (rarely 2 or 5) united carpels. The partition walls are present, forming an equal number of chambers. The ovary is positioned inferior, within a floral cup (hypanthium). The ovary matures as a capsule with many seeds, or sometimes as a berry or drupe (a fleshy fruit with a stony seed).

Worldwide, there are about 20 genera and 650 species. North American genera are listed below. Some species of evening primrose (*Oenothera*) bloom in the evening to be pollinated by moths after dark. The ornamental *Fuchsia* and *Lopezia* are members of this family. Taxonomic reshuffling has muddied the who's who of this family, as noted in individual entries below. Plants of this family are mostly edible, with astringent, mucilaginous, and antispasmodic properties.

Key Words: Flower parts usually in fours, including a four-lobed stigma.

Calylophus—sundrops (6/6/1) Formerly included in *Oenothera*. Native to most of North America, except the coast states.

Camissonia—suncups, evening primrose (58/58/7) • Plants of this genus were formerly included within *Oenothera* and are labeled as such in many books. All *Camissonia* are native to western North America. Newer sources have adapted to the new name, but taxonomists are now splitting this genera apart into yet newer ones.

Chamerion—fireweed (8/2/2) • Our fireweeds were formerly included within *Epilobium* as *E. angustifolium* and *E. latifolium*. The new genus has become fairly well accepted, but not universally embraced by all taxonomists.

The common name, fireweed, comes from its tendency to colonize bare ground after a disturbance such as a forest fire or a volcanic eruption. The pith of the plant is edible and sweet (Angier). The young leaves and shoots are edible as a potherb and mildly mucilaginous, but also bitter and astringent. A strong tea is used as a mild laxative and to settle the stomach (Tilford). Fireweed is useful internally for sore throat and ulcers, and externally for burns and other skin irritations. The flowers were reportedly rubbed on rawhide for waterproofing, and the powdered core of the plant will somehow help protect the hands and face from the cold. It prevents the stinging sensation when rewarming the skin (Willard). The fibrous bark of the stalk is a great material for making string. (See *Participating in Nature*.)

Circaea—enchanter's nightshade (7/3/1) 2 sepals, 2 petals, 2 stamens. Found throughout most of North America. Unrelated to the Nightshade family.

Clarkia—clarkia (40/40/2) • The seeds are edible (Sweet).

Epilobium (including *Boisduvalia* and *Zauschneria*)—willowherb (183/40/10) • The plants somewhat resemble young willows, hence the common name. Fireweed (*Chamerion*) was formerly included in this genus.

Gaura (including *Stenosiphon*)—beeblossom (22/22/2) • The flowers may be somewhat irregular. All species are native to North America.

Gayophytum—ground smoke (8/8/5) Native to western North America.

Ludwigia (including *Jussiaea*)—primrose-willow (85/30/0) Native and introduced species are found throughout North America, except the Northern Rockies.

Oenothera—evening primrose (125/65/9) • The seeds are edible (Olsen), although they seem quite astringent. The carrot-like tap root, especially of *O. biennis*, is edible cooked. Collect the roots of the first-year plant in the fall or early spring. The roots have a biting flavor, which may be minimized by boiling in several changes of water. The young leaves and shoots are edible as a salad or potherb (Harrington).

Medicinally, the plant contains mucilage and tannins (Lust). The seeds contain tryptophan, potassium nitrate, and the essential oils linoleic and gamma-linoleic acid. Gamma-linoleic acid has a regulatory effect on systemic fatty acid imbalances and metabolism in the liver (Tilford), also useful for lowering cholesterol (Klein). Tryptophan is commonly used as an over-the-counter sedative. The sprouts also contain alpha-linoleic acid (Duke, Tyler). The fibrous bark of the stalk is a great material for making string (see *Participating in Nature* for instructions).

70

Evening Primrose Family

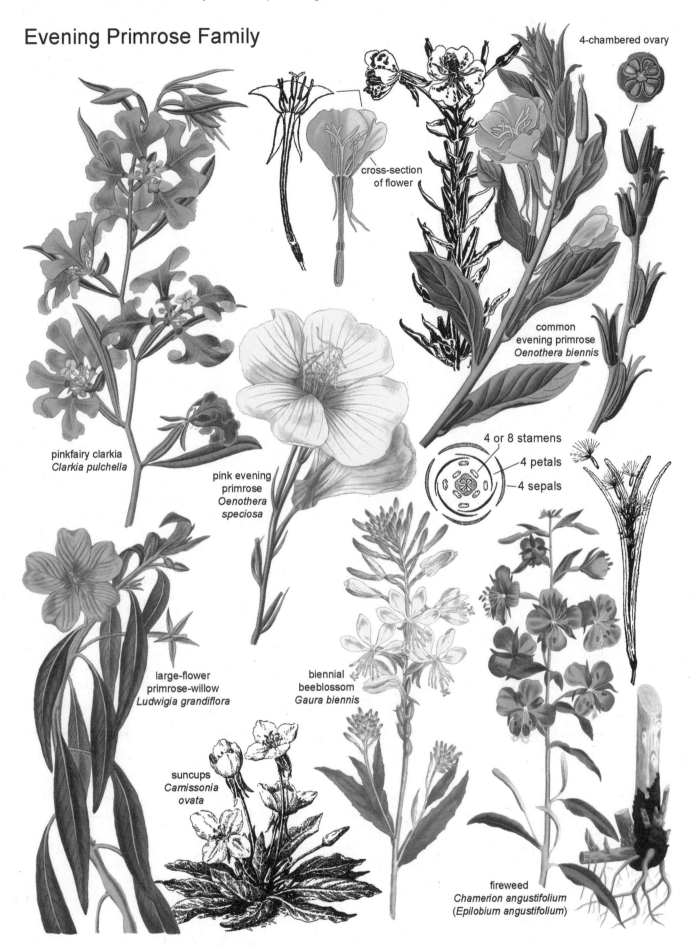

4-chambered ovary

cross-section
of flower

common
evening primrose
Oenothera biennis

pinkfairy clarkia
Clarkia pulchella

pink evening
primrose
*Oenothera
speciosa*

4 or 8 stamens
4 petals
4 sepals

large-flower
primrose-willow
Ludwigia grandiflora

biennial
beeblossom
Gaura biennis

suncups
*Camissonia
ovata*

fireweed
Chamerion angustifolium
(*Epilobium angustifolium*)

71

Patterns of the Caltrop Family

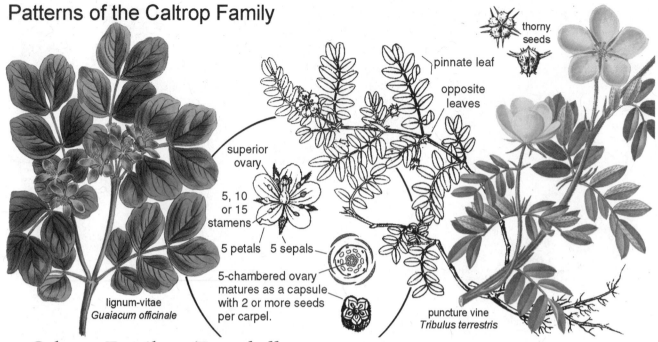

thorny seeds

pinnate leaf

opposite leaves

superior ovary

5, 10 or 15 stamens

5 petals   5 sepals

5-chambered ovary matures as a capsule with 2 or more seeds per carpel.

lignum-vitae
Guaiacum officinale

puncture vine
Tribulus terrestris

Caltrop Family—*Zygophyllaceae*

Have you ever pulled thorns from your bicycle tires, shoes, or bare feet? If you live in the South, then you may have encountered the troublesome seeds of the puncture vine (*Tribulus terrestris*). Plants of the Caltrop family have opposite, usually pinnately divided leaves. They are usually herbs or shrubs, but a few are trees. The Caltrops are largely adapted to warm climates and deserts. They are rare in the northern latitudes. A typical flower from this family is regular and bisexual, with 5 separate sepals and 5 separate petals (rarely 4 of each), and either 5, 10, or 15 stamens. The ovary is positioned superior and consists of 5 united carpels with the partition walls present, forming an equal number of chambers. It matures as a capsule with 2 or more seeds per cell, or rarely as a drupe (a fleshy fruit with a stony seed). Worldwide there are about 26 genera and 200 species. North American genera are listed below.

Key Words: Desert plants with parts in fives, and opposite, usually pinnately divided leaves.

Fagonia—fagonbushes (40/1/0) *F. californica.* Native to the desert southwest.

Guaiacum—lignum vitae (6/3/0) Native to Texas and Florida.

Kallstroemia—Arizona poppy (17/7/0) Native to the southern half of the U.S. The plant is astringent. A tea of the plant is used externally as an eyewash and internally for diarrhea or excess menstruation (Moore).

Larrea—chaparral, creosote bush (5/1/0) • *L. tridentata.* Native to the desert Southwest. Some individual plants are more than 10,000 years old. Chaparral has a sticky resin containing a potent antioxidant called nordihydroguaiaretic acid, or NDGA. It is especially effective at preserving fats and oils. The substance inhibits cellular metabolism. For many years it was thought to inhibit cancer, but new studies indicate that it can also stimulate it. Chaparral is used as an antiseptic for cuts and wounds, as an antioxidant and to treat liver and blood disorders (Bigfoot, Hutchins, Moore). A tea of the plant is strong and repulsive to many people. It tastes like water from an old garden hose to me. Herbal use (or abuse) of chaparral has led to some cases of liver damage in recent years (Tilford). When NDGA was fed to mosquitoes it lengthened the average lifespan from 29 to 45 days (Tyler).

Peganum—Syrian rue, African rue (5/2/0) Syrian rue is an introduced weed from southwest Asia. It is now common in many western states. Traditionally classified within *Zygophyllaceae*, taxonomists have recently reclassified *Peganum* as a member of the distantly related Nitre Bush family, *Nitrariaceae*. The plant is reported to have an awful taste. A tea of the plant is used for many skin conditions and also to strengthen the heart while decreasing blood pressure (Moore). The seeds contain psychoactive alkaloids (Smith).

Tribulus—puncture vine (20/2/1) • Puncture vine is an introduced weed. The young shoots, leaves and seed capsules may be cooked and eaten, but it is considered an emergency food only. Medicinally, the seeds or leaves can be used in tea to reduce blood cholesterol and improve heart function. The tea is also used as a diuretic to dissolve urate deposits and therefore relieve pain from arthritis and gout, but excess dosage can harm the kidneys (Bigfoot, Moore).

Zygophyllum—bean caper (80/1/1) *Z. fabago.* Introduced. The flowers are used as a substitute for capers (Sturtevant).

Woodsorrel Family—*Oxalidaceae*

If you celebrate St. Patrick's Day, then you will like the Woodsorrel family. Also known as "shamrocks," the little green leaves (or cut-outs like them) are seen everywhere when the Irish spirit is in the air. Woodsorrels could be mistaken for clover (*Trifolium*) from the Pea family, with its three-parted leaves, but Woodsorrels are delicate plants full of acidic, oxalate juice, and the flowers are very different. The flowers are solitary, regular, and bisexual with 5 sepals, 5 petals, and 10 stamens. The length of the stamens may vary.

The ovary is positioned superior and consists of 5 united carpels, as indicated by the 5 styles. Partition walls are present, forming an equal number of chambers. The ovary matures as an explosive capsule.

Worldwide, there are about 6 genera and 800 species. Only *Oxalis* is native to North America. The star fruit (*Averrhoa carambola*) is a tropical plant included in the Woodsorrel Family or sometimes split out into its own, *Averrhoaceae*.

Plants with oxalic acid have been used in external cancer remedies to literally etch away an offending tumor. One recipe suggests fermenting the bruised, oxalate-rich leaves in a crock-pot in the ground or 6 to 8 weeks. The resulting black salve is placed on the tumor and left in place until it draws out the cancer and falls off. It is reported to be extremely painful (Cummings).

**Key Words: Small plants with shamrock leaves
and flower parts in fives.**

Oxalis—woodsorrel, shamrock (800/31/2) • Oxalic acid gives a tart, lemon-like flavor. The leaves can be eaten as a trail nibble, used sparingly in salads, cooked as a sour soup (Lincoff), or steeped and chilled for ice-tea. Some species have edible, tuberous roots (Zomlefer). Medicinally, oxalic acid is an irritating stimulant to the digestive system, helpful for digestive problems. It is used externally as an astringent wash for skin problems. Read more about oxalic acid in the *Medicinal Properties* section of this book.

5 separate petals

10 stamens

woodsorrel
Oxalis acetosella

shamrock
leaves

Patterns of the
Woodsorrel Family

creeping woodsorrel
Oxalis corniculata

Saint John's Wort Family—*Hypericaceae*

If you've been troubled by depression then you may be delighted to learn about the Saint John's Wort family.

Saint John's wort (*Hypericum perforatum*) is a well-known herbal alternative to antidepressants. North American members of this family are perennial herbs with simple, opposite leaves. The leaves are often covered with dark glands or clear dots.

The flowers are regular and bisexual with 4 or 5 sepals and 4 or 5 petals. The petals are usually yellow, but may be tinged with red or orange spots. At least one species has pink blossoms. There are 10 or more stamens. The ovary is positioned superior and consists of 3 to 5 united carpels, as indicated by the same number of styles. Partition walls are present, forming an equal number of chambers. The ovary matures as a capsule.

Worldwide, there are about 9 genera and 356 species in the family, mostly of *Hypericum*. North American genera are listed below. *Hypericaceae* is often considered a subfamily of the larger *Clusiaceae* (also known as *Guttiferae*).

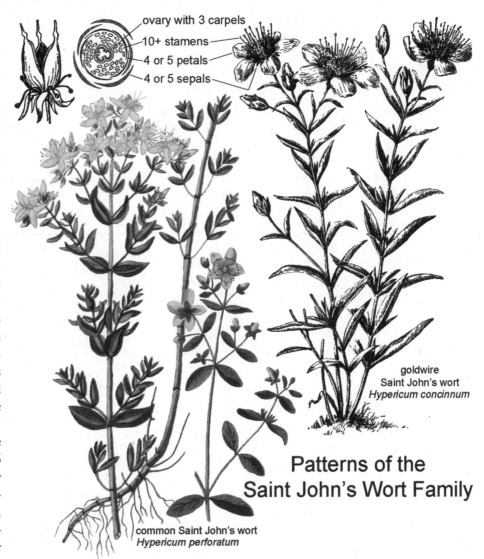

ovary with 3 carpels
10+ stamens
4 or 5 petals
4 or 5 sepals

goldwire
Saint John's wort
Hypericum concinnum

Patterns of the Saint John's Wort Family

common Saint John's wort
Hypericum perforatum

Key Words: Yellow flowers with parts in fours or fives. Opposite leaves with clear dots.

Ascyrum—St. Peterswort, St. Andrew's cross (5/5/0) These flowers are found in the eastern and southern states. The genus is now considered part of *Hypericum*.

Crookea—flatwoods St. John's wort (1/1/0) *C. microsepala*. Two narrow petals and two broad petals. Native to Georgia and Florida. It has been renamed *Hypericum microsepalum*.

Hypericum—St. John's wort (350/25/4) • The leaves of some species are edible as salad (Sweet), and the plants were dried by Native Americans and used as meal (Hutchins). A tea of the plant is antispasmodic, nervine, expectorant, astringent and diuretic. It is used for nervous conditions such as insomnia and bed-wetting (Lust). A pigment in the leaves and flower dots, called hypericin, is used as an antidepressant alternative. Saint John's wort has been demonstrated to significantly increase the healing of burns. Internal use of the plant may cause temporary sensitivity to intense sunlight (Klein).

H. perforatum, shown above, is an import from Europe and an invasive weed on this continent. It is being planted as a crop in some places and sprayed as a weed in others. Native plants are threatened by habitat loss to invasive species like this. Spraying the invasives with herbicides also kills native species. It would make a lot more sense to stop both the spraying and the planting of St. John's wort in favor of intensive wild harvesting to control its population, with subsidies if necessary. The savings from not buying herbicides would help cover the cost of any subsidy.

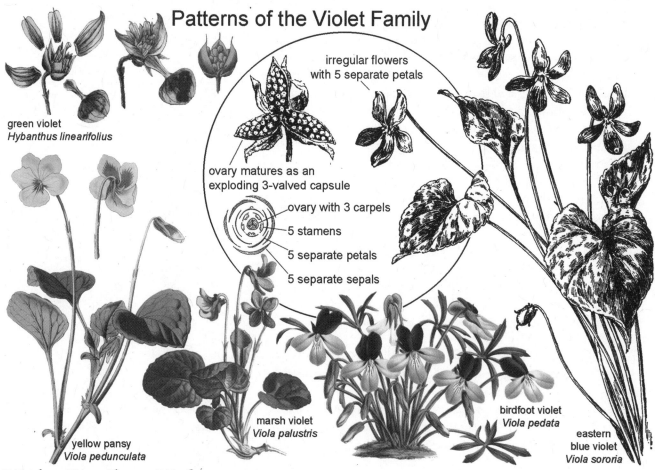

Patterns of the Violet Family

green violet
Hybanthus linearifolius

irregular flowers
with 5 separate petals

ovary matures as an
exploding 3-valved capsule

ovary with 3 carpels

5 stamens

5 separate petals

5 separate sepals

yellow pansy
Viola pedunculata

marsh violet
Viola palustris

birdfoot violet
Viola pedata

eastern
blue violet
Viola sororia

Violet Family—*Violaceae*

Violets have a distinctive, slightly irregular flower. Pansies and Johnny-jump-ups are members of the *Viola* genus; if you have seen them, then you will recognize other flowers of this group. Botanically, the violets are perennial plants with simple leaves, either basal or alternate. The nodding flowers have 5 separate sepals and 5 separate petals, with the lower petal being larger than the side and top petal pairs. The 5 stamens alternate with the petals. The ovary is positioned superior and consists of 3 united carpels forming a single chamber. It matures as an explosive 3-valved capsule. Worldwide, there are about 22 genera and 900 species. North American genera are listed below. Note that the African violet (*Saintpaulia*) is not a member of this family. It belongs to the family *Gesneriaceae*.

Key Words: Slightly irregular pansy-like flowers.

Hybanthus—green violet (80/4/0) Native from Arizona to Ontario, east to the Atlantic.

Viola—violet, pansy (450/60/13) • Native and introduced species are found throughout North America. Violets are edible as a salad green or potherb. Some are better than others. Violets make an excellent tea. They are high in vitamins A and C (Willard). As a child, I collected blue violets with my grandmother every summer. We dried them for winter tea; it is still one of my favorites.

Violet leaves contain varying amounts of saponin. Medicinally, they are diuretic, expectorant, alterative, and mildly laxative. Yellow violets are more laxative than others. Violets are sometimes used in cancer cases as "blood purifiers" to aid the liver in eliminating waste from the blood (Willard). Violets can also be used externally as a poultice on cancer (Kloss). Violets are mildly astringent, as well as mucilaginous, and thus useful for treating ulcers (Kloss). The roots of some species contain saponins and alkaloids useful for expectorant and emetic properties (Zomlefer).

Willow Family—*Salicaceae*

It would be hard to miss the Willow family. Willows, aspens, cottonwoods, and poplars are common along nearly any stream, lake, or mountain meadow. Botanically, the Willow family consists of bushes and trees with simple, alternate leaves. The flowers are unisexual with male and female flowers appearing in catkins on separate plants (dioecious). The sepals are greatly reduced or absent, and there are no petals. Male flowers have 2 or more stamens. In the pistillate (female) flower, the ovary is positioned superior and consists of 2 to 4 united carpels, as indicated by the number of stigmas. The carpels are united to form a single chamber which matures as a capsule, usually with silky "cotton" to help transport seeds by air. Worldwide, there are 2 genera and about 350 to 500 species in the traditional family. There are also numerous natural hybrids between the species, which can complicate identification down to the species level. Recent research places *Flacourtiaceae* within the Willow family, adding about 52 genera, but since the newcomers are largely tropical, the traditional family is conserved for this text.

Medicinally, the Willow family is analgesic, anti-inflammatory, astringent, and diuretic. Members of this family contain varying amounts of the simple phenol glycosides populin, salicin, and methyl salicylate from which the common aspirin was originally derived. These properties are strongest in the inner bark, but are also present in the leaves. Like aspirin, the willow family is used for fevers, headaches, arthritis, and other inflammations, particularly in the urinary tract. Unfortunately, the presence of tannic acid in the bark makes it difficult to ingest enough salicin to relieve a common headache. A strong tea of the leaves might prove more effective, without the bad taste. A strip of the bark can be tied over a cut to serve as an astringent-antiseptic band-aid. Members of the Willow family may also help expel worms (Hart).

Patterns of the Willow Family

black cottonwood
Populus trichocarpa

bract
(modified leaf)

pistil
(female flower)

ovary matures
as a capsule

stamens
(male flower)

Key Words: Trees/bushes with alternate leaves in moist soil. Catkins form many small capsules.

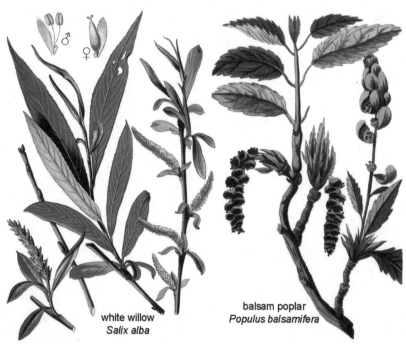

white willow
Salix alba

balsam poplar
Populus balsamifera

Populus—poplar, cottonwood, aspen (40/18/7) • Aphids sometimes produce an edible honeydew that can be scraped or boiled off the leaves and buds and eaten (Olsen). The inner bark and sap of the cottonwood is reportedly sweet early in the spring and was eaten by Native Americans.

Medicinally, the buds are diaphoretic, expectorant and diuretic (Lust). The leaves were used as a poultice (Hart). Cottonwood and aspen leaf buds contain a sticky, aromatic resin that can be collected early in the spring and used in an oil-based ointment for bruises, burns, and skin irritations. It is popularly known as "Balm of Gilead." The buds are soaked in olive oil for a week to extract constituents (Moore).

Salix—willow (350/75/28) • Willow is a commonly known wilderness medicine due to its aspirin-like qualities. It is used for headaches, fevers, hay fever, neuralgia, and inflammations of the joints. Some of the salicylic acid is excreted in the urine, making it useful as an analgesic to the urethra and bladder (Moore).

Spurge Family—*Euphorbiaceae*

If you have seen a poinsettia (*Euphorbia pulcherrima*) at Christmas, then you have met the Spurge family. This is an immensely diverse family, and *Euphorbia* is an improbably diverse genus, varying from succulent plants to cactus-like specimens, as illustrated here. North American members of the Spurge family have milky juice and simple, but varied, leaves. Colorful petal-like bracts (modified leaves) are common.

Flowers are non-showy and mostly regular and unisexual, with staminate (male) and pistillate (female) flowers usually appearing separately on the same plant. (Male flowers sometimes surround the female flowers.) There are 0 or 5 sepals and petals, plus 5, 10, or numerous stamens (up to 1,000). The ovary is positioned superior, and consists of 3 (sometimes 2, 4, or up to 30) united carpels, as indicated by the number of styles. Partition walls are usually present, forming an equal number of chambers. It matures as a capsule with one seed per cell.

Worldwide, there are about 250 genera and 6,300 species, including about 25 genera in North America. The croton (*Codiaeum*) and crown-of-thorns (*Euphorbia milii*) are cultivated as ornamentals. The *Hevea* tree provides rubber. *Aleurites* is the source for tung oil. Tapioca is made from the starchy roots of *Manihot*. The Mexican jumping bean (*Sebastiana*) "jumps" due to the rapid movements of a moth larvae inside the seed. Most members of this family contain an acrid latex (which can be made into rubber) with poisonous alkaloids. Saponins are also common in the family.

Key Words:
Plants with milky juice and often colored bracts.

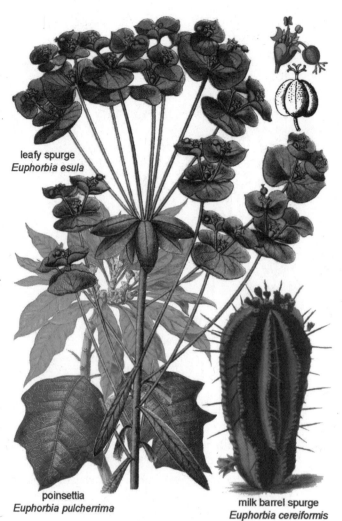

leafy spurge
Euphorbia esula

poinsettia
Euphorbia pulcherrima

milk barrel spurge
Euphorbia cereiformis

castor bean
Ricinus communis

Acalypha—copper leaf (400/19/0) Grows in southern and eastern states.

Croton—croton, turkey mullein (1,300/30/0) Turkey mullein (*C. setigerus*) was formerly classified as *Eremocarpus*. The plant was used by Native Americans to poison fish (Nyerges).

Euphorbia—spurge, poinsettia (2,400/75/8) • The spurges contain an acrid latex sap which may cause a rash when the sap on the skin is exposed to sunlight. The sap is considered carcinogenic if it is handled a lot (Fern). The whole plant contains latex but it is most concentrated in the roots. The acrid sap is useful externally on warts, or internally to irritate and open up the body—functioning as an emetic, anthelmintic, vasodilator, and potentially violent purgative. A European species is considered too toxic for medicinal use (Fern). Large doses have a depressant effect on the heart and can be fatal to people (Lust). Leafy spurge (*E. esula*) is an invasive species, but can be controlled with sheep and goats.

Ricinus—castor bean (1/1/0) *R. communis*. Castor beans are cultivated as an oil crop in warm parts of the country. The plant and seeds are poisonous, but the toxin is water-soluble and is separated out when the oil is pressed from the seeds. The seeds contain 35 to 55% oil. Medicinally, castor oil is well known as a potent laxative; the oil lubricates the bowels to facilitate movement. Castor oil is also used as an industrial lubricant, and as an ingredient in soaps, polishes, paints, varnishes, and fly paper. The living plant is said to repel flies and mosquitoes. The stem is a source of fiber (Fern).

77

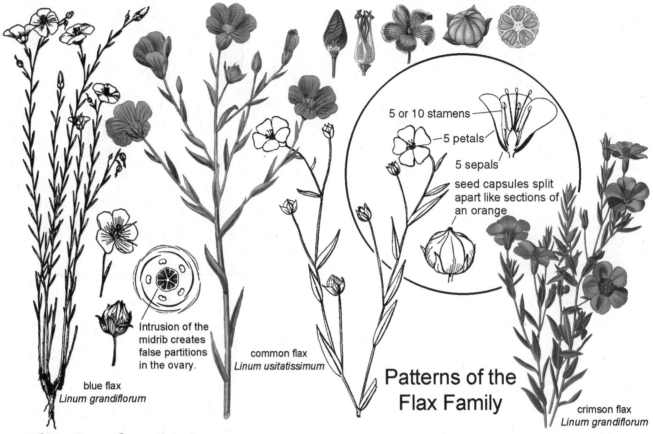

5 or 10 stamens

5 petals

5 sepals

seed capsules split apart like sections of an orange

Intrusion of the midrib creates false partitions in the ovary.

common flax
Linum usitatissimum

blue flax
Linum grandiflorum

Patterns of the
Flax Family

crimson flax
Linum grandiflorum

Flax Family—Linaceae

Flax plants wake up with a cheer every morning. In spite of their wispy little stems and small leaves that may nearly disappear in dry weather, flax plants open up a whole bouquet of fresh flowers each day with the rising sun. The plants often droop under the weight of their own exuberance, and all the petals fall off by noon—but just wait until tomorrow, and a whole new batch of flowers will bloom. Flax is often planted in wildflower mixes used along highways in the West. The flowers are bisexual and regular, with 5 separate sepals, 5 separate petals, and 5 or 10 stamens. The sepals are alternate with the petals. The ovary is positioned superior and consists of 5 (rarely 3 or 4) united carpels, with the partition walls present, forming an equal number of chambers. It often looks like 10 carpels due to intrusion of the midrib. The ovary matures as a capsule (rarely a drupe) with each cell containing 1 or 2 seeds. The capsule splits apart longitudinally like the sections of an orange.

Worldwide, there are about 18 genera and 180 species. North American genera are listed below. Flax plants supply fibers for linen and seeds for linseed oil. Linseed oil is used as a drying agent in paints and varnishes and is also used in the manufacture of linoleum.

Key Words: Flower parts in fives. Seed capsules like the sections of an orange.

Hesperolinon—dwarf flax (93/12/0) *Hesperolinon* is sometimes included within *Linum*. It is native to the Pacific Coast states.

Linum—flax (160/35/4) • The seeds contain cyanide, but it is easily destroyed by cooking, after which the seeds are quite edible and nutritious. Flax seed is rich in oils, including linoleic and linolenic essential fatty acids, also known as omega 6 and omega 3. Essential means that we need the substances to function normally, but our bodies do not produce them (Healthy Cell News). These substances help lower cholesterol and block platelets from clumping together in the bloodstream (Willard). They also help relieve arthritis, PMS, auto-immune disorders and chronic inflammation of the colon (Hobbs). In order for our bodies to properly utilize these essential fatty acids, they should be consumed together with a sulfur-rich protein source; for example, flaxseed oil combined with cottage cheese. This combination reportedly alleviates anemia, reduces cancerous tumors, and increases vitality in patients (Healthy Cell News).

Flax fibers make an excellent cordage material. Bundles of mature stalks are soaked in water for up to two weeks to loosen the fibrous outer bark. The fibers can then be stripped and twisted into cordage while wet or dry. Learn more about making cordage in my book *Participating in Nature*.

Sclerolinon—northwestern yellowflax (1/1/0) *S. digynum.* Native to the Pacific Coast states.

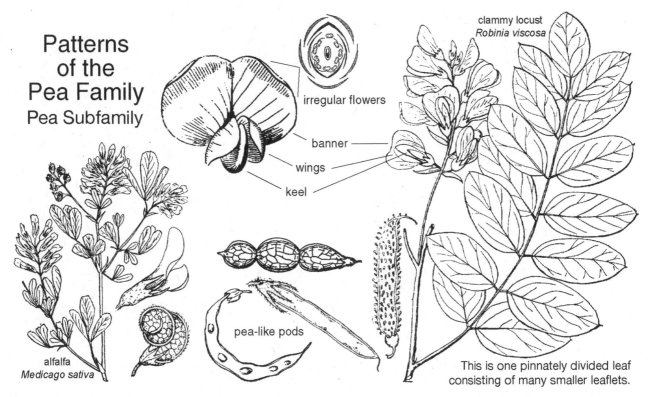

Patterns of the Pea Family
Pea Subfamily

clammy locust
Robinia viscosa

irregular flowers

banner

wings

keel

pea-like pods

alfalfa
Medicago sativa

This is one pinnately divided leaf
consisting of many smaller leaflets.

Pea Family—*Fabaceae* (*Leguminosae, Papilionaceae*)

Key Words: Banner, wings and keel. Pea-like pods and often pinnate leaves.

If you have seen a pea or bean blossom in the garden, then you will be able to recognize members of the Pea family, also known as "legumes." There are 5 united sepals. The 5 petals form a distinctive "banner, wings, and keel," as illustrated above. The banner is a single petal with two lobes, although it looks like two that are fused together. Two more petals form the wings. The remaining two petals make up the keel and are usually fused together. There are usually 10 (sometimes 5) stamens. The ovary is positioned perigynous (partially inferior) and consists of a single carpel. It matures as a pea-like pod with several seeds.

Identifying the banner, wings, and keel is sufficient to recognize all Peas across the northern latitudes, which belong to the **Pea subfamily**. As you move south you will encounter Peas from two additional subfamilies, the **Mimosa subfamily** and the **Caesalpinia subfamily**. Both of these subfamilies include mostly trees and shrubs, but also a few herbs. Their flowers are significantly different from the flowers of the Pea subfamily. However, most of these trees have pinnate leave and distinctive pea-like pods that open along two seams. Once you recognize a plant as a member of the Pea family by these characteristics, then read more about each of the subfamilies to narrow down the identity. Remember, if the flowers have a distinctive banner, wings, and keel, then the plant is a member of the Pea subfamily, and you can read about the different tribes of the Pea subfamily to search for the best match.

Worldwide, there are about 630 genera and 18,000 species in the Pea family, including peas, beans, and peanuts. This is the third largest family after the Orchid and Aster families. Most Peas form a symbiotic relationship with nitrogen-fixing bacteria in the soil. The bacteria absorb nitrogen from the atmosphere and feed it to the plants. Look for little bumps, often pink, on the roots. The nitrogen is "fixed" in the soil as vegetation decomposes.

Plants of the Pea family range from edible to mildly poisonous. Several species contain toxic alkaloids, which tend to be more concentrated in the seed coats. Locoweed (*Astragalus*), for example, contains an alkaloid which inhibits an enzyme necessary for metabolism in mammals. Excessive consumption can be fatal to livestock. In his book *Into the Wild*, author John Krakauer speculated that Christopher McCandless died from similar poisoning on a wilderness survival outing in 1992. McCandless was harvesting and eating large quantities of *Hedysarum* seeds, which Krakauer proposed to be poisonous. But later research failed to turn up any toxins in the seeds, disproving the theory, as noted in an extensive rebuttal by Samuel Thayer in his book, *Nature's Garden: A Guide to Identifying, Harvesting, and Preparing Edible Wild Plants.*

Pea Family/Mimosa Subfamily

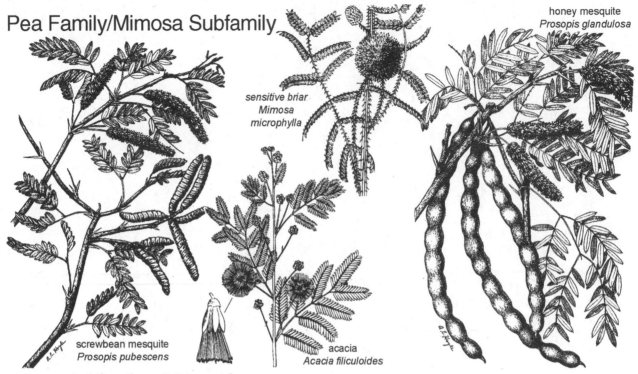

honey mesquite
Prosopis glandulosa

sensitive briar
Mimosa microphylla

screwbean mesquite
Prosopis pubescens

acacia
Acacia filiculoides

Mimosa Subfamily—*Mimosoideae*

The Mimosa subfamily consists of mostly trees and shrubs, plus a few herbs. The leaves are alternate and usually distinctively bipinnate (see the leaf terms illustrated on the opposite page). There are 5 small, united sepals, 5 separate petals, and often 10 or more stamens (sometimes only 4). These are usually small flowers in dense clusters with long stamens radiating out. The filaments (the stamen stems) are often brightly colored. The ovary is positioned superior, consisting of a single carpel, which matures as a typical pea pod. Worldwide, there are about 78 genera and 3,200 species in mostly tropical regions. Some North American genera include:

Acacia—acacia (1,000/5/0) Native across the southern half of the U.S. The *Acacias* produce gum arabic, used in many sore throat, cough and diarrhea formulas. The seeds of many species have been used as food (Sturtevant).

Calliandra—fairy duster (150/11/0) • Native from California to Florida.

Desmanthus—bundleflower (40/15/0) Native across the U.S., except the Pacific northwest.

Leucaena—lead tree (24/4/0) Native and introduced species are found from California to Florida.

Lysiloma—(7/3/0) Native to parts of Florida and Arizona.

Mimosa (including *Schrankia*)—sensitive plant (500/20/0) Native from Arizona to North Dakota, east to the Atlantic.

Prosopis—mesquite, screw bean (45/7/0) • Native from California to Missouri and south. The pods and seeds were pounded, cooked and eaten. The flowers are also edible (Harrington).

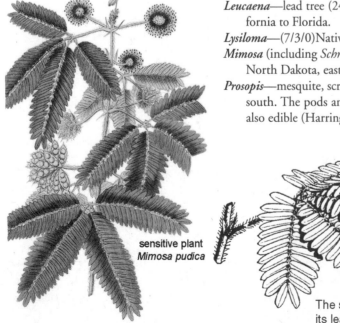

sensitive plant
Mimosa pudica

The sensitive plant folds its leaves when touched.

Pea Family / Caesalpinia Subfamily

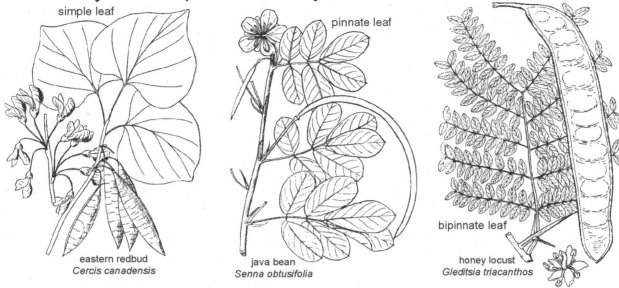

simple leaf

pinnate leaf

bipinnate leaf

eastern redbud
Cercis canadensis

java bean
Senna obtusifolia

honey locust
Gleditsia triacanthos

Caesalpinia Subfamily—*Caesalpinioideae*

The Caesalpinia subfamily (also known as the Senna subfamily or Bird-of-Paradise Tree subfamily), includes mostly trees and shrubs (rarely herbs) with showy, slightly irregular flowers. The leaves may be simple, pinnate, or bipinnate (see illustration above). There are 5 separate sepals and 5 petals, with one petal enclosed inside the others. There are usually 10 (sometimes fewer) stamens. The ovary is positioned superior, consisting of a single carpel, which matures as a typical pea pod. Worldwide, there are about 170 genera and 2,200 species, mostly in the Old World tropics. North American genera include:

Caesalpinia—bird-of-paradise tree (125/10/0) Introduced from India as an ornamental, it now grows from Arizona to Florida. This genus includes species formally classified as *Guilandina*. These plants are not related to the Bird-of-Paradise Flower (*Strelitzia reginae*) of the Banana family (*Musaceae*), which is not covered in this text.

Cassia—senna (500/4/0) Many species formerly classified as *Cassia* are now *Senna*.

Cercis—redbud, Judas tree (7/2/0) The flowers and pods have been used in salads (Sturtevant).

Chamaecrista—sensitive pea (330/12/0) Native from Arizona to Minnesota, east to the Atlantic.

Gleditsia—honey locust (12/3/0) • The immature, raw seeds taste like green peas. The mature seeds can be boiled and eaten, or roasted and ground for use as a coffee substitute. The pulp inside the seedpods is sweet. It can be eaten raw or processed into sugar (Fern). See *Robinia* for the locust or honey locust tree.

Gymnocladus—Kentucky coffee bean tree (3/1/0) *G. dioicus*. The pods are edible. Seeds are used as a coffee substitute (Sturtevant).

Kentucky
coffee bean
*Gymnocladus
dioica*

Parkinsonia (including *Cercidium*)—palo verde (12/3/0) • The common name is Spanish for "bark green," which is a distinctive identifying characteristic for palo verde trees. I have harvested Palo verde beans both green and dried. The beans should be shelled to separate them from the pods, then boiled until tender. They are often abundant and quite delicious. This is a prime wild food resource.

Senna—senna (300/28/0) Includes many species formerly classified as *Cassia*.

Tamarindus—tamarind (1/1/0) *T. indica*. Originally native to eastern Africa, the tamarind tree is widely cultivated in the tropics worldwide, including Mexico and as far north as Florida. The fruit, known as tamarindo or Indian date, is a thick, dark brown or reddish-brown pulp surrounding small seeds inside a hard, brittle bean-shaped pod. Tamarindos contains 20% fruit acids and up to 35% sugar, plus pectin. We bought a bottle of tamarindo concentrate on a trip to Mexico. The flavor is both sweet and sour, not quite like any other fruit I know. The taste is sometimes described as a combination of apricots, dates, and lemons. Tamarindos are widely used in cooking in India and Asia.

Pea Subfamily—*Faboideae*

The Pea subfamily includes all members of the Pea family with a distinctive "banner, wings, and keel." These are mostly of herbs, but some are shrubs and trees. When you've identified a plant as a member of this subfamily, then read about each of the tribes that follow to see which one best fits your sample.

Golden Pea Tribe—*Thermopsideae*

Plants of the Golden Pea tribe could easily be mistaken for lupine of the Broom tribe, but lupine has a palmately divided leaf while members of the Golden Pea tribe have trifoliate (three-parted) leaves, often with stipules.

Baptisia—wild indigo (35/25/0) Native to eastern and southern states.

Thermopsis—golden pea (23/9/2) • My grandmother always called these beautiful yellow flowers "cowslips." They grew in large patches in the fields near her home, and we often picked bouquets of the flowers to bring home. Golden pea may be poisonous to some livestock.

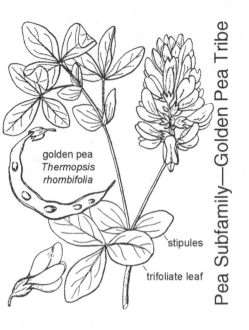

golden pea
*Thermopsis
rhombifolia*

stipules

trifoliate leaf

Hedysarum Tribe—*Hedysareae*

Members of the Hedysarum tribe have either trifoliate (three-parted) or pinnate leaves, but no tendrils. The distinctive feature of these plants is that the pods on most species are deeply constricted between the seeds (see illustration). A few are not constricted, but the pods still tend to break apart transversely (cross-wise instead of lengthwise).

Coronilla—crown vetch (25/1/1) *C. varia*. Introduced from Eurasia. The plant may contain cardiac glycosides. A British species is considered highly toxic, so all species should be suspect (Fern).

Desmodium—tick trefoil (400/45/0) Now segregated into its own tribe, *Desmodieae*.

Hedysarum—sweetvetch (300/8/4) The roots of some species are known to be edible (Willard).

Onobrychis—sainfoin (180/1/1) *O. viciifolia*, also known as *O. sativa*. Cultivated as forage for livestock.

alpine sweetvetch
Hedysarum alpinum

Broom Tribe—*Genisteae*

The Broom tribe includes mostly shrubs, some with spines. The leaves can be simple, trifoliate, or palmately divided (*Lupinus*), but not pinnately divided. (See the *Guide to Leaf Terms* inside the back cover.)

Crotalaria—rattle box (600/13/0) Grows from Arizona to Minnesota and east.

Cytisus—scotch broom (60/6/0) • Scotch broom was introduced from Europe. It is now found along the Atlantic and Pacific Coasts. *C. scoparius* contains the alkaloid sparteine, which slows the heart and stimulates uterine contractions (Tyler).

Genista—broom (90/7/0) Introduced.

Lupinus—lupine (200/150/10) • The root and seeds of some species may be edible after cooking, but some are known to contain poisonous alkaloids (Harrington). More research needs to be done in this area.

Spartium—Spanish broom (1/1/0) *S. junceum*. Introduced.

Ulex—gorse (15/1/0) *U. europaeus*. Introduced.

sundial lupine
Lupinus perennis

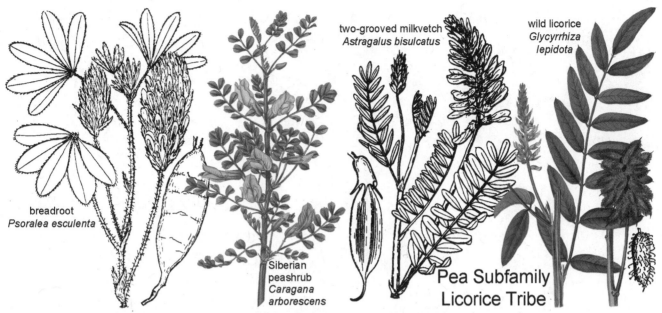

breadroot
Psoralea esculenta

Siberian
peashrub
*Caragana
arborescens*

two-grooved milkvetch
Astragalus bisulcatus

wild licorice
*Glycyrrhiza
lepidota*

Pea Subfamily
Licorice Tribe

Licorice Tribe (including the False Indigo, Breadroot, and Locust tribes)—*Galegeae*

Aside from *Psoralea*, most plants of the Licorice tribe have pinnately divided leaves. None of the plants have tendrils like the Pea tribe, or deeply constricted pods like the Hedysarum tribe. Taxonomists have recently segregated several genera from the Licorice tribe into new tribes of their own, as noted in the text below.

Amorpha—false indigo, lead plant (20/20/1) False Indigo tribe. *Amorpha* has a banner petal, but no wing or keel petals. The true indigo plant (*Indigofera*), a source of dye, is in its own tribe.

Astragalus—locoweed, milk vetch, ground plum (2000/375/43) • Ground plum (*A. succulentus*) has swollen, plum-like pods, easy to distinguish from other members of this genus. The whole pods are edible when young, and the "peas" are still good, even when the pods become tough. Members of this genus are known accumulators of selenium from the soil, and some contain poisonous alkaloids. Medicinally, *A. americanus* may be similar to a popular Chinese herb of this genus (Willard). Several species produce a gum called tragacanth, used to stabilize medicinal preparations by keeping them from separating into solids and liquids (Klein).

Caragana—caragana (80/3/1) • Introduced and often cultivated as a hedge or windbreak. The drying pods audibly snap and twist to eject the seeds. The flowers, seeds, and young pods are edible, but should probably be cooked.

Dalea (including *Petalostemon*)—prairie clover, indigo bush (165/30/4) • False Indigo tribe. The root is sweet and edible raw. The fresh plant is emetic, but a beverage tea can be made from the dried leaves (Fern).

Glycyrrhiza—wild licorice (15/1/1) • *G. lepidota*. Native west of the Mississippi. A European species, *G. glabra*, was the original source of licorice flavor. Chop and boil the root in hot water to extract the flavor. Our native species can be used similarly but doesn't taste like licorice. It usually has small, woody roots, but I have seen a few large ones sticking out of the soil along river banks. Most licorice candies are artificially flavored.

Medicinally, licorice root contains chemicals similar to the human adrenal hormone; it is used to regulate women's hormones for PMS and menstrual cramps (Willard). It can stimulate higher levels of adrenocorticosteroids and estrogen (Moore). Licorice root has an anti-inflammatory effect that mimics cortisone in the body, but without the side effects of steroid drugs. In studies of cough suppression medicines, licorice root was as effective as codeine, a narcotic drug often added to commercial cough remedies (Tilford). When taken over an extended period, licorice can cause the body to excrete more potassium and retain sodium (Hobbs), leading to water retention and elevated blood pressure. People have been hospitalized after consuming too much licorice (Tyler).

Oxytropis—pointloco, vetch (350/36/11) Several species contain toxic alkaloids.

Psoralea—breadroot, scurf pea (150/40/5) • Breadroot tribe. There are many species of *Psoralea* across the U.S., and all apparently have edible roots (Sturtevant). *P. esculenta* is abundant in eastern Montana. The starchy root is dug in the spring when the ground is moist. The bark is peeled off and the root is eaten raw or cooked. It is a first-class food plant where it is available. Caution is advised, however, as it is somewhat similar in appearance to *Lupinus* of the Broom Tribe. The seed-coat contains the lactone glycoside coumarin.

Robinia—locust tree, black locust (20/5/1) Locust tribe. The leaves and bark are poisonous. Locust seeds are acidic and high in oil, but may be edible after thorough boiling (Sturtevant). Some sources suggest that the seeds are poisonous. Note that honey locust (*Gleditsia*) belongs to the Caesalpinia subfamily.

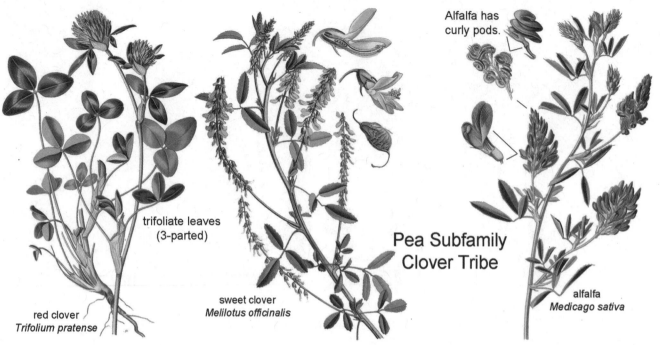

trifoliate leaves
(3-parted)

Alfalfa has
curly pods.

**Pea Subfamily
Clover Tribe**

red clover
Trifolium pratense

sweet clover
Melilotus officinalis

alfalfa
Medicago sativa

Clover Tribe—*Trifolieae*

A distinctive trait of the Clover tribe is its trifoliate (3-parted), clover-like leaves. These species also tend to have smaller flowers than most other peas, and they are often tightly clustered together. Fenugreek (*Trigonella*), a native of India, is a member of this tribe.

Medicago—alfalfa, black medic (110/12/4) • Alfalfa is an introduced crop plant from the Middle East. The mature plant has deep roots (up to sixty feet) and accumulates many mineral nutrients. It contains calcium, chlorine, iron, magnesium, phosphorus, potassium, silica, sodium and trace minerals, plus significant quantities of the vitamins A, B1, B6, B12, C, E, K1, and P. Alfalfa also contains dozens of amino acids, making the plant high in protein. A tea of the plant or a few leaves in a salad makes a highly nutritional health tonic. Tonics like this are useful for helping the body deal with chronic ailments such as arthritis, rheumatism and ulcers. Alfalfa also contains coumarins, mildly useful for lowering cholesterol, except that coumarins are destructive to red blood cells and interfere with the utilization of vitamin E. This is believed to be one of the causes of bloating in farm animals. Please note that alfalfa *sprouts* contain a toxic substance called canavanine, which can lead to scarred lesions on the face and scalp with excessive use.

Pea Subfamily / Trefoil Tribe

stipules

bird's-foot trefoil
Lotus corniculatus

trifoliate leaf

Melilotus—sweet clover (25/6/3) • The sweet odor of these plants is due to the presence of coumarin. A concentrated dose is sometimes administered internally as an anticoagulant to break up blood clots. Excessive use may lead to poisoning (Lust). Coumarin can break down into toxins if it is allowed to spoil (as in moldy hay); these toxins reduce prothrombin content of the blood and prevent the blood from clotting in a wound (Craighead).

Trifolium—clover (300/95/20) • The leaves, stems, and flowers are edible as salad greens or potherbs, but are minimally digestible and may cause bloating. Soaking them in salt water apparently counteracts this effect (Kirk). Red clover seems more edible than other species. Clover seeds are also edible (Olsen). Medicinally, red clover is a diuretic and expectorant (Willard). A tea of the flowers is used to stimulate liver and gall bladder activity (Lust). Red clover contains some coumarins, saponins, and flavonoids (Hobbs).

Trefoil Tribe—*Loteae*

Members of the Trefoil tribe have trifoliate (three-parted) or pinnately divided leaves, sometimes with stipules at the base of the leaves.

Lotus—bird's foot trefoil (125/60/3) • The fresh plant can produce cyanide and may be toxic raw. The young seed pods may be cooked and eaten. The plant has carminative, antispasmodic and hypoglycemic properties. It is also used as a poultice for skin inflammations (Fern).

Pea Tribe—*Fabeae*

Plants of the Pea tribe can be distinguished by their pinnate leaves and tendrils. This tribe includes sweet peas (*Lathyrus*), lentils (*Lens*) and the garden pea (*Pisum*). Note that the chick pea or garbanzo bean (*Cicer*) has been segregated into its own tribe, *Cicereae*. The seeds of some species of the Pea tribe can cause nervous disorders if consumed in excess. Most poisonings occur in hot climates.

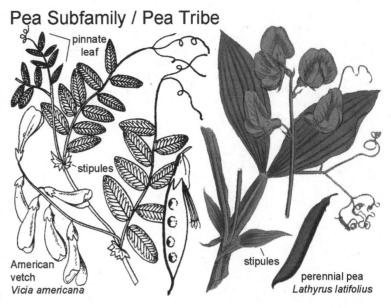

Pea Subfamily / Pea Tribe

pinnate leaf

stipules

American vetch
Vicia americana

stipules

perennial pea
Lathyrus latifolius

- *Lathyrus*—sweet pea (150/45/6) • A few species are edible in moderation, but may cause nervous disorders if eaten excessively over an extended period of time. Other species are toxic (Kirk).
- *Vicia*—vetch (140/30/5) • The seeds and young stems are edible (Craighead). The plants may contain cyanide (Phillips).

Bean Tribe—*Phaseoleae*

Most species of the Bean tribe are twining plants that climb by growing their vine-like stems around poles or other objects. The leaves are usually three-parted. This tribe includes many common beans (*Phaseolus*), the soybean (*Glycine*), as well as cow peas and black-eyed peas (*Vigna*).

- *Amphicarpaea*—hog peanut (2/1/0) *A. bracteata*. Native east of the Rocky Mountains. Hog Peanut is native to the southeastern U.S. The pods are edible (Sturtevant, Hall).
- *Apios*—ground nut, hopniss (8/2/0) Pinnate leaves. Native to the eastern half of North America. Starchy tubers form on its roots much like beads on a string. They are edible raw and reportedly taste "like Idaho potatoes" when cooked (Kallas).
- *Erythrina*—coralbean (104/3/0) Grows from Arizona to Virginia.
- *Galactia*—milkpea (112/17/0) Native from Arizona to New York, south to Florida.
- *Pueraria*—kudzu vine (15/1/0) *P. montana*. Introduced from Asia. It is common across the southeastern states, where it can engulf trees and sometimes kill them by taking all the light. The tubers can be added to stews, or pounded into flour. The young leaves, shoots, and blossoms are all edible as potherbs. The roots are high in flavonoids (Duke)
- *Rhynchosia*—snoutbean (200/15/0) Native from Arizona to Maryland, south to Florida.
- *Strophostyles*—fuzzybean (4/3/0) Native from Arizona to Ontario, east to the Atlantic.

least snoutbean
Rhynchosia minima

twining snoutbean
Rhynchosia tomentosa

kudzu vine
Pueraria montana

redcardinal coralbean
Erythrina herbacea

Pea Subfamily / Bean Tribe

85

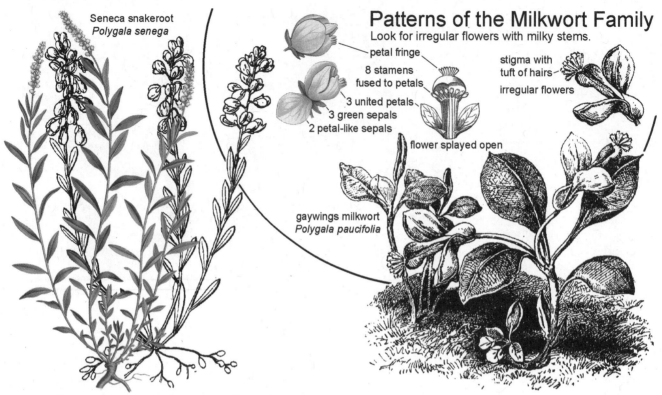

Seneca snakeroot
Polygala senega

Patterns of the Milkwort Family
Look for irregular flowers with milky stems.

petal fringe

8 stamens
fused to petals

3 united petals

3 green sepals

2 petal-like sepals

stigma with
tuft of hairs

irregular flowers

flower splayed open

gaywings milkwort
Polygala paucifolia

Milkwort Family—*Polygalaceae*

Flowers of the Milkwort family look superficially like those of the Pea family, but there are some significant differences. Milkwort flowers are irregular and bisexual. There are 5 sepals—but usually 3 green outer sepals and 2 petal-like inner sepals. There are 3 (sometimes 5) united petals, usually fused with the stamens, and the lower petal is often fringed. There are 8 (sometimes fewer) stamens, fused to the petals. The ovary is positioned superior. It consists of 2 (rarely 5) united carpels with the partition walls present, forming an equal number of chambers. It matures as a capsule, nut, or drupe (a fleshy fruit with a stony seed.)

Worldwide, there are about 17 genera and 850 species in the Milkwort family. The genera below are found in North America. Milkworts are found in patchy distribution mostly across the southern states.

Key Words: Irregular flowers with milky stems.

Monnina—pygmyflower (125/1/0) *M. wrightii.* Native to Arizona and New Mexico.
Polygala—milkwort, snakeroot (550/60/2) Seneca snakeroot (*P. senega*) is native to eastern North America. The roots contain 8 to 16% triterpenoid saponins. The saponins irritate the stomach lining, causing nausea, which subsequently stimulates bronchial secretions and the sweat glands (Tyler). A tea of the dried root stimulates salivation and circulation; it is considered beneficial for lung disorders, but it is irritating to inflamed tissues. (Hutchins). A tea of the leaves is taken for coughs, bronchitis, and other chronic lung ailments. The plants are useful as digestive stimulants (Lust). Some species of milkwort were once believed to increase milk production in cows (Schauenberg). Herbal books still list milkwort as an herb for stimulating milk flow from nursing mothers (Lust). Milkwort is also used as an expectorant (Weiner).

Patterns of the Elm Family

Look for trees or shrubs with simple leaves that are asymmetrical at the base.

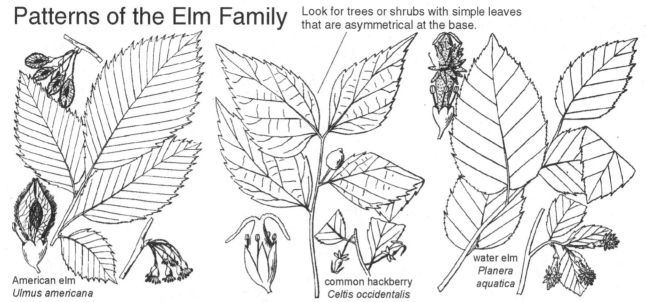

American elm
Ulmus americana

common hackberry
Celtis occidentalis

water elm
*Planera
aquatica*

Elm Family—*Ulmaceae*

The Elm family consists of a handful of trees and shrubs in the eastern and southern parts of the country, some of which are planted elsewhere as ornamentals. The leaves are simple and alternate, but often a little bit asymmetrical at the base. The flowers are bisexual in the elms and unisexual in the other genera. There are 4 or 8 separate sepals and 0 petals, plus 4 to 8 stamens. The ovary is positioned superior and consists of 2 (rarely 3) united carpels forming a single chamber. It matures as a samara (a winged seed) or a drupe (a fleshy fruit with a stony seed).

Worldwide, there are about 15 genera and 130 species in the Elm family. Our native genera are listed below. Only the hackberry is found naturally in the West. Other cultivated genera from the family include *Aphananthe, Hemiptelea, Pteroceltis,* and *Zelkova.* The native elm population has suffered greatly from Dutch elm disease.

Key Words: Trees and shrubs with simple leaves asymmetrical at the base.

Celtis—hackberry (70/5/1) • Genetic evidence suggests that *Celtis* belongs to the closely related Hemp family, *Cannabaceae,* but the traditional grouping is retained here for ease of identification. The fruits are edible (Sturtevant, Moerman).

Planera—water elm (1/1/0) *P. aquatica.* Native to the southeastern states. The fruit is a prickly nut.

Ulmus—elm, slippery elm (25/7/2) • The young leaves are edible raw or cooked (Fern). The bark may be dried and ground into flour; it is used in times of scarcity. The green fruits are also edible (Sturtevant).

slippery elm
Ulmus rubra
(a.k.a. *U. fulva*)

The immature winged seeds of Siberian elm (*U. pumila*) are a sweet treat to nibble on and an excellent addition to a salad. The introduced trees are incredibly hardy and drought tolerant, but invasive in many woodlands. However, they seem to fill an open niche here in arid Montana, often surviving where little else can grow. Read more about Siberian elms in *Foraging the Mountain West* and Samuel Thayer's *The Forager's Harvest.*

The inner bark of slippery elm (*U. rubra,* a.k.a. *U. fulva*) is highly mucilaginous and somewhat astringent. It is used as a soothing remedy, applied externally as an emollient for burns, or taken internally as a demulcent for sore throats and other internal inflammations, including diarrhea (Lust). It is the kind of remedy that can be used for just about anything. A friend once gave me some in tea to reduce a fever on an expedition. I recall that it was very effective. The inner bark can also be used as cordage material.

samaras
(winged seeds)

Patterns of the Mulberry Family

Look for trees and shrubs with alternate leaves and milky sap. Male and female flowers form separately on the same or different trees.

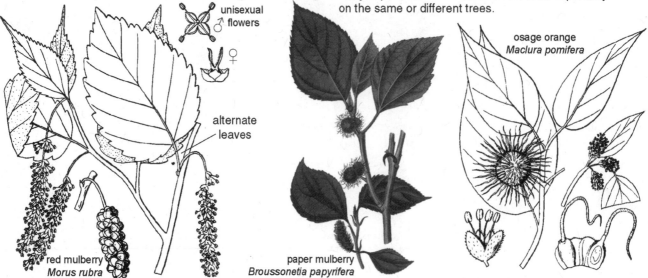

unisexual ♂ flowers

alternate leaves

red mulberry
Morus rubra

paper mulberry
Broussonetia papyrifera

osage orange
Maclura pomifera

Mulberry Family—*Moraceae*

Have you ever seen a tree with milky sap? If so, you have likely met a member of the Mulberry family. These trees and shrubs have alternate leaves and milky latex sap. The unisexual flowers are small and usually tightly clustered, with male and female flowers appearing on the same or different trees. Male flowers have 4 (sometimes 0) sepals, 0 petals and 4 stamens. Female flowers have 4 (sometimes 0) sepals and 0 petals. The ovary is positioned superior or inferior and consists of usually 2 (rarely 3) united carpels, as indicated by the same number of styles. One carpel is usually aborted, forming a single chamber. In species with tightly clustered flowers, the fruits merge together as a single mass, creating a false fruit known as an "aggregate" or "multiple."

Figs are highly unusual in that the flowers are borne in the hollow end of a branch, which later swells around the developing seeds to become the fruit, called a "syconium." Other members of the family produce a nut or a drupe (a fleshy fruit with a stony seed).

Worldwide, there are about 53 genera and 1,500 species in the family. About 800 species are *Ficus*, including figs, the banyan tree, the Indian rubber tree, and the bodhi tree, where the Buddha became enlightened. Breadfruit and jackfruit belong to *Artocarpus*. Other cultivated genera (mostly tropical) include *Antiaris*, *Brosimum*, *Cecropia*, *Chlorophora*, *Cudrania*, *Coussapoa*, *Dorstenia*, *Musanga*, and *Treculia*. North American genera, native and introduced, are listed below.

Key Words: Trees and shrubs w/ alternate leaves and milky sap.

Broussonetia—paper mulberry (7/1/0) *B. papyrifera*. Introduced from Asia.

Fatoua—crabweed (3/1/0) *F. villosa*. Introduced to the southeastern and Pacific states.

Maclura—osage orange (12/1/0) Osage orange is valued as one of the premier woods for bow-making in this country, even though the wood is almost all knots.

Morus—mulberry (12/3/0) • The aggregate fruits are edible, varying from sweet to acidic. Eat them raw or cooked into jelly, pies, or added to ice cream (Lincoff).

When I was a kid, we lived in Los Altos, California. I don't recall that we ever ate the fruits from the mulberry trees in our yard, but we fed the leaves to our pet silkworms.

Medicinally, a tea of the bark is used as a laxative and to expel tapeworms. The milky juice and the unripe fruit may cause hallucinations, nervousness and an upset stomach (Lust).

osage orange
Maclura pomifera

Fruit is a "multiple."

Hemp Family—*Cannabaceae*

The plants of the Hemp family may not have much in the way of showy flowers, but the family does claim one of the most recognized plants on earth: marijuana (*Cannabis sativa*).

Members of the Hemp family are dioecious, meaning that male and female flowers form on separate plants. Male flowers grow in loose racemes or panicles, each flower with 5 sepals, 0 petals and 5 stamens. Female flowers form in dense clusters, sometimes hidden by leafy bracts, with 5 sepals and 0 petals. The ovary is positioned superior and consists of 2 united carpels, as indicated by the same number of styles. One carpel is usually aborted, forming a single chamber. It matures as an achene (a dry seed).

Worldwide, the traditional family includes only 2 genera and 3 to 5 different species. However, genetic evidence suggests that hackberries (*Celtis*) should be transferred here from the closely related Elm family.

Key Words: Coarse, aromatic plants with palmate or pinnate leaves and no petals.

Cannabis—marijuana, hemp (1/1/1) *C. sativa*. Some botanists recognize three different species instead of one. Medicinally, marijuana is often used to stimulate appetite, control nausea, and manage chronic pain. The drug can help patients suffering from neuropathic pain, commonly caused by degenerative diseases like multiple sclerosis or fibromyalgia, and as a side effect of chemotherapy and radiation (Wilson).

Marijuana is also a popular recreational drug with euphoric properties. It is theoretically impossible to get a fatal overdose of unadulterated marijuana, regardless of potency or quantity, but the substance is considered addictive for about 9 percent of users. The main psychoactive ingredient in *Cannabis* is delta-9-tetrahydrocannabinol, also known as THC. The human body produces natural cannabinoids, active chemicals that make us feel good, and THC has a similar effect on the body. The safety or risk of the drug has been a topic of intense debate. A 2011 study found that marijuana has little long-term effect on learning and memory in adults. But another study showed long-term harm to adolescent marijuana users. Teens who smoked pot at least four days a week lost an average of eight IQ points between the ages of 13 and 38. Adults who smoked pot as teenagers had pronounced deficits in memory, concentration, and overall brainpower compared to their peers (Wilson).

Pot is ubiquitous in our culture. It seems like just about every teenager and adult in the country, including our recent Presidents, have all tried it. My singular experience with marijuana went badly. After the emotionally devastating loss of my marriage, I felt curious to try new experiments in life, so I tried half a pot brownie. Nothing happened at first, but then I blacked out. The following day was miserable, with brief moments of coherence and long gaps in consciousness. I was told I had a *very low* tolerance for marijuana. I succeeded in driving home a day later, but experienced gaps in consciousness for months afterwards. People could walk across a room in front of me without me noticing it. They just appeared on the opposite side of the room. I also suffered intermittent, sudden drowsiness that made ten miles of driving seem like a thousand. It took my body about six months to cleanse itself from the experience. Other people obviously don't react as badly as I do, but it is hard to imagine that it is doing them any good!

Cannabis is also famous for its fiber. Most of our ropes and paper and much of our fabric was once made from hemp fibers. Outlawing this plant eliminated an extremely valuable resource. There are some varieties of hemp with virtually no psychoactive properties that should be legalized and utilized.

Humulus—hops vine (2/2/1) • The young leaves, shoots, and roots may be cooked and eaten, and the seeds contain gamma-linolenic acid. The female flowers have a powdery appearance due to many small, translucent-yellow glands; this appears to be the source of the bitter and antibacterial properties that are valued in beer making (Fern). Hops is also rich in pectin (Duke). Stuffing a pillow with dried hops, or brewing a tea of the plant or flowers, produces a sedative effect. The tea is a bitter tonic that stimulates digestive functions while acting as a general antispasmodic. Hops can be used for cordage if the vines are soaked over winter before separating the fibers. The fibers are also used in making paper (Fern).

Patterns of the Hemp Family

hops vine
Humulus lupulus

Coarse, mildly aromatic plants with palmate leaves. Male and female flowers without petals form in clusters on separate plants.

female flowers with bract

2 styles

bracts

89

Stinging Nettle Family—*Urticaceae*

Many plants in the Stinging Nettle family have a memorable way of identifying themselves to you. Hairs underneath the leaves function as hypodermic needles, injecting formic acid into the skin when you come in contact with them. Several genera have stinging hairs, including *Urtica*, *Laportea*, *Hesperocnide*, *Urera*, and *Dendrocnide*.

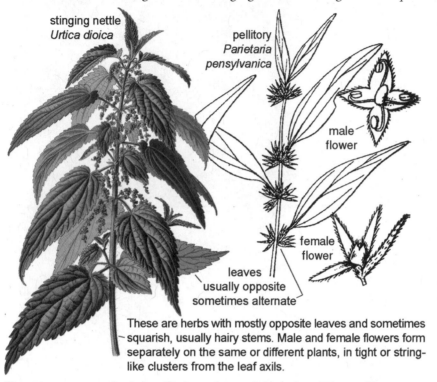

stinging nettle
Urtica dioica

pellitory
Parietaria pensylvanica

male flower

female flower

leaves usually opposite sometimes alternate

These are herbs with mostly opposite leaves and sometimes squarish, usually hairy stems. Male and female flowers form separately on the same or different plants, in tight or string-like clusters from the leaf axils.

Members of the Stinging Nettle family are mostly herbs with simple, usually opposite leaves and occasionally squarish, usually hairy stems. The green or brownish flowers are mostly unisexual with male and female flowers on the same or different plants. There are 4 or 5 sepals, 0 petals, and 4 to 5 stamens. The ovary is positioned superior and has only one carpel. It matures as a dry seed, called an achene.

Worldwide, there are about 54 genera and 2600 species. Six genera are found in North America, as listed below. Most plants in the family are edible as potherbs. The stalks have strong fibers for making cordage.

**Key Words:
Usually hairy plants with petalless flowers in string-like clusters at the leaf axils.**

Patterns of the Stinging Nettle Family

Boehmeria—silkplant, false nettle (80/16/0) Silkplant is said to have the longest fibers known in the plant kingdom, with a tensile strength eight times greater than cotton (Fern).

Hesperocnide—western nettle (2/1/0) *H. tenella*. Native to California and Baja California.

Laportea—wood nettle (45/5/0) The young leaves are edible after cooking to destroy the stinging hairs. They are said to taste better than stinging nettles (Thayer). Fiber from the stems is up to 50 times stronger than cotton (Fern).

Parietaria—pellitory (20/6/1) The young plant is edible raw or cooked (Sturtevant). The plant has both astringent and demulcent properties; it is used externally as a poultice for burns and wounds. A tea of the plant is taken internally for bladder stones and as a laxative. The whole plant may be crushed and used to clean windows or copperware (Fern).

Pilea—clearweed (600/7/0) Clearweed is reportedly a delicious potherb and tasty raw when young (Cook).

Urtica—stinging nettle (35/4/2) • Stinging nettles are edible as a potherb, or added to soups, pesto, sauces, and custard. In Turkey, the leaves are layered onto a circular flat of dough, then rolled, baked, and sliced (Lincoff). I like chopped nettles blended into scrambled eggs. Nettles should be harvested young, before blooming. The plants may accumulate nitrates (see also the Amaranth family) or form calcium carbonate cystoliths as they age (Kallas). It is best to pick them with gloves and a knife. Lacking gloves or a reasonable substitute, carefully grab the plants by the stems and avoid the stinging hairs beneath the leaves. Dried, powdered nettles can be used as a flour additive and stew thickener. Nettles are high in nutrients, including vitamins A, C, and D, the minerals calcium, iron, phosphorus, potassium, sodium, silica, and albuminoids (Willard), and relatively high in protein. The plants are reportedly edible raw if properly crushed first (Kramer). Nettle tea can be used to curdle milk for making cheese (Moore).

Nettles have been used medicinally as a rubefacient to irritate rheumatic joints by whipping them with the plant (Coon), or by applying crushed leaves as a poultice (Lust) to stimulate healing activity in the area. Remembering this advice, a friend with an ill-fitting boot on a walkabout whipped his swollen ankle with nettles until it went numb. But by morning the pain was worse than ever. The tendonitis was obvious when he finally hobbled into a clinic, but the nettle rash was awkward to explain! Nettle tea is a good astringent, useful externally as a wash and hair cleanser or internally for bleeding (Kloss). Nettles are diuretic, but may irritate the kidneys with prolonged use. The plant is also known to bind up immunoglobulin G, reducing sensitivity to food allergies (Willard).

The dead stalks make excellent cordage material (see *Participating in Nature*) and were used in Germany in World War I for weaving when cotton was unavailable. (Coon).

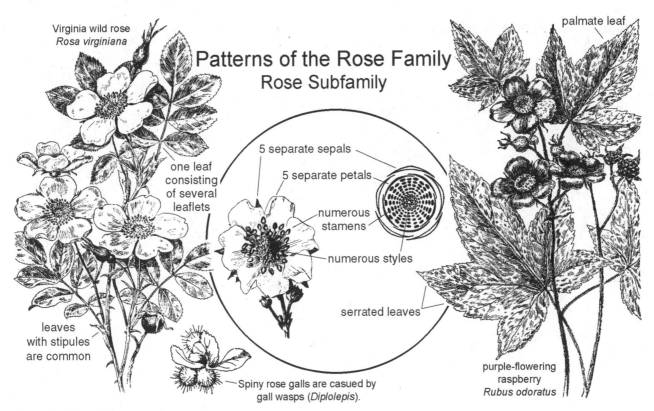

Patterns of the Rose Family
Rose Subfamily

Virginia wild rose
Rosa virginiana

one leaf consisting of several leaflets

leaves with stipules are common

5 separate sepals
5 separate petals
numerous stamens
numerous styles
serrated leaves

Spiny rose galls are casued by gall wasps (*Diplolepis*).

palmate leaf

purple-flowering raspberry
Rubus odoratus

Rose Family—*Rosaceae*

Key Words: 5 sepals and 5 petals with usually numerous stamens. Oval, serrated leaves.

If you have ever buried your nose into an apple, rose, strawberry, or cherry blossom, then you know the Rose family. Roses have alternate leaves, which vary from simple to trifoliate, palmate, or pinnate. The whole leaves or smaller leaflets are frequently more or less oval-shaped with serrated edges, which is a good secondary pattern for recognizing the Rose family. As for the flowers, there are typically 5 (rarely 3 to 10) separate sepals and a similar number of petals. There are a minimum of 5 stamens, but often many more, usually in multiples of five. Many flowers of the Rose family, especially those of the Rose subfamily, have several to numerous simple pistils, or the pistils may be united at the base, with the styles separate, making a single compound pistil with numerous styles. Either way, the result is a distinctive, fuzzy-looking center surrounded by lots of stamens. Plants of the Rose family form many different fruits, varying from fleshy fruits to various false fruits, dry seeds, capsules, or follicles, as described on the following pages.

Worldwide, there are about 100 genera and 3,000 species. About 50 genera are found in North America. The Rose family produces many edible fruits. Tannins are common in the vegetation, giving astringent properties. Cyanide compounds are found in the leaves and fruits of some species.

In the early 1900s, botanists reclassified the Spirea, Plum, and Apple families as subfamilies within the Rose family. In response, Robert Frost poemed, *"The rose is a rose and was always a rose. But the theory now goes that the apple's a rose, and the pear is, and so's the plum, I suppose. The dear [Lord] only knows what will next prove a rose. You, of course, are a rose - but were always a rose."*

Taxonomists have since determined that the Spiraea, Plum, and Apple subfamilies did not represent genetically distinct lines, but should more properly combined as a single subfamily, now known as the Almond subfamily, *Amygdaloideae*. When you have a specimen in hand, then read through each of the subfamilies to narrow down the choices for identification.

purple avens
Geum rivale

Rose Family / Rose Subfamily

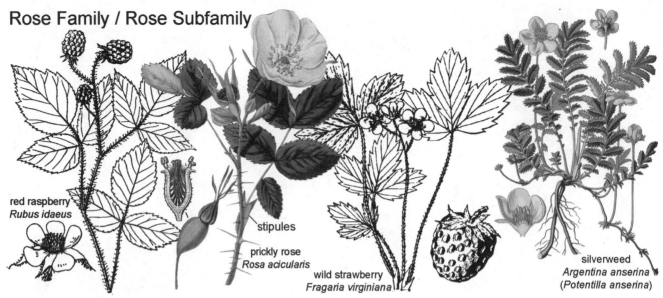

red raspberry
Rubus idaeus

stipules

prickly rose
Rosa acicularis

wild strawberry
Fragaria virginiana

silverweed
Argentina anserina
(Potentilla anserina)

Rose Subfamily—*Rosoideae*

Most flowers of the Rose subfamily have a slightly domed receptacle beneath the pistils. Some species resemble Buttercups with their numerous stamens and numerous simple pistils attached to a cone-like receptacle. But it is easy to determine the difference. There are often stipules at the base of leaves in the Rose subfamily, but never in the Buttercups. Stipules are small, leaf-like growths at the base of the leaf stems (see *Rosa acicularis* above).

Plants of the Rose subfamily have multiple separate pistils (sometimes basally united). Botanically speaking, the ovary from each pistil matures into its own fruit, which is a dry seed (achene) in most Roses. However, there are some interesting false fruits. In the rose, for example, each ovary produces a dry seed, all of which are enclosed within a fleshy receptical that greatly resembles a fleshy ovary. The strawberry is similar, but inverted, with the dry seeds embedded on the surface of a fleshy receptical. The raspberry, however, does have fleshy fruits; the ovary of each simple pistil swells to create an aggregate fruit covering a domed receptacle.

Agrimonia—agrimony (12/8/1) Agrimony is astringent and diuretic, containing malic and tannic acid (Moore, Lust).

Alchemilla—lady's mantle (300/7/1) Various species may have 4, 5, or 10 petals. The plant is astringent (Lust).

Argentina—silverweed (3/2/1) • Includes species formerly included in *Potentilla*.

Chamaerhodes—little rose (8/1/1) *C. erecta*. Native to the Rockies, Canada, and Alaska.

Fragaria—strawberry (20/8/2) • The domestic strawberry is a hybrid of *F. virginiana* and *F. chiloensis*. Wild strawberries are small, but usually flavorful. On camping trips I like to use the fruits in wild strawberry ashcake pies, as described in *Participating in Nature*. Strawberry leaves are mildly astringent and mucilaginous.

Fallugia—Apache plume (1/1/0) • *F. paradoxa*. Native to arid habitats from California to Texas.

Geum—avens (56/18/6) • The root of *G. rivale* can reportedly be boiled and sugar added for a "chocolate substitute" (Hall). *Geum* contains tannic acid and bitters, and releases volatile oils with hydrolysis (Schauenberg).

Horkelia—pink root (19/19/1) The root of at least one species has a pink sap. A tea of the root is taken as a "tonic" (Murphey).

Kelseya—kelseya (1/1/1) *K. uniflora*. Found on rocky outcroppings in Montana, Idaho, and Colorado.

Luetkea—partridge foot (1/1/1) *L. pectinata*. Native from Alaska to California, east to the Rockies.

Potentilla—cinquefoil, silverweed (300/120/26) • All potentillas are astringent; the roots of some contain up to 20% tannin. Some bitter principles are also present (Densmore, Schauenberg).

Rosa—rose (100/54/6) • Rose hip tea is one of my all-time favorites, even better left in the kettle overnight. Rose hips cling to the bushes through most of the winter. Depending on the species, rose hips vary from dry to fleshy and pleasant as a trail nibble. I eat most fleshy rose hips whole, but other people caution that the hairy seeds could be a choking hazard. If in doubt, clean it out. Rose hips are extremely rich in vitamin C and often included as an ingredient in vitamin tablets.

Rubus—raspberry, blackberry, salmonberry, thimbleberry (700/240/6) • Wild raspberries contain citric and malic acids (Densmore). The vegetation is mildly astringent and diuretic, generally recommended during pregnancies (Willard). It is also mildly mucilaginous (Geller). It is used for diarrhea (Lust). The wilted vegetation may produce cyanide (Tilford). Read more about raspberries, blackberries, and their kin in *Foraging the Mountain West*.

Sanguisorba—burnet (30/8/1) • 4 petal-like sepals. 0 petals. 2 to 12 stamens. 1 to 3 pistils. A tea of the root is highly astringent, used for diarrhea, hemorrhaging and varicose veins (Lust).

Sibbaldia—sibbaldia (1/1/1) *S. procumbens*. This is an arctic plant, also found in higher elevations in western states.

Dryad Subfamily—*Dryadoideae*

In the flowers and shrubs of the Dryad subfamily, the ovary matures as a dry seed (achene). The style remains attached to the ovary, usually forming a distinctive feathery plume attached to each seed. (Also found in *Geum triflorum* and *Fallugia paradoxa* of the Rose subfamily.) Like members of the Pea family, Dryads associate with nitrogen-fixing bacteria in the soil, forming nodules on the roots. The bacteria absorb nitrogen from the air and make it available to the plants. In exchange, the plants photosynthesize sugars for the bacteria.

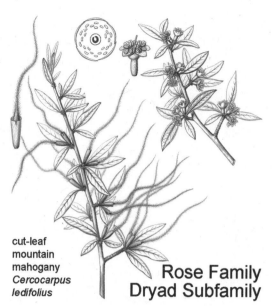

cut-leaf mountain mahogany *Cercocarpus ledifolius*

Rose Family
Dryad Subfamily

Cercocarpus—mountain mahogany (10/4/2) • Astringent, yet laxative (Moore). It contains some hydrocyanic acid (Phillips).

Chamaebatia—mountain misery (2/2/0) Native to California. The vegetation has a strong odor, the source of the common name.

Dryas—dryad, mountain avens (5/5/3) • Dryads are dwarf perennial plants native to arctic and alpine regions of the northern hemisphere. Fossils of eight-petal mountain avens (*D. octopetala*) are used as indicators to mark geological periods of cold temperature known as the Younger Dryas and Older Dryas stadials. Medicinally, the astringent leaves are used in tea (Sturtevant). *Dryas* is also the scientific name for a genera of butterflies.

Purshia—(including *Cowania*) bitterbrush (7/2/1) • Native to the West. The vegetation is an important food for antelope and other wildlife. The seeds are collected and stored in quantity by mice (Craighead).

Almond Subfamily: Spiraeas—*Amygdaloideae*

The Almond subfamily includes the former Spiraea, Plum, and Apple subfamilies. There was some genetic overlap between these groups, which necessitated combining them. For example, some genera listed below were previously classified as Spiraeas, but are more closely related to Plums or Apples. Nevertheless, the traditional grouping remains useful for the purposes of identification.

Spiraea-type plants are mostly shrubs with foamy-looking, dense clusters of usually small white or pink flowers, often with stamens dangling beyond the petals. Unlike the Rose subfamily, these plants do not have stipules on the leaves. The ovary is positioned superior with 2 to 5 (rarely 1 to 12) simple pistils, which may be partially fused at the base. Fruits of this group include capsules, follicles (unicarpellate dry fruits that split along a seam), or sometimes achenes (dry seeds).

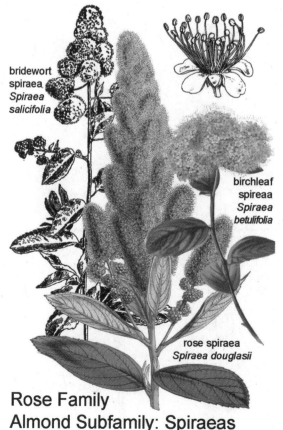

bridewort spiraea *Spiraea salicifolia*

birchleaf spireaa *Spiraea betulifolia*

rose spiraea *Spiraea douglasii*

Rose Family
Almond Subfamily: Spiraeas

Aruncus—bride's feathers (1/1/0) *A. dioicus*. Eastern and western states.

Chamaebatiaria—desert sweet (1/1/0) *C. millefolium*. Native to the West.

Gillenia—Indian physic (2/2/0) Native to the eastern states.

Holodiscus—ocean spray (8/2/1) • The small, dry fruits were reportedly eaten by Native Americans (Craighead).

Lyonothamnus—Catalina ironwood (1/1/0) *L. floribundus*. Found only on California's Catalina Islands.

Petrophyton—rock mat (4/4/1) Native to the western states.

Physocarpus—ninebark (10/5/2) • The palmate leaves resemble the Gooseberry family. Genetic evidence now places this genus closer to *Prunus* than *Spiraea*.

Spiraea—spiraea, meadowsweet (100/22/3) • Spiraea is astringent, diuretic, and it contains methyl salicylate (oil of wintergreen) and other salicylates, similar to aspirin or willow. It is used especially for arthritis, rheumatism, and urinary tract infections (Schauenberg). Spiraea is becoming a popular herb because the salicylate content is much more reliable from plant to plant than willows or poplars.

Vauquelinia—Arizona rosewood (2/2/0) Grows from Arizona to Texas. Genetically, this genus is closer to apples (*Malus*) than *Spiraea*.

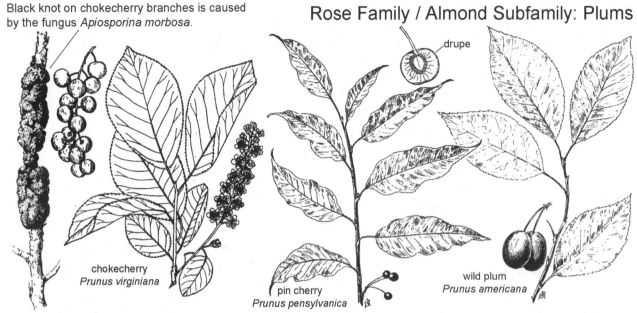

Black knot on chokecherry branches is caused by the fungus *Apiosporina morbosa*.

Rose Family / Almond Subfamily: Plums

drupe

chokecherry
Prunus virginiana

pin cherry
Prunus pensylvanica

wild plum
Prunus americana

Almond Subfamily: Plums—*Amygdaloideae*

Plums, cherries, apricots, peaches, nectarines, and almonds are all included in the *Prunus* genus. With most of these species, we eat the fleshy fruit and throw the pit away, but in the almond (*P. dulcis*), we discard the fleshy fruit and crack open the pit to eat the nut. The ovary is positioned mostly or wholly superior and usually consists of a single carpel (unicarpellate) (2 to 5 carpels in *Oemleria*) forming a single chamber that matures as a drupe (a fleshy fruit with a stony seed). Next time you see one of these fleshy fruits, notice the "seam" down one side, and the almond-like pit in the middle; those are the obvious marks of *Prunus* and it closest allies.

The fruits and/or nuts of any species of *Prunus* are technically edible, but the nuts contain amygdalin, a glycoside that breaks down into benzaldehyde and cyanide. Benzaldehyde is the source of the bitter almond flavor, often utilized in cooking. The degree of bitterness is a good indicator of the concentration of amygdalin in the raw nut. Amygdalin, also known as laetrile or Vitamin B17, is considered beneficial in small doses, but excess consumption leads to cyanide poisoning. Cyanide prevents cells from utilizing oxygen in the bloodstream, resulting in asphyxiation at the cellular level. Proper cooking, drying, and/or oxidation destroys the cyanide, making the pit—or rather the nut inside the pit—edible.

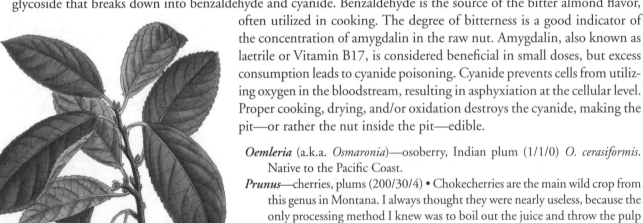

beach plum
Prunus maritima

Oemleria (a.k.a. *Osmaronia*)—osoberry, Indian plum (1/1/0) *O. cerasiformis*. Native to the Pacific Coast.

Prunus—cherries, plums (200/30/4) • Chokecherries are the main wild crop from this genus in Montana. I always thought they were nearly useless, because the only processing method I knew was to boil out the juice and throw the pulp away. As a "survivalist," I like real food, and the juice was never quite good enough. Then a Crow Indian woman showed me the native way of processing them. Put the fresh berries on a metate stone and mash them up, pits and all, and dry the mash. The nut inside the pit has an almond-like aroma. The combination cherry-almond odor is richly intoxicating to work with when mashing them on a rock. Like most of other members of this genus, chokecherry pits contain a form of cyanide, but cyanide is easily destroyed by heat, sunlight, and oxygen. Mashing and drying the chokecherries renders them safe to eat. The pit shells are crunchy, but surprisingly edible. I cook the fresh mash and use it as a filling in "chokecherry ashcake turnovers." The dried mash makes a passable trail mix. I can hand-pick one gallon of cherries per hour, which take another forty minutes to mash with a rock. Read more about chokecherries and plums in *Foraging the Mountain West*.

Rose Family / Almond Subfamily: Apples

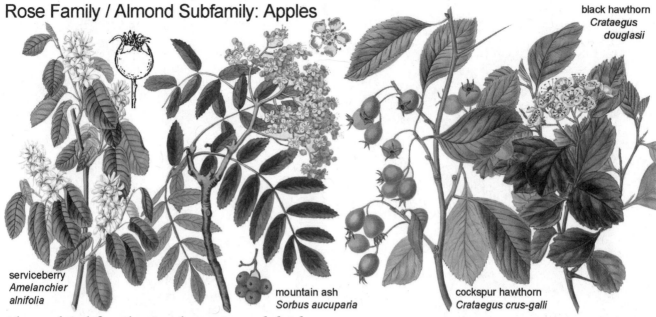

black hawthorn
Crataegus douglasii

serviceberry
Amelanchier alnifolia

mountain ash
Sorbus aucuparia

cockspur hawthorn
Crataegus crus-galli

Almond Subfamily: Apples—*Amygdaloideae*

If you find a Rose family plant with fleshy fruits and a five-pointed star on the bottom then it belongs to the apple group of the Almond Subfamily. The only other fleshy fruit of the Rose family with a five-pointed star is the rose itself (see the Rose subfamily). In apple-type flowers, the ovary is positioned inferior, leaving the remains of the flower attached to the tip of the fruit. The fruit is a false fruit known as a pome. Rather than being formed as a swollen ovary, the fleshy fruit is formed from the enlarged receptacle around the ovary.

All of these apple-type fruits are more or less edible, although some, like the mountain ash (*Sorbus*), can be highly sour-astringent. Other cultivated members of the Apple subfamily include the apple (*Malus*), pear (*Pyrus*), quince (*Cydonia*), loquat (*Eriobotrya*), Christmasberry (*Photinia*), and *Pyracantha*. The fruits of most of these plants are sweeter after a frost. Note that berries from the Heath family / Blueberry subfamily have a similar five-pointed star from the leftover sepals.

Aronia—chokeberry (3/3/0) Aronia juice is available in many stores. The juice is best cold-pressed from the fruits, but it can also be extracted through boiling and used for making jelly or syrup. See *Nature's Garden* by Samuel Thayer.

Amelanchier—saskatoon, serviceberry (20/17/2) • Many wild berries are all juice, but serviceberries are more fleshy, without being too sweet or acidic. They are among my favorite berries, and I can easily eat a quart of them on site when I find a good thicket. Serviceberries are good in pies and jams, or perhaps best utilized as Native Americans did, dried in berry cakes or used in pemmican. See *Foraging the Mountain West* for more details. Medicinally, the berries may be laxative, while the leaves and bark are astringent (Willard).

Cotoneaster—cotoneaster (95/16/1) • Introduced. Cotoneaster is often cultivated as a hedge. The Peking cotoneaster (*C. acutifolius*) is common in Montana towns. The purple fruits are edible and often cling to the bushes into winter.

Crataegus—hawthorn (200/170/4) • All hawthorn berries are edible: black, blue, red or yellow. Blue-black fruits tend to be pulpy and delicious, whereas red fruits are more seedy and astringent. Hawthorns are packed with pectin; the fruits can be boiled down and the juice added to jams and jellies to help them set. The western black hawthorn (*C. douglasii*) is especially pulpy. To separate the seeds, mash the fruit in a bowl, mix in a small amount of water, load into a clean sock, and squeeze out the pulpy juice. The juice has so much pectin that it jells shortly after squeezing. The pectin-rich pulpy juice can be served as a dish that resembles cranberries, or combined with egg whites and sugar and frothed into something resembling ice cream, as described in *Foraging the Mountain West*.

    Medicinally, the leaves, flowers and fruit are rich in flavonoids, especially beneficial to the heart. Hawthorn is used to normalize arrhythmia, high or low blood pressure, and to reduce blood clots. It makes the blood vessels more flexible, reducing vascular resistance so the heart doesn't have to pump so hard (Klein).

Sorbus—mountain ash (100/10/2) • Western mountain ash (*S. scopulina*) is commonly cultivated in towns, where the fruits can be gathered in great abundance. Unfortunately, the fruit has such a sour-astringent flavor that we have not yet been successful in making anything palatable from it. The European service tree (*S. domestica*) has a good fruit and could be a good candidate for edible landscaping here.

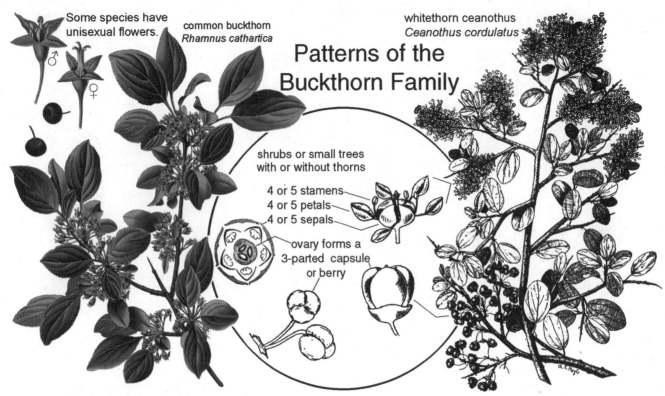

Some species have unisexual flowers.

common buckthorn
Rhamnus cathartica

whitethorn ceanothus
Ceanothus cordulatus

Patterns of the Buckthorn Family

shrubs or small trees with or without thorns

4 or 5 stamens
4 or 5 petals
4 or 5 sepals

ovary forms a 3-parted capsule or berry

Buckthorn Family—*Rhamnaceae*

If you find a dicot shrub or small tree with visibly three-parted capsules or berries, then it is likely a member of the Buckthorn family. The foamy, white, greenish, or even blue spray of flowers of *Ceanothus* is also hard to miss, when in season. These shrubs have simple, and usually serrated, alternate or opposite leaves and sometimes thorns. The flowers are mostly regular and usually, but not always, bisexual. There are 4 or 5 sepals, 4 or 5 (sometimes 0) petals, and 4 or 5 stamens. The stamens are alternate with the sepals and opposite the petals. The ovary is positioned superior or partly inferior, consisting of 3 (sometimes 2 or 4) united carpels, as indicated by the same number of styles. Partition walls are usually present, forming an equal number of chambers. It matures as a capsule or berry with 1 (rarely 2) seeds per chamber. The sections of the ovary are often readily visible on the surface. Worldwide, there are 58 genera and 900 species. Ten genera are found in North America, including *Berchemia*, *Colubrina*, *Condalia*, *Gouania*, *Krugiodendron*, *Reynosia*, *Sageretia* and *Ziziphus*, plus the genera below.

Key Words: Shrubs or small trees with visibly three-parted capsules or berries.

Ceanothus—buckbrush, ceanothus, red root (80/50/3) • The flowers and fruits of New Jersey tea (*C. americanus*) contain saponin and can be used for soap (Craighead). The leaves are popular for tea. The root can be used for a red dye (Hall). The root contains many acids, including tannin, and thus astringent, used in the conventional ways for inflamed tonsils, sore throat, nosebleeds, menstrual hemorrhage, etc. Additionally, the root somehow stimulates "electrical repelling" between the blood vessels and the red blood cells. Increasing the blood charge helps keep the red blood cells flowing without clumping up. The enhanced flow is especially beneficial for headaches triggered by a heavy dinner, when fats flood into the bloodstream. Increasing the blood charge also facilitates a better exchange between the blood vessels and the lymph nodes to expedite the break down and removal of wastes. Red root helps to "tone" or improve and strengthen the lymph tissues. It is beneficial to "healthy people under stress," but it is not a heroic herb to treat sick people. For more information please refer to Michael Moore's *Medicinal Plants of the Pacific West*.

Rhamnus—buckthorn, cascara sagrada (155/12/3) • The berries of many species found in North America are reported to be edible (Sturtevant), but may have laxative properties (Schauenberg). *Rhamnus* bark contains anthroquinone glycosides. It is used as a powerful laxative that does not result in dependency (Willard). It is available commercially; the total trade consumes 1 to 3 million pounds each year. It is recommended that the bark be aged for a year (Hall) or baked at 212ºF for ten minutes (Bigfoot) before use. The fresh bark can cause severe diarrhea and vomiting. Native Americans sometimes used it as an emetic to expel ingested poisons (Tilford).

Patterns of the Oleaster Family

These are shrubs or small trees, often with silvery leaves and gray or red-orange fruits.

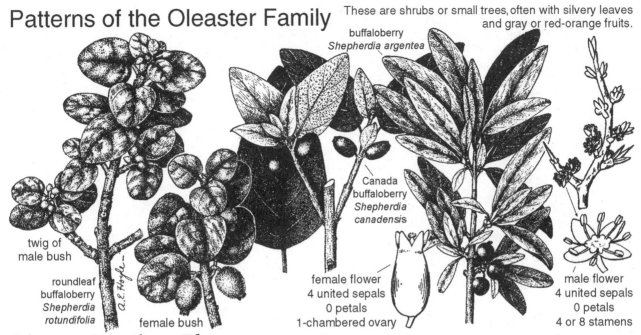

buffaloberry
Shepherdia argentea

twig of
male bush

roundleaf
buffaloberry
*Shepherdia
rotundifolia*

female bush

Canada
buffaloberry
*Shepherdia
canadensis*

female flower
4 united sepals
0 petals
1-chambered ovary

male flower
4 united sepals
0 petals
4 or 8 stamens

Oleaster Family—*Elaeagnaceae*

The Oleaster family consists of usually thorny shrubs and trees with alternate or sometimes opposite leaves, usually silvery in appearance due to the presence of minute hairs. Some species have small orange dots under the leaves. Several members of this family prosper in valley bottoms where the soil is dry, but the water table is not far below. Flowers are regular and mostly bisexual, but sometimes unisexual, with male and female flowers often appearing on separate plants. There are 4 united sepals, often petal-like, and 0 petals. There are 4 or 8 stamens. The ovary is positioned partly or wholly inferior, consisting of a single carpel. It matures as an achene (a dry seed), but looks like a drupe (a fleshy fruit with a stony seed). The fleshy part is the swollen calyx (the sepals), not the ovary. Worldwide, there are 3 genera and about 50 species, all native to the northern hemisphere. All associate with nitrogen-fixing bacteria.

Key Words: Shrubs or trees often with silvery leaves and gray or red-orange fruits.

Elaeagnus—Russian olive, oleaster, silverberry, autumn olive (45/5/3) • The introduced Russian olive (*E. angustifolia*) is well adapted to arid lands and alkaline soil. It is cultivated in many areas, but naturalized in the countryside, and often invasive. The fruits are astringent and marginally edible. Our native silverberry (*E. commutata*) also produces edible fruit, and unlike Russian olive it has no thorns. The inner bark was used extensively for cordage material by Native Americans (Turner). The ripe fruits of the introduced autumn olive (*E. umbellata*) have 7 to 17 times as much of the antioxidant lycopene as tomatoes.

Hippophae—seaberry, sea-buckthorn (3/1/1) *H. rhamnoides*. An introduced ornamental shrub from Russia with large yellow-orange, edible fruits.

Shepherdia—buffaloberry (3/3/2) • Red-orange fruits. Buffaloberries ripen in late summer, but frequently remain on the bushes all winter. The fresh berries are quite astringent, and they will really pucker your mouth. Picking them after a hard freeze helps sweeten them. I like the berries dried whole; they sweeten up quite a bit that way. It is much more efficient to beat the berries out of the bushes with sticks than to handpick them. Read more in *Foraging the Mountain West*.

Russet buffaloberry (*S. canadensis*) grows in the mountains. The saponin-rich berries are bitter, but were dried and eaten by the Inuit (Heywood). The berries can be whipped into a froth and mixed with sugar to make "Indian ice-cream" (Hart).

Russian olive
Elaeagnus angustifolia

97

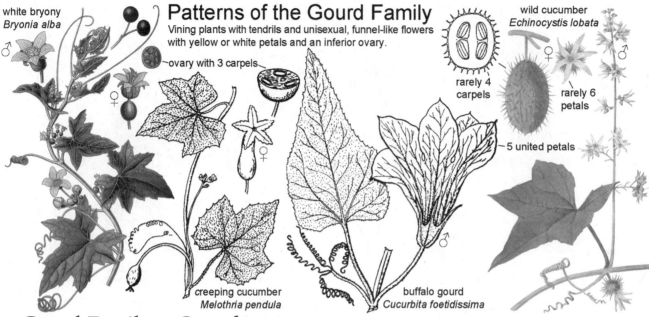

Patterns of the Gourd Family

Vining plants with tendrils and unisexual, funnel-like flowers with yellow or white petals and an inferior ovary.

white bryony
Bryonia alba

ovary with 3 carpels

wild cucumber
Echinocystis lobata

rarely 4 carpels

rarely 6 petals

5 united petals

creeping cucumber
Melothria pendula

buffalo gourd
Cucurbita foetidissima

Gourd Family—*Cucurbitaceae*

The Gourd family is as easy to recognize as pumpkins and squash in the garden. These are vining plants with tendrils and typically palmate or palmately-veined leaves. The flowers are regular and unisexual, with male and female flowers appearing on the same or separate plants. There are 5 separate sepals and 5 united petals (rarely 6 of each), forming a funnel-shaped flower. In the staminate (male) flower, the 5 stamens (sometimes 3) are often twisted together. In the pistillate (female) flower, the ovary is positioned inferior and consists of 3 united carpels (sometimes 4, as in *Echinocystis* above), as indicated by the same number of stigmas. Partition walls are present, forming an equal number of chambers. Notice the pattern when you cut across a zucchini or cucumber.

Worldwide, there are about 120 genera and 850 species, including 14 genera in North America. Pumpkins, squash, zucchini, and gourds belong to the *Cucurbita* genus of this family. Muskmelon, cantaloupe, honeydew, and cucumbers belong to *Cucumis*. Other family members include watermelons (*Citrullus*), chayote (*Sechium*) and the *Luffa* vegetable sponge. Pumpkin seeds contain alkaloids capable of arresting cell division, useful for certain types of cancer (Schauenberg). **Warning:** Some genera contain toxic alkaloids.

Key Words: Vining plants with tendrils. Funnel-shaped flowers form 3-chambered fruits.

Bryonia—bryony (12/3/1) Introduced. The whole plant is poisonous. The root is used in minute quantities as an irritating stimulant. Externally it may be used to irritate sore muscles or joints (a rubefacient) to stimulate healing. Internally, it functions as an irritating expectorant, beneficial for congested lungs, or as an irritating purgative-cathartic to clear out the digestive tract. Toxicity varies between species, but an overdose may lead to severe diarrhea, vomiting and death within a few hours (Fern). This plant is not for amateurs.

Cucurbita—wild gourd, pumpkins, squash, etc. (20/8/0) • The raw seeds of pumpkins and other species contain cucurbitin acid, a popular treatment for internal parasites. The concentration is extremely variable within the genus, even among the many varieties of pumpkins (Tyler). Wild gourds (*C. foetidissima* and *C. digitata*), are not native to Montana, but I have grown them from seed. The plants never put on fruit, apparently due to the short growing season in Montana, but surprisingly, the plants prosper in spite of our extreme winters. The massive root of these plants contains large amounts of saponin. It can be chopped and used for soap or fish poison. The seeds are edible after complete drying and roasting. The plant and the gourd flesh have a strongly laxative effect (Bigfoot), possibly due to the saponins.

Echinocystis—wild cucumber (25/1/1) • *E. lobata*. Native across most of North America, except the southwest and southeast. The fruit is not edible, but the seeds were roasted and eaten for kidney trouble (Murphey). The root has analgesic properties. It may be pulverized and used as a poultice for headaches or brewed as a bitter tea and taken internally (Fern).

Marah—wild cucumber, manroot (7/6/0) • The fruits and seeds of the plants appear to contain saponins and narcotic alkaloids. The whole fruits can be crushed and used to stun fish, but with variable results. At least one death is attributed to this plant. The victim made a tea of the seeds, possibly for its narcotic effect (Nyerges).

Melothria—creeping cucumber (12/1/0) *M. pendula*. Native from Texas to Pennsylvania to Florida. The green fruits are edible, while the fully ripe black fruits are strongly laxative.

Patterns of the Walnut Family
Aromatic trees with pinnate leaves and walnut-like fruits.

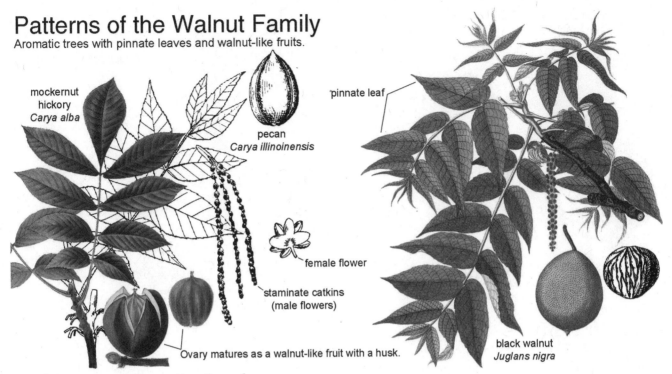

mockernut
hickory
Carya alba

pecan
Carya illinoinensis

pinnate leaf

female flower

staminate catkins
(male flowers)

Ovary matures as a walnut-like fruit with a husk.

black walnut
Juglans nigra

Walnut Family—*Juglandaceae*

Members of the Walnut family are generally resinous, aromatic trees with alternate, pinnately divided leaves. Glandular dots beneath the leaves help to identify this family. Flowers are unisexual and wind-pollinated, with male and female flowers usually appearing on the same trees (monoecious). Male flowers are borne in catkins, with 3 to 6 (sometimes 0) sepals, 0 petals, and 3 to 40 stamens (sometimes 100). Female flowers have 4 sepals and 0 petals. The pistil consists of 2 to 3 united carpels fused together to make a single-chambered ovary. The extra carpels are aborted and the ovary matures as a single hard-shelled nut enclosed in a husk. Worldwide, there are about 8 genera and 60 species, mostly walnuts. Our natives are listed below. Other cultivated genera include *Platycarya* and *Pterocarya*.

Key Words: Aromatic trees with pinnate leaves and walnut-like fruits.

Carya—pecan, hickory, bitternut, pignut (27/16/0) Hickory and its kin are processed and used similarly to walnuts. The trees can be tapped for syrup (Hall, Gilmore).

Juglans—walnut, butternut (20/4/0) • There are about twenty species of walnuts in the world. They all produce edible nuts, but of varying quality. Walnuts are not native to the West, however some species are cultivated, especially the black walnut (*J. nigra*). Black walnuts are mostly shell with little nutmeat inside. On a springtime walkabout in eastern Oregon, some friends and I collected a bunch of black walnuts at an abandoned homestead. Cracking the shells and picking out the meat with a sharp stick was tedious. I was able to extract only about one cup of nutmeat per hour of effort, but it sure was good! One author recommends gathering the nuts in the fall and drying them before removing the husks. After husking, the nuts should be crushed then slowly boiled in water. The oil and nut meats rise to the top, while the shells settle to the bottom. The oil and meats can be used separately, or blended together to make walnut butter. The trees can also be tapped for syrup in the springtime (Hall). (See the Soapberry family: Maples for more information on wild syrup.)

Medicinally, the leaves, bark, and husks are rich in tannic acid, with some bitter components. Walnut is used mostly as an astringent, but also as vermifuge, internally to get rid of worms, externally for ringworm fungus. The green husk is rich in vitamin C (Schauenberg). Butternut bark contains a naphthoquinone laxative (Hobbs). (Read about the similar anthraquinone glycosides in the *Medicinal Properties* section of this book.)

Walnut husks are rich in tannins, especially useful for dye. Butternut husks make a rich purple dye, while walnuts procude a black dye. Boil the husks to extract the pigment (Hall).

Patterns of the Beech Family

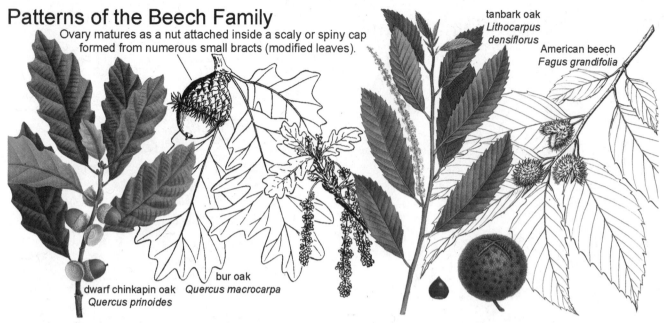

Ovary matures as a nut attached inside a scaly or spiny cap formed from numerous small bracts (modified leaves).

tanbark oak
Lithocarpus densiflorus

American beech
Fagus grandifolia

bur oak
Quercus macrocarpa

dwarf chinkapin oak
Quercus prinoides

Beech Family—*Fagaceae*

Members of the Beech family are trees or shrubs, either deciduous or evergreen. The leaves are simple, alternate and often toothed or lobed. The flowers are typically unisexual, with both male and female flowers appearing on the same plant (monoecious). Most are wind-pollinated. Staminate (male) flowers have 4 to 6 sepals, 0 petals and 4 to 40 stamens. The pistillate (female) flowers have 4 to 6 sepals and 0 petals. The ovary is positioned inferior and consists of 3 (sometimes 6) united carpels, as indicated by the same number of styles. The extra carpels are aborted and the ovary matures as a nut, usually attached to a scaly or spiny cap formed of numerous small, overlapping bracts.

Worldwide, there are about 8 genera and 900 species in the family. Five genera are native to North America, as listed below. Cork comes from the bark of the cork oak (*Quercus suber*). Members of this family contain varying amounts of tannic acid, making them astringent and diuretic.

Key Words: Trees or shrubs with single nuts attached to scaly or spiny caps.

Castanea—chestnut (8/6/0) Chestnuts are edible raw or cooked (Fern). Collect the fruit with gloves, then step on them to break the husk and free the nuts. Score and ovenroast the nuts until the scores pull back to expose the yellowish seed inside (Lincoff). The American chestnut (*C. dentata*) was abundant in eastern North America until the chestnut blight was accidentally imported from Asia and wiped out about four billion trees.

Chrysolepis—chinquapin (2/2/0) Native to Pacific coast states. The nuts are edible raw or cooked (Fern).

Fagus—beech (10/2/0) Beech leaves are edible raw or cooked early in the spring. The seeds are rich in oil and high in protein, edible raw or cooked, but should not be eaten in large quantities due to an alkaloid in the outer covering (Schauenberg). The seeds may be dried and ground into flour. The roasted seed is used as a coffee substitute. The sprouted seeds are also edible and reportedly delicious. Oil from the seeds may be used in cooking and salad dressings or in lamps (Fern).

Lithocarpus—tanbark oak (100/1/0) *L. densiflorus*. Native to California and Oregon. The nuts are edible like acorns after leaching out the tannins, as described for *Quercus*, below (Thayer).

Quercus—oak (450/80/1) • Acorns are edible and highly nutritious, rich in carbohydrates, oil, and protein, but they also contain tannins which must be leached out prior to use. The acorns should be cracked open and the nuts removed. The nuts can be slow-leached whole or in chunks by suspending a net bag full of nuts in a stream for several weeks until the tannins leach out. A faster method is to grind the nuts into flour, then stir the flour into a large quantity of cold water and let it set for a few hours. Then pour off the water and repeat the leaching process through multiple changes (typically six to twenty changes of water), until the acorn flour loses its astringent quality. For super-comprehensive coverage of acorn harvesting and processing, be sure to read Samuel Thayer's *Nature's Garden*.

Medicinally, oaks are astringent throughout, due to the tannins. The bark also contains quercin, a compound similar to salicin (like aspirin). The astringency is used internally for gum inflammations, sore throat and diarrhea. Externally it is used for first and second degree burns. The tannin binds the proteins and amino acids, sealing off the burns from weeping and from bacterial infection. The leaves can be chewed into a mash for use as an astringent poultice (Moore). Oak galls, distorted growths caused by the gall wasp, also have a high tannin content; as much as 60–70% in the galls of *Q. lusitanica* (plus 2–4 % gallic acid). The galls can be collected and used as dye (Pammel).

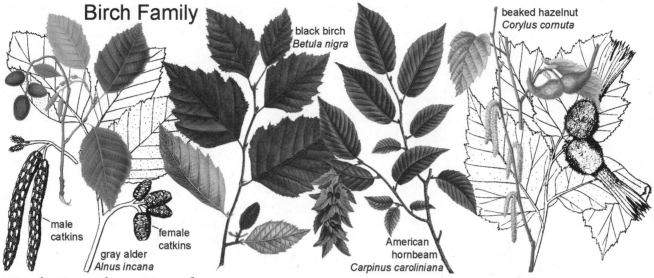

Birch Family—*Betulaceae* (*Cupuliferae*)

The Birch family includes deciduous trees and shrubs with simple, toothed, alternate leaves with pinnate veins. Flowers are wind-pollinated, with male and female catkins forming separately on the same tree (monoecious). Staminate (male) catkins have small flowers with either 0 or 4 sepals, 0 petals, and 2 to 20 stamens. Pistillate (female) catkins also have numerous small flowers, with 0 sepals and 0 petals. The catkins include bracts (modified leaves) that may be mistaken for sepals. The ovary is usually positioned inferior and consists of 2 united carpels, as indicated by the same number of styles. It matures as a nut or a winged seed. Worldwide, there are about 6 genera and 150 species, including filberts or hazelnuts (*Corylus*), which produce edible nuts. Members of the Birch family contain varying amounts of tannic acid, making them somewhat astringent and diuretic. North American genera are listed below.

Key Words: Trees or shrubs with cone-like catkins or nuts with attached bracts.

Alnus—alder (30/8/2) • Alders are rich in tannins and excellent for producing orange or brown dyes for dying hides, cloth, or yarn. Some Native Americans even dyed their hair. Medicinally, alder bark can be used as a potent astringent for wounds, diarrhea, and so forth. It may be possible to make syrup from the sap of large alders.

Like plants of the Pea family, alders associate with nitrogen-fixing bacteria in the soil, forming nodules on the roots. The bacteria absorb nitrogen from the air and make it available to the trees. In exchange, the trees photosynthesize sugars for the bacteria. The growth and decomposition of these trees is important for boosting soil fertility in northern climates where cold temperatures otherwise limit nitrogen accumulation.

Betula—birch (50/10/3) • Birch trees can be tapped for syrup like maples in the early spring. The sap is about 50 to 60 parts water to 1 part syrup, so it must be boiled down extensively to get the syrup. (See the Soapberry family for more information.) Birches also contain some amount of methyl salicylate oil, a substitute for wintergreen oil (Coon). The bark and twigs are chopped, then simmered overnight and distilled. Medicinally, methyl salicylate oil is synthesized by the body into salicylic acid (like willow bark), useful as an analgesic. A strong tea of bark or leaves can be used externally as a wash for poison ivy or acne, or internally as a mild sedative (Brown). A compound called betulinic acid, derived from the bark, is being tested on some types of skin cancer. The bark also can be boiled and then folded into a variety of useful containers. The highly resinous bark is useful for fire-starting, even when wet.

Hazelnut Subfamily—*Coryloideae*

The Hazelnuts are variously treated as a subfamily or tribe of the Birch family, or as its own family, *Corylaceae*.

Carpinus—American hornbeam, blue beech, musclewood (35/2/0) The seed is reportedly edible in emergencies. The leaves are astringent, used in conventional ways (Fern).

Corylus—hazelnut, filbert (15/3/1) The nuts of all species are edible raw or cooked. The nuts are sweet and comprised of up to 65% oil. The nut is sweetest during the "milk" stage, prior to maturity. Medicinally, oil from the nut is said to be a gentle remedy for pinworm and threadworm infections in babies and small children. The leaves and bark are astringent. The inner bark of at least some species is fibrous, suitable for making cordage or paper (Fern).

Ostrya—ironwood, hop-hornbeam (8/2/0) A tea of the bark is taken for intermittent fevers and nervousness (Hutchins).

wingleaf soapberry
Sapindus saponaria

Soapberry Family

Soapberry Family—*Sapindaceae*

If you need to get clean, the Soapberry family can help. Some trees have nut-like seeds that are rich in soapy saponins. North American members of the Soapberry family are trees with either pinnate (*Sapidus*) or palm-like digitate (*Aesculus*) leaves. The flowers are bisexual and regular or slightly irregular, grouped in a cluster at the end of a stem. There are typically 5 united sepals and 5 separate or basally united petals, plus 5 to 10 stamens. The ovary is positioned superior, consisting of usually 3 united carpels, but only one carpel normally develops into a fruit, typically a single, large nut-like seed encased inside a leathery or translucent "peel."

Worldwide, there are about 150 genera and 2,000 species, but the description here is specific to North American genera, as listed below. Taxonomists now include the former Horse Chestnut family (*Hippocastanaceae*) and Maple family (*Aceraceae*) within the Soapberry family. Maples are described separately on the facing page for ease of identification.

Saponins can be extracted by mixing the crushed seeds with water. The mix can be worked into a soapy lather and used to wash your hair or added to your laundry. Saponins are effective at removing dirt but not oils. Saponins also break down red blood cells. Saponin-rich plants can be mixed into slow moving waters to stun fish, since the saponins are absorbed directly into the bloodstream through their gills. Read more about saponins in the Medicinal Properties section of this book.

Key Words: Trees with large, nut-like seeds encased in a leathery or translucent "peel."

Aesculus—buckeye, horse chestnut (13/8/0) • The name "horse chestnut" could be confused with the true chestnut (*Castanea*) of the Beech family.

I once puréed slices of a fresh buckeye seed in the blender and used the resulting soap in the washing machine, which worked quite well. It is one of the easiest sources to obtain saponins. Buckeyes can be used for fish poison (Weiner).

Despite the high saponin content, buckeyes may be somewhat edible. The seeds must be crushed and the bitterness leached away by soaking in cold water (Sturtevant), making it more of a survival food than a real staple. Caution is advised, as there are reports of poisonings from consuming the green seed casings (Schauenberg). Roasting apparently renders them safe (Lust).

Medicinally, in addition to the saponins, there is tannic acid and coumarin glycoside in the seeds. An extract of the seeds increases blood circulation, in this case apparently helpful to stimulate digestion (Schauenberg). An extract from the seeds can be used to treat varicose veins (Cook).

Sapindus—Soapberry (12/2/0) Beneath the hard peel, the seed is covered by a sweet-sour pulp that is edible (Sturtevant), but most people consider it repulsive (Fern).

Eco Nuts® and NaturOli™ laundry soaps, available online, are made from the dried husks of *S. mukorossi*, originally native to India.

horse chestnut
Aesculus hippocastanum

3-chambered ovary

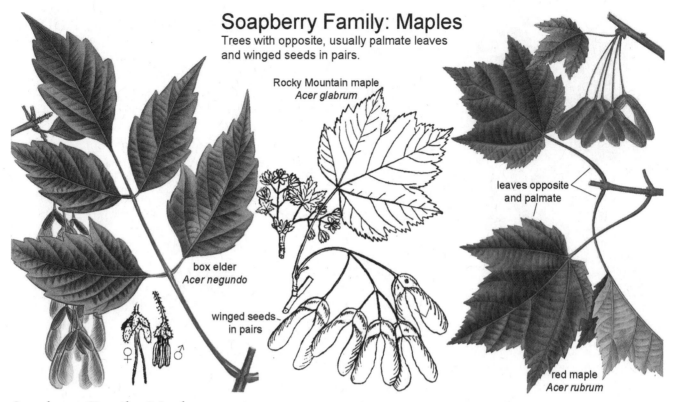

Soapberry Family: Maples

Trees with opposite, usually palmate leaves and winged seeds in pairs.

Rocky Mountain maple
Acer glabrum

box elder
Acer negundo

winged seeds
in pairs

♀   ♂

leaves opposite
and palmate

red maple
Acer rubrum

Soapberry Family: Maples

Almost everyone recognizes the maple leaf from the Canadian flag, if not from trees themselves. The opposite, usually palmate leaves are a good pattern for recognizing maples. Many people will also remember tossing the winged seeds into the air to make "helicopters." If you examine the flowers in springtime, you will find 4 or 5 separate sepals, sometimes colored like petals, and 4 or 5 (sometimes 0) separate petals. The flowers are typically, but not always, unisexual, with male and female blossoms appearing in separate blossoms, often on separate trees. Male flowers have 4 to 10 stamens. In female flowers the ovary is positioned superior and consists of 2 united carpels with partition walls usually present. The ovary matures as two winged seeds, called samaras. Based on genetic evidence, taxonomists reclassified the traditional Maple family as part of the Soapberry family. Note that ash (*Fraxinus*) of the Olive family has similar clusters of winged seeds, but the seeds are not in touching pairs.

Key Words: Trees with opposite leaves and winged seeds in pairs.

Acer—maple, box elder (110/15/3) • Most maple syrup comes from the sugar maple (*A. saccharum*), but all other maples can be tapped for syrup as well, with varying results. The box elder was once used extensively for syrup production where sugar maples were not available (Harrington). I put two taps in my neighbor's tree in mid March (late in the season) and collected about six gallons of sap in three weeks. This boiled down to 1.5 cups of thick, rich syrup—a real treat.

The sap "runs" in the trees on warm days from January to May, depending on where you live. To collect the sap, drill a hole 1 inch in diameter and 3 inches deep into the trunk of the tree, about 2 feet above the ground and on the south side. I use a short length of 3/4 inch PVC pipe for a spout. The hole should be drilled in at a slight upward angle and the spout tapped in only partway. A notch can be made into the top of the PVC pipe to hold the wire handle of a bucket, or you can use sheetrock screws to attach the bucket or its handle to the tree trunk. A large tree (16+ inches in diameter) can have more than one tap. The sap is mostly water, so it is boiled down to remove at least 30 parts of water to get 1 part pure maple syrup. The sap is high in B vitamins, calcium, phosphorus and enzymes (Angier).

The Rocky Mountain maples (*A. glabrum*) native to my area are more like bushes than trees, with a maximum trunk diameter of about 3 inches. The best method for these little trees is to drill a 1/4-inch hole an inch at an angle into the trunk. Make two slashes in the bark, forming a V down to the hole. (Do not slash all the way around the tree—that will kill it.) Pound a stick into the hole, and the sap will run out and drip off the end of the stick. I use a battery-powered drill to screw a plastic bucket below the drip stick. These small trees only produce a pint of sap per day and the syrup content is low. It took me a month to get a pint of syrup from eight trees!

Maple seeds are bitter, but edible after boiling (Couplan).

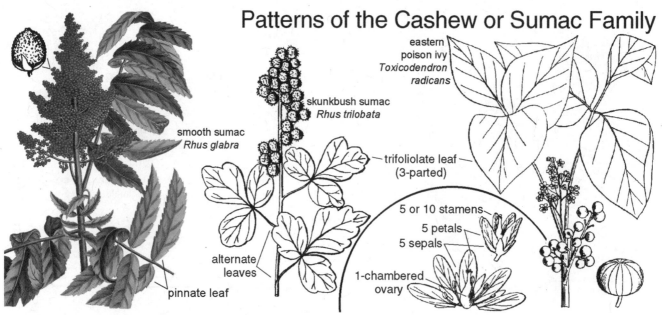

Patterns of the Cashew or Sumac Family

Cashew or Sumac Family—*Anacardiaceae*

If you have ever had a rash from poison ivy or poison oak, then you have met the Cashew family. These are trees or shrubs with alternate, often trifoliate or pinnate leaves, and usually resinous bark. The flowers can be either unisexual or bisexual, with 5 (sometimes 3) sepals united at the base and 5 (sometimes 3 or 0) petals. There are 5 or 10 stamens. The ovary is positioned superior and consists of 3 (sometimes 1 to 5) united carpels forming a single chamber. Only one carpel matures, forming a drupe (a fleshy fruit with a stony seed).

Worldwide, there are about 70 genera and 600 species. North American genera are listed below. Several members of the family produce oils, resins and lacquers. Zebrawood (*Astronium*) is well-known as an exotic hardwood for furniture. The family name comes from the cashew tree (*Anacardium*). *Rhus* and *Toxicodendron* are the only genera found across the frost belt of North America. Most other members of the family live in the tropics, with a few representatives cultivated across the southern states, including the Peruvian pepper tree (*Schinus*), mango (*Mangifera*) and pistachio (*Pistacia*). The introduced hog plum or mombin (*Spondias*) grows on disturbed sites in southern Florida.

Key Words: Shrubs with three-lobed or pinnate leaves and single-seeded red or white fruits.

Cotinus—smoketree (2/2/0) Native and introduced species are found from Texas to Ontario.
Malosma—laurel sumac (1/1/0) *M. laurina*. Native to southern California and Mexico.
Metopium—Florida poisontree (1/1/0) *M. toxiferum*. Native to Florida.
Pistacia—pistachio (15/3/0) Our native pistachio (*P. mexicana*) grows in Texas and Mexico. Other species are cultivated.
Rhus—sumac, lemonade berry (100/15/2) • The bright red berries are high in calcium and potassium malates, and the leaves and bark contain gallic and tannic acid (Moore, Densmore). The berries can be infused into cold water to make a good lemonade-type drink. The leaves and bark are astringent (the berries less so), used in the typical ways: sore throat, diarrhea, etc., with particular reference to cold sores (Moore). The leaf tea is recommended for asthma (Willard).
Toxicodendron—poison ivy, poison oak, poison sumac (30/5/1) • These plants were formerly included within *Rhus*. The fruits of all *Rhus* species are orange or red, while *Toxicodendron* species have white or yellowish berries.

Poison ivy contains a non-volatile phenol-type oil, called 3-n-pentadecylcatechol, or more commonly, urushiol. Urushiol gives the leaves a shiny, waxy appearance and is the agent that causes dermatitis. Not everyone is susceptible to poison ivy and the potency changes throughout the year (Harrington), usually becoming stronger with age. I am not usually bothered by poison ivy, but I did once lead a friend through a leafless patch in winter, causing unbelievable rashes and swelling. She is so allergic that she even reacts to mango (*Mangifera*) juice on her skin, which is from the same family.

On the other hand, Peter Bigfoot wrote that he was allergic to poison ivy until he saw a deer browsing on the foliage in the spring-time when it is sweet, then he started eating it too. The poisonous oil may be dilute enough at that time of year to mildly stimulate the immune system without causing an adverse reaction. This practice could be extremely dangerous. The effects would certainly vary from one individual to another and a toxic reaction could cause your throat to swell shut, leading to asphyxiation. Likewise, burning the plant puts the oil in the air, where it can be inhaled into the lungs. Medicinally, poison ivy was once used externally to treat the symptoms of herpes (Weiner).

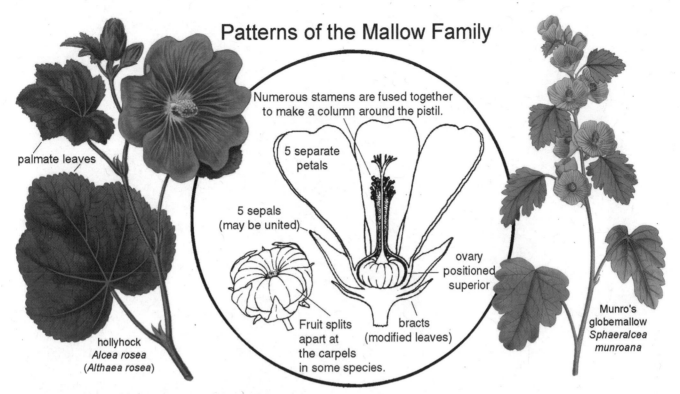

Patterns of the Mallow Family

Numerous stamens are fused together to make a column around the pistil.

5 separate petals

5 sepals (may be united)

palmate leaves

ovary positioned superior

Fruit splits apart at the carpels in some species.

bracts (modified leaves)

hollyhock
Alcea rosea
(*Althaea rosea*)

Munro's globemallow
Sphaeralcea munroana

Mallow Family—*Malvaceae*

If you have seen a hollyhock or hibiscus, then you know the Mallow family. Mallow leaves are alternate and usually palmately lobed. Crushed leaves and flowers have a mucilaginous or slimy quality, which can help identify the family. The Mallows have distinct, funnel-shaped flowers. The flowers are regular and often surrounded by several bracts, with 3 to 5 partially united sepals and 5 separate petals. There are numerous stamens united to form a distinctive column around the pistil. The ovary is positioned superior and typically consists of 5 (rarely 1, but sometimes up to 20) united carpels, as indicated by the same number of styles. Partition walls are present, forming an equal number of chambers. The ovary matures as a capsule, a schizocarp (the round "cheese" in the illustration), or rarely as a winged seed or berry. Worldwide, the traditional family includes about 85 genera and 1,500 species. Genera common to North America are listed below. There are many additional genera in Texas and/or other southern states. Taxonomists now consider the former Basswood (*Tiliaceae*) and Cacao (*Sterculiaceae*) families (and several others) as subfamilies of the Mallow family, as treated on the following page.

Many plants from the traditional Mallow family contain natural gums called mucilage, pectin, and asparagin, which can be whipped into a marshmallow-like froth. Most Mallow family greens and flowers are edible, but not widely used, probably due to their slimy consistency. However, okra (*Abelmoschus*) is favored for its mucilaginous quality in gumbo. Medicinally, the Mallows tend to be mucilaginous, like *Aloe vera* or cactus. They are useful externally as an emollient for soothing sunburns and other inflamed skin conditions, and internally as a demulcent and expectorant for soothing sore throats.

Key Words: Mucilaginous plants and flowers with numerous stamens fused into a central column.

Abutilon—Indian mallow (150/18/1) Native and introduced species are found throughout North America. *A. indicus* is a source of fibers (Pammel). The flowers of two foreign species are known to be edible (Sturtevant), but our *A. theophrasti* has a strong odor and may be poisonous (Pammel).

Alcea—hollyhock, marshmallow (60/2/1) • Introduced. Taxonomists split hollyhocks out of *Althaea* to form *Alcea*. The leaves are edible as a salad green or potherb. Marshmallows were originally derived from *A. officinalis*. Medicinally, these plants are listed as demulcent, diuretic, and emollient (Lust). Hollyhocks make acceptable cordage material in the winter when the dead stalks have lain in the snow long enough for the outer layer to moisten and separate.

Anoda—anoda (23/7/0) Native from California to New York, south to Florida.

Callirhoe—poppymallow (9/9/0) Native from Arizona to North Dakota, east to the Atlantic.

Gossypium—cotton (50/2/0) • Originally native to Florida, Mexico, and south. The seeds of cotton are mucilaginous and oily. The oil from the seeds is sometimes used in cooking. A tea from the bark of the root has been used as a stimulant

Mallow Family Plants

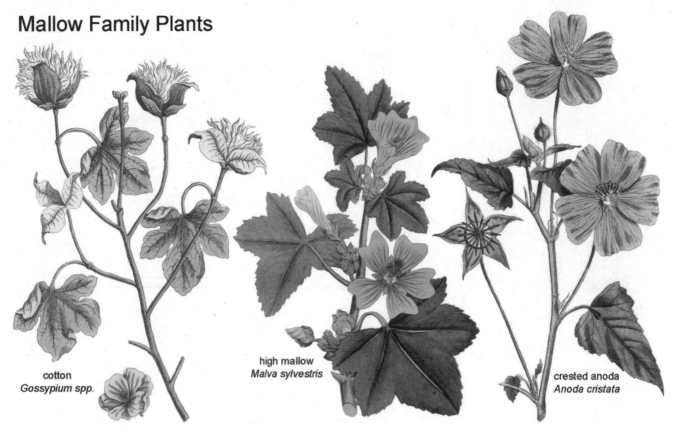

cotton
Gossypium spp.

high mallow
Malva sylvestris

crested anoda
Anoda cristata

for menstruation, contractions during birth, and abortions. Cotton is the only member of this family with documented poisonous properties (Pammel). Do not use without medical supervision (Lust).

Herissantia—bladdermallow (5/1/0) *H. crispa.* Native to the southern states from California to Florida.

Horsfordia—velvetmallow (4/2/0) Native to California and Nevada.

Hibiscus—hibiscus, rosemallow (200/24/1) • Native and introduced species are found across North America. The various species are generally mucilaginous, emollient, and demulcent. (Lust). The flowers of some species are commonly used in commercial herbal teas. They are rich in citric, malic, and tartaric acids (Schauenberg). Kenaf (*H. cannabinus*) is grown as a fiber crop for making paper. *H. syriacus* is popularly known as Rose of Sharon.

Iliamna—wild hollyhock (8/6/1) Native from the Pacific Ocean to the Rocky Mountains.

Lavatera—tree mallow (5/5/0) Mostly introduced species are scattered across the continent.

Malva—mallow, cheeseweed (30/8/6) • Introduced and naturalized throughout North America. *M. neglecta* is edible as a salad green or potherb and works as a good stew thickener. The green fruits are a popular snack found in the lawn and garden. Learn how to make wild marshmallows in *Edible Wild Plants: Wild Foods from Dirt to Plate* by John Kallas. Medicinally, a poultice of the leaves helps to break down and remove damaged tissues while increasing white blood cell activity in the area (Moore).

Malvastrum—false mallow (19/6/0) Native and introduced species are found from Arizona to Pennsylvania and south.

Modiola—bristlemallow (1/1/0) *M. caroliniana.* Native to the southern states, from California to Virginia.

Napaea—glademallow (1/1/1) *N. dioica.* Native to the northeastern states.

Sidalcea—checkermallow (25/25/2) Native from Alaska to Texas.

Sphaeralcea—globemallow (60/22/2) • Native to the western two-thirds of North America. The plant and root are mucilaginous and soothing (Bigfoot). The tea is used for lower urinary tract infections. (Moore).

scarlet globemallow
Sphaeralcea coccinea

106

Cacao Subfamily—*Sterculioideae*

Everyone knows the Cacao subfamily—at least in the form of chocolate. The seeds of the cacao tree (*Theobroma cacao*) are processed to make cocoa powder and cocoa butter, used in innumerable popular sweets. Flowers from this subfamily resemble true Mallows, but typically with only 5 or 10 stamens (sometimes numerous), which are *not* fused together as a column. The fruit is a leathery or woody follicle or capsule. Like true Mallows, the vegetation has a mucilaginous quality.

The traditional family included about 70 genera and 1,500 species of tropical trees and shrubs. North American genera are listed below. Further taxonomic research may significantly revise this subfamily.

Ayenia—ayenia (50/9/0) Native from California to Florida.
Fremontodendron—flannelbush (3/3/0) • 3 sepals. Native to California and Arizona.
Melochia—pyramidflower (54/4/0) Native and introduced species are found from Texas to New York.
Waltheria—uhaloa (50/1/0) Native from Arizona to Florida.

Mallow Family / Cacao Subfamily

California flannelbush
Fremontodendron californicum

Basswood Subfamily—*Tilioideae*

To the casual observer, Basswoods do not share an obvious connection to the true Mallows. These are trees and shrubs with simple, alternate leaves, often asymmetrical at the base. Basswoods generally have narrow petals and numerous stamens, which are *not* fused together as a column. The traditional family included about about 50 genera and 450 species, mostly in the tropics. But Taxonomists demoted the Basswoods to a subfamily of the Mallow family and segregated all but 3 genera into other subfamilies. Only *Tilia* is native to North America.

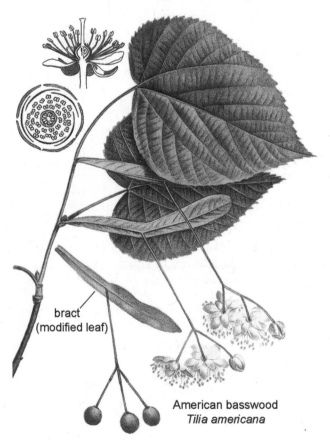

bract
(modified leaf)

American basswood
Tilia americana

Mallow Family / Basswood Subfamily

Key Words: Trees with the flower/berry cluster suspended from a leaf-like bract.

Tilia—basswood, linden tree (50/5/0) • Linden trees can be distinguished from other trees by the slender, leaf-like bract that supports the flower cluster. Linden trees are native to eastern forests, but are often cultivated in the West.

Reportedly, the fruit and flowers can be ground up to produce a chocolate flavor. There were attempts long ago to commercialize it as a chocolate substitute, but it was too perishable for shipping and storage. The tree may also be tapped for syrup (Sturtevant) (see the Soapberry family for more information). The young leaves are somewhat mucilaginous and edible raw. The flowers are also edible, but caution is advised, as narcotics may develop as they age (Fern).

Linden provides quality cordage material. Cut long strips of bark from the tree (please use some ethics here) and soak them in water for at least a week to separate the inner and outer bark. The inner bark can be split into narrower strips with the aid of a fingernail. The material can be made into cordage at this point, or for extra strength you can boil the fibers in a mix of ashes and water for about twenty-four hours (Jaeger).

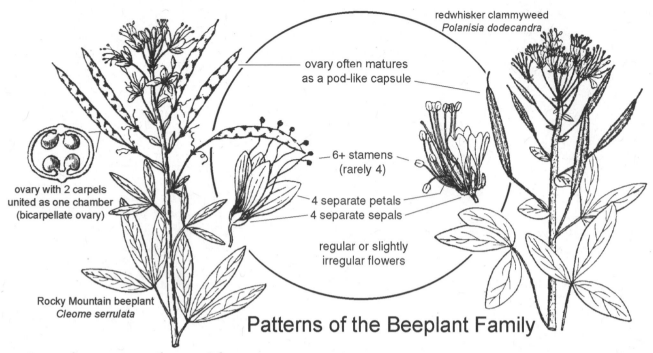

redwhisker clammyweed
Polanisia dodecandra

ovary often matures
as a pod-like capsule

6+ stamens
(rarely 4)

4 separate petals
4 separate sepals

regular or slightly
irregular flowers

ovary with 2 carpels
united as one chamber
(bicarpellate ovary)

Rocky Mountain beeplant
Cleome serrulata

Patterns of the Beeplant Family

Beeplant Family—*Cleomaceae*

If you find a plant that looks like a hybrid between the Mustard and Pea families, it is likely a member of the Beeplant family. Beeplants are closely related to the Mustard family, but resemble Pea family plants in the shape and curvature of the seed pods. Many species also have trifoliate or palmate leaves like clovers and lupines of the Pea family. Beeplants were formerly placed within the Caper family, *Capparaceae*, but genetic research places them closer to Mustards than Capers, earning them a new family of their own.

yellow beeplant
Cleome lutea

The Beeplants are mostly herbs or shrubs with trifoliate, alternate leaves, like those shown above. The flowers are regular or slightly irregular, and bisexual with 4 separate sepals, 4 separate petals, and 4 to numerous stamens. The ovary is positioned superior and consists of 2 united carpels forming a single chamber. It matures as a capsule with 1 or more kidney-shaped seeds. Worldwide, there are about 8 genera and 275 species. North American genera are listed below. Many species are adapted to desert or tropical conditions. Only *Cleome* and *Polanisia* are widespread across the continent.

Key Words: Mustard-like flowers with pea-like pods.

Cleome—beeplant (200/12/2) • The young shoots and leaves can be used as a potherb, boiled in two or three changes of water. The seeds are edible. Native Americans boiled the plant down for an extended time to produce a dark paint (Harrington). Medicinally, the tea is reported to be taken for a fever (Murphey).

Cleomella—stinkweed (20/11/0) Native to the desert Southwest.

Isomeris—California bladderpod (1/1/0) *I. arborea*. Also known as *Cleome isomeris*. Native to southern California.

Polanisia—clammy weed (5/5/1) Redwhisker clammyweed (*P. dodecandra*) is widespread across North America.

Oxystylis—spiny caper (1/1/0) *O. lutea*. Native to the Mojave Desert in southern California and adjacent Nevada.

Wislizenia—spectacle fruit (10/1/0) *W. refracta*. Native to the Southwest.

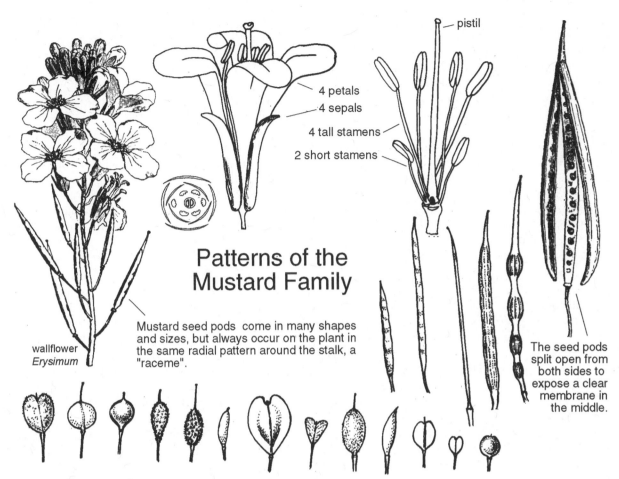

pistil

4 petals

4 sepals

4 tall stamens

2 short stamens

Patterns of the Mustard Family

Mustard seed pods come in many shapes and sizes, but always occur on the plant in the same radial pattern around the stalk, a "raceme".

wallflower
Erysimum

The seed pods split open from both sides to expose a clear membrane in the middle.

Mustard Family—*Brassicaceae* (*Cruciferae*)

Key Words: 4 petals and 6 stamens—4 tall and 2 short

Mustards are as easy to recognize as radishes (*Raphanus*) in the garden. In fact, many plants in the Mustard family have a similar life cycle: they shoot up fast in the spring, bloom, and then set seed and die while other plants are just getting going. Mustards are adapted to colonizing barren ground, so they tend to grow and reproduce quickly, before the soil dries out. If you see a bunch of weedy-looking plants in newly disturbed soil, at least some of them are sure to be Mustards! Look close at the flowers. There are 4 sepals, 4 petals, and 6 stamens (2 short, 4 long). The petals are often arranged like either the letters X or H, and they may be deeply split, making it appear as eight petals. The ovary is positioned superior and consists of 2 united carpels forming a single chamber. It matures as a silicle or silique, meaning a pod where the outside walls fall away leaving the translucent interior partition intact. Look for it on dried specimens. Mustard seed pods come in many shapes and sizes, but they always form a raceme on the flower stalk, which looks something like a spiral staircase for the little people (see illustrations). The crushed leaves usually smell more-or-less like mustard.

Worldwide, there are about 340 genera and 3,400 species. About 55 genera are found in North America. Horseradish (*Armoracia*, page 218) has been propagated with pieces of the root for so long that it no longer produces viable seed. Other cultivated mustards include watercress (*Nasturtium*), turnip and mustard (*Brassica*). Commercial mustard is usually made from the seeds of the black mustard (*B. nigra*) mixed with vinegar. Canola oil comes from the seeds of *B. napus* and *B. rapa*. Interestingly, six of our common vegetables—cabbage, cauliflower, kohlrabi, Brussels sprouts, broccoli, and kale—were all bred from a single species, *B. oleracea*. Plant breeders bred up the starch-storage abilities in different parts of the plant to come up with each unique vegetable.

Medicinally, Mustards contain varying concentrations of acrid sulfur glycosides, which are basically irritants. Mustards can help stimulate digestion, or in concentration be used as a "mustard plaster" on the chest to warm the chest and help stimulate coughing to clear the lungs. Read more about sulfur glycosides in the *Medicinal Properties* section of this book.

109

Edible and Medicinal Properties of Mustard Family Plants

Alyssum—alyssum (150/8/2) • Introduced. The common garden alyssum (*A. maritimum*) has been reclassified as *Lobularia maritima*. It is edible.

Arabidopsis—mouse-ear cress (12/3/1) *A. thaliana* was the first plant to have its entire genome sequenced.

Arabis—rock cress (100/70/15) • The flowers and basal leaves are edible. The stem leaves may be too bitter (Angier).

Barbarea—bittercress, creasy greens (12/3/1) • The leaves can be used as a salad green or potherb (Hall).

Berteroa—false alyssum (5/2/1) Introduced. Petals are deeply split.

Brassica—mustard (50/10/5) • The leaves can be used as a salad green or potherb. The seeds can be used for seasoning. Medicinally, the seeds can be ground into a powder and mixed with flour and water to make a mustard plaster (Hall). Applied externally like a poultice, the plaster is an irritant, stimulating activity underneath the skin. Prolonged contact can cause serious inflammation (Lust). Members of this genus contain sulfur glycosides (Geller).

Cardaria—whitetop (3/3/3) • Introduced from Eurasia. Most mustards are annuals that spread by seeds, but the *C. draba* is an invasive perennial plant that also spreads by lateral underground stems, called rhizomes. Once established, a patch may continue to spread by several feet per year.

Camelina—false flax (8/3/2) Introduced from Eurasia. *C. sativa* is cultivated as an oil crop. (Sturtevant).

Capsella—shepherd's purse (8/1/1) • *C. bursa-pastoris*. Introduced. The seeds are used for seasoning (Hall) or cooked and ground into meal (Olsen). The root is a substitute for ginger (Harrington). The seeds dumped into still water will kill mosquito larvae (Willard). Medicinally, shepherd's purse is astringent and diuretic; it is especially known as a potent vasoconstrictor and coagulant. The tea can be used internally or externally to stop bleeding; it is commonly used for women's mid-cycle bleeding. It may also equalize blood pressure (Willard), but it can have inconsistent effects, causing either vasodilation or hypertension. As an astringent and diuretic, shepherd's purse is good for the urinary tract and bladder, and it stimulates phosphate recycling in the kidneys. It is given during birth to stimulate uterine contractions (Moore). It is also a remedy for diarrhea (Kloss).

Cardamine—bittercress (170/45/5) The whole plant is edible as a salad green or potherb. The root is hot like horseradish.

Chorispora—crossflower (13/1/1) *C. tenella*. Introduced from Asia. The plant is edible (Sturtevant).

Conringia—hare's ear mustard (6/1/1) *C. orientalis*. Introduced from Eurasia, and now widespread in North America. Edible.

Descurainia—tansy mustard (46/8/3) • Native and introduced species are found across the continent. The plant can be used as a potherb; boil in two or three changes of water. The seeds can be used as meal (Harrington). It is unrelated to common tansy (*Tanacetum*) from the Aster family.

Draba—whitlow grass (350/100/18)

Eruca—rocket salad (3/1/1) *E. sativa*. Introduced from Europe. The plant is edible as a salad green (Sturtevant).

Erysimum—wallflower (180/22/3) • The plant, mashed with water, can be applied to prevent sunburn (Weiner).

Hesperis—rocket (60/1/1) • *H. matronalis*. Introduced and often cultivated for its purple or pale flowers. Rocket is edible as a salad green.

Isatis—dyer's woad (30/1/1) *I. tinctoria*. Dyer's woad was introduced from Europe and cultivated as a source of blue dye. It is the same dye extracted from true indigo (*Indigofera tinctoria*) of the Pea family, but it is less concentrated in *Isatis*.

Lepidium—pepperweed (170/40/1) • Native and introduced species are found across the continent. Clasping pepperweed (*L. perfoliatum*) was one of the very first edible plants I learned as a child. It is edible in a salad or as a potherb (Duke). The freshly bruised plant has been used as a treatment for poison ivy (Vogel).

Lesquerella—bladderpod (78/78/3) • This genus is being merged into *Physaria*.

Nasturtium—watercress (50/5/1) • Watercress (*N. officinale*) was introduced from Europe. It is now widespread and one of our few greens of winter. It can be found growing in the water near natural springs. Rice cooked with watercress is one of my favorite meals on camping trips. Watercress is rich in vitamin C, iron and iodine (Lust). Medicinally, watercress is a mild diuretic and stimulant. Prolonged use may lead to kidney problems, and consumption is not advised during pregnancy (Lust). Note that the common garden nasturtium (*Tropaeolum majus*) belongs to its own family, *Tropaeolaceae*.

Physaria—twinpod (85/14/3) Native to the western half of North America. Used as a cure for sore throat (Murphey).

Rorippa—yellowcress (80/20/7) • Native and introduced species are found across North America. The plants are edible.

Sisymbrium—tumble mustard (80/10/4) • Introduced. Tall tumble mustard (*S. altissimum*) is a delicious wild edible. The tender young tops look and taste a lot like broccoli, but with a sharp mustard bite. The plant can be used as a salad or potherb. The seeds can be gathered and used for meal or seasoning. Read more in *Foraging the Mountain West*. Medicinally, tumble mustards are used similarly to the *Brassicas* (Lust).

Stanleya—prince's plume (6/6/2) • Native to the western half of North America. The fresh plant has an emetic effect, but is reportedly safe to eat after boiling in several changes of water (Murphey). The plant requires selenium in the soil for proper growth and is used as an indicator of this mineral.

Thlaspi—pennycress (70/6/2) • Introduced and widespread across North America. The plant can be used as a salad green or potherb in small amounts, but the flavor is disagreeable in any quantity.

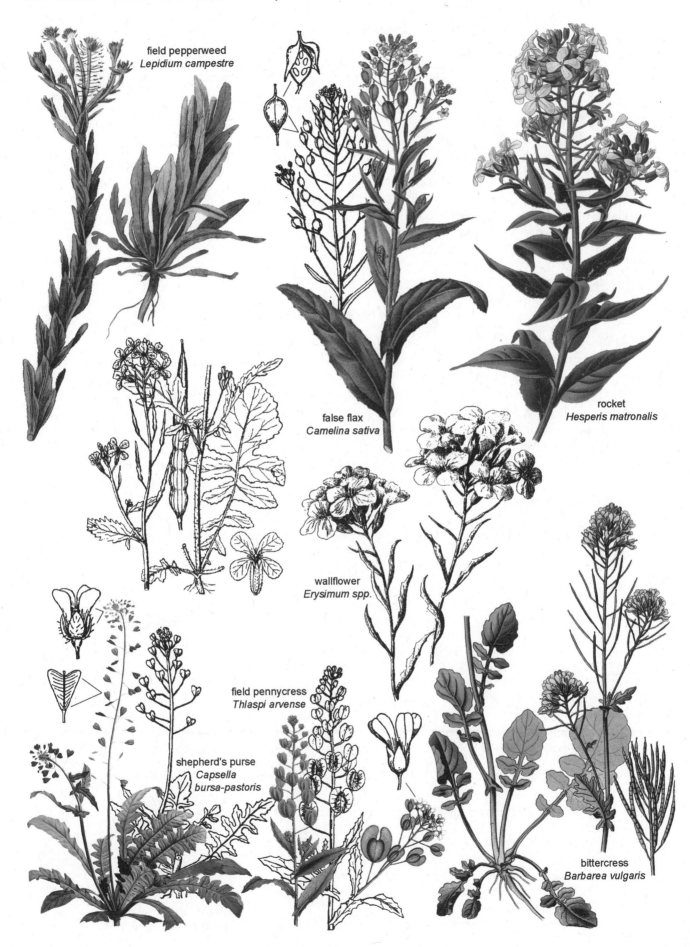

field pepperweed
Lepidium campestre

false flax
Camelina sativa

rocket
Hesperis matronalis

wallflower
Erysimum spp.

field pennycress
Thlaspi arvense

shepherd's purse
*Capsella
bursa-pastoris*

bittercress
Barbarea vulgaris

111

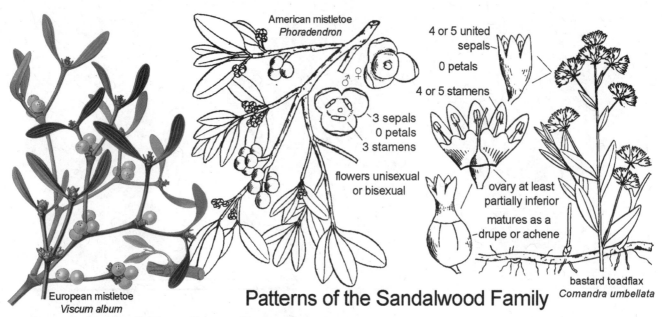

American mistletoe
Phoradendron

3 sepals
0 petals
3 stamens

flowers unisexual
or bisexual

4 or 5 united
sepals

0 petals

4 or 5 stamens

ovary at least
partially inferior

matures as a
drupe or achene

bastard toadflax
Comandra umbellata

European mistletoe
Viscum album

Patterns of the Sandalwood Family

Sandalwood Family—*Santalaceae* (including *Viscaceae*)

Have you ever been kissed under a mistletoe? If so, you have met one member of the Sandalwood family. Sandalwoods are parasitic plants that feed off of other plants, but they also have chlorophyll for photosynthesis.

In past classification systems, the Sandalwood family was separate from the Mistletoe family (*Viscaceae*). Sandalwoods are ground-dwelling plants parasitic on the roots of other plants, while Mistletoes are arboreal plants that feed off tree branches. But genetic testing consolidated these two families within the Sandalwoods.

The flowers are regular and either bisexual or unisexual, with 3, 4, or 5 sepals (rarely 2), but 0 petals and the same number of stamens as sepals. The stamens are aligned opposite the sepals (meaning in the middle of them), instead of alternating with them. The ovary is positioned partly or wholly inferior and consists of 2 to 5 united carpels forming a single chamber. It matures as a drupe (a fleshy fruit with a stony seed) or sometimes as an achene (a dry seed). Worldwide, there are about 40 genera and 950 species. Note that parasitic plants can absorb toxins from their hosts. North American genera are listed below.

Key Words: Parasitic green or grayish plants without true petals.

Arceuthobium—dwarf mistletoe (42/19/5) • Parasitic on the Pine and Cypress families. Dwarf mistletoes often blend in and vaguely resemble the tree's own foilage. A single species of mistletoe is often parasitic on a single species of tree. Native Americans drank a tea of the plant for tuberculosis and lung or mouth hemorrhages (Moerman).

Buckleya—piratebush (4/1/0) *B. distichophylla*. A rare shrub, parasitic on hemlock trees in the Appalachian Mtns (Cook).

Comandra—bastard toadflax (1/1/1) • *C. umbellata*. The common name is misleading since there is a flower in the Plantain family called "butter and eggs toadflax." The berries are edible. A tea of the plant was used for canker sores by the Native Americans (Moerman).

Geocaulon—false toadflax (1/1/1) *G. lividum*. Formerly *Comandra lividum*. Native to moist boreal forests from Alaska to Newfoundland.

Nestronia—leechbush (1/1/0) *N. umbellula*. Native to southeastern states.

Phoradendron—American mistletoe (300/13/0) • American mistletoe contains the alkaloid acetylcholine (Moore). It has been prescribed for epilepsy, stroke, and tuberculosis (Klein). A tea of the plant or the raw leaves acts as a strong vasoconstrictor and thus raises blood pressure. It has been used to stimulate contractions during childbirth with variable results. It can be dangerous (Moore).

Pyrularia—buffalo nut (1/1/0) *P. pubera*. Parasitic on deciduous trees in the Appalachian Mountains (Cook).

Thesium—thesium (325/1/1) *T. arvense*. Introduced to Montana and North Dakota from the Old World.

Viscum—mistletoe (70/1/1) *V. album*. Introduced to California.

pineland dwarf mistletoe
Arceuthobium vaginitum

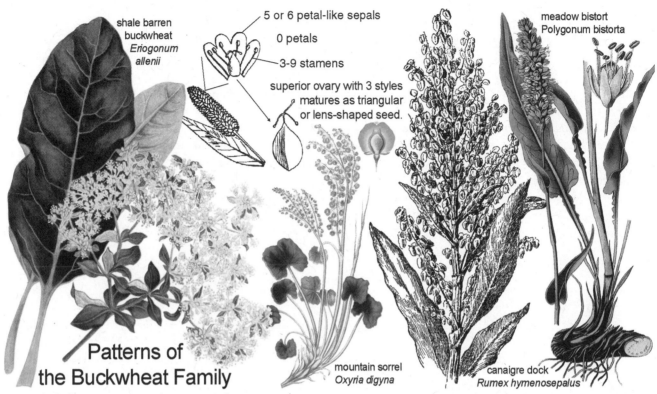

shale barren
buckwheat
*Eriogonum
allenii*

5 or 6 petal-like sepals

0 petals

3-9 stamens

superior ovary with 3 styles
matures as triangular
or lens-shaped seed.

meadow bistort
Polygonum bistorta

mountain sorrel
Oxyria digyna

canaigre dock
Rumex hymenosepalus

Patterns of the Buckwheat Family

Buckwheat Family—*Polygonaceae*

The Buckwheats have simple, toothless leaves and often swollen joints, or nodes, on the stems (polygonum = "many knees"), plus lots of small flowers in clusters or spikes. There are typically 5 or 6 sepals, sometimes colored like petals and often in two layers, but no true petals, and 3 to 9 stamens. The ovary is positioned superior and consists of 3 united carpels, as indicated by the same number of styles. The carpels are united to form a single chamber. It matures as a dry seed, usually brown or black and triangular or lens-shaped, sometimes with wings.

Worldwide, there are about 40 genera and 800 species, including 15 genera in North America. Sour juice, from oxalic acid, is common in this family. Many plants of this family also contain tannic acid and anthraquinone glycosides. (See the *Medicinal Properties* section.)

Key Words: Small flowers with colored sepals, 0 petals, and triangular seeds.

Eriogonum—wild buckwheat (250/230/15) • The leaves are edible as a potherb. The seeds are ground into meal or flour (Olsen). These are astringent plants, useful internally and externally (Sweet).

Fagopyrum—buckwheat (15/2/1) *Fagopyrum* is a "pseudocereal." True cereal grains come from the Grass family, but buckwheat is used similarly. My grandmother frequently made buckwheat pancakes.

Oxyria—mountain sorrel (1/1/1) • *O. digyna*. Mountain sorrel is edible as a salad or potherb. It contains oxalic acid (Willard).

Polygonum—smartweed, knotweed, bistort (200/70/23) • The leaves and shoots of many species are edible in the spring before becoming too astringent (Angier). American bistort (*P. bistortoides*) roots are also astringent, but quite edible when cooked, with a flavor like nuts. The seeds are also edible. I sometimes snack on the whole flowers.

Rheum—rhubarb (40/1/1) • *R. rhabarbarum*. Rhubarb was often planted by homesteaders and miners. It often survives long after the people and buildings are gone. The chopped stems make great pies, but the leaves contain toxic levels of anthraquinone glycosides.

Rumex—dock, sorrel, canaigre (200/50/12) • The docks and sorrels are all edible to varying degrees. Generally "sorrels" are lemony-tasting, while "docks" are more astringent. Changing the water once or twice while cooking can tame the flavor The seeds are said to be edible, but require leaching to take away their astringent nature. The roots are even more astringent. Anthraquinone glycosides with purgative properties appear in numerous species of *Rumex* (Geller, Schauenerg). The leaves of *R. hymenosepalus* may be toxic (Bigfoot), probably due to concentrated anthraquinones.

sheep
sorrel
*Rumex
acetosella*

Pink Family—*Caryophyllaceae*

The next time you see a carnation or pink (*Dianthus*), stop and examine the vegetation and flowers. The coarse, durable stem and leaves are characteristic of this family. The leaves are usually positioned opposite on the stems, but are sometimes whorled. Members of the Pink family have regular, bisexual flowers with 5 sepals (rarely 4). The sepals can be united or separate. There are 5 usually separate petals (rarely 4, or sometimes numerous in domestic varieties). The petals are often split at the ends. There are 5 or 10 stamens (rarely 3 or 4), appearing in one or two whorls. The ovary is positioned superior and consists of 2 to 5 (rarely 1) united carpels, as indicated by the same number of styles. Carpels are united to form a single chamber. The ovary matures as a dry capsule with numerous seeds and opens by valves at the top. Worldwide, there are about 80 genera and 2,000 species, including about 40 genera found in North America.

Many species of the family contain at least a small amount of saponin, most notably the soapwort plant (*Saponaria*). Plants with a significant saponin content can be mashed in water and used as a soap substitute. Read more about saponin under the "Glycosides" heading of the *Medicinal Properties* section of this book. Several plants in the Pink family have edible greens or seeds.

Key Words: Coarse plants with parts in 5s and split petal-ends.

Achyronychia—onyxflower (1/1/0) *A. cooperi*. Colored sepals. 0 petals. Native to the deserts of California and Arizona.

Agrostemma—corncockle (2/1/1) *A. githago*. Introduced from Europe. The plant and especially the seeds contain saponin. People and livestock have been poisoned when large quantities (over 40%) of *Agrostema* seed have been mixed in feeds and flour (Pammel).

Arenaria—sandwort (210/22/12) • The plant is boiled as a vegetable or fermented like sauerkraut (Sturtevant). A tea of the plant has diuretic properties (Kadans); it is also used as an eye wash (Murphey).

Cardionema—sandcarpet (6/1/0) *C. ramosissimum*. Grows on west coast beaches. Often encouraged for erosion control.

Cerastium—field chickweed (100/25/5) • Field chickweed isn't as tender as *Stellaria*, but still very edible.

Dianthus—carnation, pink, sweet william (300/12/3) • Introduced throughout North America.

Drymaria—drymary (48/8/0) Found from Arizona to Florida.

Geocarpon—tinytim (1/1/0) *G. minimum*. A rare plant, native to Missouri and the surrounding states.

Gypsophila—baby's breath (126/8/1) • Showy baby's breath (*G. elegans*) is used in floral arrangements. *G. paniculata* is invasive in many areas. A species of baby's breath from Spain is known to contain saponin and a sapotoxin (Pammel).

common chickweed
Stellaria media

Holosteum—jagged chickweed (3/1/1). *H. umbellatum*. Introduced from Eurasia.

Lychnis—campion (10/5/3) • Several species from this genera were reclassified as *Silene*.

Minuartia—stitchwort (175/32/6) Formerly included within *Arenaria*.

Paronychia—nailwort (40/28/1) Native throughout North America, except the Pacific Northwest.

Pseudostellaria—starwort (21/2/1) Grows from Montana to Texas, west to the Pacific.

Sagina—pearlwort (30/10/1) Native and introduced species are found throughout North America.

Saponaria—soapwort, bouncing bet (30/1/1) • *S. officinalis*. Introduced from Europe. I love the sweet, sweet smell of the flowers. The plant contains saponin. It can be crushed in water for use as a soap substitute. I used a blender and added it to the washing machine. It works! A tea of the root is used as an expectorant, purgative and diuretic (Lust).

Scleranthus—knotgrass (10/2/1) Introduced from Eurasia.

Silene—moss campion, Indian pink (400/50/13) At least some species are edible as potherbs (Kirk, Willard), although many species may be too dry and woody to eat. Medicinally, *S. stellata* and *S. virginica* have been used to expel worms (Coon).

Spergula—spurry (5/2/1) The seeds are edible; they have been harvested in times of scarcity (Sturtevant).

Spergularia—sand spurry (60/12/3) Found throughout North America.

Stellaria—chickweed (100/30/14) • The common chickweed, *S. media*, is an import from Europe. Sometimes the green plants can be found growing in the midst of winter in snow-free space underneath trees. The whole plant is edible and delicious as a salad green or potherb. Chickweed has demulcent, diuretic, laxative and mildly anti-inflammatory properties. A poultice or tincture is used externally to reduce swellings from sprains or arthritis (Moore), or to sooth minor burns and itchy, dry skin (Tilford). It contains at least some saponin (Densmore).

Vaccaria—cow cockle (1/1/1) *Vaccaria hispanica*. Introduced from Europe. It is found across much of North America.

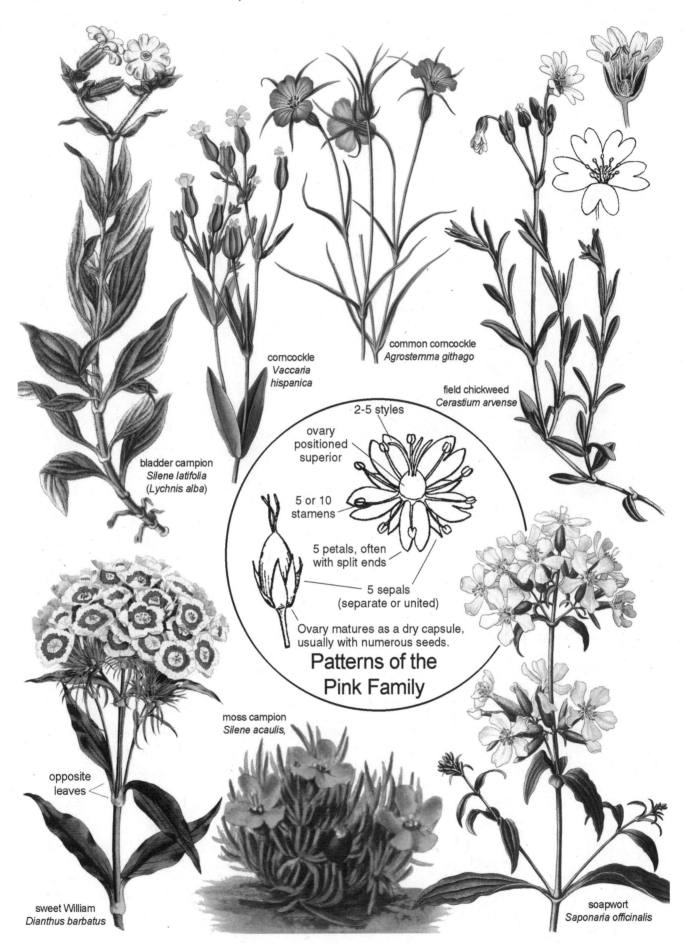

corncockle
Vaccaria hispanica

common corncockle
Agrostemma githago

field chickweed
Cerastium arvense

bladder campion
Silene latifolia
(*Lychnis alba*)

2-5 styles

ovary positioned superior

5 or 10 stamens

5 petals, often with split ends

5 sepals (separate or united)

Ovary matures as a dry capsule, usually with numerous seeds.

Patterns of the Pink Family

moss campion
Silene acaulis,

opposite leaves

sweet William
Dianthus barbatus

soapwort
Saponaria officinalis

115

Sundew Family—*Droseraceae*

Sundew family plants have an appetite for bugs. These are rare plants, often found in moist, but nutrient-poor soils. They have specialized leaves with sensitive appendages, called trichomes, that respond to the light touch of insects. The Venus flytrap leaf (*Dionaea*) snaps shut when triggered. The sundew leaf (*Drosera*) is covered with sticky mucilage that initially traps an insect, while other trichomes wrap around an insect as the leaf folds closed. The plants digest the insects with enzymes and acids, then open the leaf to drop away the indigestible exoskeleton.

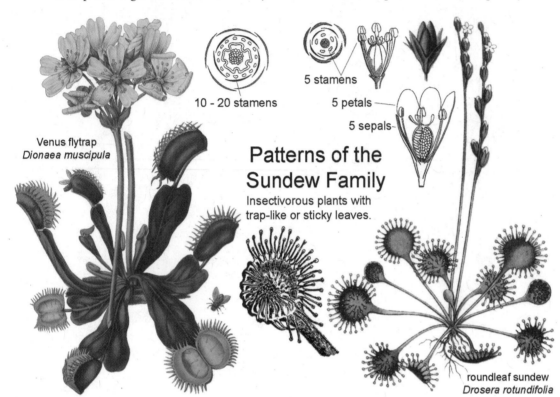

Venus flytrap
Dionaea muscipula

10 - 20 stamens

5 stamens

5 petals

5 sepals

Patterns of the Sundew Family

Insectivorous plants with trap-like or sticky leaves.

roundleaf sundew
Drosera rotundifolia

The flowers have 5 sepals united at the base and 5 separate petals (rarely 4 of each). Most species have 5 stamens, but there are 10 to 20 in *Dionaea*. The ovary is positioned superior and consists of 2, 3, or 5 united carpels forming a single chamber, at least at the base. It matures as a capsule with several to many seeds per carpel.

Worldwide, there are 3 genera and about 200 species. The waterwheel plant (*Aldrovanda*) is native to the Old World. The Portuguese sundew (*Drosophyllum*) has been segregated into its own family, *Drosophyllaceae*. The distant Bladderwort and Pitcher Plant families are also insectivorous. Our native Sundews are listed below. Do not harvest these plants in the wild and buy only those that have been propagated from cultivated stock.

Key Words: Insectivorous plants with active trapping systems

Dionaea—Venus fly trap (1/1/0) *D. muscipula*. The Venus fly trap is native to the East Coast, primarily in North and South Carolina.

Drosera—sundew (194/10/2) The juice of the plant is acrid; it has been used to remove warts and even freckles, but it can raise a blister on the skin (Willard). For tea, the plant is usually boiled, instead of steeped. These plants have antispasmodic, expectorant and antibiotic properties. An alcohol tincture may be required to extract the antibiotic properties. Caution is advised with this plant. Larger doses can irritate your system (Lust).

Amaranth/Goosefoot Family—*Amaranthaceae* (including *Chenopodiaceae*)

If you have ever weeded a garden then you have probably encountered more than one member of this family. Pigweeds (*Amaranthus*) and lamb's quarters (*Chenopodium*) thrive in disturbed garden soils and manure-rich barnyards. These weeds are as edible and tasty as anything else that can be grown in a garden.

The traditionally separate Amaranth and Goosefoot families were known to be closely related, and are now considered a single family with multiple subfamilies, based on genetic research. Plants from the traditional Amaranth family are included on this page, while those of the former Goosefoot family follow on the next two pages.

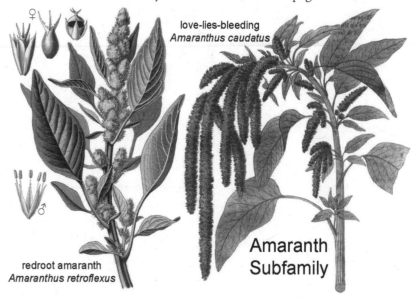

love-lies-bleeding
Amaranthus caudatus

Amaranths usually have dense clusters of flowers without any petals, although each flower may be enclosed by 3 green or colored, often pointed bracts. Flowers are usually, but not always bisexual. There are 4 or 5 sepals, 0 petals, and the same number of stamens as sepals. The ovary is positioned superior and consists of 2 or 3 united carpels forming a single chamber. It matures as a lidded capsule, called a pyxis, usually with only one seed per flower. In some species it forms a utricle instead, a one-seeded bladder-like fruit, or rarely a drupe (a fleshy fruit with a stony seed).

The traditional Amaranth family included about 60 genera and 900 species worldwide, mostly in the tropics. North American genera are listed below. Only *Amaranthus* is widespread in the northern latitudes.

redroot amaranth
Amaranthus retroflexus

Amaranth
Subfamily

Key Words: Plants with dense clusters of small flowers enclosed by 3 colored bracts and 0 petals.

Amaranth Subfamily—*Amaranthoideae*

Achyranthes—chaff flower (13/2/0) Introduced. Found from Texas to Maryland.

Amaranthus—amaranth, pigweed (70/40/7) • Amaranth leaves and tender stem tips are edible as a salad or potherb and rank among the most nutritious wild greens, being especially high in iron, calcium, protein, and vitamin C. (Kallas). *A. caudatus* was cultivated by the Aztecs. The seeds are now a common ingredient in many food products. The seeds of our weedy amaranths can also be harvested. Cut the whole, dead stalks in the fall and place them on a tarp, then beat the seeds out with a stick and winnow away the chaff. The seeds are small and hard and thus may need to be ground into flour to be reasonably digestible.

Celosia—cockscomb (50/4/0) Native and introduced species are found from Texas to Vermont. Often cultivated.

Globe Amaranth Subfamily—*Gomphrenoideae*

Alternanthera—(80 /11/0) Native and introduced species are found across the southern and eastern states. Alligatorweed (*A. philoxeroides*) is an invasive plant that forms dense, sprawling mats on southern waters.

Blutaparon—silverweed (4/1/0) *B. vermiculare*. Texas to Florida.

Froelichia—snake cotton (15/5/0) From California to the northeast.

Gomphrena—globe amaranth (100/8/0) Arizona to Massachusetts.

Gossypianthus—cotton flower (2/1/0) *G. lanuginosus*. Native from New Mexico to Louisiana.

Guilleminea—matweed (5/1/0) *G. densa*. From California to Texas.

Iresine—bloodleaf (70/5/0) Native from Arizona to Pennsylvania. Often cultivated.

Tidestromia—honeysweet (6/5/0) Native from California to Illinois.

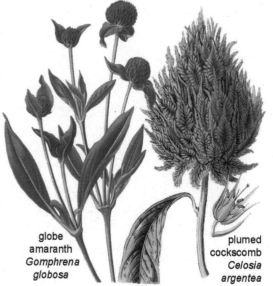

globe
amaranth
*Gomphrena
globosa*

plumed
cockscomb
*Celosia
argentea*

Globe Amaranth Subfamily

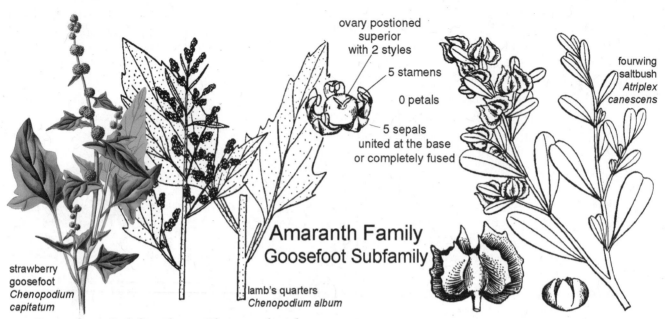

ovary postioned
superior
with 2 styles

5 stamens

0 petals

5 sepals
united at the base
or completely fused

fourwing
saltbush
*Atriplex
canescens*

Amaranth Family
Goosefoot Subfamily

strawberry
goosefoot
*Chenopodium
capitatum*

lamb's quarters
Chenopodium album

Goosefoot Subfamily—*Chenopodioideae*

Look closely at a spinach plant the next time you see one going to seed in the garden. Notice the little green "globs" forming along the upright stalk, sometimes colored with specks of yellow, the sign of pollen and stamens... yes, these globs are true flowers! If you find a weedy plant without petals, but with either globby or prickly flowers clustered along the stems, it is likely you have a Goosefoot or one of its allies. Examine the flowers with a lens to see 5 (sometimes fewer) sepals, often united, and 0 petals. There are an equal number of stamens as sepals. The ovary is positioned superior and consists of 2 (rarely 3 to 5) united carpels forming a single chamber. It matures as a nutlet. Ragweeds (page 172) of the Aster family can superficially resemble Goosefoots.

The traditional Goosefoot family included about 100 genera and 1,500 species, which are now segregated into this and the following subfamilies. Spinach (*Spinacia*) belongs to the Goosefoot subfamily. Domestic chard and beets belong to the Beet subfamily. Both were bred from *Beta vulgaris,* originally from the coast of France. Note that greasewood (*Sarcobatus*) has been segregated out into its own family, *Sarcobataceae*.

Most Goosefoots are edible in salads or as potherbs. The plants are rich in calcium and other minerals, but may accumulate nitrates when there is excess chemical or manure fertilizer in the soil and no irrigation. (Nitrate accumulation can also occur in crops such as lettuce, corn, celery, broccoli, and wheat.) Nitrates are harmless for normal, healthy adults, but can be converted to nitrites in the immature digestive systems of infants under six months of age, theoretically blocking oxygen uptake and potentially resulting in suffocation. Nitrates are not generally considered a threat to people over six months of age (Kallas). The seeds of most species are also edible. Many species accumulate salts from the soil. They can be utilized as salt substitutes, either whole or burned and the ashes used. A salty taste is a good indicator for any of the following subfamilies. Saponins are also common.

Key Words: Weedy plants with globby or prickly flowers, found in disturbed or alkaline soils.

Atriplex—saltbush, orache (150/90/10) • This genus is exceptionally variable. Four-wing saltbush (*A. canescens*) and other saltbushes are rugged, grey bushes adapted to desert conditions, while the common orache (*A. hortensis*) greatly resembles spinach-like edible goosefoots (*Chenopodium*). Orache is one of my favorite, introduced, semi-wild greens. (Read more in *Foraging the Mountain West*.) Pinole is a Southwestern drink made with the parched, ground seeds of four-wing saltbush, plus sugar and water (Bigfoot). The seeds from all species are likely edible.

Axyris—Russian pigweed (5/1/1) *A. amaranthoides*. Introduced. Grows across Canada and the northern states.

Krascheninnikovia (formerly *Ceratoides* or *Eurotia*)—winterfat (8/1/1) *K. lanata*. As the common name implies, winterfat is an important winter range plant.

Chenopodium—goosefoot, lamb's quarters, quinoa, epazote, wormseed (200/50/11) • The Latin "*Cheno-podium*" means "goose-foot," in reference to the shape of the leaves. Lamb's quarters (*C. album*) was introduced from Europe, and is often found in gardens. It thrives is disturbed, manure rich soils, hence the common name. It contains more calcium than any other plant ever analyzed, plus lots of riboflavin, vitamins A and C, and protein (Kallas). Most goosefoots are delicious as salad greens or potherbs, and highly nutritious. Read more in *Foraging the Mountain West*.

Quinoa (*C. quinoa*) seed is sold as a hot cereal at many health food stores. Blite goosefoot (*C. capitatum*) and leafy goosefoot (*C. foliosum*) develop fleshy bright red berries around the seeds. The berries are bland and uninteresting compared to real berries, but easy to gather and highly nutritious.

Epazote or wormseed (*C. ambrosioides*) is found from coast-to-coast across the southern states, most common in the Southwest. The seeds contain a potent and bitter oil used as an anthelmintic to kill intestinal parasites. Excess consumption could be toxic (Moore).

Cycloloma—winged pigweed (1/1/1) *C. atriplicifolium*. Seeds are edible (Kirk).

Grayia—hop sage (1/1/1) *G. spinosa*. Native to the West.

Monolepis—poverty weed (3/3/1) The plant is edible as a potherb (Harrington).

Suckleya—suckleya (1/1/1) *S. suckleyana*. The plant contains a poisonous cyanogenic substance that can form hydrocyanic or prussic acid in the digestive system (Harrington). Similar cyanide compounds in other plants are typically destroyed by cooking.

Camphorosma Subfamily—*Camphorosmoideae*

Bassia (including *Kochia*)—smotherweed, kochia (20/6/4) The plants contain some saponins. The young leaves or seeds of *B. scoparia* are known to be edible in moderate quantities. Also known as "burning bush," the plant turns red as it ages.

burning bush
Bassia scoparia

Camphorosma Subfamily

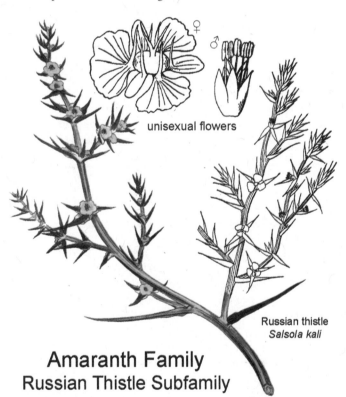

unisexual flowers

Russian thistle
Salsola kali

Amaranth Family
Russian Thistle Subfamily

Russian Thistle Subfamily—*Salsoloideae*

Halogeton—saltlover (5/1/1) *H. glomeratus*. Native to the West. *Halogeton* contains an oxalate that may poison sheep (Booth).

Salsola—Russian thistle (100/6/2) • Introduced. One of the most common tumbleweeds in the West, along with tumble mustard (*Sisymbrium altissimum*) of the Mustard family. The young plant is edible as a potherb. The seeds are also edible (Harrington). The dry plants are spiky.

Bugseed Subfamily—*Corispermoideae*

Corispermum—Bugseed (65/9/2) Grows in all states and provinces west of the Mississippi.

Seepweed Subfamily—*Suaedoideae*

Suaeda—Seepweed (110/13/3) The plant is edible as a potherb; it has a salty flavor. The seeds are also edible. (Kirk).

Seepweed Subfamily

herbaceous seepweed
Suaeda maritima

Pickleweed Subfamily—*Salicornioideae*

Allenrolfea—iodine bush (3/1/0) • *A. occidentalis*. Grows in desert alkaline environments, from Oregon to Texas.

Salicornia—pickleweed, glasswort (30/4/1) The plant is edible as a salad, pickle, or potherb (Kirk). It is high in salt and can be added to stews to provide salt flavoring (Olsen). *Salicornia* and several other salty plants were used in early glass-making. The plants were dried, then burned in a heap. The ashes were added to sand for crude glass-making, or leached with lime water to make caustic soda. The moisture was then evaporated away to leave crystals of mostly pure sodium hydroxide, used for making finer glass (Mabey).

Miner's Lettuce Family—*Montiaceae*

What would you eat if you joined the gold rush, and set up camp miles away from the nearest garden or grocer? You might try miner's lettuce. The name has been given to many edible plants found near mining camps, but especially stuck with a few plants in the Miner's Lettuce family.

Plants of the Miner's Lettuce family are succulent herbs with regular, bisexual flowers. There are usually 2 sepals and 5 petals, but a few species have 2, 3, 4, or 6 petals, and the bitterroot (*Lewisia*) has up to 18 petals. (In some books the 2 sepals are considered bracts (modified leaves) and the petals are considered colored sepals.) There may be an equal or double number of stamens as petals, or they may be numerous. The ovary is positioned superior and consists of 2 to 8 united carpels forming a single chamber. It matures as a capsule that opens along three seams, or by a cap-like top. A few species prefer the shade of trees, but most members of this family seem particularly adapted to dry areas with intense sunlight. Worldwide, there are about 19 genera and 580 species. North America genera are listed below. Most are found in the western states. The bitterroot (*Lewisia*) is the state flower of Montana. Many plants in the family contain some amount of oxalic acid, giving a a mild lemon-like taste. Read more about oxalic acid in the *Medicinal Properties* section of this book. The plants of this family were previously included in the Purslane family (below).

Key Words: Succulent plants often growing in intense sunlight. Two sepals.

Calandrinia—red maids (150/2/0) Red maids are native to the Pacific Coast states. The plants and seeds are edible.

Cistanthe—pussypaws (35/11/1) This genus includes plants formerly included in *Calyptridium*, *Calandrinia*, and *Sprague*.

Claytonia—spring beauty, miner's lettuce (26/26/11) • Several species have small, potato-like roots that are edible raw or cooked. I can only harvest about a cup of roots per hour of work, but it is very much worth the effort. Cooked spring beauty roots taste as good or better than buttery "new potatoes." Read more in *Foraging the Mountain West*. The whole plant is good as a salad or potherb. The spring beauty was a favored crop of Native Americans here in Montana (Hart). See also *Montia*, below.

Lewisia—bitterroot (19/19/4) • Bitterroot is the state flower of Montana, and it *is* legal to harvest it, but be sure to dig only in areas of extreme abundance. The starchy roots are edible. Kirk says to peel the roots or rub them vigorously between the hands to remove the bitter bark, or to boil the bitterness out. Sweet says to boil them and then peel them.

    Bitterroot has a well-known history as one of Montana's premiere native food crops. In an experiment, I collected over a gallon of the whole plants in a one-hour harvest in May. Trimming away the vegetation left approximately 1.5 quarts of roots. Peeling off the bitter bark took another eight hours! The peeled roots cook up nicely in a stew. They are starchy, gelatinous, and filling. However, it is important to remove *all* of the red bark. Even a little bit will make the whole stew bitter beyond edibility.

    The Flathead Indians monitor the bitterroot crop each spring to see when the bark slips easily off the root, usually late April or early May. Then they have a big harvesting day to collect the year's supply. I have stumbled across a few plants at just the right time, and yes, the bark slides right off.

Montia—miner's lettuce (12/8/4) • Several members of the genus have been shuffled to *Claytonia*. The plant is succulent and tasty as a salad green or potherb. Medicinally, the tea may be used as a laxative (Sweet). The common name "miner's lettuce" is confusing, because the same name was given to many different wild plants that were eaten by early miners.

Phemeranthus—fameflower (25/17/0) Various species found primarily from the Rockies east to the Atlantic.

Talinum—flame flower (15/3/0) Flame flower grows in the Southwest. Several species were shuffled to other genera, with the remaining *Talinum* segregated into an independent family, *Talinaceae*.

Talinopsis—arroyo fameflower (1/1/0) *T. frutescens*. Native to Texas and New Mexico.

Purslane Family—*Portulacaceae*

The Purslane family originally included all the plants of the Miner's Lettuce family (above), but genetic analysis revealed that *Portulaca* is more distinct and should be an independent family. Purslanes are mostly fleshy, succulent annual herbs with 2 sepals, 5 to 7 short-lived petals, and typically 6 to 40 stamens (sometimes more or less). The ovary is positioned at least half inferior, and consists of 2 to 8 united carpels forming a single chamber. It matures as a lidded capsule with many seeds. The family has been reduced to just the one genus.

Portulaca—purslane, moss rose (100/11/1) • Common purslane (*P. oleracea*) is a succulent, edible, reddish-green plant found growing flat on the ground, with fat stems and small, fat leaves. The whole plant is edible raw or cooked. Try frying some in a little oil or butter. Purslane is surprisingly high in carbohydrates (Harrington, Storer), as well as proteins, omega 3 fatty acids, antioxidants and vitamin E (Gillaspy). Moss rose (*P. grandiflora*) is also edible, as is likely the case with all *Portulaca*.

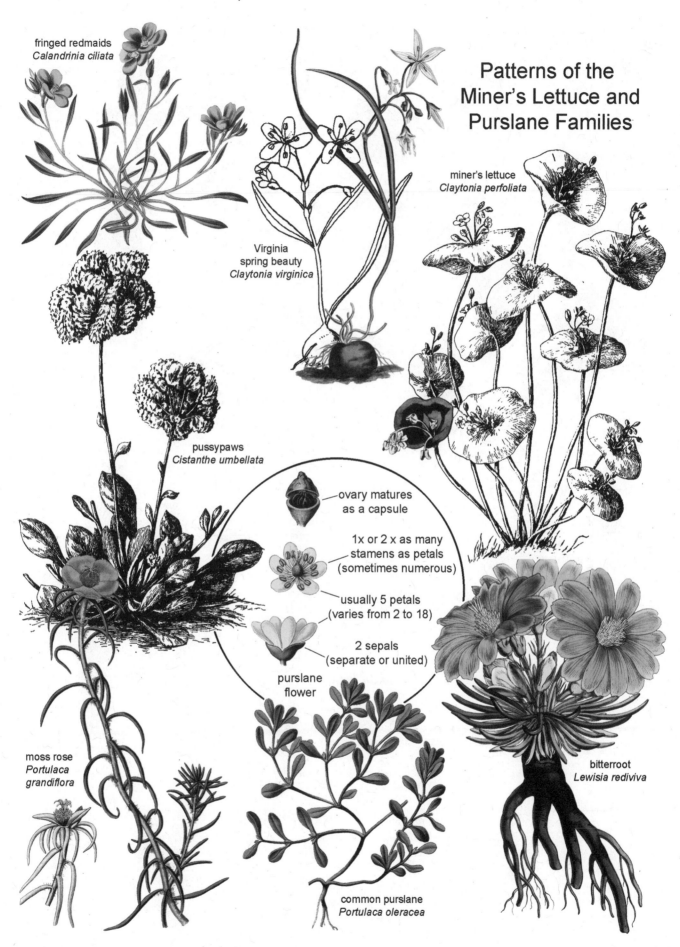

fringed redmaids
Calandrinia ciliata

Patterns of the
Miner's Lettuce and
Purslane Families

Virginia
spring beauty
Claytonia virginica

miner's lettuce
Claytonia perfoliata

pussypaws
Cistanthe umbellata

ovary matures
as a capsule

1x or 2 x as many
stamens as petals
(sometimes numerous)

usually 5 petals
(varies from 2 to 18)

2 sepals
(separate or united)

purslane
flower

moss rose
*Portulaca
grandiflora*

common purslane
Portulaca oleracea

bitterroot
Lewisia rediviva

121

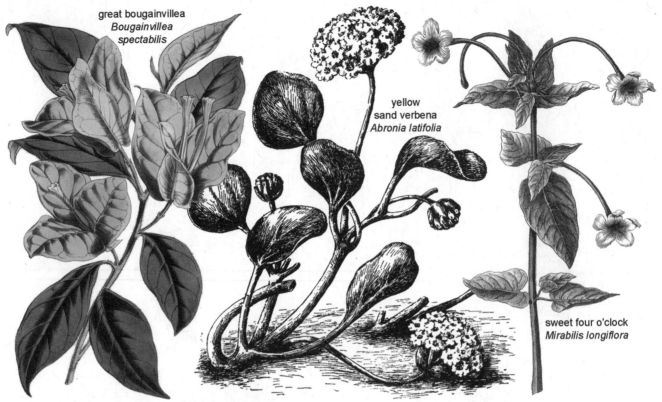

great bougainvillea
Bougainvillea spectabilis

yellow
sand verbena
Abronia latifolia

sweet four o'clock
Mirabilis longiflora

Four O'Clock Family—*Nyctaginaceae*

If you live or travel to southern states, then you have likely encountered the ornamental *Bougainvillea*, with its showy red or pink bracts (modified leaves). Next time, take a closer look at the flowers. Plants of the Four O'Clock family sometimes have colored bracts, plus typically funnel-shaped flowers with 5 (rarely 3 to 10) united sepals colored like petals, and 0 petals. There are usually 5 (sometimes 1 to 3) stamens. The ovary is positioned superior and consists of a single carpel. It matures as a dry seed (an achene). The sepals persist as the ovary matures.

Worldwide, there are about 30 genera and 300 species. Fifteen genera are native to North America, mostly found in warmer climates. Only a few species are found in the northern latitudes. The flowers of *Mirabilis* bloom late in the day, hence the common name for the family.

Key Words:
Tubular flowers with 5 colored sepals and no petals.

Four O'Clock Family

5 petal-like sepals
united as a tube

0 petals

usually 5 stamens
(sometimes 1 to 3)

superior
ovary

Abronia—sand verbena (50/23/2) The name "sand verbena" could be confused with the unrelated Verbena family. The roots of three species are known to be edible, with some specimens reportedly large and sweet (Fern). Another species was used by the Ute as a remedy for stomach and bowel troubles. The tea is also reported to be diuretic (Murphey).

Allionia—windmills (2/2/0) Native to the Southwest.

Boerhavia—spiderling (40/16/0) Among the species listed, the leaves are edible (Zomlefer), as are the cooked seeds and roots. The roots are rich in carbohydrates and proteins, but may have a woody texture. The roots contain an alkaloid that causes a rise in blood pressure (Fern).

Mirabilis—four o'clock (60/35/3) Some four o'clocks have large roots rich in carbohydrates and proteins, but they may have mildly narcotic properties. The mashed root is used as a local analgesic. Taken internally, the root raises blood sugar levels, acting as a temporary stimulant and appetite depressant. Larger doses lead to a feeling of well-being and hyperactivity followed by slurred speech and befuddlement. It also has a purgative and gas-producing effect (Moore).

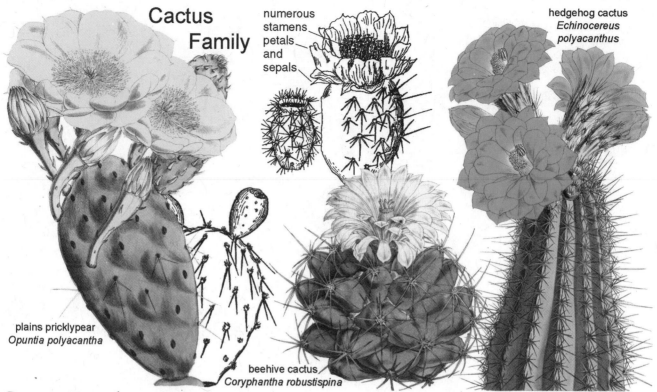

Cactus Family

numerous stamens petals and sepals

hedgehog cactus
Echinocereus polyacanthus

plains pricklypear
Opuntia polyacantha

beehive cactus
Coryphantha robustispina

Cactus Family—*Cactaceae*

Plants of the Cactus family are easy to recognize with their fleshy stems and spines. The spines are actually highly modified leaves. The regular, bisexual flowers are showy with numerous sepals, petals, and stamens. The ovary is positioned inferior and consists of 3 to 100 united carpels, as indicated by the same number of styles. The carpels are united to form a single chamber, which matures as a pulpy, often spiny "berry" with numerous seeds. The cacti originated in the New World. Worldwide, there are about 125 genera and more than 2,000 species. Sixteen genera are found in North America. Some well-known members of this family include peyote (*Lophophora williamsii*), saguaro (*Carnegiea* or *Cereus*), Christmas cactus (*Zygocactus*), and the barrel cactus (*Ferocactus*). The spines of some species were once used as phonograph needles (Smith). Some plants from the Spurge family resemble cacti.

Key Words: Succulent desert plants with spines. Flower parts numerous.

Coryphantha—beehive cactus (300/7/2) • *Coyphantha* are sometimes included in *Mammillaria*. The plant and fruit are edible raw or cooked (Olsen). *C. missouriensis* barely rises above the soil surface, making it nearly invisible underfoot.

Echinocereus—hedgehog cactus (70/40/0) • Hedgehog cactus grows in the Southwest. It is easy to collect and peel. It can be used as a poultice for cuts and burns, or eaten raw or cooked. It is rare and should be used sparingly.

Opuntia—prickly pear (200/60/2) • Spiny fruits and cactus pads are edible. The large pads of some species are cultivated as food in Mexico and can be purcased in ethnic grocery stores. The texture is slimy like ocra, but interesting to explore. The big spiny "berries" of some species become quite colorful and sweet as they ripen. Trim away the spines and make jelly much as you would for any other fruit.

The plains pricklypear (*O. polyacantha*), common in northern states, has small pads, big spines, and lots of prickly hair-like "glochids." The plant isn't very useful as food, but fun to taste, and it makes an excellent salve for sunburns. To get the slimy flesh, select a thicker pad, but leave it attached to the plant. Hold the pad still with a stick or rock in one hand, and slice it in half with a knife to make two flat halves. Scrape out the slimy green goo with the edge of a knife. Medicinally, the mucilage can be used like *Aloe vera*. It osmotically draws out waste material from bruised, burned, or other injured tissues, while soothing those tissues with its slimy quality (Moore). This mucilage is a complex sugar called a mucopolysaccharide. A similar mucopolysaccharide forms a "hydrogel" between your body's cells. This gel can dry out or break down after an injury, especially from a burn or sunburn. Wipe a cactus pad over the burn to replenish your own mucopolysaccharide gel. Repeated applications can heal a bad sunburn and prevent peeling. Prickly pear has a hypoglycemic effect for adult-onset diabetes. Refer to Michael Moore's *Medicinal Plants of the Desert and Canyon West* for more information. Prickly pear juice is also used as a mordant for setting dyes (Hart).

Pediocactus—ball cactus (8/8/1) Native from Washington to New Mexico.

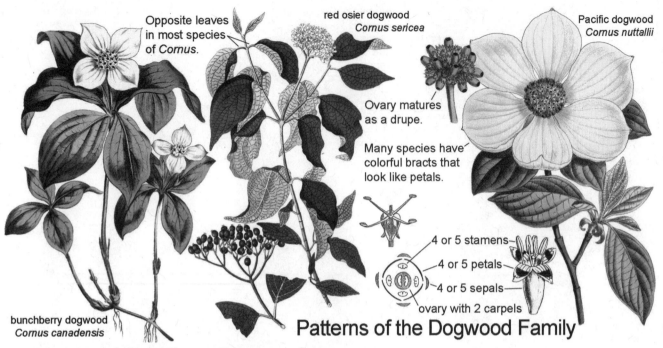

Opposite leaves in most species of *Cornus*.

red osier dogwood
Cornus sericea

Pacific dogwood
Cornus nuttallii

Ovary matures as a drupe.

Many species have colorful bracts that look like petals.

4 or 5 stamens
4 or 5 petals
4 or 5 sepals
ovary with 2 carpels

bunchberry dogwood
Cornus canadensis

Patterns of the Dogwood Family

Dogwood Family—*Cornaceae* (including *Nyssaceae*)

The flowers of many dogwoods (*Cornus*) are illusionary. There are often 4 (sometimes more or none) showy white or pinkish bracts (modified leaves) that look like petals, while the actual flowers are much smaller and clustered together in the center. The individual flowers are regular and usually, but not always, bisexual, with 4 or 5 (rarely 0) small, separate sepals, and a similar number of usually white, separate petals. There are 4 or 5 stamens (double in *Nyssa*). The ovary is positioned inferior, consisting of 2 (sometimes 1, 3, or 4) united carpels, usually (not always) forming a single chamber. It matures as a drupe (a fleshy fruit with a stony pit), or rarely as a berry. As currently described, the Dogwood family includes 7 genera and about 110 species, of which only dogwoods (*Cornus*) and tupelo (*Nyssa*) are native to North America. Most species of *Cornus* have opposite (rarely whorled) leaves. Only *Cornus alternifolia* has alternate leaves, as do all species of *Nyssa*.

Key Words (*Cornus*):
Trees, shrubs, or woody plants with opposite or whorled leaves, showy bracts and fleshy fruits.

blackgum tupelo
Nyssa sylvatica

Cornus—dogwood, bunchberry (58/22/2) • The red, white, and black fruits of at least eight species are known to be edible, although some are very bitter or acid tasting (Sturtevant), and some may be strongly laxative in excess. The cornelian cherry (*C. mas*), introduced from Europe for cultivation, has a tart, cherry-like drupe, which is edible raw or made into jelly. And the kousa dogwood (C. kousa), introduced from Asia, has an aggregate fruit (like a raspberry), which is also edible raw or made into jelly (Lincoff).

Medicinally, the berries may reduce the potency of some poisons when ingested or applied as a poultice (Willard). Dogwoods contain varying amounts of cornic acid and the alkaloid cornine, mostly in the bark and/or the inner bark. It has a mildly narcotic and analgesic effect, especially helpful for individuals who have a negative reaction to salicylates like willow or aspirin. The bark is also quite astringent, which further helps to draw down inflamed tissues (Moore, Willard). The aromatic greenish inner bark of the red osier dogwood (*C. stolonifera*) was often added to smoking mixtures. It should be used in moderation due to its narcotic effect (Harrington, Willard).

Tupelo Subfamily—*Nyssoideae*
The Tupelos are sometimes treated as a separate family, *Nyssaceae*.

Nyssa—tupelo (10/5/0) Native from Texas to Ontario, east to the Atlantic.

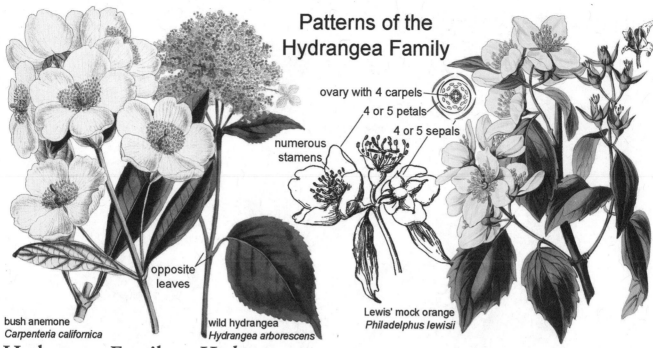

Patterns of the Hydrangea Family

ovary with 4 carpels
4 or 5 petals
4 or 5 sepals
numerous stamens
opposite leaves

bush anemone
Carpenteria californica

wild hydrangea
Hydrangea arborescens

Lewis' mock orange
Philadelphus lewisii

Hydrangea Family—*Hydrangeaceae*

If you have a mock orange (*Philadelphus*) or *Hydrangea* in your yard, then you have met the Hydrangea family. The family includes mostly shrubs with usually opposite leaves and showy flowers. The flowers are bisexual and regular, with 4 or 5 (rarely 10) united sepals and 4 or 5 (rarely 10) separate petals. There are often numerous stamens (but sometimes only 4, 5, or 8). The ovary is positioned either superior or inferior and consists of usually 4 (sometimes 2 to 5) united carpels, as usually indicated by the number of styles. Partition walls are present, forming an equal number of chambers. The ovary matures as a capsule containing numerous seeds. Worldwide, there are 17 genera and 250 species. North American genera are listed below. Pride of Rochester (*Deutzia*) is an introduced ornamental.

Key Words: Shrubs with opposite leaves and showy flowers with parts in fours and fives.

Carpenteria—bush anenome (1/1/0) *C. californica*. Native to California.

Decumaria—woodvamp (2/1/0) *D. barbara*. Native to the eastern states.

Fendlera—fendlerbush (3/3/0) Native from Nevada to Texas.

Fendlerella—Utah fendlerbush (1/1/0) *F. utahensis*. Native across the Southwest.

Hydrangea—hydrangea (70/5/0) • Native and introduced species are often cultivated in warm climates. The cluster of showy flowers are sterile. The fertile flowers are smaller and shorter, appearing in the middle of the group. The fresh leaves contain cyanide, but some species are dried and powdered for use as a tea sweetener. Medicinally, the roots are emetic and cathartic, diaphoretic, diuretic, and anthelmintic. The plant might contain an antimalarial alkaloid (Fern).

Itea—sweet spire (8/1/0) *I. virginica*. Grows from Texas to New Jersey.

Jamesia—cliffbush (2/2/0) Native to the southwest. The seeds were sometimes eaten by Native Americans (Moerman).

Philadelphus—mock orange, syringa (71/29/1) • I love to bury my nose in the sweet blossoms. The common name "syringa" is misleading, since that is the botanical name of lilacs from the Olive family. The fruits of at least one species were eaten by Native Americans. The leaves and flowers contain saponin and were crushed in water for use as soap (Moerman). *Philadelphus* and its allies are sometimes segregated into their own family, *Philadelphaceae*.

Whipplea—yerba de selva (1/1/0) *W. modesta*. Native to the Pacific Coast states.

cliff fendlerbush
Fendlera rupicola

125

Patterns of the Loasa Family

yellow stingbush
Eucnide bartonioides

numerous stamens

5 petals (rarely 4 or 10)

5 sepals

inferior ovary

Lindley's blazingstar
Mentzelia lindleyi

ovary matures as a capsule with numerous seeds

tenpetal blazingstar
Mentzelia decapetala

Loasa Family—*Loasaceae*

Plants of the Loasa family typically have coarse vegetation with rough, hooked, or even stinging hairs. These are mostly desert and tropical plants, but a few species can be found in arid environments throughout the Rocky Mountains. The flowers are bisexual and regular and often 2 to 4 inches in diameter. There are typically 5 (rarely 4) separate sepals and 5 (rarely 4 or 10) usually separate petals, and numerous stamens—as many as 200! The ovary is positioned inferior and consists of 4 to 7 (rarely 3 or 8) united carpels forming a single chamber. The ovary matures as a capsule with numerous seeds (only 1 seed in *Petalonyx*).

Worldwide, there are 15 genera and 250 species, mostly in South America and southern North America. Our genera are listed below. In *Mentzelia laevicaulis* the outer ring of stamens can be flat, wide, and missing the anthers, so they look like petals. In some specimens from southern California the sepals, petals, and styles even resemble leaves.

Key Words: Coarse, hairy plants of arid lands with 5 or 10 petals and numerous stamens.

Cevallia—stinging serpent (1/1/0) *C. sinuata*. Native from Arizona to Texas. The plant is covered with hairs, some of which cause a stinging sensation.

Eucnide—stingbush (14/3/0) Native from California to Texas. The plant is covered with stinging hairs.

Mentzelia—blazing star (70/53/5) • The seeds can be parched or roasted and ground into a flour, for use as mush or bread (Olsen). Reportedly, they could be used to thicken gravy (Murphey).

    Medicinally, a tea of the plant may be beneficial for hardened arteries if taken over a long period of time (Bigfoot). The seeds were used in burn dressings by Native Americans. The leaves were used as an aid for toothache (Moerman).

Petalonyx—Sandpaper Plant (4/4/0) The sandpaper plant is a native of the desert Southwest.

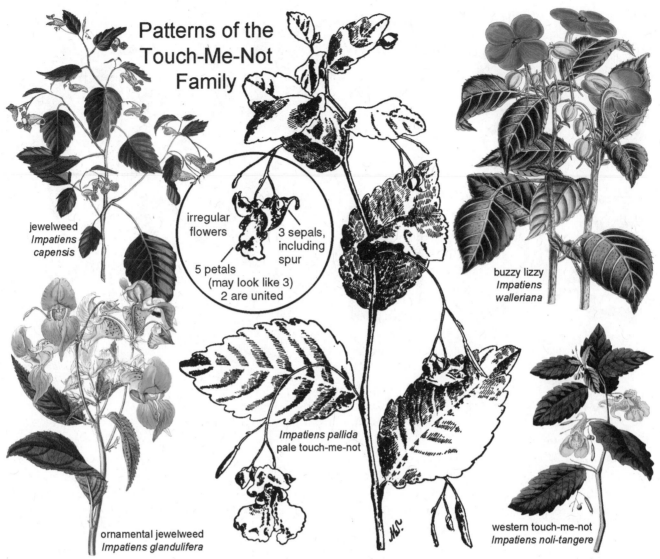

Patterns of the Touch-Me-Not Family

jewelweed
Impatiens capensis

irregular flowers

5 petals
(may look like 3)
2 are united

3 sepals, including spur

buzzy lizzy
Impatiens walleriana

Impatiens pallida
pale touch-me-not

ornamental jewelweed
Impatiens glandulifera

western touch-me-not
Impatiens noli-tangere

Touch-Me-Not Family—*Balsaminaceae*

Jewelweed (*Impatiens*) really stands out when you come across it. It has translucent, watery stems and a distinctive irregular blossom. There are 3 (rarely 5) sepals of unequal size, the lowest one forming a spur. There are 5 petals, 2 of which are united, plus 5 stamens. The ovary is positioned superior. It consists of 5 united carpels with the partition walls present, forming an equal number of chambers. Each carpel produces 2 to numerous seeds. In many species the ovary matures as a capsule that explodes when touched, hence the common name of the family. The leaf has a silvery appearance when held underwater.

Worldwide, there are 2 genera and more than 850 species. *Hydrocera triflora* is native to southern India and southern China. Everything else in the family has been classified or reclassified within *Impatiens*. Buzzy lizzy (*I. walleriana*) and several other species are cultivated as garden flowers and house plants. Be sure to look for the spur on the back. Some species of *Impatiens* have been used to produce red, yellow and black dyes.

Key Words: Delicate, juicy plants with irregular flowers and spurs.

Impatiens—jewelweed, touch-me-not (850/10/3) • Young jewelweed shoots up to 6 inches tall are reported to be a good potherb. The seeds are also edible. Medicinally, jewelweed is astringent; it is often used as a poultice or wash for skin irritations, especially for poison ivy, bee stings, and athlete's foot. A European species also contains a bitter principle; it is used as a laxative. Jewelweed is not common in Montana. I have only seen a half-dozen plants, and they are all gone now. I think it prefers a more humid environment.

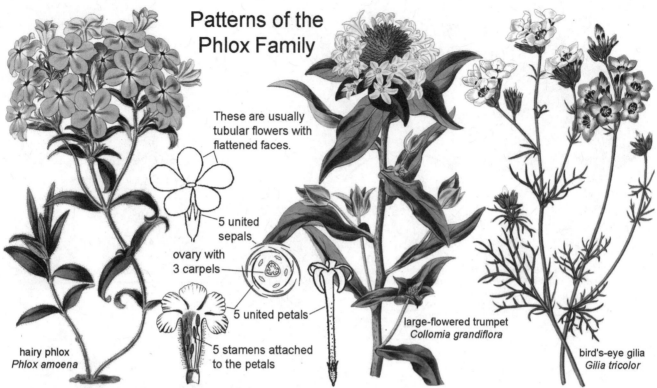

Patterns of the Phlox Family

These are usually tubular flowers with flattened faces.

5 united sepals

ovary with 3 carpels

5 united petals

5 stamens attached to the petals

hairy phlox
Phlox amoena

large-flowered trumpet
Collomia grandiflora

bird's-eye gilia
Gilia tricolor

Phlox Family—*Polemoniaceae*

Most members of the Phlox family are small plants with narrow, alternate or opposite leaves. They are adapted to arid environments, especially in the western states. A few species take the form of shrubs or trees in other parts of the world. The delicate flowers are regular and bisexual, usually forming a tube at the base, which flattens out to form a dish-like face. There are 5 united sepals, but they may appear mostly separate. There are 5 united petals, usually twisted in the bud stage. There are 5 stamens attached to, and alternate with, the petals. (In a few species there are 4 sepals, petals, and stamens.) The ovary is positioned superior. It consists of 3 (sometimes 2 or 5) united carpels, as indicated by the number of styles. Partition walls are present, forming an equal number of chambers. The ovary matures as a capsule with 1 to numerous seeds.

Worldwide, there are 18 genera and 320 species, mostly in the western hemisphere. Eleven genera are present in North America, as listed below. Medicinally, many of these plants have seeds containing mucilage. The plants also contain inulin polysaccharides, saponins and flavonoids (Zomlefer).

Key Words: Five united petals forming tubular flowers with a flat face. Usually narrow leaves.

Collomia—trumpet (14/11/4) • The seeds contain significant amounts of mucilage (Craighead).

Eriastrum—woollystar (15/15/0) Includes plants formerly classified as *Hugelia*.

Gilia—gilia (50/33/1) The herb and flowers sometimes have an acrid smell when crushed. Some species may contain saponin (Craighead).

Ipomopsis—scarlet trumpet, scarlet gilia (25/25/5) • Some species were formerly classified as part of *Gilia*.

Langloisia—langloisia (1/1/0) *L. setosissima*. Grows in the Great Basin Desert.

Leptosiphon—babystars (28/28/1) Native to the western states.

Linanthus—linanthus (22/22/2) Many species from this genus are now classified as *Leptosiphon*.

Microsteris—slender phlox (1/1/1) • *M. gracilis*. Found from Alaska to Baja California, east to the Rocky Mountains.

Navarretia—pincushion plant (30/30/3) The seeds of *N. squarrosa* are reported to be edible, typically parched and pulverized. A tea of *N. leucocephala* was used on swellings (Sweet).

Phlox—phlox (67/67/11) • We have patches of *P. longifolia* growing on our property, which florish in drought years. It makes a spectacular carpet of white and pinkish flowers with dozens of blossoms on every little plant. It is a refreshing reminder that drought is not the tragedy we often make it out to be, but part of the natural flow of things. Medicinally, the boiled leaves are used as a drawing poultice (Murphey).

Polemonium—Jacob's ladder (23/20/4) • Several species have a skunk-like odor when crushed. A tea of the herb has diaphoretic properties (Kadans).

Patterns of the Pitcher Plant Family

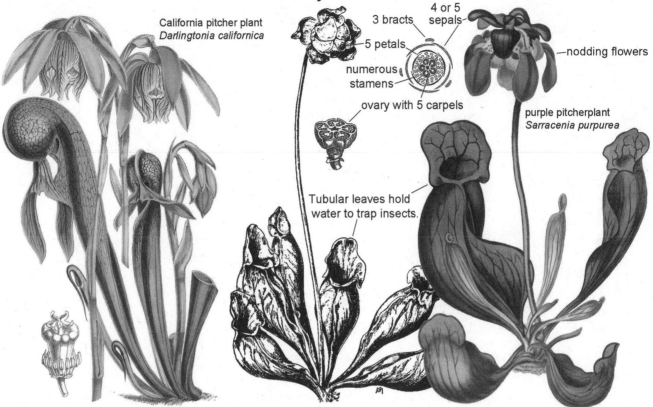

California pitcher plant
Darlingtonia californica

3 bracts

4 or 5 sepals

5 petals

numerous stamens

ovary with 5 carpels

—nodding flowers

purple pitcherplant
Sarracenia purpurea

Tubular leaves hold water to trap insects.

Pitcher Plant Family—*Sarraceniaceae*

Pitcher Plants have tubular, vase-like leaves that hold water to drown insects. As with other carnivorous plants, Pitcher Plants typically live in acidic or nutrient poor soil and depend on insects as a nutritional supplement. Brilliant colors and nectar help attract insects in some species, while downward pointing hairs and waxy secretions help to hinder escape. Digestive enzymes and/or bacteria in the water break down the insects so that the plants can absorb the nutrients, often giving the plants a putrid odor. The flowers often have 3 bracts, plus typically 4 or 5 sepals (sometimes colored like petals) and 5 petals (rarely 0). There are numerous stamens. The ovary is positioned superior and consists of 5 (rarely 3) united carpels forming an equal number of chambers. It matures as a capsule containing numerous seeds.

Worldwide, there are 3 genera and 17 species, found only in the New World. These plants are sometimes over-collected as novelties. To better conserve the plants, do not harvest them in the wild and buy only those plants that have been propagated from cultivated stock.

Key Words: Plants with tubular leaves to trap insects.

Darlingtonia—cobra lily, California pitcher plant (1/1/0) *D. Californica*. Native to northern California and southern Oregon.
Sarracenia—pitcher plant (9/9/0) The pitcher plants are native to the East Coast of North America.
Heliamphora—marsh pitcher plant (6/0/0) *Heliamphora* is found only in Venezuela and Guyana.

yellow pitcherplant
Sarracenia flava

129

scarlet pimpernel
Anagallis arvensis

Primrose Family—*Primulaceae*

The Primroses are herbs or slightly woody plants with usually basal or opposite leaves, but sometimes whorled. Some species are aquatic, while many others will be found near the water or at least in very moist soils. The flowers are regular and bisexual, often formed in clusters above a bract (modified leaf) on the main stem. There are usually 5 (rarely 4 to 9) sepals united at the base, and a similar number of petals and stamens. The petals may be united (often at the base) or separate and the stamens are aligned opposite (in the middle of) the petals. The ovary is positioned superior or partly inferior and consists of 5 united carpels forming a single chamber. It matures as a capsule, often with a circumscissile lid (like a lid on a pot), containing 1 to numerous seeds.

Worldwide, there are about 28 genera and 800 species. North American genera are listed below. The *Cyclamen* is a popular houseplant that looks similar to our wild shooting stars (*Dodecatheon*). The common names of this family can be the source of some confusion. The Primrose family is not related to the Evening Primrose family, nor is loosestrife (*Lysimachia*) related to the loosestrife (*Lythrum*) of the Loosestrife family.

Key Words: Plants in moist soil with parts in fives and stamens aligned opposite the petals.

Anagallis—pimpernel (40/4/1) • *A. arvensis* was introduced from Europe. Some species of pimpernel are used in salads, but otherwise the plants are diaphoretic, expectorant, diuretic, and purgative. Small doses cause sweating and increased kidney activity. Larger doses act on the central nervous system and the brain, leading to trembling, watery stools, and excessive urination (Lust). The plants contain some saponin; it is used for fishing in India (Schauenberg).

Androsace (including *Douglasia*)—rock jasmine (110/15/5) • A tea of the plant was taken for birth injuries and postpartum bleeding, or taken cold for internal pain (Moerman). Dwarf primrose (*A. montana*, previously *Douglasia montana*), grows abundantly on windswept ridges above my home. It blooms prolifically in May and June, yet individual blossoms can be found during midwinter warm spells.

Dodecatheon—shooting star (15/15/3) • The whole plant is edible as a salad green or potherb (Willard). Shooting stars are mildly astringent. I like to pick the flowers and present them to whomever I am with, then gobble them down!

Glaux—sea milkwort (1/1/1) *G. maritima.* The young shoots and cooked roots are edible. The roots have a sedative quality (Fern, Moerman).

Hottonia—featherfoil (2/1/0) *H. inflata.* An aquatic plant with feathery leaves found from Texas to Maine.

Lysimachia (including *Steironema*)—loosestrife (200/16/1) The cooked leaves are edible. Various species are largely astringent with some diaphoretic and emetic properties. The live plant is reported to repel gnats and flies; it can also be burned as a smudge (Fern).

Primula—primrose (540/20/2) The flowers or young leaves are edible and can often be found in winter. Some species contain saponins and salicin. The saponins have an expectorant effect, while the salicin is a pain reliever like aspirin. (Fern).

Samolus—brookweed (7/4/0) Found in shallow water or moist soils across much of North America.

Trientalis—starflower (3/3/0) • Sepals, petals, and stamens can come in multiples of 5 to 9. Found across North America, except the Rockies and Great Plains.

shooting stars
Dodecatheon meadia

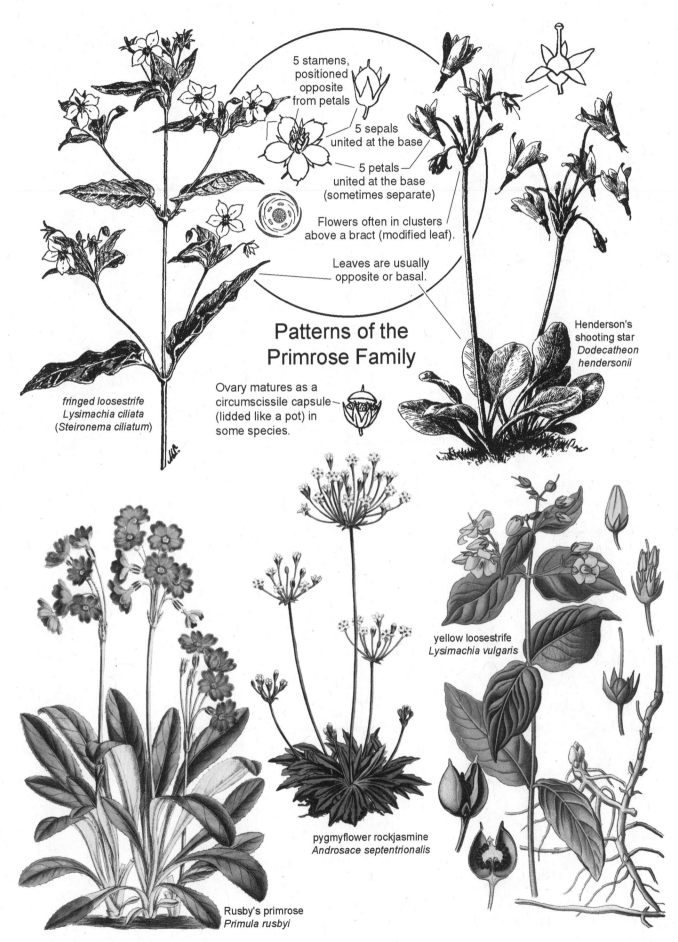

5 stamens, positioned opposite from petals

5 sepals united at the base

5 petals united at the base (sometimes separate)

Flowers often in clusters above a bract (modified leaf).

Leaves are usually opposite or basal.

Patterns of the Primrose Family

Ovary matures as a circumscissile capsule (lidded like a pot) in some species.

fringed loosestrife
Lysimachia ciliata
(*Steironema ciliatum*)

Henderson's shooting star
Dodecatheon hendersonii

Rusby's primrose
Primula rusbyi

pygmyflower rockjasmine
Androsace septentrionalis

yellow loosestrife
Lysimachia vulgaris

131

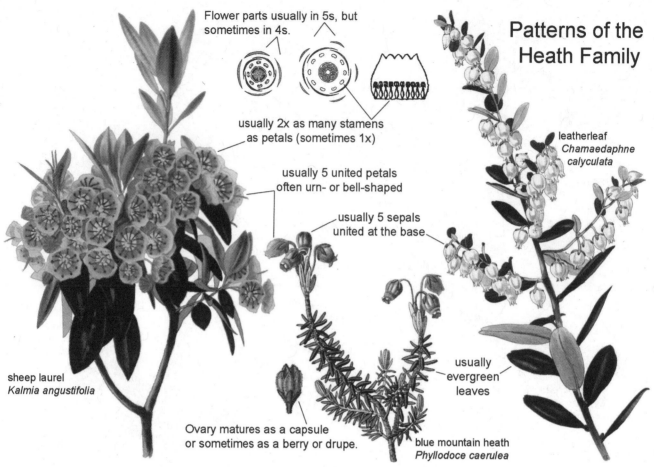

Flower parts usually in 5s, but sometimes in 4s.

usually 2x as many stamens as petals (sometimes 1x)

usually 5 united petals often urn- or bell-shaped

usually 5 sepals united at the base

Patterns of the Heath Family

leatherleaf
Chamaedaphne calyculata

usually evergreen leaves

sheep laurel
Kalmia angustifolia

Ovary matures as a capsule or sometimes as a berry or drupe.

blue mountain heath
Phyllodoce caerulea

Heath Family—*Ericaceae*

The Heath family is as exciting to know as blueberries and huckleberries (*Vaccinium*). This family includes mostly shrubs (some herbs and trees) with usually alternate, often evergreen leaves. The plants typically grow in poor, acidic soils or bogs. The bisexual and regular or nearly regular flowers typically have 5 sepals united at the base and 5 usually united petals (sometimes 4 of each or rarely more or less), often in a bell shape and white to pink or red in color. Expect to find the same number or twice as many stamens as petals. The ovary is positioned either superior or inferior and consists of usually 5 (sometimes 4, and rarely more or less) united carpels with the partition walls present, forming an equal number of chambers. It matures as a capsule, a berry, or rarely as a drupe (a fleshy fruit with a stony pit).

Worldwide there are about 126 genera and 4,000 species. Taxonomists have expanded the family to include the Pyrola and Indian Pipe families as subfamilies of the Heath family. For clarity of identification, these subfamilies retain separate descriptions in the text that follows. In addition, the Crowberry family has been folded into this family as a tribe of the Heath subfamily.

Key Words: Mostly red, pink, or white bell-shaped flowers with flower parts in fives. Leaves often evergreen.

White Heather Subfamily—*Cassiopoideae*

Leaves are small and needlelike. Flowers are urn- or bell-shaped.

Cassiope—white heather (12/3/2) Found from California to Alaska, inland to Montana. Formerly included in the Heath subfamily.

White Heather Subfamily

white mountain heather
Cassiope tetragona

132

Heath Subfamily—*Ericoideae*

Taxonomists expanded the Heath subfamily to include the former Rhododendron subfamily, as well as the entire Crowberry family (formerly *Empetraceae*). The resulting mishmash is less intuitive than previous classification systems. Genera are grouped into tribes below to clarify relationships.

Crowberry Tribe—*Empetreae*

The leaves are small and needlelike. Urn-shaped flowers with parts in 3s. The ovary is positioned superior and matures as a drupe or berry. The tribe was previously considered a family unto itself, *Empetraceae*.

Ceratiola—sand heath (1/1/0) *C. ericoides*. From Mississippi to South Carolina.
Corema—broom crowberry (2/1/0) *C. conradii*. The fruit is edible (Fern).
Empetrum—crowberry (4/2/0) Native across Canada and the Pacific Coast states. The fruit is edible.

Heath Tribe—*Ericeae*

Leaves are small and needlelike, and the plants do not have leaf buds present in winter. Fruit is a capsule.

Calluna—heather (1/1/0) *C. vulgaris*. Introduced to northern states.
Erica—heath (860/3/0) Introduced.

Mountain Heath Tribe—*Phyllodoceae*

Flowers vary from urn-shaped to parachute-like, or nearly separate petals. Fruit is a capsule.
Bejaria—flyweed (15/1/0) *B. racemosa*. Native from Alabama to South Carolina. Insects get trapped in sticky secretions on the flowers.
Elliottia—copper bush (4/2/0) Native from Alaska to Oregon, plus Georgia and South Carolina.
Epigaea—trailing arbutus (3/1/0) *E. repens*. Native from Manitoba to Mississippi, east to the Atlantic.
Kalmia (including *Leiophyllum* and *Loiseleuria*)—laurel (6/2/1) The common name could be confused with laurel (*Laurus*) of the Laurel family. *Kalmia* contains andromedotoxin (Craighead), used in small doses as a sedative and for neuralgia. A tea of the leaves has been used to commit suicide (Lust).
Kalmiopsis—kalmiopsis (2/2/0) Native to Oregon.
Phyllodoce—mountain heath (5/5/2) • Western mountains and Canada.

Rhododendron Tribe—*Rhodoreae*

Leaf buds are present in winter. The ovary is positioned superior and matures as a capsule. The seeds are usually winged. Some species contain andromedotoxins. Genetic evidence suggests that *Ledum* and *Menziesia* should be included within *Rhododendron*.

Ledum—Labrador tea (5/3/1) • Labrador tea contains the volatile oil ledol or ledum, a mildly narcotic substance with the potential to cause abortions, heart palpitations, drowsiness or temporary paralysis if used in excess. However, the substance is not readily soluble in water and the plant has a long history of use as an aromatic, mildly bitter tea, drunk either hot or cold (Moore). Medicinally, the tea is antispasmodic, diuretic, diaphoretic and expectorant (Lust).
Menziesia—false huckleberry (2/2/1) • Vegetation resembles true huckleberries. The fruits (capsules) are edible (Fern).
Rhododendron—azalea, rhododendron (1,000/30/1) • The flowers can be made into jelly, but may have an intoxicating effect (Sturtevant). Rhododendrons contain andromedotoxin, like that found in *Kalmia*. Usage can lead to paralysis and heart failure (Klein). Some species are highly toxic to horses.

black crowberry
Empetrum nigrum

flower parts in 3s

bracts

Heath Family
Heath Subfamily

copperbush
Elliottia pyroliflora

smooth azalea
Rhododendron arborescens

cross-section of seed capsule

salal
Gaultheria shallon

Blueberry Subfamily—*Vaccinioideae*

Members of the Blueberry subfamily typically have leaf buds that can be seen in winter. Flower petals are united into an urn- or bell-shape. The ovary is positioned inferior in berry-producing genera, but superior in genera that form seed capsules. Genera are grouped into tribes below to clarify relationships.

Blueberry Tribe—*Vaccinieae*

Gaylussacia—huckleberry (50/8/0) Native from Ontario to Louisiana, east to the Atlantic. The fruit is edible.

Vaccinium—blueberry, huckleberry, cranberry, bilberry, lignonberry (200/40/8) • The berries are edible and delicious. I love to gorge on the berries until the fruit acids make my gums and teeth sore, but even that doesn't stop me! The vegetation and berries are rich in flavonoids, which are consumed for their antioxidant effects. The berries benefit night vision by increasing the number of purple receptor rods in the eyes (Klein). See also *Foraging the Mountain West*.

Salal Tribe—*Gaultherieae*

Chamaedaphne—leatherleaf (1/1/0) *C. calyculata*. Fruit is a capsule. Native across Canada and from Minnesota to Georgia.

Gaultheria—salal, wintergreen (150/6/2) • The berries are edible and tasty. Read more in *Foraging the Mountain West*. The leaves contain the phenolic glycoside, methyl salicylate, and like willow, it can be used as aspirin (Brown, Hall, Lust). *G. procumbens*, from the eastern U.S., was the original source of wintergreen oil, a volatile oil and spice later extracted from the twigs of black birch and finally produced synthetically (Hall). Other species may have similar properties (Harrington).

Andromeda Tribe—*Andromedeae*

Andromeda—andromeda, bog rosemary (1/1/0) *A. polifolia*. Fruit is a capsule. Native to Canada and the northeastern states. The plant contains an andromedotoxin, which lowers blood pressure and can cause respiratory problems, dizziness, vomiting, or diarrhea.

Sourwood Tribe—*Oxydendreae*

Oxydendrum—sourwood (1/1/0) *O. arboreum*. Fruit is a capsule. Native from Louisiana to New York.

Staggerbush Tribe—*Lyonieae*

Lyonia—staggerbush (30/5/0) Fruit is a capsule. Native from Texas to Maine.

Pieris—fetterbush (5/2/0) Fruit is a capsule. Native from Mississippi to Virginia.

Madrone Subfamily—*Arbutoideae*

Plants of the Madrone subfamily were formerly included within the Blueberry subfamily. The fruit is usually a berry, soft and mushy in *Arbutus*, but dry, mealy, and usually astringent in other genera.

Arbutus—madrone (20/4/0) Native from British Columbia to Texas. The big berries are edible, but hardly exciting. Medicinally, the plant contains simple phenol glycosides and tannic acid similar to *Arctostaphylos* (Moore).

Arctostaphylos—kinnikinnick, bearberry, manzanita (78/78/3) • The mealy berries are edible. The plants are rich in the astringent tannic and gallic acids and the simple phenol glycosides, arbutin and ericolin (Schauenberg). In the presence of bacteria and alkaline urine, the phenols are hydrolized in the bladder into the disinfectant hydroquinone, useful for urinary tract ulcerations and inflammation and as a solvent for calcium stones in the urinary tract. (Read about *Glycosides* in the *Medicinal Properties* section for more information.) In cases of acid urine, sodium bicarbonate must be taken with the herbs to activate the reaction. (Also read about *Tannic Acid* in the *Medicinal Properties* section of this book.)

Comarostaphylis—summer holly (10/1/0) *C. diversifolia*. Native to California. Fruit is a drupe.

Ornithostaphylos—Baja birdbush (1/1/0) *O. oppositifolia*. Native to Baja California. Fruit is a drupe.

Xylococcus—mission manzanita (1/1/0) *X. bicolor*. Native to coastal California.

134

dwarf bilberry
*Vaccinium
cespitosum*

dwarf huckleberry
Gaylussacia dumosa

oval-leaf
blueberry
*Vaccinium
ovalifolium*

wintergreen
*Gaultheria
procumbens*

whiteleaf manzanita
Arctostaphylos manzanita

Heath Family
Blueberry & Madrone Subfamilies

kinnikinnick
Arctostaphylos uva-ursi

Pacific madrone
Arbutus menziesii

135

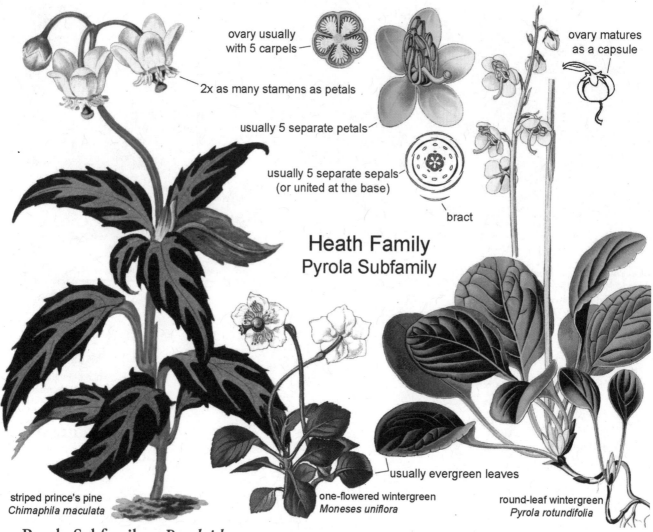

ovary usually with 5 carpels

2x as many stamens as petals

usually 5 separate petals

usually 5 separate sepals (or united at the base)

bract

ovary matures as a capsule

Heath Family
Pyrola Subfamily

usually evergreen leaves

striped prince's pine
Chimaphila maculata

one-flowered wintergreen
Moneses uniflora

round-leaf wintergreen
Pyrola rotundifolia

Pyrola Subfamily—*Pyroloideae*

The Pyrolas are forest dwellers. They thrive in the shade of others. These plants have evergreen leaves and slightly woody stems. The waxy-looking flowers are bisexual with 5 (sometimes 4) separate sepals (sometimes united at the base) and 5 (sometimes 4) separate petals. There are twice as many stamens as petals. The ovary is positioned superior and consists of 5 (sometimes 4) carpels with the partition walls present, forming an equal number of chambers. It matures as a round capsule with numerous seeds. The Pyrola subfamily has at times been classified as its own family, *Pyrolaceae*.

Key Words: Evergreen forest plants with waxy-looking flowers and parts in fives.

Chimaphila—pipsissewa, prince's pine (4/3/2) • The leaves have a mild wintergreen flavor and can be eaten as a trail nibble, brewed into a tea, or used to flavor homemade root beer. In some places pipsissewa has been overharvested as an ingredient for soft drinks. Medicinally, a tea of the leaves is astringent, diuretic, and diaphoretic, useful internally and externally (Lust).

Moneses—one-flowered wintergreen (1/1/1) *M. uniflora*. Native to the mountains and northern latitudes of North America.

Orthilia—sidebells wintergreen (3/1/1) *O. secunda*. Native to the mountains and northern latitudes of North America.

Pyrola—wintergreen, pyrola (40/7/5) • Pyrola contains tannic acid and simple phenol glycosides, especially useful as a diuretic for the kidneys and urinary tract infections (Schauenberg), and helpful for sore throats. Externally, the plant is used to stop bleeding and to heal bruises and insect bites. Its antispasmodic properties make the plant useful for nervous disorders, such as epilepsy. The chewed roots were used as throat lozenges (Willard).

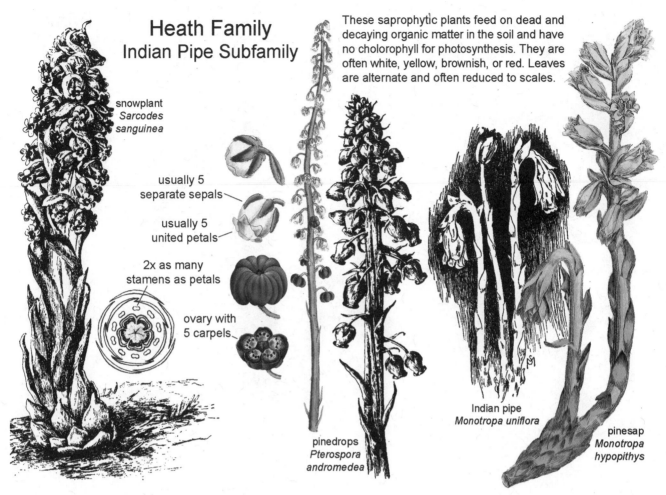

Heath Family
Indian Pipe Subfamily

These saprophytic plants feed on dead and decaying organic matter in the soil and have no cholorophyll for photosynthesis. They are often white, yellow, brownish, or red. Leaves are alternate and often reduced to scales.

snowplant
Sarcodes sanguinea

usually 5 separate sepals

usually 5 united petals

2x as many stamens as petals

ovary with 5 carpels

pinedrops
Pterospora andromedea

Indian pipe
Monotropa uniflora

pinesap
Monotropa hypopithys

Indian Pipe Subfamily—*Monotropoideae*

Have you ever found a plant that isn't green? Plants of the Indian Pipe subfamily are saprophytes, meaning that they have no chlorophyll and they feed on dead organic matter in the soil. They are often white, yellow, brownish, or even candy-striped red and white. Flowers are regular and bisexual with usually 5 (sometimes 2 to 6) separate sepals, 5 (sometimes 3 to 6) separate or united petals, and usually twice as many stamens as petals. The ovary is positioned superior and consists of usually 5 (sometimes 4 or 6) united carpels forming an equal number of chambers. It matures as a capsule. The Indian Pipe subfamily has at times been classified as its own family, *Monotropaceae*. Be sure to read about other plants lacking chlorophyll in the Broomrape and Orchid families, plus *Cuscuta* in the Morning Glory family.

Key Words: Saprophytic plants with regular flowers.

Allotropa—candystick (1/1/1) *A. virgata.* Native to the Pacific Coast states, inland to Montana.
Hemitomes—coneplant (1/1/0) *H. congestum.* Native from California to British Columbia.
Monotropa—Indian pipe, pinesap (3/2/2) • A tea of the root is antispasmodic, nervine, and sedative (Lust), suggesting the possible presence of alkaloids.
Monotropsis—pigmy pipes, sweet pinesap (2/1/0) *M. odorata.* Native to sandy pine forests of the southeastern states.
Pityopus—pinefoot (1/1/0) *P. californica.* Native from California to Washington.
Pleuricospora—fringed pinesap (1/1/0) *P. fimbriolata.* Native to deep woods from California to British Columbia.
Pterospora—pinedrops (1/1/1) • *P. andromedea.* The Cheyenne used a tea of the stems and berries to prevent bleeding from the nose and lungs (Vogel).
Sarcodes—snow plant (1/1/0) *S. sanguinea.* Native to the mountains California, Oregon, and Nevada.

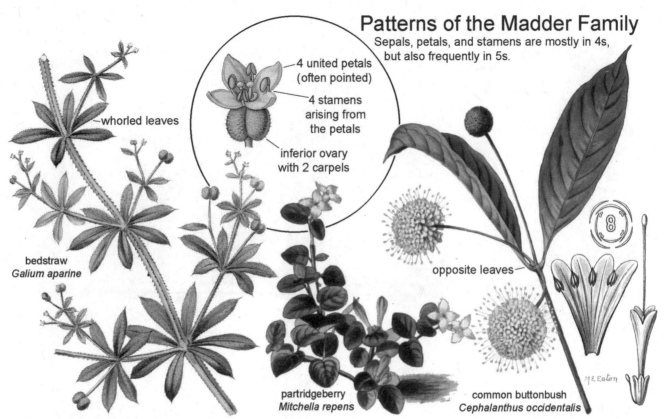

Patterns of the Madder Family
Sepals, petals, and stamens are mostly in 4s, but also frequently in 5s.

- 4 united petals (often pointed)
- 4 stamens arising from the petals
- inferior ovary with 2 carpels

whorled leaves

bedstraw
Galium aparine

opposite leaves

partridgeberry
Mitchella repens

common buttonbush
Cephalanthus occidentalis

M.E.Eaton

Madder Family—*Rubiaceae*

If you are a coffee drinker, then the Madder family could be a real eye-opener. Coffee beans (*Coffea*) contain caffeine, a purine-type alkaloid that stimulates production of hormones, including adrenaline. Botanically, plants of the madder family have simple, usually opposite, or sometimes whorled leaves. An outgrowth called a stipule is often found along the stem between each set of leaves. Flowers are regular and bisexual with 4 or 5 (sometimes 0) separate or united sepals, 4 or 5 united petals (often pointed), and 4 or 5 stamens. The ovary is positioned inferior (rarely superior) and consists of 2 (sometimes 4) united carpels with partition walls present, forming an equal number of chambers. The ovary matures as a capsule or berry with numerous seeds in most species, but as a 2-seeded fruit in *Galium* that looks like fuzzy, green testicles.

The Madder family is large, consisting of about 600 genera and 13,000 species of mostly trees and shrubs in tropical climates. About 20 genera, mostly herbs, are native to North America, primarily in Florida. Genera listed below are widespread, especially bedstraw (*Galium*).

Key Words: Opposite or whorled leaves, with 4 (or 5) united petals, and an ovary with 2 carpels.

Cephalanthus—button bush (10/2/0) Native to moist habitats from Texas to Ontario, east to the Atlantic.

Galium—bedstraw, cleavers (300/78/6) • Squarish stems. *G. aparine* is a fun plant to play with. The vines are covered with Velcro-like stickers that cling to the clothing of whomever you throw them at! The common name "bedstraw" comes from the practice of filling mattresses with the plants. Apparently the plants do not pack down flat, but retain some loft.

The young shoots are edible as a salad green or potherb (Hall), but hairy species may irritate the throat. A tea of the plant is recommended for dissolving calcium stones and as a general diuretic, astringent (Willard), anti-inflammatory, and lymphatic tonic. Pure bedstraw juice is considered very beneficial for stomach ulcers (Tilford). Bedstraw is also useful for modest healing without irritation in cases of hepatitis (Moore). The roots of some species yield a bright red dye (Willard). Sweet-scented bedstraw (*G. odoratum)* contains high levels of coumarins (Duke).

Houstonia—bluets (38/18/0) Various species of bluets grow from the East Coast to the Midwest and across the southern states.

Mitchella—partridge berry (3/1/0) *M. repens*. Native from Texas to Ontario, east to the Atlantic. Twin flowers are joined at the ovaries, producing a single berry. The berry is edible, but nearly tasteless. The plant is used medicinally to tone the prostate and womb (Cook).

Patterns of the Gentian Family

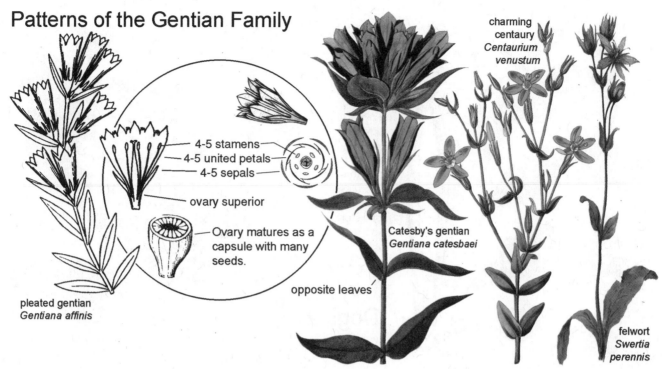

4-5 stamens
4-5 united petals
4-5 sepals

ovary superior

Ovary matures as a capsule with many seeds.

charming centaury
Centaurium venustum

Catesby's gentian
Gentiana catesbaei

opposite leaves

pleated gentian
Gentiana affinis

felwort
Swertia perennis

Gentian Family—*Gentianaceae*

Gentians are as beautiful as they are bitter. The plants have mostly opposite leaves, but species of *Frasera* have leaves in whorls of three or four. The flowers are mostly bisexual and regular and often twisted in the bud stage. There are usually 5 (sometimes 4) separate sepals, 5 (sometimes 4) united petals, and a similar number of stamens, which are attached to the petals and alternate with the lobes. The ovary is positioned superior. It consists of 2 united carpels forming a single chamber. It matures as a capsule with many seeds.

Worldwide, there are 87 genera and 1,500 species. Thirteen genera are native to North America, including *Bartonia, Eustoma, Obolaria, Nymphoides, Sabbatia* and the genera listed below. Most members of the Gentian family contain potent bitter principles that stimulate the digestive system. Read more in the *Medicinal Properties* section of this book.

Key Words: Plants with opposite leaves and tubular flowers with parts in 4s or 5s.

Centaurium—centaury (40/15/1) The plant stimulates digestion, benefiting the liver and kidneys; also used as a diaphoretic (Hutchins).

Frasera—deer's tongue (15/13/2) • The plant is mildly bitter, while the raw root is emetic and cathartic. The dried, powdered root is used as a bitter, but large doses can be fatal (Fern). The seeds are very bitter.

Gentiana—gentian (200/56/7) • Gentian roots contain some of the most bitter compounds known in the plant world, previously used in beer-making and medicines (Fern). The root or chopped herb is steeped for use as a bitter tonic for indigestion and as an appetite stimulant (Moore). Gentian is used as a blood-builder to increase the number of white blood cells (Lust). It is also used to expel worms (Bigfoot). Excess consumption can lead to nausea, vomiting or diarrhea.

Gentianella—dwarf gentian (275/10/5) Similar to the true gentians (*Gentiana*).

Halenia—spurred gentian (47/2/1) Native to northern states and provinces and the southern Rocky Mountains.

Lomatogonium—marsh felwort (18/1/1) *L. rotatum*. Native from Alaska to Maine and south through the Rocky Mountains.

Swertia—felwort (100/15/1) *S. perennis*. The powdered, dried root is steeped for a bitter tonic; it is stronger than *Gentiana*, potentially laxative or cathartic. The root can be used as a fungicide for ringworm, athlete's foot, also for lice and scabies (Moore). The leaves may be toxic (Bigfoot).

soapwort gentian
Gentiana saponaria

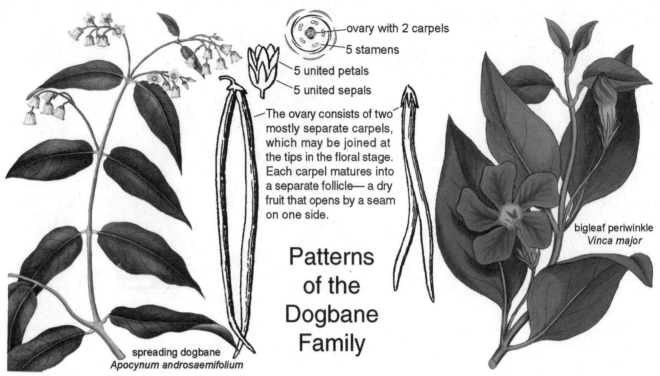

ovary with 2 carpels
5 stamens
5 united petals
5 united sepals

The ovary consists of two mostly separate carpels, which may be joined at the tips in the floral stage. Each carpel matures into a separate follicle— a dry fruit that opens by a seam on one side.

Patterns of the Dogbane Family

bigleaf periwinkle
Vinca major

spreading dogbane
Apocynum androsaemifolium

Dogbane Family—*Apocynaceae*

The herbs, shrubs, and trees of the Dogbane family have opposite leaves (rarely alternate) and a milky, latex sap. Most are poisonous to some degree. The flowers are bisexual and regular, with 5 united sepals, 5 united petals, and 5 stamens. Stamens attach at the base of the petals, alternate with the lobes. The ovary is positioned wholly or mostly superior. It consists of 2 carpels, usually separate in North American genera, united only at the styles. Each carpel matures as a separate follicle, a dry, pod-like fruit with a seam down one side. There are many seeds, often with a tuft of hair attached at one end. Some genera produce berries or capsules.

The traditional family included about 200 genera and 2,000 species, including 11 genera in North America, mostly in Florida. Periwinkle (*Vinca*) is often used in landscaping. The oleander (*Nerium oleander)* is grown as an ornamental (and toxic) shrub in warmer parts of our country. Oleander contains cardiac glycosides (Geller). Children have died after roasting hot dogs on the sticks. Taxonomists have reclassified the former Milkweed family as a subfamily of the Dogbanes, greatly expanding the size of the family.

Key Words: Plants with opposite leaves and milky juice. Tubular flowers with parts in 5s.

Amsonia—blue star (18/18/0) Native to the southern states, often cultivated.

Apocynum—dogbane (7/6/3) • The bark contains durable fibers that can be spun into cordage. Common dogbane (*A. cannabinum)* is tallest and best to work with. (Learn how in *Participating in Nature*.) Common dogbane is more potent than other species and should not be used medicinally (Moore). The root of *A. androsaemifolium* is used internally as a vasoconstrictor. It raises blood pressure and slows, but strengthens, the heart rate. It is a potent diuretic, an irritating stimulant to the kidneys. Externally the root can be used as an irritating poultice to stimulate blood flow (vasodilator) and speed healing, or as a rinse to irritate the scalp and stimulate hair growth (Moore). Dogbane contains resins, a volatile oil, a bitter substance (Densmore) and cardiac glycosides (Phillips). It should not be used internally by amateurs.

Haplophyton—cockroach plant (1/1/0) *H. crooksii.* The milky sap or dried leaves are mixed with molasses as a poison for cockroaches, flies, and lice, and as a lotion to repel mosquitoes and fleas.

Mandevilla (*Macrosiphonia*)—rock trumpet (4/4/0) Native from Arizona to Texas.

Trachelospermum—climbing dogbane (11/2/0) Grows from Texas to Virginia.

Vinca—periwinkle (5/2/1) • *Vinca* and *Catharanthus* are closely related and both called periwinkle. They are often cultivated, but escape into the wild. *Vinca* is used medicinally as an internal astringent for excess menstruation, hemorrhoids, bleeding ulcers and diarrhea (Willard). As a capillary constrictor it may be useful for migraine headaches (Tilford). The dried leaves have been smoked as a hallucinogen, but with serious side effects. It causes an immediate reduction in the white blood cell count and makes the hair fall out (Emboden). Vinblastine and vincristine are two indole alkaloids derived from a species of periwinkle that are used in the treatment of blood and lymph cancers.

Dogbane Family / Milkweed Subfamily

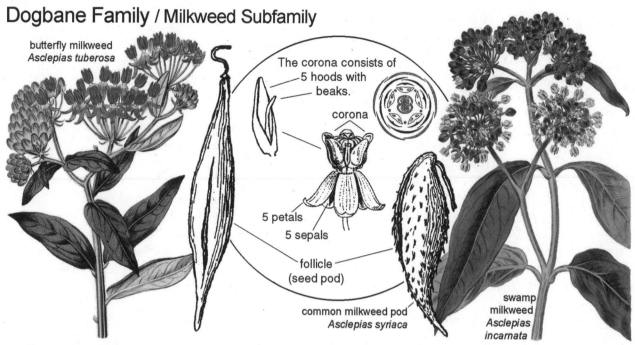

butterfly milkweed
Asclepias tuberosa

The corona consists of 5 hoods with beaks.

corona

5 petals

5 sepals

follicle (seed pod)

common milkweed pod
Asclepias syriaca

swamp milkweed
Asclepias incarnata

Milkweed Subfamily—*Asclepiadoideae*

Milkweeds are perennial herbs, shrubs, or rarely trees, usually with acrid, milky juice and opposite or sometimes whorled leaves. The flowers are bisexual and regular, typically grouped in clusters. There are 5 separate sepals and 5 united petals, plus in some species a corona that looks like an extra set of petals. The corona consists of 5 hood-like forms facing towards the center of the flower. Inside the corona there are 5 stamens fused to the ovary. The ovary is positioned superior. It consists of 2 mostly-separate carpels. Each carpel, or often only one by abortion, matures as a separate follicle, a pod-like dry fruit with a seam down one side. The pods are filled with numerous seeds with silky tufts. Traditionally, the Milkweeds were classified as an independent family, *Asclepiadaceae*, but taxonomists now believe the Milkweeds arose from within the Dogbane family. Worldwide, there are 250 genera and 2,000 species, mostly native to the tropics. The waxplant (*Hoya*) is a common houseplant from this subfamily. There are 5 genera in North America, including *Cynanchum*, *Gonolobus*, *Matelea*, and *Sarcostemma*.

Key Words: Plants with opposite leaves, milky juice, and big pods. Irregular, crown-like flowers.

Asclepias—milkweed (140/77/5) • The young stalks of the common milkweed (*A. syriaca*) and showy milkweed (*A. speciosa*) can be cooked much like asparagus: put the stalks in a pan of water and simmer for fifteen or twenty minutes, then drain off the water. Coincidentally, the taste is similar to asparagus, too. Do not eat the milkweed if it is bitter. It may be the wrong species, a different variety, or possibly dogbane.

It was once believed that milkweed was poisonous raw and needed to be placed in several changes of boiling water to remove its poisonous properties. With a reputation like that, many foragers like myself never bothered to mess with it at all. But fortunately, Sam Thayer, author of *The Forager's Harvest*, experimented with milkweed enough to find that it wasn't bitter and didn't require any special preparation. This widespread disbelief may have started when one forager mistook dogbane for milkweed and tried to remove its bitterness through repeated boiling. The mistake was then copied and pasted into nearly every foraging book since, without anyone testing the original assumption (Thayer). The blossoms are high in sugar and can be boiled down to make a syrup (Willard).

Medicinally, at least some milkweeds have a bitter latex sap that can be used to irritate and stimulate the body. The boiled root dilates the bronchioles, stimulating lymph drainage from the lungs for lung infections. It is used as a menstrual stimulant, lactose stimulant, laxative, bitter diuretic, diaphoretic and expectorant. The root powder can be snuffed to promote sneezing to clear the sinuses. Some species may produce nausea (Moore). Long-term consumption may lead to depression or death (Willard). The latex sap can be applied repeatedly to remove a wart (Hutchins). A boiled tea of the herb applied to the eyes may have some effect on blindness (Hart).

Butterfly weed (*A. tuberosa*) is diaphoretic, carminative, expectorant, and diuretic. A tea of the dried or cooked root is used for colds, flu, and bronchitis. The raw root may be poisonous (Lust).

Milkweed, particularly *A. speciosa*, is an excellent fiber plant like its cousin the dogbane. It produces beautiful, silky, white cordage. This species can frequently be found growing in semi-moist ditches along the highways.

Borage Family—*Boraginaceae*

If you have ever found flat, teardrop-shaped burrs stuck on your clothes, then you have met one member of the Borage family, known as beggarstick or houndstongue (*Cynoglossum*). Plants of this family are often rough and hairy, usually with simple, alternate leaves. The flower spikes often curl like a scorpion's tail, with flowers blooming on the upper surface. Individual flowers are bisexual and mostly regular. They have 5 separate sepals and 5 united petals. There are 5 stamens, which are attached to the corolla tube, alternate with the petals. The ovary is positioned superior. It consists of 2 united carpels, but false partitions may make the ovary appear 4-chambered. It typically matures as 4 separate nutlets or sometimes achenes (dry seeds). Some genera produce fewer than 4 nutlets due to abortion. You may be able to see the aborted nutlets around the developing ones.

Worldwide, the traditional Borage family included approximately 100 genera and about 2,000 species, including about 22 genera in North America. Taxonomists have expanded the family to include the previously separate Waterleaf family as a subfamily, which retains its own description on the following page. Hairs on the vegetation may irritate the skin and cause dermatitis on some individuals. Medicinally, these plants are mildly astringent, good internally as tea or externally as a poultice for any wounds or excretions that need an astringent to tighten up tissues. Some species are mildly mucilaginous, useful for their emollient properties. However, many species contain minute amounts of poisonous alkaloids and may be toxic with sustained use.

Key Words: Hairy plants with flower parts in fives. Four nutlets.

Amsinckia—fiddleneck (20/14/2) The seeds are reported to be edible when ground on a metate and used as flour (Olsen). The protective hairs may irritate the skin. The seeds may be poisonous to cattle (Kinucan).

Anchusa—Alkanet (35/3/3) Introduced. The leaves of at least some species are edible as a salad green (Sturtevant). *A. officinale* contains alkaloids, tannin and mucilage, used internally as an expectorant, "blood purifier," and to stop diarrhea. (Schauenberg).

Asperugo—catchweed, German madwort (1/1/1) • *A. procumbens*. Introduced from Europe.

Borago—borage (3/1/1) • *B. officinale*. This is a European herb often cultivated in the U.S. The very young leaves can be used in salads or as potherbs. The plants have mucilaginous, astringent, diuretic and diaphoretic properties. It is used to reduce fevers, stimulate milk production and calm nerves. As with other members of this family, long-term consumption is not recommended.

Cryptantha—miner's candle (150/113/13) • Native to western North America.

Cynoglossum—houndstongue, beggarstick (68/6/1) • No doubt you have pulled the flat, tear-drop-shaped seeds of this plant from your socks or woolens. *C. officinale* is a European weed that is now widespread across this country. Medicinally, hound's tongue contains allantoin (Tilford). The plant or root is principally astringent and demulcent, useful externally as a poultice for burns, internally for sore throat or diarrhea (Hutchins). Hound's tongue is similar to comfrey (Moore) and includes similar, potentially carcinogenic alkaloids (Tilford). One alkaloid, cynoglossine, is toxic to cold-blood animals, but has little effect on mammals (Schauenberg); it may be useful as a fish poison.

Eritrichium—alpine forget-me-not (25/3/2) • Native to the mountain West.

Hackelia—stickseed forget-me-not (40/25/5) •

Heliotropium—heliotrope (220/23/1) A tea of the plant was reportedly taken as an emetic (Murphey). A European species contains a poisonous alkaloid (Pammel).

Lithospermum—stoneseed, gromwell (50/18/3) • Native Americans reportedly ate the root of *L. incisum* (Craighead), and *L. linearifolium* (A. Brown). However, some species of gromwell contain toxic alkaloids and estrogen-like compounds that interfere with hormonal balances in the female reproductive system (Tilford). Some species were used by Native American women as a female contraceptive. Extended use may cause sterility (Vogel).

Mertensia—bluebell (40/23/8) • On camping trips, I often do my cooking in an old tin miner's gold pan. Some species of bluebells have wide leaves that serve well as a lid on my pan for steaming foods. I eat bluebell leaves in limited quantities. They seem mildly astringent and mucilaginous.

Myosotis—forget-me-not (80/10/3) • Native and introduced species are found across North America.

Symphytum—comfrey (17/4/1) • Comfrey is often planted domestically for its herbal properties. The root and leaves are astringent, mucilaginous and contain allantoin, useful externally on cuts and burns, and internally as an expectorant and demulcent. The astringency makes comfrey useful for stopping bleeding and healing ulcers, while the mucilage soothes the irritated tissues. Comfrey contains pyrrolizidine alkaloids which are toxic to the liver tissues. Toxicity is variable from species to species. People have died from chronic use of this herb (Tyler), but many herbalists consider it safe in moderation.

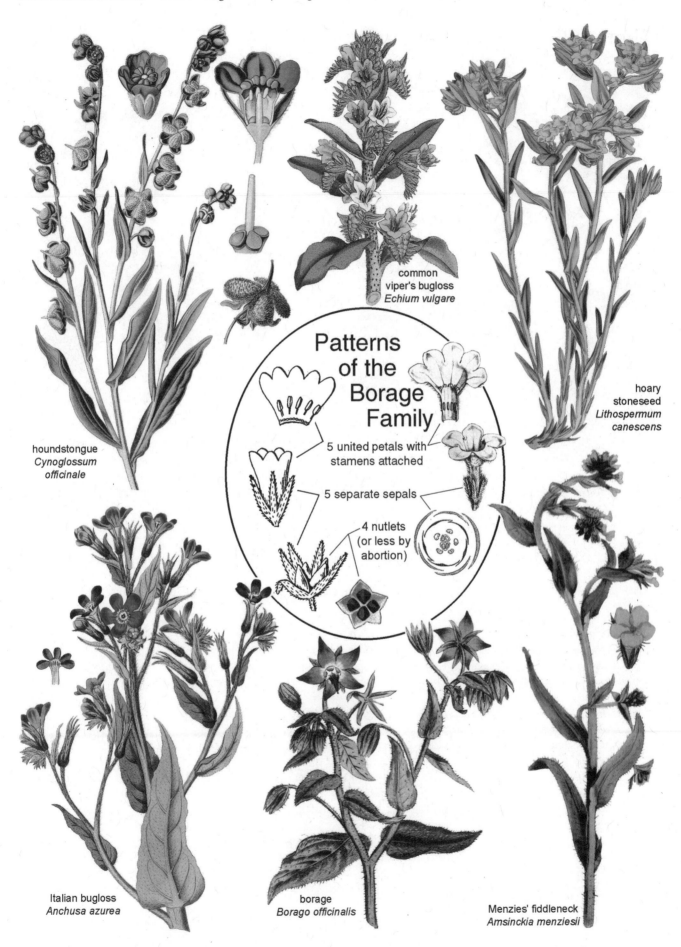

common
viper's bugloss
Echium vulgare

houndstongue
*Cynoglossum
officinale*

hoary
stoneseed
*Lithospermum
canescens*

Patterns
of the
Borage
Family

5 united petals with
stamens attached

5 separate sepals

4 nutlets
(or less by
abortion)

Italian bugloss
Anchusa azurea

borage
Borago officinalis

Menzies' fiddleneck
Amsinckia menziesii

Borage Family
Waterleaf Subfamily

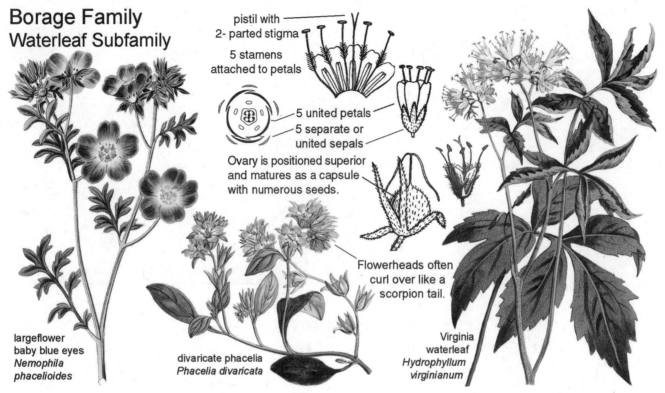

pistil with
2- parted stigma

5 stamens
attached to petals

5 united petals
5 separate or
united sepals

Ovary is positioned superior
and matures as a capsule
with numerous seeds.

Flowerheads often
curl over like a
scorpion tail.

largeflower
baby blue eyes
*Nemophila
phacelioides*

divaricate phacelia
Phacelia divaricata

Virginia
waterleaf
*Hydrophyllum
virginianum*

Waterleaf Subfamily—*Hydrophylloideae*

More than other members of the Borage family, the Waterleafs are typically hairy and the flower spikes often curl over like a scorpion tail. These are usually small plants. The flowers are regular and bisexual with 5 separate or united sepals, 5 united petals, and 5 stamens attached to the base of the petals. The stamens typically dangle beyond the petals, giving the flowers a dainty appearance. The ovary is positioned superior. It consists of 2 (rarely 4) united carpels, usually forming a single chamber. It matures as a capsule with a variable number of seeds. The Waterleafs were formerly considered an independent family, *Hydrophyllaceae*, but taxonomists now classify them as a subfamily of the Borage family. Worldwide, there are 20 genera and 270 species. North American genera are listed blow. Note that some common names overlap between the Waterleafs and the Borages.

Key Words: Small, hairy plants with parts in fives, united.

Draperia—draperia (1/1/0) *D. systyla*. Native to the mountains of northern California.

Ellisia—Aunt Lucy (1/1/0) *E. nyctelea*. Native across much of North America.

Emmenanthe—whispering bells (1/1/0) *E. penduliflora*. Native to the desert southwest.

Eriodictyon—mountain balm, yerba santa (9/8/0) The plant contains resins and phenols; it is smoked or made into tea for use as an expectorant and bronchial dilator. It is used for mild urinary tract infections (Moore).

Eucrypta—hideseed (2/2/0) Native to the desert southwest.

Hesperochiron—hesperochiron (2/2/2) Native from the Rocky Mountains west to the Pacific.

Hydrophyllum—waterleaf (9/9/1) • The leaves and shoots are edible in a salad. The roots are edible cooked (Kirk).

Nama (including *Lemmonia*)—fiddleleaf (21/21/0) Native from the Pacific Coast east to Montana and Louisiana.

Nemophila—baby blue eyes (11/11/1) • Native to the West and South.

Phacelia—phacelia, scorpionweed, heliotrope (140/130/8) • *P. racemosissima* was reportedly used by Native Americans as a potherb (Kinucan). The flowers of some species have a unique smell that is sweet to some people and very offensive to others. The name heliotrope is also used in the borage family.

Pholistoma—fiestaflower (3/3/0) Native to the Southwest.

Romanzoffia—mist maiden (5/5/1) Native from Alaska to California and Montana.

Tricardia—threehearts (1/1/0) *T. watsonii*. Native to the Southwest.

Turricula—poodle-dog bush (1/1/1) *T. parryi*. Native to the mountains of southern California. The vegetation can cause severe irritation, dermatitis, and blisters when touched.

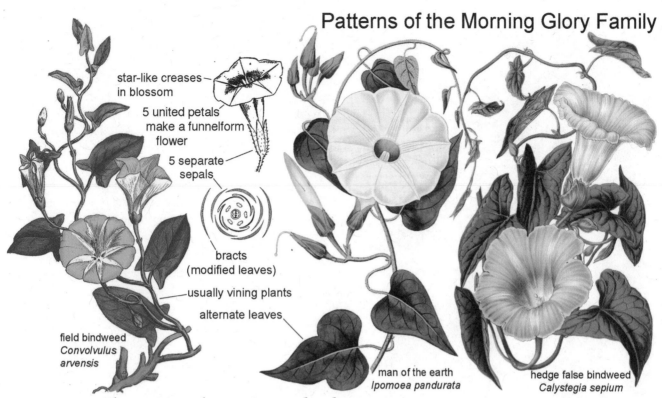

Patterns of the Morning Glory Family

star-like creases in blossom

5 united petals make a funnelform flower

5 separate sepals

bracts (modified leaves)

usually vining plants

alternate leaves

field bindweed
Convolvulus arvensis

man of the earth
Ipomoea pandurata

hedge false bindweed
Calystegia sepium

Morning Glory Family—*Convolvulaceae*

Morning Glories get noticed. You may have some in your yard or neighborhood already. These are often vining plants with alternate leaves and funnel-like flowers with a star-like pattern of creases embossed in the petals. The flowers are regular and bisexual with 5 separate sepals and 5 united petals. There are 5 stamens attached at the base of the flower tube. The ovary is positioned superior. It consists of 2 (sometimes 3 to 5) united carpels with the partition walls present, forming an equal number of chambers. It matures as a capsule with 1 to 2 seeds per carpel. Worldwide, there are about 60 genera and 1,650 species. The sweet potato is *Ipomoea batatas*. The seeds of *I. tricolor* and *Turbina corymbosa* contain ergoline alkaloids with psychedelic properties, producing a similar effect to LSD in large doses. (Read about ergot fungus in the Grass family.) Seeds from commercial sources are often coated in toxic pesticides.

Key Words: Usually vining plants with star-like creases in funnelform flowers.

Calystegia—false bindweed (25/17/4) Similar to *Convolvulus*.
Convolvulus—bindweed (250/28/2) • The bindweeds contain glycosides with potent purgative properties (Pammel).
Cressa—alkaliweed (5/2/0) Found in alkaline soils, mostly in the Southwest.
Cuscuta—dodder (170/46/7) • Dodder is a parasitic plant. It attaches itself to another plant, wraps itself around it, and taps into the host's vascular system to feed, ultimately allowing its own roots to die off. At maturity, the plant is generally yellow-orange in color, with no apparent roots or leaves. It has sometimes been segregated into its own family, *Cuscutaceae*.
Dichondra—ponysfoot (10/8/0) Ponysfoot forms a dense mat, often used as a grass substitute for southern lawns.
Evolvulus—dwarf morning glory (64/7/1) Native to the Great Plains and South.
Ipomoea—morning glory, man of the earth, sweet potato (400/51/1) • Many species have enlarged, starchy taproots that are generally edible, but sometimes bitter due to a milky sap in the fresh roots. The bush morning glory (*I. leptophylla*) of the Great Plains can have roots 1 foot thick and 4 feet deep. The boiled or roasted root is reported to be exceptional, but older plants may be bitter (Harrington). The wild potato vine (*I. pandurata*) of the southeastern states also has large roots. It is edible, but may require a couple changes of the water to remove the bitterness (Hall).
  Medicinally, the root of *I. jalapa* is listed as cathartic (Lust). The seeds of many *Ipomoea* species have psycho-active properties (Emboden). Note that the yam (*Dioscorea*) is a monocot vine with its own family, *Dioscoreaceae*.
Jacquemontia—clustervine (46/5/0) These species are mostly native to Florida and the southeastern states. They can be confused with *Convolvulus*.
Merremia—woodrose (58/6/0) Native to the coastal plain from Florida to Texas.
Stylisma—(6/6/0) Native to the southeastern states.

red pepper
Capsicum annuum

Nightshade Family—*Solanaceae*

The Nightshade family is as familiar as the petunia (*Petunia*) and tomato (*Solanum lycopersicum*). These are mostly herbs (sometimes vines, shrubs, or trees) with alternate, often fuzzy leaves and colorless juice. Memorize the texture of a petunia leaf to aid in identifying many wild members of this family. The flowers are typically solitary, bisexual, and regular with usually 5 united sepals and 5 united petals (rarely 3 to 7 of each). Flowers vary from funnel-form, like the petunia, to reflexed, with only partially united petals, like a tomato blossom. There are 5 (rarely 4 to 7) stamens attached to the petals. The ovary is positioned superior. It consists of usually 2 united carpels with the partition walls often present, forming an equal number of chambers (sometimes more, due to false partitions, exceptions, or breeding). Cut across a maturing fruit, such as the capsule of a petunia, and you will usually see two chambers inside. Tomatoes and peppers are highly variable due to breeding.

Worldwide, there are about 85 genera and 2,300 species, including many popular food plants. Many varieties of hot peppers come from *Capsicum*. *Physalis* is the tomatillo. *Solanum* includes the potato (*S. tuberosum*) and eggplant (*S. melongena*).

The Nightshade family is rich in alkaloids. Solanine is the bitter glyco-alkaloid found in green potato skins, as well as the vegetation and fruits of most *Solanum* species. In large amounts (several pounds of green potatoes) it can cause vomiting, diarrhea, headaches, and possible paralysis of the central nervous system. Children are more vulnerable than adults. Many Nightshades also include narcotic alkaloids, some addictive, such as nicotine from tobacco (*Nicotiana*). Most narcotic alkaloids are useful as analgesics to numb the body's sense of pain. In addition, scopolamine is used to treat seasickness or vertigo. Soldiers in the Persian Gulf War carried the alkaloid atropine with them as a treatment for nerve gas attacks (Duke). The juice of *Atropa* was used by Italian ladies as eye drops to dilate the pupils, hence the common name belladonna, meaning "fair-lady" (Klein).

Some narcotic Nightshades can cause hallucinations, including *Atropa*, *Datura*, *Hyoscyamus* and *Mandragora*. Our European heritage of witches flying on broomsticks comes from these hallucinogenic plants. An ointment containing *Atropa* and *Hyoscyamus* was rubbed on the broomstick then absorbed through the vaginal tissues by "riding" the broom (Emboden). The "witches" then experienced "flying." These plants are highly poisonous, with a toxicity that varies from plant to plant. People have died using Nightshades as psychedelics. Symptoms of poisoning include an unquenchable thirst, dilation of the pupils, delirium, hallucinations, convulsions and coma.

Key Words: Alternate leaves. Flower parts in fives with united petals and a two-chambered ovary.

Atropa—belladonna (4/1/0) *A. bella-donna.* Introduced.
Bouchetia—painted tongue (4/1/0) *B. erecta.* Native to Texas.
Browallia—bush violet (7/2/0) *B. eludens* is native to Arizona. *B. americana* is introduced from Jamaica.
Calibrachoa—seaside petunia (28/1/0) *C. parviflora.* Native from Oregon to Virginia and south.
Capsicum—bell pepper, chili pepper, pimento, jalapeno, cayenne, tabasco (35/1/0) • *C. annuum* is the native pepper, which has been bred into many varieties, including bell peppers, chili peppers, cayenne peppers, banana peppers, jalapeno, pequins, and more. Spicy peppers contain capsaicin, which stimulates sensory receptors that normally respond to heat or pain, creating the illusory sensation of heat. Repeated exposure to capsaicin reduces sensitivity of the nerves, increasing tolerence for spicy food. Used as a topical treatment, capsaicin also reduces sensitivity, providing pain relief for arthritis and other inflammatory disorders. It works by depleting "substance P," the compound that mediates transmission of pain impulses from the peripheral nerves to the spinal cord. Capsaicin doesn't stop the pain, but it prevents the signal from reaching the brain. It is especially helpful for people who still feel pain weeks or months after surgery. A commercial product is marketed as "Capsaicin P." It takes about three days to become effective. Cayenne pepper is good

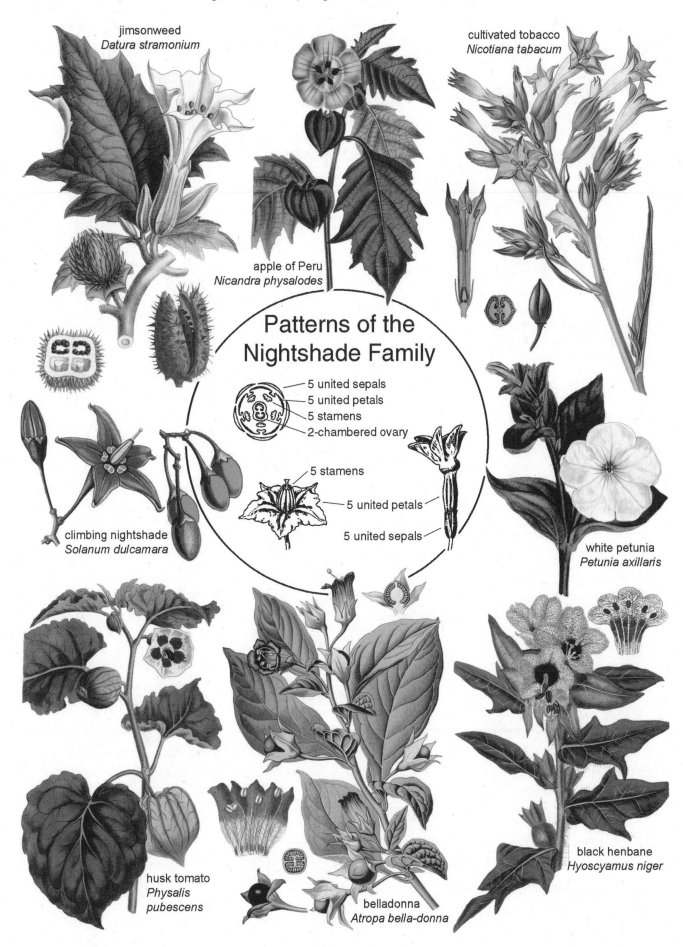

jimsonweed
Datura stramonium

apple of Peru
Nicandra physalodes

cultivated tobacco
Nicotiana tabacum

Patterns of the Nightshade Family

5 united sepals
5 united petals
5 stamens
2-chambered ovary

5 stamens

5 united petals

5 united sepals

climbing nightshade
Solanum dulcamara

white petunia
Petunia axillaris

husk tomato
*Physalis
pubescens*

belladonna
Atropa bella-donna

black henbane
Hyoscyamus niger

147

to have in the first aid kit. Internally, it increases circulation, stimulates digestion and helps to treat shock. Externally, the powder can be applied to stop bleeding, reduce pain and increase circulation (Sheff).

Chamaesaracha—five eyes (9/7/0) Native to the southwest. The fruits of at least some species are edible when cooked.

Datura—Jimsonweed, thorn-apple (18/7/1) • Narcotic. Contains scopolamine, hyoscyamine, and atropine. *Datura* is a dangerous plant, and many individuals have died from misusing it. Do not ingest any part of the plant, period. A small amount of smoke from the leaves numbs and relaxes the bronchials for asthma and bronchitis, and it brings temporary sinus relief. A poultice or bath of the fresh plant is used for its analgesic properties (aching joints, etc.). However, an extended bath can result in absorption of alkaloids through the skin and lead to drowsiness (Moore). The poultice may have some effect on rattlesnake or tarantula bites (Hutchins).

Hunzikeria—cupflower (3/1/0) *H. texana*. Native to Texas.

Hyoscyamus—henbane (15/1/1) • *H. niger*. Introduced from Europe. It is now widespread in areas of disturbed soils. My grandmother picked henbane during World War II. It was used as an analgesic for wounded soldiers. Henbane contains atropine, hyoscyamin, and scopolamine (Schauenberg). It should never be eaten. The plant is used similarly to *Datura* (Hutchins).

Jaltomata—false holly (27/1/0) *J. procumbens*. Native to Arizona.

Lycium—wolfberry, boxthorn, goji berry (110/19/1) • The red, tomato-like berries are edible fresh or cooked. The fruit isn't sweet, and palatability varies from species to species, but it is one of few berries available in the desert southwest. I have picked them in quantity in Arizona. The commercially available goji berries come from the introduced *L. barbarum* and *L. chinense*.

Nectouxia—stinkleaf (1/1/0) *N. formosa*. Native to Texas and Mexico.

Nicandra—apple of Peru (1/1/0) *N. physalodes*. Introduced from Peru. The sepals encompass the fruit like *Physalis*.

goji berry
Lycium barbarum

Nicotiana—tobacco (100/15/1) • Wild tobacco is rare in the North, but fairly common in the South. The fresh herb is used as a poultice or bath for an analgesic. The leaves can be smoked (Moore). Nicotine is a toxic alkaloid, chemically similar to the poisonous water hemlock. It was once used as a pesticide, but caused numerous human fatalities (Schauenberg). It should never be taken internally.

Oryctes—oryctes (1/1/0) *O. nevadensis*. A rare plant native to the California-Nevada border.

Petunia—petunia (14/2/0) • Introduced. Sometimes included within *Nicotiana*. The flowers may be used as an edible garnish.

Physalis (including *Margaranthus*)— husk tomato, ground cherry, tomatillo (110/34/3) • The sepals enlarge to loosely encompass the developing fruit. Most (not all) species produce edible fruits. The tomatillo (*P. philadelphica*), commonly used in green salsa, originated in Mexico. Wild ground cherries I have found produce yellow fruits. They are initially sweet, but with a slightly bitter, lingering after taste. I think they are a real treat when I can find them. The fruit can be used for salsa or made into pie (Lincoff). Green fruits should not be eaten raw (Bigfoot).

Quincula—Chinese lantern (1/1/0) *Q. lobata*. Sometimes included in *Physalis*. Native from California to Texas and Kansas.

Solanum—(including *Lycopersicon*) nightshade, bittersweet, potato, eggplant, buffalobur, tomato (1500/40/5) • Carl Linnaeus classified the tomato as *S. lycopersicum* in 1753. It was later segregated into its own genus, *Lycopersicon*. But the original name has been restored based on genetics.

buffalobur nightshade
Solanum rostratum

Most cultivated potatoes are varieties of *S. tuberosum*, originally from the Andes. Most species of *Solanum* contain the toxic alkaloid solanine, especially in green parts of the plants (such as green potato peels). The wild potato (*S. jamesii*) is native to southwestern states. While camping in Arizona I was surprised and delighted to dig up one of these small (marble-sized) wild potatoes while building a primitive shelter.

The introduced black nightshade (*S. nigrum*) has edible black berries, but American black nightshade (*S. americanum*) as well as species with green or red tomato-like berries are toxic. Members of this genus are used externally as an analgesic poultice or bath (Hutchins). The fresh plant is too dangerous to be used internally without expert assistance.

148

Patterns of the Olive Family

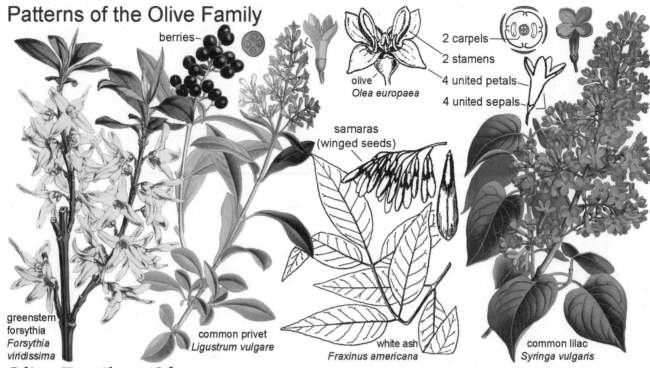

berries

2 carpels
2 stamens
4 united petals
4 united sepals

olive
Olea europaea

samaras
(winged seeds)

greenstem
forsythia
*Forsythia
viridissima*

common privet
Ligustrum vulgare

white ash
Fraxinus americana

common lilac
Syringa vulgaris

Olive Family—*Oleaceae*

The Olive family is often close at hand. Ash trees (*Fraxinus*) provide summer shade on college campuses and city streets in northern latitudes. Lilacs (*Syringa*) and *Forsythia* dazzle yards and parks with an early spring show of flowers. In Mediterranean climates, olive trees (*Olea*) draw attention with their grey leaves and purple-black fruits that are often mashed into the ground below. Stop and take a closer look. Most members of the family are shrubs and trees, generally deciduous in northern latitudes and evergreen in the South. The leaves are usually opposite, sometimes on squarish stems, as in *Forsythia* above. The flowers are regular, bisexual, and often aromatic. There are typically 4 (rarely 5 or more) united sepals and 4 (rarely 0, 5, or more) united petals, plus usually 2 (rarely 4, 5, or more) stamens. The ovary is positioned superior and consists of 2 united carpels with the partition walls present, forming 2 chambers. It matures as a capsule, a pair of winged seeds, a drupe (a fleshy fruit with a stony pit like the olive), or rarely as a berry. Worldwide, there are about 29 genera and about 600 species. Jasmine fragrance comes from *Jasminum* (page 221). Many genera are cultivated.

Key Words: Shrubs or trees with opposite leaves and 4 sepals, 4 petals, and 2 stamens.

Chionanthus—fringetree (80/2/0) Flower petals are long and sometimes thread-like. The fruit is a blue-purple drupe, prepared like an olive. Native from Texas to New York.

Forestiera—swampprivet (20/8/0) 4, 5, or more stamens. The fruit is a blue-purple drupe, prepared like an olive. Native to the southern half of North America.

Forsythia—forsythia (11/3/1) • Yellow flowers may emerge prior to leaves. Fruit is a capsule. Introduced and widely cultivated.

Fraxinus—Ash (60/16/2) • Some species lack petals. The fruit is a winged seed. Native and introduced species are found across North America. Ash is stimulating, diaphoretic, diuretic and laxative. Drink a tea of the inner bark for depression or tiredness; a strong tea for a laxative (Willard). A tea of the bark is used to reduce fever and to expel worms (Lust).

Ligustrum—privet (50/8/1) The flowers look similar to lilacs (*Syringa*), but the odor is unpleasant and the fruit is an inedible purple berry. Introduced and sometimes invasive. The plant is considered poisonous to horses.

Menodora—menodora (23/5/0) 5 to 10 sepals and 4 to 6 petals. Fruit is a capsule. Native from California to Texas.

Olea—Olive (20/1/0) • *O. europaea*. Introduced. The green-purple-black fruits are bitter fresh, but the bitterness can be leached out in a saltwater brine or by a variety of other methods. Medicinally, olive oil is used internally as a laxative, or externally as an emollient to soothe the skin (Lust). It is often added to herbal salves.

Osmanthus—devilwood, wild olive (30/1/0) *O. americanus*. The fruit is a blue-purple drupe, prepared like an olive. Native from Texas to Virginia.

Syringa—Lilac (25/5/1) • Fruit is a capsule. Introduced and widely cultivated. I like to add the blossoms to a salad for color. The Latin *Syringa* is confusing, because it is also one of the common names of *Philadelphus* of the Hydrangea family.

Figwort Family—*Scrophulariaceae*

The Figwort family got gutted in the taxononic name game. This was a magnificent family with fairly intuitive patterns for identification, but most Figwort genera have been reclassified according to genetic evidence into the closely related **Plantain**, **Lopseed**, and **Broomrape** families. The **Acanthus** and **Bladderwort** families also have figwort-like flowers. Unfortunately, all of these families are now more complicated to identify, and the remaining genera in the Figwort family lack strong patterns between them. Nevertheless, being able to recognize a typical figwort-like flower remains an essential step for identifying any of these six closely related families.

The Figworts and their allies typically have irregular, bisexual flowers with 5 united sepals and 5 united petals (sometimes 4 of each), usually 2-lipped with 2 lobes up and 3 lobes down. There are 4 or 5 stamens, often in two pairs, plus a shortened fifth stamen. The ovary is positioned superior and consists of 2 united carpels with the partition walls present, forming 2 chambers. It typically matures as a capsule containing many seeds. The dried up style of the pistil can often be seen at the tip of the capsule. Be sure to cross-check your specimen with each of the figwort-like families listed above.

Key Words: Irregular flowers with 2 petal lobes up and 3 down. Capsules with numerous seeds.

Buddleja—butterfly bush (150/11/0) • Flower parts in 4s or 5s. Introduced for cultivation. The wavy petal edges resemble the Verbena family, but it has been historically classified in the Logania family (*Loganiaceae*) or its own family (*Buddlejaceae*), and now in the Figwort family.

Limosella—mudwort (15/4/1) Native across North America, except the southeastern states.

Scrophularia—figwort, California bee plant (150/8/1) • Figwort contains saponins (Schauenberg). It has sedative, astringent and antifungal properties (Moore). It is also diuretic. It is used especially as a skin wash (Lust).

Verbascum—mullein (320/7/2) • 5 equal stamens. Introduced. Mullein has sedative, astringent, and mildly mucilaginous properties. The leaves can be smoked or made into tea to relax the bronchioles in the initial stages of an infection. A tea of the root is diuretic and astringent for the urinary tract (Moore). A strong tea or dry powder of the leaves can be applied to a wound as an effective astringent (Brown). Its mucilaginous quality makes the tea useful as a demulcent to soothe a sore throat. The dried flower stalk makes a great drill for handdrill fire-starting. Learn how in *Participating in Nature*.

Lopseed Family—*Phrymaceae*

Plants of the Lopseed family are figwort-like flowers with only four stamens.

Mimulus—monkey flower (120/89/9) • The plant is edible, but bitter, as a salad green or potherb (Craighead). The root is astringent (Sweet). Juice of the plant is soothing on minor burns (Tilford).

Phryma—lopseed (1/1/0) *P. leptostachya*. Native to all states and provinces east of the Rocky Mountains. Previously classified as a member of the Verbena family.

Plantain Family—*Plantaginaceae*

The traditional Plantain family was small, consisting of only 3 genera and 270 species, almost all of them plantain (*Plantago*). However, based on genetic evidence, most members of the Figwort family have been moved into the Plantain family, making this the new "figwort family." In addition, the former Mare's Tail family (*Hippuridaceae*) and Water Starwort family (*Callitrichaceae*) were also merged into the Plantain family. The resulting hodgepodge of plants are genetically related, but don't share any over-arching patterns for identification. Additional details for identification are included for each tribe here and on the following pages.

Plantain Tribe—*Plantagineae*

These are low, green plants with inconspicuous flowers. The leaves appear to have parallel venation like monocts, but there are smaller, netted veins between the main veins. The flowers are greenish and small, forming on a slender stalk. They are regular and bisexual with 4 united sepals, 4 united petals, and 4 stamens. The ovary is positioned superior and consists of 2 united carpels forming a single chamber. It matures as a circumscissile (lidded) capsule with 1 or more seeds per cell, or sometimes as a nut. See illustrations, pages 37 and 214.

Littorella—shoreweed (3/1/0) *L. uniflora*. Native from Minnesota to Labrador.

Plantago—plantain (260/34/8) • Broad-leaf plantain (*P. major*) was introduced from Eurasia. The leaves are delicious batter-fried, or the young leaves can be added to a salad. They are rich in the vitamins A, C, and K (Tilford). The leaves contain allantoin, useful for soothing skin sores (Duke), or secured over a wound as a bandage (Willard). Plantain is a gentle astringent useful for stomach ulcers, bee stings, and such. Sand plantain (*P. psyllium*) is the source of psyllium seed, used as a bulk laxative in products like Metamucil®. The seed husks swell up in water, resulting in soft, large stools that are easier to pass. Plantain seeds have also been used to absorb toxins (Klein) or bad cholesterol from the intestinal tract.

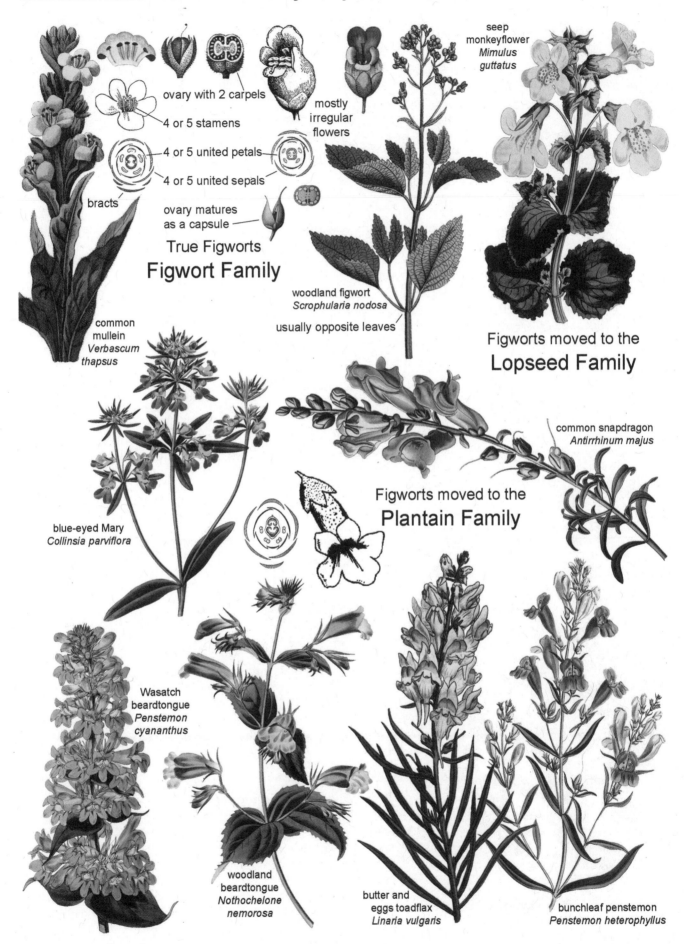

ovary with 2 carpels

4 or 5 stamens

mostly irregular flowers

4 or 5 united petals

4 or 5 united sepals

bracts

ovary matures as a capsule

True Figworts
Figwort Family

common mullein
Verbascum thapsus

seep monkeyflower
Mimulus guttatus

woodland figwort
Scrophularia nodosa

usually opposite leaves

Figworts moved to the
Lopseed Family

blue-eyed Mary
Collinsia parviflora

Figworts moved to the
Plantain Family

common snapdragon
Antirrhinum majus

Wasatch beardtongue
Penstemon cyananthus

woodland beardtongue
Nothochelone nemorosa

butter and eggs toadflax
Linaria vulgaris

bunchleaf penstemon
Penstemon heterophyllus

151

Water Starwort Tribe—*Callitricheae*

These are aquatic plants with usually whorled or opposite leaves and usually bisexual flowers. The sepals are greatly reduced or absent, and there are no petals. There is only one 1 stamen. The ovary consists of 1 carpel in *Callitriche*) or 2 carpels with false partitions, making a four-chambered ovary in *Hippuris*. Also read about the Water Milfoil family.

Callitriche—water starwort (7/12/4) Native throughout North America.

Hippuris—mare's tail (1/1/1) • Mare's tail is edible as a potherb any time of year (Harrington). Reportedly, the plants are best harvested between fall and spring, and even the browned, over-wintered stems can be eaten. Alaska natives once stored mare's tail in big piles to eat in winter. Medicinally, the juice of the plant is used internally or externally as a vulnerary (Fern), meaning the plant aids the healing process, without specifying how.

Snapdragon Tribe—*Antirrhineae*

These are often highly ornate figwort-like flowers with a distinctive "mouth." Squeeze and release the sides of the flower to make the mouth open and close.

Antirrhinum—snapdragon (20/1/1) *A. majus*. Widely cultivated and sometimes locally naturalized.

Gambelia—greenbright (4/1/0) *G. speciosa*. Native to California.

Linaria—toadflax (150/12/1) • Introduced, and sometimes invasive. *Linaria* is astringent, diuretic and cathartic. It is primarily used for its diuretic and antilithic properties (Lust).

Mohavea—desert snapdragon (2/2/0) Native to the southwestern states.

Nuttallanthus—toadflax (4/3/1) Native to North America, except for the Great Basin states.

Turtlehead Tribe—*Cheloneae*

These are classic figwort-like flowers, elongated, usually with well defined petal lobes, 2 up and 3 down.

Chelone—turtlehead (4/4/0) Native to the eastern states. See illustration, page ii.

Collinsia—blue-eyed Mary (20/19/1) • Native to most of North America, except the southeastern states.

Keckiella—keckiella (7/7/0) May resemble *Penstemon*. Native from Oregon to Arizona.

Nothochelone—woodland beardtongue (1/1/0) *N. nemorosa*. Formerly included in *Penstemon*. Native to the Pacific Coast.

Penstemon—penstemon (300/210/25) • Many species found across the continent. Astringent (Moore) and diuretic (Sweet).

Foxglove Tribe—*Digitalideae*

These obvious figwort-like flowers, but often with less-pronounced petal lobes.

Digitalis—foxglove (21/5/1) • Introduced and often cultivated for its flowers. It contains dangerous cardiac glycosides used for heart arrhythmia. Handling the plant may cause rashes, nausea, and headache in some individuals (Lust).

Plantain Family / Speedwell Tribe

corn speedwell
Veronica arvensis

Hedge Hyssop Tribe—*Gratioleae*

These flowers generally have shorter floral tubes than the Turtlehead tribe, and some are only slightly irregular.

Gratiola—hedge hyssop (20/13/2) Native to all of North America. *Gratiola* contains cardiac glycosides (Schauenberg). It is listed as cardiac, diuretic, purgative and vermifuge. It is considered too dangerous for amateurs to use (Lust).

Bacopa—waterhyssop (100/7/1) Native to most states. The crushed leaves have a lemon-like scent.

Capraria—goatweed (27/1/0) *C. biflora*. Native to Texas and Florida.

Limnophila—marshweed (40/2/0) Introduced to California, Texas, and Florida.

Scoparia—licorice weed (10/2/0) Native and introduced species are found from Texas to Virginia.

Speedwell Tribe—*Veroniceae*

Plants of the Speedwell tribe typically have irregular or nearly regular flowers with 4 sepals, 4 petals, and only 2 stamens.

Besseya—kittentail (8/8/2) • Native to the western and northern states. They are among the first flowers to bloom in spring.

Synthyris—kittentail (14/9/3) Native to the western states.

Veronica—speedwell, brooklime (300/30/9) • Found throughout North America. The plant is edible raw or cooked, but bitter (Harrington). Medicinally, the various species are mildly diuretic, diaphoretic and expectorant (Lust).

Veronicastrum—Culver's root (14/1/0) *V. virginicum*. Native east of the Rockies.

Patterns of the Bladderwort Family
These are insectivorous plants with figwort-like flowers.

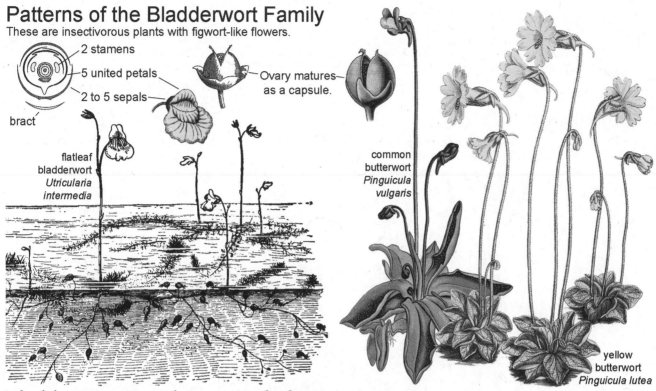

- 2 stamens
- 5 united petals
- 2 to 5 sepals
- bract
- Ovary matures as a capsule.

flatleaf bladderwort
Utricularia intermedia

common butterwort
Pinguicula vulgaris

yellow butterwort
Pinguicula lutea

Bladderwort Family—*Lentibulariaceae*

The Bladderworts are primarily insectivorous plants of humid, moist, or sometimes aquatic habitats, but a few species in seasonally arid climates have adapted by going dormant during the dry season. Like other insectivorous plants, the Bladderworts are adapted to nutrient-poor soils and compensate by preying on insects. Each genera uses a different method for trapping their prey, as described below. Like other insectivorous plants, the Bladderworts have tall flower stems to separate potential pollinators from the traps below. The flowers are irregular and bisexual with figwort-like characteristics. There are usually 2 (sometimes 4 or 5) united sepals and 5 united petals, and usually just 2 stamens (sometimes 4). The ovary is positioned superior and consists of 2 united carpels forming a single chamber. It matures as a capsule. Worldwide there are 3 genera and 300 species, with 2 genera in North America. Two former genera, *Polypompholyx* and *Biovularia*, have been reclassified within *Utricularia*.

Key Words: Insectivorous plants with figwort-like flowers.

Genlisea—corkscrew plant (27/0/0) Native to Central and South America and Africa, but not found in North America. The plants trap minute microfauna, such as protozoans, with the aid of highly modified hollow underground leaves. Prey organisms enter the hollow tubes and then move deeper and deeper inside, guided by directional hairs that allow the organisms to pass forward more easily than backward.

Pinguicula—butterwort (35/8/1) The petals form a spur on the back of the flower with nectar to attract pollinators. Various native species are found in the northern states and Canada, as well as in the southeast, but not in the horizontal band from Nevada to Virginia and New Jersey. Butterworts capture insects with sticky leaves, much like plants of the Sundew family. When an insect comes in contact with a leaf, glands in the leaf release additional sticky mucilage and digestive enzymes. The nutrients are absorbed through the leaf surface, leaving only the exoskeleton behind on the surface of the leaf.

Utricularia—bladderwort (250/21/3) Native throughout North America and found worldwide. The plants are adapted to fresh water and wet soil, and use sophisticated bladder traps to catch their prey. Terrestrial species typically prey on minute rotifers and protozoa in water-saturated soil, while aquatic species have larger traps to catch nematodes, water fleas, mosquito larvae, small tadpoles, and even fish fry. The trap door springs open when an organism brushes up against it. Due to negative pressure inside the trap, the organism and the water surrounding it are swept inside the trap before the door closes again.

Broomrape Family—*Orobanchaceae*

The Broomrape family consists of plants with figwort-like flowers that are parasitic on other plants, typically feeding off their root systems. The traditional family included only genera lacking chlorophyll, which are easy to recognize, since the vegetation isn't green. Taxonomists have expanded the family to include partially parasitic (hemiparasitic) genera, which were formerly included in the Figwort family. These plants have chlorophyll and produce their own energy through photosynthesis, so they are not wholly dependent on their host plants.

Unfortunately, the casual observer would not recognize them as hemiparasitic plants, so the connection to the Broomrape family is not obvious. But these new additions to the family often have highly modified or contorted flowers. There are typical figwort-like features, such as irregular, tubular flowers, often with 2 petal lobes up and 3 down, but most flowers are contorted such that they do not look like other figworts, either. There are several tribes of closely related genera within the Broomrape family, but for convenience in identification, all are lumped into two groups below, those with and without chlorophyll.

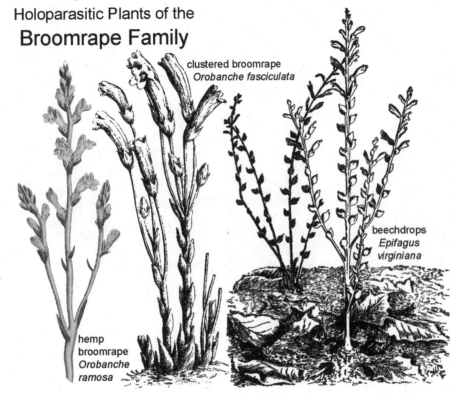

Holoparasitic Plants of the **Broomrape Family**

clustered broomrape
Orobanche fasciculata

beechdrops
Epifagus virginiana

hemp broomrape
Orobanche ramosa

Key Words: Parasitic plants with figwort-like flowers.

Holoparasitic Genera (Plants without chlorophyll)

Orobanche—broomrape (100/16/4) • Native and introduced species are found across North America. Some species have swollen, starchy, edible roots (Olsen). *O. fasciculata* is edible in salad or roasted. Medicinally, broomrapes are highly astringent, useful externally as a powerful drawing poultice; internally, the tea is a uterine homeostatic (Moore). A tea of the blanched or powdered seeds reduces swelling for toothaches or joint inflammation (Willard). These are often rare plants, so utilize them conscientiously.

Boschniakia—groundcone (3/3/0) Native from Alaska to California.

Conopholis—cancer root (2/2/0) Found in the southwest, as well as eastern North America.

Epifagus—beechdrops (1/1/0) *E. virginiana.* Associated with beech trees. It is native from Texas to Ontario, east to the Atlantic.

Hemiparasitic Genera (Plants with chlorophyll)

Agalinis—false foxglove (70/33/0) Native to North America east of the Rocky Mountains.

Castilleja—Indian paintbrush (200/109/22) • The blossoms are edible, but they may absorb selenium from the soil, so you should not eat too many of them. The plants have been used for womens' ailments and for rheumatism; the uses are possibly related to the selenium content (Willard). It functions as an astringent to stop menstrual flow (Vogel).

Cordylanthus—bird's beak (18/18/2) Hemiparasitic. Native to the western United States.

Euphrasia—eyebright (450/11/1) Native to the northern states and Canada. Astringent, often used as an eye-wash (Lust).

Melampyrum—cowwheat (10/1/1) *M. lineare.* Native to Canada and the northern and eastern states.

Orthocarpus—owl clover (9/9/2) • Native from New Mexico to Ontario, west to the Pacific. Many species have been reclassified as *Castilleja.*

Pedicularis—lousewort, elephant head (600/40/10) • Native throughout the continent. The root and plant of some species are edible raw or cooked (Willard), but the plants are partly parasitic and may absorb toxins from nearby poisonous plants such as groundsels (*Senecio*). Please refer to Michael Moore's *Medicinal Plants of the Pacific West* for detailed information on this plant.

Rhinanthus—rattleweed (30/3/1) Native to the northern states, the Rockies, and all of Canada.

Triphysaria—owl clover (5/5/0) Native from California to British Columbia. Closely related to *Castilleja* and *Orthocarpus.*

giant red
Indian paintbrush
Castilleja miniata

Hemiparasitic Plants of the
Broomrape Family
(Formerly in the Figwort Family)

common eyebright
Euphrasia nemorosa

Canadian lousewort
Pedicularis canadensis

little yellow rattle
Rhinanthus minor

redrattle
Pedicularis flammea

155

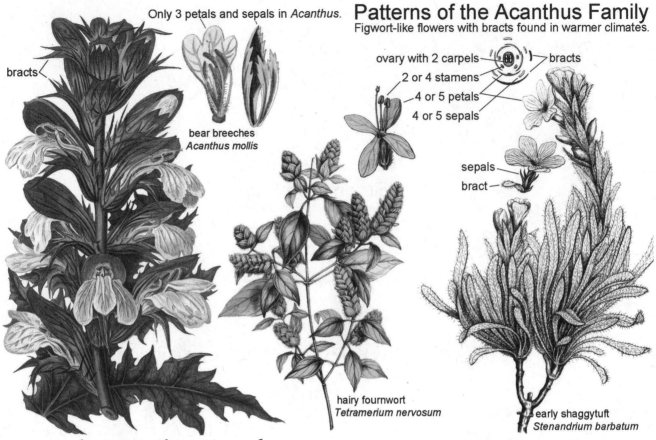

Only 3 petals and sepals in *Acanthus*.

bracts

bear breeches
Acanthus mollis

Patterns of the Acanthus Family
Figwort-like flowers with bracts found in warmer climates.

ovary with 2 carpels — bracts
2 or 4 stamens
4 or 5 petals
4 or 5 sepals

sepals
bract

hairy fournwort
Tetramerium nervosum

early shaggytuft
Stenandrium barbatum

Acanthus Family—*Acanthaceae*

If you live in a Mediterranean or tropical climate, then you are likely to encounter the figwort-like flowers of the Acanthus family, such as the cultivated bear breeches (*Acanthus*). Plants of this family are mostly herbs and shrubs with simple and opposite or sometimes basal leaves. Flowers are usually grouped in a spike, often with one or more bracts (modified leaves) by each blossom. Bracts may be colorful and petal-like. The flowers are irregular (sometimes only slightly) with typically 4 or 5 (rarely 3) united sepals and 4 or 5 (rarely 3) united petals. There are 2 or 4 stamens, which are attached to the petals. The ovary is positioned superior and consists of 2 united carpels forming a single chamber. It matures as a capsule, which often explosively ejects the seeds. Worldwide there are about 220 genera and 4000 species, mostly in the tropics. North American genera are listed below.

Key Words: Figwort-like flowers with bracts found in warmer climates.

Acanthus—acanthus, bear breeches (30/1/0) • *A. mollis*. Only 3 sepals and 3 petals. Introduced to California for cultivation. I became acquainted with this plant and its unusual flowers as a child, since my parents grew a row of *Acanthus* next to my sandbox.

Carlowrightia—wrightwort (24/8/0) Native from California to Texas.

Dicliptera—foldwing (230/3/0) Native from Arizona to Virginia.

Dyschoriste—snakeherb (110/6/0) Native from Arizona to South Carolina.

Hygrophila—swampweed (125/5/0) Native and introduced species are found from Texas to Georgia.

Justicia—waterwillow (420/16/0) Native from California to Quebec.

Ruellia—wild petunia (168/18/0) Some species resemble the true *Petunia* of the Nightshade family. Native from Arizona to Minnesota, east to the Atlantic.

Stenandrium—shaggytuft (38/2/0) Native from Arizona to Florida.

Tetramerium—fournwort (60/4/0) *T. nervosum*. Native from Arizona to Texas.

Yeatesia—bractspike (2/2/0) Native from Texas to Florida.

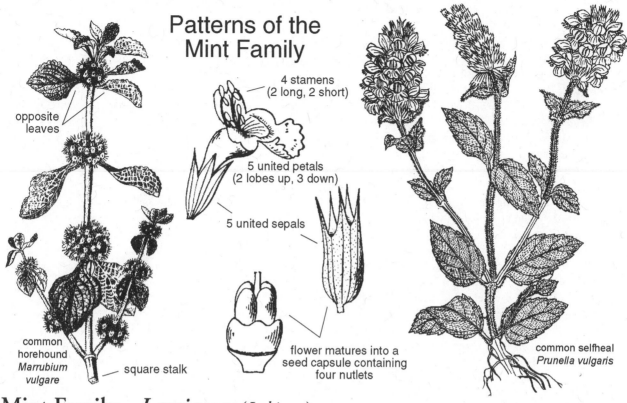

Patterns of the Mint Family

opposite leaves

4 stamens (2 long, 2 short)

5 united petals (2 lobes up, 3 down)

5 united sepals

common horehound *Marrubium vulgare*

square stalk

flower matures into a seed capsule containing four nutlets

common selfheal *Prunella vulgaris*

Mint Family—*Lamiaceae* (*Labiatae*)

Key Words: Square stalks and opposite leaves. Usually aromatic.

If you find a plant with a square stalk and simple, opposite leaves it may be a member of the Mint family. If it is also aromatic (crush and smell a leaf), then it is almost certainly a member of this family. Mint flowers are bisexual and irregular. Technically, Mint flowers are similar to Figwort flowers, with 5 united sepals and 5 united petals, usually 2-lipped with 2 lobes up and 3 lobes down. And yet, there are distinct differences between Mints and Figworts that are easy to see, but difficult to describe. (Compare the illustrations in this book, and you will see the similarities and differences.) Inside the flower, there are 4 stamens, with one pair longer than the other. The ovary is positioned superior. It consists of 2 united carpels and matures as a capsule containing 4 nutlets. (False partitions may make it appear 4-chambered.) Worldwide there are about 180 genera and 3,500 species. Approximately 50 genera are found in North America. Other plants with square stems and opposite leaves which may be confused with the Mints are found in the Loosestrife, Verbena, and Stinging Nettle families.

Many species from the Mint family are popular kitchen spices, including: basil (*Ocimum*), rosemary (*Rosmarinus*), lavender (*Lavandula*), marjoram (*Origanum*), mint, peppermint, spearmint (*Mentha*), germander (*Teucrium*), thyme (*Thymus*), savory (*Satureja*), horehound (*Marrubium*), and sage (*Salvia*). (Note that sagebrush (*Artemisia*) is in the Aster family.) The *Coleus* is a popular ornamental houseplant from the Mint family.

Medicinally, this family is rich in volatile oils, especially menthol. Spicy and stimulating, volatile oils warm the body, open the pores, and encourage sweating. This diaphoretic property is useful to help break a fever. A fever is the body's way of "cooking" the microorganisms that cause infections. Spicy teas and food can help raise a mild fever just high enough to "cook" a virus, thus ending the fever. Spicy foods also have a vasodilator effect, opening up the blood vessels to facilitate circulation. This property is useful in cases of hypertension, or for stimulating delayed menstruation, called an emmenagogue. Most members of this family are astringent, but a few are bitter, resulting in different uses between them. Astringent mints are often recommended as menstrual regulators, apparently because the volatile oils stimulate menstruation, while the astringents suppress it—a balancing effect, in theory. Bitter mints like false pennyroyal (*Hedeoma*), horehound (*Marrubium*), mints (*Mentha*), and coyote mint (*Monardella*) tend to have a more pronounced vasodilating effect. Some of these herbs may be dangerous during pregnancies, due to their anthelmintic (worm-killing) and menstrual-stimulating properties. The most dangerous ones are those that are also bitter (irritating). Read more about volatile oils in the *Medicinal Properties* section of this book.

Edible and Medicinal Properties of the Mint Family plants

Agastache—giant hyssop (22/14/2) • *Agastache* is astringent, diaphoretic and carminative.

Dracocephalum (including *Moldavica*)—false dragonhead (75/4/1) • The seeds can be ground into flour, or cooked into mush, and eaten (Olsen). The plant is probably astringent.

Glechoma—ground ivy (12/1/1) *G. hederacea.* Introduced from Europe. It contains tannins, bitters and volatile oils (Schauenberg). The herb has been used for respiratory ailments, including bronchitis, pneumonia and coughs (Tilford).

Galeopsis—hempnettle (10/3/1) A tea of the plant is astringent, diuretic and expectorant. It is used especially for clearing bronchial congestion. Also used as a blood purifier (Lust).

Hedeoma—false pennyroyal (38/14/2) Found throughout North America. Image on page 213. See also *Mentha*.

Hyssopus—hyssop (10/1/1) *H. officinalis.* Introduced from Europe. It is carminative, tonic, expectorant, vasodilator and anthelmintic (Hutchins). Also reported as astringent and an emmenagogue (Lust); used for nose and throat infections.

Lamium—dead nettle, henbit (40/5/2) • Dead nettle contains tannin, mucilage, and many flavonoids; it is used as a mild astringent and expectorant (Schauenberg). The whole plant is edible (Tilford).

Leonurus—motherwort (20/3/1) Antispasmodic, nervine, anthelmintic, laxative and an emmenagogue (Hutchins). Also astringent (Lust). The plant contains bitters, tannins, volatile oils, and an alkaloid (Schauenberg). Motherwort is used to slow and strengthen the heartbeat while lowering high blood pressure. It is also used as a uterine tonic and antispasmodic, hence the common name (Tilford).

Lycopus—bugleweed, water horehound (12/10/3) Bugleweed is edible, but tough and bitter (Tilford). Medicinally, bugleweed is mildly astringent, useful internally or externally to stop bleeding (Moore). It also contains some bitters (Schauenberg) and is useful as an expectorant (Tilford). Bugleweed is often used for its mild antispasmodic, nervine, and sedative properties, much like hops vines from the Hemp family (Moore).

Marrubium—horehound (30/1/1) • *M. vulgare.* Introduced from Europe. The plant is aromatic and very bitter and therefore useful as a digestive aid or as a cough suppressant and expectorant. The herb is often added to cough syrups. Horehound candy is much easier to consume than the bitter herb or tea. Excessive use may lead to hypertension (Moore). Horehound also contains tannic acid (Schauenberg).

Mentha—mint, spearmint, peppermint, pennyroyal (15/11/2) • As a child I loved picking peppermint (*M. piperita*—image on page 212) on outings with my grandmother. Today I still nibble on the leaves to freshen my breath as I walk. I often eat peppermint when drinking from streams to help kill microbes in the water. Mints are the main source of menthol, a volatile oil used for its penetrating vapors to relieve congestion or as a carminative to aid digestion. These are the original "after dinner mints."

> Pennyroyal (*M. pulegium*—image on page 213) is diaphoretic, antispasmodic, and bitter. It is used as a tea to stimulate a sweat, or to stimulate digestion. The tea is also a menstrual stimulant and vasodilator and can be used to stimulate contractions in an overdue pregnancy (Moore). At least one person has died from ingesting pure, distilled pennyroyal oil to cause an abortion. It is also a nervine (Hutchins) and carminative (Lust).

Monarda—horsemint, bee balm, bergamot (18/18/1) • Horsemint is diaphoretic, refrigerant, carminative, anthelmintic, mildly sedative and diuretic. A poultice can be use for headaches (Willard). The cool tea is used as an emmenagogue (Moore). At least some species contain tymol, an antiseptic compound used in commercial mouthwashes. Native Americans used it as a tea for mouth and throat infections (Tilford). Oil of bergamot is reported to have a calming effect on birds if it is rubbed on the bill, near the nostrils (Verrill).

Monardella—coyote mint, false horsemint (20/22/0) The plant is used identically to *Hedeoma* (*see above*) (Moore).

Nepeta—catnip (150/2/1) • The young leaves and buds may be added to a salad (Tilford). Medicinally, catnip contains volatile oils (Densmore) with mild antispasmodic, nervine, and sedative properties (Moore). It makes a wonderful and mildly relaxing tea. Catnip is also carminative, useful to expel gas or aid indigestion (Tilford). It is an effective emmenagogue (Hutchins). The reason cats like the smell of catnip is because it is chemically similar to the secretions from the anal glands of cats (Klein)! Lions, tigers, leopards, and jaguars are affected by lavender instead (Verrill).

Prunella—self heal (5/2/1) • Not aromatic. Heal-all is edible as a salad green or potherb (Tilford). Medicinally it is carminative, anthelmintic, diuretic, antispasmodic, astringent, and mildly bitter. (Willard, Klein).

Salvia—sage, chia (500/56/2) • *S. columbarae* is chia; the seeds are edible, high in protein and mucilaginous (Bigfoot). Many species of *Salvia* are richly aromatic and can be used as spices or antimicrobials. Ornamental varieties often lack aromatics. Sagebrush (*Artemisia*) belongs to the Aster family, and tastes nothing like culinary sage.

Scutellaria—skullcap (200/42/3) • Skullcap contains a flavonoid called scutellarin, with antispasmodic, nervine, and sedative properties, used especially in cases of acute or chronic nervous tension or anxiety (Tilford). It also acts as a vasodilator to reduce high blood pressure (Hutchins) and to increase menstruation (Lust).

Stachys—hedge nettle, betony (200/30/1) • The roots of some species are starchy and edible (Sturtevant). The seeds are edible parched or roasted and ground into meal (Olsen). *Stachys* contains up to 15 percent tannic acid (Schauenberg); useful for diarrhea and irritations of the mucous membranes (Tyler).

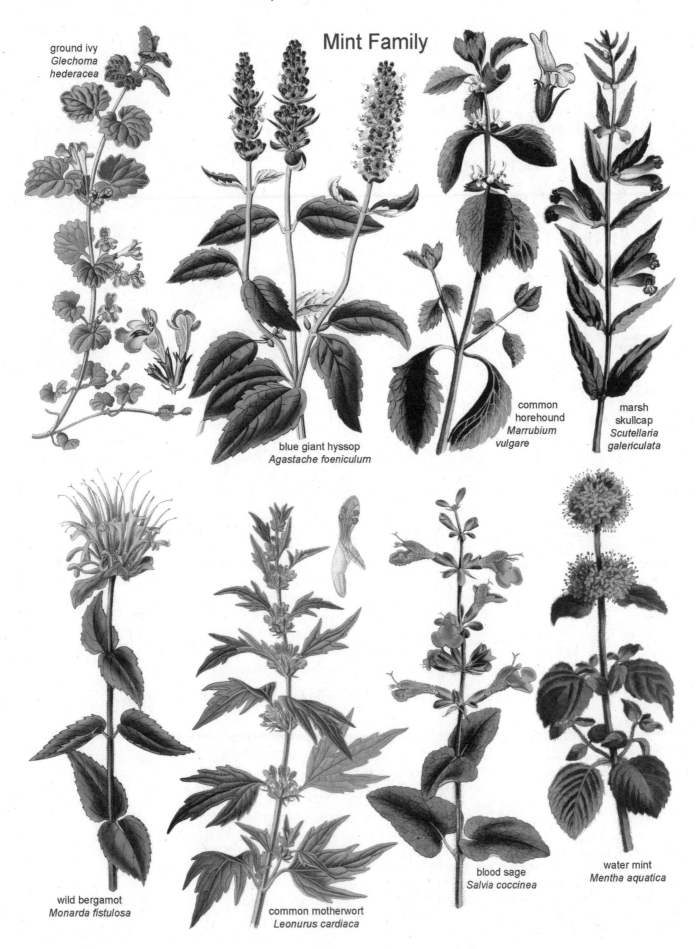

Mint Family

ground ivy
*Glechoma
hederacea*

blue giant hyssop
Agastache foeniculum

common
horehound
*Marrubium
vulgare*

marsh
skullcap
*Scutellaria
galericulata*

wild bergamot
Monarda fistulosa

common motherwort
Leonurus cardiaca

blood sage
Salvia coccinea

water mint
Mentha aquatica

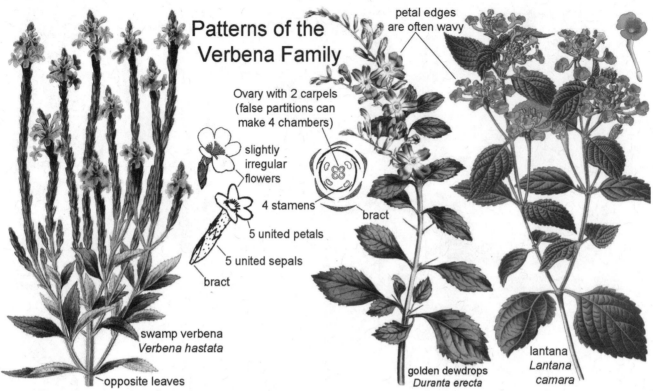

Patterns of the Verbena Family

petal edges are often wavy

Ovary with 2 carpels (false partitions can make 4 chambers)

slightly irregular flowers

4 stamens

5 united petals

5 united sepals

bract

bract

swamp verbena
Verbena hastata

opposite leaves

golden dewdrops
Duranta erecta

lantana
Lantana camara

Verbena Family—*Verbenaceae*

The Verbena family is common in the South, with only a few species found in the northern latitudes. The family includes mostly herbs and shrubs, but also a few trees. The leaves are usually opposite or whorled and occasionally aromatic. The flowers are mostly bisexual and slightly irregular. They bloom in elongated spikes, often with wavy petal edges that are a good clue to the family. There are usually 5 united sepals and 5 united petals, forming a tube with unequal lobes. There are 4 stamens (sometimes 2 or 5 outside the continent). The ovary is positioned superior. It consists of 2 (rarely 4 or 5) united carpels with the partition walls present, forming an equal number of chambers. Additional false partitions may be present in some species. The fruit matures as 1 to 2 nutlets per carpel or sometimes as a drupe (a fleshy fruit with a stony pit). Worldwide, there are about 35 genera and 1,200 species. Only *Verbena* is widespread across the continent. It has squarish stems and may be confused with the Mints. Note that an unrelated plant in the Four-O'Clock family is known as "sand verbena."

Based on genetic evidence, taxonomists have moved several genera from the Verbena family into the Mint family. North America genera include: beautyberry (*Callicarpa*), glorybowers (*Clerodendrum*), and chastetree (*Vitex*). In addition, black mangrove (*Avicennia*) is now in the Acanthus family, and lopseed (*Phryma*) has a family of its own. The unrelated butterfly bush (*Buddleja*) greatly superficially resembles plants of the Verbena family.

Key Words: Slightly irregular flowers with parts in 5s and often wavy petals.

Bouchea— bouchea (3/3/0) Native from Arizona to Texas.

Citharexylum—fiddlewood (70/3/0) These are trees and shrubs native to Florida and Texas, south to Argentina.

Duranta—dewdrops (17/1/0) *D. erecta*. Native from California to Florida.

Lantana—lantana, shrub verbena (160/8/0) The native and introduced shrubs are often cultivated for their flowers in the southern states. The vegetation is generally considered toxic, and may be useful as a pesticide (Cook).

Lippia—lippia (200/2/0) These tropical flowering plants are found in Florida, Texas, and New Mexico. The vegetation is fragrant. *L. graveolens* may be used in cooking like oregano.

Phyla—fogfruit (15/8/0) Various species are found across North America, except for the northwestern states and provinces.

Priva—catstongue (24/1/0) *P. lappulacea*. Native to Texas and Florida.

Stachytarpheta (11/2/0) *S. jamaicensis* is native to Florida and southern Alabama.

Verbena—verbena, vervain (230/47/3) • *Verbena* contains glycosides, tannins, bitters, and volatile oils (Schauenberg). Medicinally, it is sedative, diaphoretic, diuretic, antispasmodic and bitter tonic. The tea is taken to relieve cold symptoms and to settle the stomach, but it is bitter, and too much can cause nausea and vomiting (Moore).

Harebell Family—*Campanulaceae*

If you find a plant with beautiful flowers, alternate leaves, and milky sap, it may belong to the Harebell family. Excluding the Lobelias (described below), members of the Harbell family have delicate, bell-shaped flowers, which are bisexual and mostly regular. There are 5 (sometimes 3, 4, or 10) separate sepals, 5 (rarely 4) united petals, and 5 stamens. Flowers are most often blue, purple, or white. The ovary is positioned inferior or partly so, and consists of 3 (sometimes 2 or 5) united carpels, as indicated by the number of styles. Partition walls are present, forming an equal number of chambers. False partitions may make it seem like more chambers. The ovary matures as a capsule (rarely a berry) with numerous seeds.

Worldwide, there are about 70 genera and 2,000 species. Many species contain inulin polysaccharides and cyanogenic glycosides (Zomlefer). *Laurentia* provides isotomin, a heart poison.

Key Words: Bell-shaped flowers, usually with milky juice in the stems.

Campanula—harebell (300/29/6) • Harebells are sometimes called "bluebells," but there are also bluebells (*Mertensia*) in the Borage family. The leaves and roots are edible (Willard, Harrington, Sturtevant), as are the flowers. The roots of some species are edible and worth harvesting. Read more in *Foraging the Mountain West*.

Heterocodon—pearlflower (1/1/0) *H. rariflorum*. Pacific states.

Jasione—sheep's bit (15/1/0) *J. montana*. Imported from Europe. It is naturalized in the East Coast states.

Triodanis (including *Specularia*)—Venus' looking glass (8/7/1) Found across North America.

rampion bellflower
Campanula rapunculoides

Patterns of the Harebell Family

Lobelia Subfamily—*Lobelioideae*

The Lobelia subfamily includes irregular, figwort-like flowers, often with pointy lobes. Like other members of the Harebell family, the Lobelias have milky sap.

Key Words: Figwort-like flowers, often with pointy lobes. Milky juice in the stems.

Downingia—calicoflower (13/13/1) Native to the western states and provinces.

Howellia—water howellia (1/1/1) *H. aquatilis*. Native to the Pacific Northwest.

Lobelia—lobelia, cardinal flower (380/29/2) *L. inflata* is a popular herb for the lungs. Other species are used similarly, but vary in potency. Lobelia has milky sap containing pyridine alkaloids. It stimulates the nervous system, then depresses it. In moderate doses it dilates the bronchioles and increases respiration. Overdose leads to respiratory depression, low blood pressure and coma (Tyler). The plant can also be smoked for asthma (Bigfoot).

Porterella—porterella (1/1/1) *P. carnosula*. Native to the West.

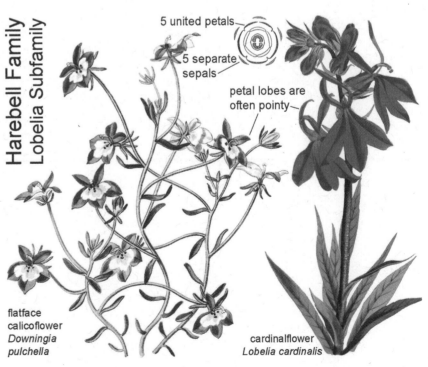

Harebell Family Lobelia Subfamily

flatface calicoflower
Downingia pulchella

cardinalflower
Lobelia cardinalis

161

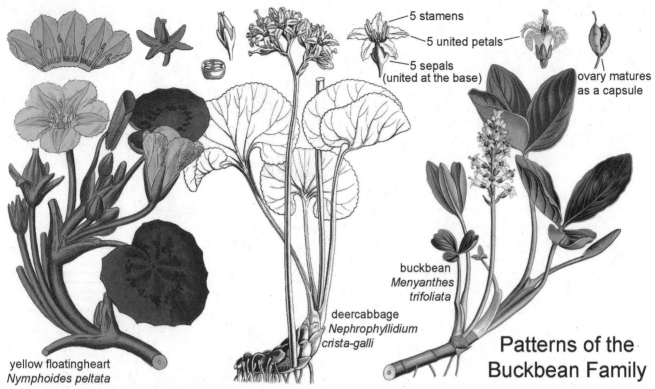

5 stamens

5 united petals

5 sepals
(united at the base)

ovary matures
as a capsule

buckbean
*Menyanthes
trifoliata*

deercabbage
*Nephrophyllidium
crista-galli*

yellow floatingheart
Nymphoides peltata

**Patterns of the
Buckbean Family**

Buckbean Family—*Menyanthaceae*

The Buckbeans are a small family of aquatic and wetland plants. The flowers are regular, bisexual, and tubular. There are 5 sepals, usually united at the base, and 5 united petals, forming a funnel. The petals are often fuzzy or imprinted with a star-like pattern. There are 5 stamens, attached to the corolla tube. The ovary is positioned superior and consists of 2 united carpels forming a single chamber. It matures as a capsule (sometimes a berry) with many seeds. Worldwide there are 5 genera and about 60 species. *Liparophyllum* and *Villarsia* are found only in the southern hemisphere. North American genera are listed below.

Key Words: Aquatic plants with flower parts in 5s and united petals.

Menyanthes—buckbean (1/1/1) *M. trifoliata*. Native throughout North America, except for the South. Buckbean contains a bitter substance. The fresh plant is emetic. The dried plant functions as a bitter to stimulate digestion, relieve gas, and act as a cathartic. It is high in vitamin C, iron and iodine, and is thus used as a tonic for general health (Willard). The roots are sometimes crushed and washed to remove the bitterness, then used as flour (Sturtevant).

Nephrophyllidium—deercabbage (1/1/0) *N. crista-galli*. Native from Oregon to Alaska.

Nymphoides—floating heart (50/6/0) Native and introduced species are distributed from Texas and Florida north to Quebec, plus the Pacific Coast states.

Patterns of the Aster or Sunflower Family

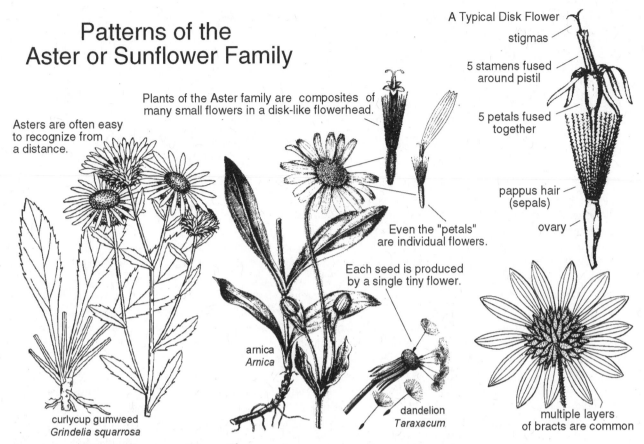

A Typical Disk Flower
stigmas
5 stamens fused around pistil
5 petals fused together
pappus hair (sepals)
ovary

Plants of the Aster family are composites of many small flowers in a disk-like flowerhead.

Asters are often easy to recognize from a distance.

Even the "petals" are individual flowers.

Each seed is produced by a single tiny flower.

arnica
Arnica

curlycup gumweed
Grindelia squarrosa

dandelion
Taraxacum

multiple layers of bracts are common

Aster or Sunflower Family—*Asteraceae* (*Compositae*)

Despite simple appearances, the Asters are highly complex plants. To identify flower parts, one normally starts on the outside of a flower and works inward: sepals, petals, stamens, pistil(s). But that doesn't work with the Asters. The "sepals" are actually bracts (modified leaves), which often appear in multiple layers. The "petals" make it appear that there is just one big flower, but look closely inside and you will discover many smaller flowers—dozens or even hundreds of them! In a sunflower (*Helianthus*), for example, each seed is produced by a small, five-petaled **disk flower** within the larger head. Each disk flower has its own itsy-bitsy petals, stamens, and pistil. The sepals have been reduced to small scales, transformed into a hairy "pappus," or sometimes eliminated altogether. Each big "petal" around the flowerhead is also an individual flower, known as a ray flower. These flowers are often infertile, without stamens or a pistil. Members of the Aster family can have disk flowers, ray flowers, or both.

The pitted disk of the flowerhead is an excellent clue to the Aster family at any time of year. Look for it on a dandelion, for example, after the seeds have blown away. I like to think of this pitted disk as the garden where all the little flowers were planted. Another good clue to the Asters is the multiple layers of bracts surrounding the flowerhead. In an artichoke those are the scale-like pieces we pull off and eat. Most members of this family do not have that many bracts, but there are frequently two or more rows. This is not a foolproof test, only a common pattern of the Aster family. Also look inside the flowerhead for the individual flowers. Disk flowers are often quite small. Even the common yarrow (*Achillea*), with its tiny flowerheads, usually has a dozen or more nearly microscopic flowers inside each head. Note that many Asters, such as sagebrush (*Artemisia*), lack an obvious outer ring of ray flowers.

The Asters are the second largest family of flowering plants, surpassed only by the mostly tropical Orchid family. Worldwide, there are about 920 genera and 19,000 species, including about 346 genera and 2,687 species in North America. Aside from lettuce (*Lactuca*), artichoke (*Cynara*), and endive (*Cichorium*), surprisingly few genera are cultivated for food. When you have identified a plant as a member of the Aster family, then read about each of the following subfamilies (Chicory/Dandelion, Thistle, Mutisia, and Aster) as well as each tribe of the Aster subfamily, to get a better sense of which group your specimen belongs to. Taxonomists have tweaked classification within the Aster family to more accurately reflect genetic relationships, so the subfamilies and tribes utilized here may differ somewhat from older sources, but most of the changes are relatively minor. For example, the Thistle and Mutisias were elevated from tribes to subfamilies, but the plants included within each group are still the same.

Chicory Subfamily—*Cichorioideae*

The Chicory or Dandelion subfamily is the most distinct sub-grouping of the Aster family. The distinguishing feature is the strap-shaped petals—the ray flowers have mostly parallel edges like a strap, instead of tapered edges like the petals of other flowers. These ray flowers often overlap all the way to the center of the flower, like a dandelion. There are no disk flowers. Another pattern of this subfamily is the milky juice in the stems. Most, if not all, members of the Chicory subfamily are edible, but bitter due to the milky juice. The bitterness makes these plants valuable as digestive aids. For example, dandelion leaves (*Taraxacum*) are known as a "spring tonic," used to cleanse the liver after a long winter of eating hard-to-digest foods. Note that many unrelated plants also have milky juice and some are poisonous, so check the flower to make sure it is a member of the Chicory subfamily before you eat it!

Agoseris—false dandelion (11/10/3) • The leaves are edible. The hardened, milky juice can be chewed as gum (Olsen).

Anisocoma—scalebud (1/1/0) *A. acaulis*. Native to the desert southwest.

Atrichoseris—gravel ghost (1/1/0) *A. platyphylla*. Native to the desert southwest.

Calycoseris—tackstem (2/2/0) Native to the desert southwest.

Chaetadelpha—skeletonweed (1/1/0) *C. wheeleri*. Native to the Southwest. See also *Lygodesmia* (below).

Cichorium—chicory, endive (8/2/1) • *C. intybus* was imported from Europe. The leaves are edible as a salad green or potherb, especially after blanching to reduce bitterness. The bitterness is useful as a digestive aid and liver stimulant. The young roots are edible raw or cooked (Willard). They contain up to 58% inulin polysaccharides, favorable for diabetics (Hobbs). Chicory is similar, but more mild than dandelion (see *Taraxacum* below) (Moore). The roots can be gently roasted and ground for a coffee substitute (Harrington). Cafix® is a coffee substitute made with chicory roots. Roasting converts the inulin into oxymethylfurfurol, the compound with the coffee-like aroma (Tyler).

Crepis—hawksbeard (200/22/9) The young leaves are edible as a potherb. (Olsen).

Glyptopleura—carveseed (2/2/0) Native to the southwest.

Hieracium—hawkweed, mouse ear (800/56/6) A tea of the plant is astringent and diuretic, used in the usual ways (Lust).

Lactuca—lettuce, prickly lettuce (100/13/5) • Prickly lettuce has a row of prickles down the midrib underneath the leaf. Sowthistle (*Sonchus*) does not. Prickly lettuce is edible as a salad green or potherb. The leaves are extremely bitter at times. Prickly lettuce is sometimes called "lettuce opium," because the sap is reminiscent of the milky white latex from the opium poppy. The sap does have a very mild analgesic effect, safe enough for children (Moore). It includes two bitter principles, lactucin and lactucopicrin, which were shown to have a depressant effect on the nervous systems of small animals. However, the bitter principles are very unstable, so commercial preparations are functionally useless (Tyler). Cultivated leaf lettuce (*L. sativa*) also belongs to this genus.

Lapsana—nipplewort (1/1/1) *L. communis*. Introduced. The plant is minimally edible as a salad green or potherb (Sturtevant).

Lygodesmia—skeletonweed (7/7/2) • A tea of the plant is used to increase lactose production (Willard).

Malacothrix—desert dandelion (22/14/1) Native to the western states.

Microseris—silverpuffs (14/14/4) The roots are edible (Sturtevant).

Prenanthes—rattlesnakeroot (15/15/1) A tea of the root is both astringent and bitter, used for diarrhea (Lust).

Prenanthella—brightwhite (1/1/0) *P. exigua*. Native from Oregon to Texas.

Rafinesquia—plumeseed (2/2/0) Native to from Oregon to Texas.

Sonchus—sowthistle (70/5/4) • Introduced. Edible as a salad green or potherb. Read more in *Foraging the Mountain West*.

Stephanomeria—wirelettuce (17/17/1) Native to the western half of North America.

Taraxacum—dandelion (70/9/5) • Dandelion leaves and roots are rich in vitamins A, B, C, and E and the minerals iron, phosphorus, potassium, and calcium (Hutchins). Dandelion greens are bitter, useful as a digestive aid. Many people think the greens are too bitter to eat at first, but try a small amount mixed in with other greens. You can develop a taste for them until they hardly seem bitter at all. Optionally, harvest them from shady locations for less bitterness. (Read more in *Foraging the Mountain West*.) Roasting dandelion roots sweetens them by breaking the inulin polysaccharides down into fructose (Hobbs). The roots make delicious coffee substitute, much like chicory roots (see above).

Medicinally, dandelion roots and leaves are most bitter in the spring, useful as a diuretic and stimulating to the liver, spleen and kidneys. The plant is safe for long-term use, making it ideal for dissolving calcium stones (Moore). Dandelions, especially the roots, are high in sodium, which is recommended for breaking down acid in the blood. Dandelions may lower blood sugar, an aid for diabetics. The latex sap from the stems is used on warts (Willard).

Tragopogon—salsify, goatsbeard (45/5/3) • Salsify produces edible, slightly bitter foliage and large edible roots. It is sometimes planted as a garden vegetable. It is a biennial, producing an edible root the first year which turns woody the second year. The purple flowered species are best. The yellow flowered species are more fibrous and bitter (Tilford). I once dug up a field mouse "cellar" with nearly two gallons of salsify and grass roots! Medicinally, salsify is used as a diuretic and digestive stimulant (Lust).

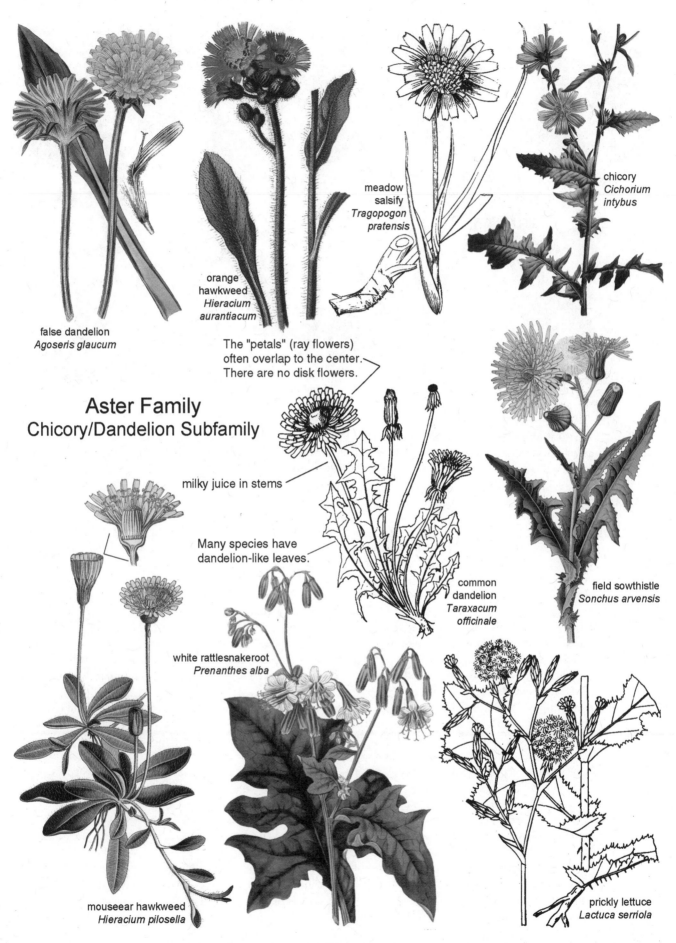

chicory
Cichorium intybus

meadow salsify
Tragopogon pratensis

orange hawkweed
Hieracium aurantiacum

false dandelion
Agoseris glaucum

The "petals" (ray flowers) often overlap to the center. There are no disk flowers.

Aster Family
Chicory/Dandelion Subfamily

milky juice in stems

Many species have dandelion-like leaves.

field sowthistle
Sonchus arvensis

common dandelion
Taraxacum officinale

white rattlesnakeroot
Prenanthes alba

mouseear hawkweed
Hieracium pilosella

prickly lettuce
Lactuca serriola

165

nodding
thistle
*Carduus
nutans*

Aster Family
Thistle Subfamily

blessed milkthistle
Silybum marianum

cornflower
*Centaurea
cyanus*

lesser burdock
Arctium minus

Thistle Subfamily—*Carduoideae*

If you find an Aster with its head protected inside a tight wrapping of bracts like an artichoke, then it belongs to the Thistle or Artichoke subfamily of the Aster family. Most of these plants have at least some prickly parts, especially the bracts around the flower heads. Aside from their spines, coarse texture, and fibrous nature, these plants are otherwise edible and often used in bitters formulas to stimulate digestion. The artichoke belongs to the *Cynara* genus. Teasel, of the family *Dipsacaceae,* could easily be mistaken for a thistle.

Arctium—burdock (6/6/2) • Introduced. Burdock is a biennial with an edible taproot. It is cultivated in Europe and Japan (Harrington). Read more about harvesting and preparing burdock root in *Foraging the Mountain West.* In addition, the big leaves are ideal for covering a steam pit to keep dirt out of the food. The burrs can be used as "Velcro®." The roots contain 45% inulin polysaccharides (Schauenberg). Burdock root is a very popular medicinal plant, especially for facilitating liver function. It is bitter and diuretic in effect (Hobbs, Tilford).

Carduus—thistle (100/5/2) • Introduced. The flowerstalk of the nodding or musk thistle (*C. nutans*) is a favorite wild snack, something like "wild celery," after peeling away the spiny outer skin. Learn how in *Foraging the Mountain West.*

Centaurea—knapweed, starthistle, cornflower, bachelor's buttons (500/27/8) • Most species were introduced and some are invasive. Spotted knapweed (*C. maculosa*) covers more than 5 million acres just in Montana, often to the exclusion of all other plants. The leaves and roots of many species of *Centaurea* are edible (Sturtevant). Medicinally, knapweed is both bitter and astringent (Klein).

Cirsium—thistle (250/92/9) • Thistles are biennial; the roots are tender and edible the first year, turning woody and fibrous the second year when the flower stalk forms. The bull thistle (*C. vulgare*) is especially delicious. The roots are crunchy but good when raw, and even better cooked. The young leaves can be cooked as greens, effectively wilting the spines (Kallas). Thistle roots and foliage contain electrolyte minerals and have an energizing effect when you are exercising (Bigfoot). The stalk of the elk thistle (*C. scariosum*) is edible and delicious, much like *Carduus* above. Medicinally, the plants are mildly bitter; some species are used in bitter formulas (Hobbs).

Onopordum—cotton thistle, scotch thistle (40/5/1) • Introduced. The roots are reasonably edible, just fibrous.

Silybum—milk thistle (2/1/0) *S. marianum.* Introduced from Europe. It is now found in the Atlantic and Pacific Coast states. The young leaves are edible as a salad green or potherb. The young stalks are edible after peeling, soaking to remove the bitterness and cooking. The root is also edible (Sturtevant).

Medicinally, milk thistle is used as a bitter to stimulate liver function. It also contains the flavonoid silymarin, which has been shown to protect the liver from toxins. It has been given to patients who ingested toxic amanita mushrooms. The silymarin molecules attach to the liver where the amanita toxins would normally attach, so the toxins pass through the body harmlessly (Klein).

Mutisia Subfamily—*Mutisioideae*

The most distinctive feature of the Mutisia subfamily of the Aster family is that the disk flowers are irregular. Look closely and you will see a two-lipped flower with 2 petal lobes up and 3 petal lobes down. Also, the blossoms have no outer ring of petals (the ray flowers). The flowers of this subfamily are found in the southern states from coast to coast, but not in the northern states.

Acourtia—desertpeony (5/5/0) Native from California to Texas.
Adenocaulon—trailplant (6/1/1) • *A. bicolor*. Native to moist forests of the Pacific and northern states. Walking through the plants turns up the silvery underside of the leaves, revealing an obvious trail.
Chaptalia—sunbonnets (68/5/0) Native from New Mexico to Virginia.
Gerbera—transvaal daisy (50/1/0) *G. jamesonii*. Introduced to Florida.
Trixis—threefold (65/2/0) Native from California to Texas.

Aster Family
Mutisia Subfamily

woolly sunbonnets
Chaptalia tomentosa

Aster Subfamily—*Asteroideae*

The Aster Subfamily includes several tribes of genera, which are more useful for identification than tribes of the other subfamilies:

Boneset Tribe—*Eupatorieae*

Members of the Boneset tribe are distinguished from other composites by the shape of their stigmas, which are thickened at the ends like a baseball bat. It is a pretty nit-picky distinction, but then, this *is* botany! Otherwise, the flowers lack an outer ring of petals (the ray flowers) and none of the blossoms are pure yellow. These plants are most easily confused with the Ironweed tribe.

Aster Family
Aster Subfamily
Boneset Tribe

shaggy blazing star
Liatris pilosa

Brickellia—thoroughwort (100/12/3) • Native throughout North America. A tea of the leaves is reported to be useful for insulin-resistant diabetes (Bigfoot).
Eupatorium—Joe Pye weed, boneset (600/50/2) Boneset contains tannins and bitters (Schauenberg). The hot tea has been used for centuries as a diaphoretic to treat fevers, including dengue, also known as "breakbone fever," from which the plant gets its common name. This common name has led to some confusion, so that some herbalists have recommend boneset to aid in knitting broken bones. There is neither the history nor a scientific basis to support that use. Boneset may act as a cathartic or emetic (Lust).
Liatris—gayfeather, blazing star (34/34/2) • Native from the Rocky Mountains to the Atlantic. In August, our place is covered with the blossoms of dotted gayfeather (*L. punctata*), one of my favorite flowers. Medicinally, it is astringent and diuretic. The roots are burned and the smoke inhaled for headache, nosebleed, sore throat and tonsil inflammation. A tea of the root is similarly used for sore throat and laryngitis (Moore).

Ironweed Tribe—*Vernonieae*

Members of the Ironweed tribe can be distinguished from the Bonesets and other composites by the shape of their stigmas, which are long, thread-like and hairy. Similar to the Bonesets, there are no ray flowers and virtually none of the blossoms are pure yellow. The Ironweeds are found in the southern and eastern states, not in the Northwest nor the Rocky Mountains.

Elephantopus—elephant's Foot (12/4/0) Native from Texas to New Jersey.
Stokesia—Stoke's aster (1/1/0) *S. laevis*. Native from Louisiana to North Carolina.
Vernonia—ironweed (1,000/22/0) Native from the Rocky Mountains east to the Atlantic.

New York ironweed
Vernonia noveboracensis

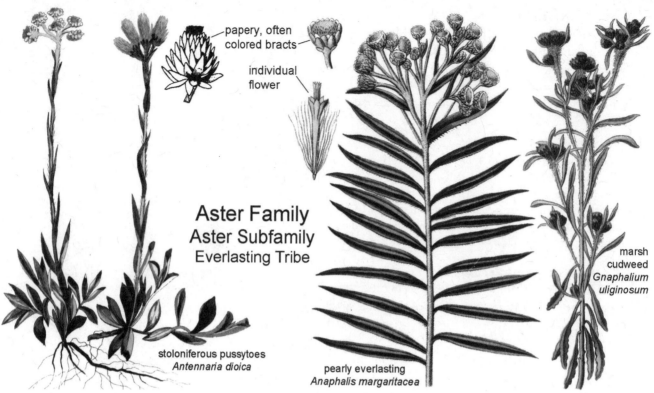

papery, often colored bracts

individual flower

Aster Family
Aster Subfamily
Everlasting Tribe

marsh cudweed
Gnaphalium uliginosum

stoloniferous pussytoes
Antennaria dioica

pearly everlasting
Anaphalis margaritacea

Everlasting Tribe—*Gnaphalieae*

If you find a member of the Aster family with grayish vegetation and papery, often colored bracts surrounding a flower with disk flowers, but no ray flowers then it is probably a member of the Everlasting tribe. The bracts around the flowers are scarious, meaning thin, dry, and translucent. Note that plants of the Chamomile tribe also have somewhat scarious bracts, but the Chamomiles have a strong odor, whereas the Everlastings do not.

Anaphalis—pearly everlasting (50/1/1) • *A. margaritacea*. A tea of the plant is principally astringent and diaphoretic, also with expectorant properties. It is used in the expected ways: for colds, fevers, sore throats and to expel worms. The smoke is inhaled to relieve headaches (Willard). Pearly everlasting has a mildly antihistamine effect. It has been used in the treatment of asthma (Tilford).

Antennaria—pussytoes (85/85/12) • *Antennaria* contains tannin, volatile oils, resin and bitters (Schauenberg). It is astringent and diuretic; the tea is used for liver inflammations and for irritations of the upper intestines. As an astringent, it is useful as a vaginal douche (Moore). It may act as a vasoconstrictor and raise blood pressure (Lust).

Filago—cottonrose (45/2/0) Introduced to the East and West coastal states and provinces of North America.

Gnaphalium—everlasting, cudweed (150/29/6) *Gnaphalium* is astringent, diuretic and diaphoretic, used especially as a gargle for sore throat; it is also smoked for headaches or used to expel worms (Lust).

Elecampane Tribe—*Inuleae*

The Elecampane tribe includes Old World plants, only a few of which have been introduced to North America.

Inula—elecampane (90/3/0) Introduced to the Pacific and north-eastern states.

elecampane
Inula helenium

Aster Family
Aster Subfamily
Elecampane Tribe

Aster Family
Aster Subfamily
Chamomile Tribe

common
yarrow
*Achillea
millefolium*

wormwood
Artemisia absinthium

common
tansy
*Tanacetum
vulgare*

oxeye daisy
Leucanthemum vulgare

Chamomile Tribe—*Anthemideae*

The Chamomile tribe includes some of the most aromatic plants of the Aster family. The other distinguishing characteristic is that the bracts surrounding the flowerhead are somewhat scarious, meaning thin, dry, and translucent (which may be more apparent when fully dried). Note that the members of the Everlasting tribe also have scarious bracts (much more translucent), but the plants lack the odor characteristic of the Chamomiles. If your specimen has *both* the odor and the translucent bracts then it belongs with the Chamomiles.

Achillea—yarrow (100/5/2) • The warrior Achilles used yarrow poultices stop bleeding (Hart). Yarrow is astringent, diuretic, and diaphoretic. The tea can be taken to decrease menstruation, shrink hemorrhoids, or to stimulate sweating in a dry fever (Moore). It will also speed up childbirth and aid in expelling the afterbirth. It is taken to ease the transition into menopause (Willard). A little yarrow tincture on a tissue, stuffed up the nostril, will stop a bloody nose in seconds. My grandmother always gave me yarrow tea with honey when I had a cold.

Anthemis—chamomile (110/8/1) Chamomile tea is useful as an antispasmodic and carminative for the digestive system or as a mild sedative, especially for restless children. The flowers can be used in a rubbing oil on painful joints (Lust). It is also used for migraine headaches (Schauenberg).

Artemisia—sagebrush, wormwood, tarragon (250/100/19) • Some species are used as a smudge for purification before entering sweat lodges and other ceremonial events. *Artemisia* contains potent volatile oils, some tannins, and a bitter substance. Medicinally, the bitter tea acts as a digestive aid, but the volatile oils in some species can lead to permanent nervous disorders with prolonged use (Schauenberg). The *Artemisias* are useful as a menstrual stimulant and as a vermifuge. Some species of *Artemisia* can decrease the effects of rancid fats (called lipid peroxides, such as in old donuts, etc.) on the liver (Moore). Tarragon (*A. dracunculus* and *A. drancunculoides*) is the culinary spice used in tartar sauce, hollandaise, and bé arnaise. But don't mistake sagebrush for culinary sage, which belongs to the Mint family.

Chrysanthemum—chrysanthemum, mums, daisy (30/2/0) • The arctic daisy (*C. arcticum*) is native to Canada.

Leucanthemum—oxeye daisy (70/4/1) • Formerly included in *Chrysanthemum*. Imported from Europe. The leaves are edible.

Matricaria (including *Tripleurospermum*)—mayweed, pineapple weed (50/4/1) • Pineapple weed (*M. discoidea* or *M. matricarioides*) is a sweet-smelling herb often found in lawns and driveways. The fresh plant is edible. It is an excellent tea, similar to, but milder than chamomile. It is listed as diaphoretic, antispasmodic, stimulant, and sedative. It is a mild remedy—safe for children—used for stomach pains, colds, fevers, and as a menstrual stimulant (Hutchins).

Tanacetum—tansy (160/7/3) • *T. vulgare* was introduced as a medicinal herb. It is now an invasive weed in many states. It contains a bitter principle (Densmore), plus resins, volatile oils, tannic and gallic acids, gums, lime- and lead-oxide. In small doses, the tea is used as a diaphoretic and emmenagogue. In large doses it can cause convulsions, vomiting, reduced heart function and coma (Hutchins). Some individuals have died using oil of tansy to cause abortions.

tansy
ragwort
*Senecio
jacobaea*

Arctic butterbur
Petasites frigidus

Texas ragwort
Senecio ampullaceus

**Aster Family
Aster Subfamily
Groundsel Tribe**

coltsfoot
Tussilago farfara

Groundsel Tribe—*Senecioneae*

Many members of the Aster family grow a pappus or tuft of white hair around each of the little flowers inside the larger head. The Groundsels are distinguished from other Asters by the soft, silky quality of the pappus hair. The hair is usually pure white and very abundant. Note that *Arnica* has been moved to the Sunflower tribe.

Petasites—butterbur, coltsfoot (17/3/1) Coltsfoot leaves and stems are edible as potherbs. The plant has a salty flavor and may be used as a salt substitute. Medicinally, coltsfoot has been used for centuries as an expectorant and cough suppressant for everything from chest colds to pneumonia. However, the plant contains potentially dangerous pyrrolizidine alkaloids (Tilford). Read more in the *Medicinal Properties* section of this book.

Senecio—groundsel, ragwort (1500/120/24) • Groundsels are diuretic, astringent and diaphoretic (Hutchins). In larger quantities the plants may be emetic or purgative (strongly laxative) (Willard). The plants contain pyrrolizidine alkaloids, which can damage the liver. The common name "ragwort" is also applied to some genera in the Sunflower tribe.

Tussilago—coltsfoot (1/1/0) *T. farfara*. Introduced. *Tussilago* and *Petasites* are closely related, and appear to share similar properties and uses.

Marigold Tribe—*Tageteae*

Most genera of the Marigold tribe are native to the highlands of Mexico, with only a few genera found as far north as our southwestern states. Some are fragrant or pungent.

Adenophyllum—dogweed (10/4/0) Native from California to New Mexico.

Nicolletia—hole-in-the-sand plant (3/2/0) Native to the Mojave Desert. There is often a hole in the sand around the base of the plant.

Pectis—chinchweed (85/18/0) Native from California to Florida. Lemonscent chinchweed (*P. angustifolia*) is aromatic.

Porophyllum—poreleaf (30/5/0) Native from California to Texas. The leaf surface has aromatic oil glands, and the leaves are often used as a spice.

Tagetes—marigold (56/6/0) • Several species are widely cultivated, including the Mexican marigold (*T. erecta*). The wild licorice marigold (*T. micrantha*) is native from Arizona to Texas.

Mexican marigold
Tagetes erecta

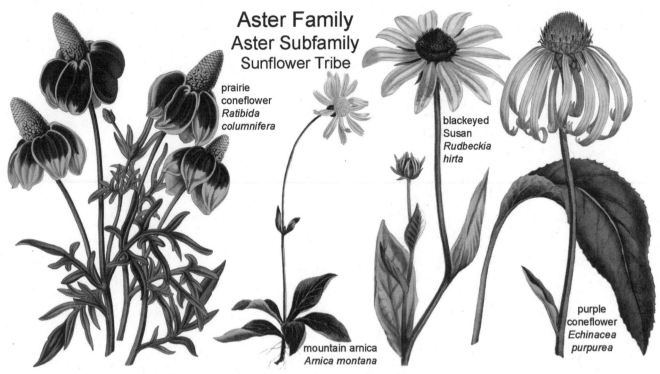

Aster Family
Aster Subfamily
Sunflower Tribe

prairie
coneflower
*Ratibida
columnifera*

blackeyed
Susan
*Rudbeckia
hirta*

mountain arnica
Arnica montana

purple
coneflower
*Echinacea
purpurea*

Sunflower Tribe—*Heliantheae* (including Ragweeds)

    Pull apart a flowerhead from your sample plant and look for a small bract attached at the base of each disk flower. The Sunflower and Tickseed tribes often have them, while other tribes usually don't. In addition, most members of the Sunflower tribe are noticeably resinous. Taste or smell any part of a sunflower head and you will notice the pitchy quality. Resins are useful as expectorants to help clear out mucous after a cold. Read more about resins in the *Medicinal Properties* section of this book.

    Taxonomists now include the former Ragweed tribe as part of the Sunflower tribe, yet to the layperson, the flowers seem distinctly different. Ragweed flowers are usually unisexual, with male and female flowers appearing separately on one plant, an oddity within the Aster family. It would be easy to confuse *Ambrosia* and *Iva* with the "green globby flowers" of the Amaranth/Goosefoot family. The cocklebur is the most noticeable member of the Ragweed tribe. Its sharp cockleburs, a "composite" of two female flowers, are often underfoot along lakes and streams across the West. Note the cross-section of the bur on the next page, showing two mature seeds inside.

Arnica—arnica (32/28/14) • Formerly in the Groundsel tribe. The plant and
    flowers are used externally as a poultice, tea, tincture, oil, or salve to treat
    bruises, arthritis, and other inflammations (Moore). Arnica stimulates
    and dilates blood vessels near the surface, improving circulation to the
    injured area. In rare cases it causes severe dermatitis (Moore). Arnica may
    be used as a mouth rinse to treat a sore throat, or taken in small doses
    to treat bruises and inflammations from the inside—but only if you
    are otherwise physically strong and healthy (Moore). Arnica contains
    sesquiterpene lactone (Tyler). It is toxic to the heart and can significantly
    raise blood pressure (Tyler). It has put children in comas (Kinucan).

Balsamorhiza—arrowleaf balsamroot (12/11/3) • The very young leaves are
    edible as they emerge from the ground in spring (before they unfold).
    Fry them in grease. Palatability varies by region and/or species. The
    young root is also supposedly good raw, boiled, or prepared in any other
    way (Willard) or when cooked in a steam pit for three days (Hart). In
    my limited experience, even young roots are too fibrous to eat. The
    seeds are edible (Willard).

        The root has thick, resinous bark. A tea of this bark coats
    the throat with the sticky resins, soothing a sore throat and acting as
    an expectorant. The root bark also contains volatile oils, useful as a

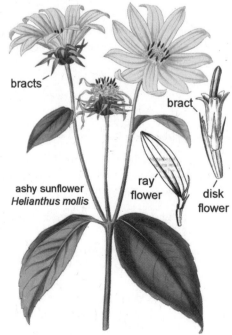

bracts

bract

ray
flower

disk
flower

ashy sunflower
Helianthus mollis

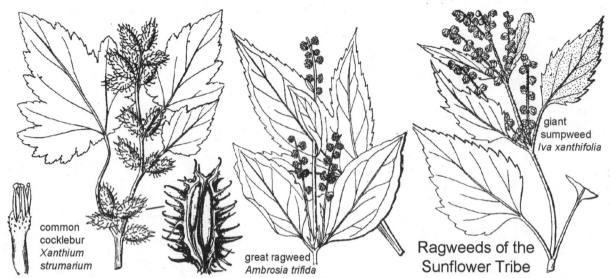

common cocklebur
Xanthium strumarium

great ragweed
Ambrosia trifida

giant sumpweed
Iva xanthifolia

Ragweeds of the Sunflower Tribe

diaphoretic. Balsamroot has immunostimulating properties similar to *Echinacea*, but not as potent (Tilford).

Chaenactis—Dusty Maiden (18/18/1) • Native to the West. A tea of the plant is used as a fever medicine for children, but it may act as a sedative on the heart (Murphey).

Echinacea—purple coneflower (7/7/1) • Native east of the Rocky Mountains. *Echinacea* plants and roots are used in many commercially available products to stimulate the immune system to prevent or fight off a cold. It is most useful for "surface" conditions like the common cold, while other herbs are more appropriate for deep immune system deficiencies (Hobbs). I got hooked on the wonders of *Echinacea* after trading copies of this book for some tincture. In addition to other measures (reduced dairy and sugar intake), the *Echinacea* helped me get through an entire winter without succumbing to the flu. Unfortunately, the herb has been seriously overharvested in the wild. Please purchase only formulas made with cultivated *Echinacea*. It is also considered highly effective for candidiasis and vaginal yeast infections (Hobbs).

Galinsoga—soldierweed (3/2/1) Introduced. Widespread throughout North America.

Helianthus—sunflower, Jerusalem artichoke, sun tubers (100/50/5) • All sunflowers produce edible seeds that are high in oil. I often eat them shells and all, which is easier than trying to extract the tiny seeds. The common wild sunflower (*H. annus*) often produce dozens of little flowerheads per plant. This native was shipped to Europe and then Russia, where it was bred to develop a single big head with big seeds (Hutchins). Wild sunflowers can be harvested with a seed beater and ground on a metate for use as mush (Olsen). The seeds are rich in phosphorus, calcium, iron, fluorine, iodine, potassium, magnesium, sodium, thiamin (vitamin B), niacin, vitamin D, and protein (Hutchins). The plants and flowerheads are quite resinous, often used for coughs, kidneys, and rheumatism (Willard).

Jerusalem artichoke *(H. tuberosus)* is a perennial sunflower often cultivated for its starchy, potato-like tubers. This common name is quizzical, since the plant is a native of eastern North America, not Jerusalem, and it doesn't look anything like an artichoke! Sun tubers seems like a better name. The tubers are high in inulin polysaccharides, good for diabetics (Gibbons). They are delicious boiled like potatoes, and even better the following day, after more of the inulin has converted to fructose.

Madia—tarweed (11/11/3) • I always smell tarweed before I see it. The odor is powerfully resinous, but also almost sweet. I like to put a stem on the dashboard of the car for fragrance, but usually have to keep the windows open to breathe! The seeds are extremely rich in oil, used in cooking (Sturtevant).

Ratibida—prairie coneflower (6/4/1) • The roots are mildly diuretic. The plant may have qualities similar to *Echinacea*.

Rudbeckia—coneflower (30/24/2) • A tea of the root or leaves is a stimulating diuretic and a mild cardiac stimulant (Moore).

Viguiera—goldeneye (150/11/1) Native from California to Texas.

Wyethia—Mule's Ears (11/10/2) • The seeds are edible. The root of *W. helianthoides* is edible after extensive cooking (Olsen). The poultice is used for rheumatism (Murphey).

Ragweeds now in the Sunflower Tribe:

Ambrosia (including *Franseria*)—ragweed (50/25/3) A tea of the plant was used by the Cheyenne as an antispasmodic and astringent for bowel cramps and bloody stools (Vogel). It is also used for menstrual cramps, but excess consumption can lead to nausea (Bigfoot). A tea of the leaves is bitter, useful especially for relief from allergies (Bigfoot).

Iva—false ragweed, giant pigweed (15/10/2) • Widespread across North America.

Xanthium—cocklebur (5/2/2) • The prickly cockleburs are the bane of every barefoot river rat. Medicinally, the seeds are a potent diuretic and astringent, with analgesic and antispasmodic effects. Excessive consumption can be toxic (Moore).

172

Tickseed Tribe—*Coreopsideae*

Plants of the Tickseed tribe are closely related to the Sunflower tribe and share some overlapping characteristics for identification. However, members of the Tickseed tribe are not resinous like those of the Sunflower tribe.

Bidens—beggarstick (200/26/4) • *B. alba* is considered edible and delicious as a potherb. A tea or tincture of some species is used for irritation, inflammation, pain, and bleeding of the urinary tract mucosa (Moore). The common name "beggarstick" also applies to houndstongue (*Cynoglossum*) of the Borage family.

Coreopsis—tickseed (35/35/1) • Native throughout North America, except for the Great Basin.

Cosmos—cosmos (20/4/0) • Native and introduced species are found primarily in the southern and eastern half of North America. Garden cosmos (*C. bipinnatus*) are widely cultivated.

Thelesperma—cota, greenthread, Navajo tea (13/13/1) Native to the western two-thirds of North America. Cota is mildly diuretic. It is a popular tea where it is abundant in the Southwest (Moore).

Aster Family
Aster Subfamily
Tickseed Tribe

golden tickseed
Coreopsis tinctoria

nodding beggartick
Bidens cernua

Sneezeweed Tribe—*Helenieae*

Most Sneezeweeds have only one row of bracts beneath the flowerhead, and none have more than three rows. Also, the Sneezeweeds often have glands or dots of resin on the leaves.

Eriophyllum—woolly sunflower (14/11/1) Native to western North America.

Gaillardia—blanket flower, brown-eyed Susan (15/12/1) • Native throughout North America. *Gaillardia* is apparently astringent (Willard).

Helenium—sneezeweed (40/20/1) • Native throughout North America. The crushed blossoms are used as an inhalant for hay fever (Murphey).

Hulsea—alpinegold (7/7/1) Native from the Pacific Coast to the Rocky Mountains.

Hymenopappus—woollywhite (11/10/1) Native to western and southern North America.

Hymenoxys—rubberweed (28/22/4) The root contains a latex that may be used as chewing gum. It is a potential source for commercial rubber (Fern), but the vegetation may be toxic to sheep.

common woolly sunflower
Eriophyllum lanatum

sneezeweed
Helenium autumnale

Aster Family
Aster Subfamily
Sneezeweed Tribe

California rubberweed
Hymenoxys californica

blanketflower
Gaillardia pulchella

173

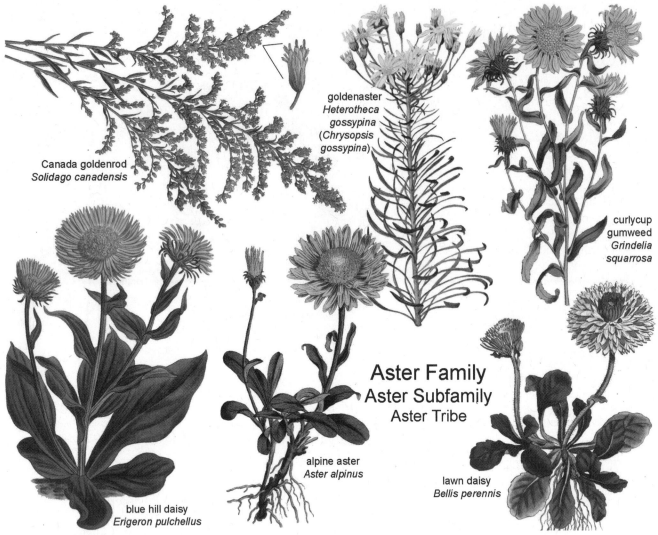

Canada goldenrod
Solidago canadensis

goldenaster
Heterotheca gossypina
(*Chrysopsis gossypina*)

curlycup gumweed
Grindelia squarrosa

Aster Family
Aster Subfamily
Aster Tribe

blue hill daisy
Erigeron pulchellus

alpine aster
Aster alpinus

lawn daisy
Bellis perennis

Aster Tribe—*Astereae*

Plants of the Aster tribe often have a great many very slender ray flowers. Also, turn the flowerhead over and look at the back. Members of the Aster tribe often have multiple layers of bracts of unequal length. Based on its resinous properties, gumweed (*Grindelia*) seems like it should be part of the Sunflower tribe.

Aster—aster (600/2/0) Most North American asters have been reclassified as *Symphyotrichum* and several other genera.

Baccharis—seepwillow (400/24/0) • The stalks make excellent drills for handdrill fire sets. (See *Participating in Nature*.)

Bellis—daisy (10/1/1) *B. perennis.* Introduced from Europe. The tea is used as a digestive aid, antispasmodic, laxative, expectorant and demulcent (Lust). The leaves can be cooked as a potherb (Sturtevant).

Chrysopsis—goldenaster (11/11/0) Many species were reclassified as *Heterotheca*. The rest are native to the southeastern states.

Chrysothamnus—rabbitbrush (16/14/2) • The young shoots are edible. The latex can be chewed as gum (Olsen).

Erigeron—fleabane daisy (250/140/30) • The fleabanes are astringent and diuretic, useful in conventional ways (Willard). *E. canadensis* is known to contain a volatile oil (Densmore).

Grindelia—gumweed (50/33/2) • *Grindelia* is rich in amorphous resins, tannic acid, volatile oils, and contains the alkaloid grindeline (Hart). A tea of the plant or flowers has expectorant properties, probably due to the resins. It is principally used for lung ailments such as coughing, asthma, and bronchitis. A poultice of the plant is used as a stimulant to bring healing to rheumatism, sores, and rashes (Willard). It is also used as a diuretic (Hutchins). Gumweed may absorb selenium from the soil (Lust).

Gutierrezia—snakeweed (25/10/1) A tea of the plant is used in a bath to reduce inflammation from arthritis and rheumatism. It is safe for repeated, long-term use. The tea is also used to decrease menstruation (Moore).

Solidago—goldenrod (100/90/11) • Goldenrod seeds are edible as mush or as a stew thickener (Olsen). The young greens are edible as a potherb. The dried flowers make a pleasant tea. Goldenrod contains saponins, tannins, bitters, flavonoids, and a volatile oil (Schauenberg). The dried, powdered plant was once used to stop bleeding on battlefields (Tilford).

Townsendia—Townsend's daisies (26/26/9) These are tightly clustered flowers close to the ground, named after a botanist.

Teasel Family—*Dipsacaceae*

Teasel flowerheads could easily be mistaken for those of the Aster family. The individual flowers are bisexual and slightly irregular, clustered in a dense head, and often protected by spiky bracts (modified leaves). There are 5 sepals and 4 or 5 united petals, plus 4 stamens. The ovary is positioned inferior and consists of 2 united carpels (bicarpellate), but aborts one, forming just 1 chamber. It produces a dry seed (an achene) enclosed in a sac. Worldwide, there are about 12 genera and 350 species.

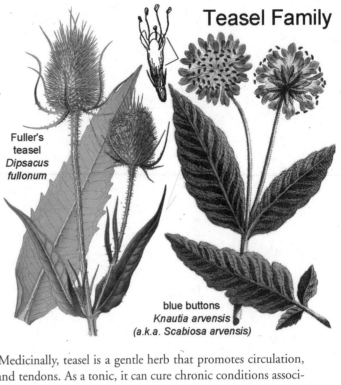

Teasel Family

Fuller's teasel
Dipsacus fullonum

blue buttons
Knautia arvensis
(a.k.a. *Scabiosa arvensis*)

Key Words: Aster-like blossoms with slightly irregular flowers.

Dipsacus—teasel (15/2/1) • Introduced and widespread across North America. Usually found in moist soil. Teasel superficially resembles a thistle. The spiky flowerheads were once used to raise the nap on new woolen textiles, a process called "teasing" or "fulling" the cloth (Baumgardt). The upper leaves of the teasel have evolved to catch water and drown insects. The nutrients are absorbed as the bodies naturally decompose (Verrill). Medicinally, teasel is a gentle herb that promotes circulation, tones the liver and kidneys, and strengthens the bones and tendons. As a tonic, it can cure chronic conditions associated with arthritis and stiff or sore muscles, including potentially lyme disease (Storl)

Knautia—blue buttons (40/1/1) • *K. arvensis*. Introduced. The plant contains tannic acid and bitter principles (Schauenberg). A tea of the plant or roots is used externally as a wash for cuts, burns, and bruises, internally as a "blood purifier."

Scabiosa—pincushion flower (80/4/0) Some species have pretty flowers like *Knautia* combined with spiky bracts like *Dipsacus*.

Valerian Family—*Valerianaceae*

North American members of this family have small flowers in clusters. The flowers can be bisexual or unisexual, regular or slightly irregular. The sepals are inconspicuous. There are 5 united petals, often with a spur at the base of the flower. There are 1 to 4 stamens. The ovary is positioned inferior and consists of 3 united carpels (tricarpellate) but aborts two, forming just 1 chamber. It produces an achene (a dry seed). Worldwide, there are 13 genera and 400 species. North American genera are listed below. Red valerian (*Centranthus*) is cultivated.

Key Words: Plants with basal and opposite leaves. Small flowers with tiny spurs. Roots with pungent aroma.

Plectritis—seablush (15/3/1) Native from the Pacific Coast to the Rocky Mountains.

Valeriana—valerian, tobacco root (250/19/5) • I live near the Tobacco Root Mountains, which are named after this plant. *V. edulis* (Harrington) and *V. obovata* (Craighead) produce large, edible roots. These are traditionally cooked in a steam pit for two days prior to being eaten. The two species in the Tobacco Root Mountains have small, inedible roots. The roots of all valerians have a characteristic "dirty sock smell," due to the presence of isovaleric acid. Many people consider the odor repelling.

Valerian is a popular sedative, but it is not related to Valium®. Valerian sedates the central nervous system, but stimulates digestion and the cardiovascular system. About one in five people react to valerian as a stimulant rather than a sedative. Long-term use can result in depression (Moore). Author Robyn Klein told of driving down the road with freshly-dug valerian roots in the front seat. The roots became very aromatic in the sun, until she grew so tired she had to pull off the road and sleep for two hours!

Valerianella—cornsalad (60/14/0) As the name implies, the plant is edible (Cook).

marsh valerian
Valeriana dioica

Valerian Family

Honeysuckle Family—*Caprifoliaceae*

If you find a bush with opposite leaves and pithy stems (what looks like Styrofoam® in the core), then it may be a member of the Honeysuckle family or the closely related Adoxa family. Many genera also have flowers and berries in pairs. The flowers are regular, except for some species of *Lonicera*. The bisexual flowers include 5 usually united sepals (sometimes very small), plus 5 united petals and usually 5 stamens (sometimes 4 of each). The ovary is positioned inferior and consists of 2, 3, 5, or 8 united carpels with the partition walls either present or absent. It matures as a fleshy berry or sometimes a drupe, a fleshy fruit with a stony pit. The remains of the sepals can be seen attached to the fruit. Worldwide, there are about 15 genera and 400 species between the two families. Many genera are cultivated as ornamentals. The genera below are native to North America. This is a chemically complex family. Many species produce minimally palatable fruits. Some species contain toxic alkaloids in the seeds or vegetation.

Key Words:
Bushes with opposite leaves and flowers/berries usually paired or in clusters. Pithy stems.

Linnaea—twinflower (1/1/1) • *L. borealis*. The plant or berries might be edible. The plant has been used as a tonic for pregnancy and for painful or difficult menstruation (Fern). It is sometimes segregated into its own family, *Linnaeaceae*.

Lonicera—honeysuckle (180/50/4) • Honeysuckle berries are edible, but usually very bitter. A frost may improve their flavor (Willard). A European species may be poisonous. The bark and leaves contain bitter principles with emetic properties (Schauenberg). The plant is also used as an expectorant and laxative (Kadans).

Symphoricarpos—snowberry (15/12/4) • The leaves, bark and berries have astringent properties; the poultice is used for wounds, and the tea as an eye wash (Hart). The berries contain saponins, and may be used as a soap substitute or fish poison (Fern). The berries are considered emetic (Willard), probably due to the taste of the saponins.

Triosteum—feverwort (8/3/0) Native to the eastern two-thirds of North America. A tea of the leaves is used as a diaphoretic to bring down a fever, hence the common name. A tea of the roots contains an alkaloid; it is considered diuretic and cathartic. In addition to urinary disorders, it is used for menstrual disorders and constipation. A poultice of the root is used on snakebites and sores (Fern).

Adoxa Family—*Adoxaceae*

Several genera previously classified within the Honeysuckle family have been segregated out into the new Adoxa family. These genera do not usually have flowers in pairs.

Adoxa—moschatel (1/1/1) *A. moschatellina*. Native across Canada, and down through the Rocky Mountains. The plant and flowers emit a musk-like scent when the dew falls in the evening.

Sambucus—elderberry (25/3/3) • The botanical and common names for North American elderberries are highly confusing. There are basically two species, plus a number of subspecies, but much disagreement about what to call them. Our blue elderberry (*S. cerulean*) is sometimes classified as a subspecies of the European black elderberry (*S. nigra*), while other botanists classify it as *S. mexicana*. And our common black elderberry, widespread at high elevations the mountain West, is actually considered a variety of the red elderberry (*S. racemosa*). Thus, our blue elderberry might be a black one and our black one is actually a red one! Elderberries are easy to gather in abundance. The light-blue berries seem to be the sweetest. The flowers can be batter-fried. Read more about harvesting, processing, and eating elderberries in *Foraging the Mountain West*.

Elderberry extract is an effective remedy for the flu. A property of the elderberries reportedly binds to the "spikes" on the flu virus, preventing it from penetrating and entering body cells. A clinical trial with an elderberry extract called "Sambucol" revealed that 90% of a flu-infected group fully recovered after three days, while most individuals in the control group needed six days to recover (Eliman). The seeds of all elderberries contain a bitter form of cyanide called sambucin, which may cause nausea and diarrhea if eaten in large enough amounts (Hutchins). Cyanide and sambucin are also present in the leaves and bark (Moore). Elderberry stems are useful for bowdrill and handdrill fire sets, as well as for making flutes, but note that the stems may be toxic until dried.

Viburnum—highbush cranberry, snowball tree, black haw, nannyberry (120/27/3) • Native and introduced species are found throughout North America, except for the Southwest. The true cranberry is a member of the Heath family. *Viburnum* berries are edible but bitter. A frost may improve them. Cook the berries with sugar and strain out the big seeds (Hall). Medicinally, the bark contains isovalerianic acid (like *Valerian*) and simple phenol glycosides (Densmore, Geller, Schauenberg). It is used for its antispasmodic, nervine, astringent and diuretic properties. The boiled tea is recommended for the last two to three months of a pregnancy to eliminate nervousness and cramps (Willard).

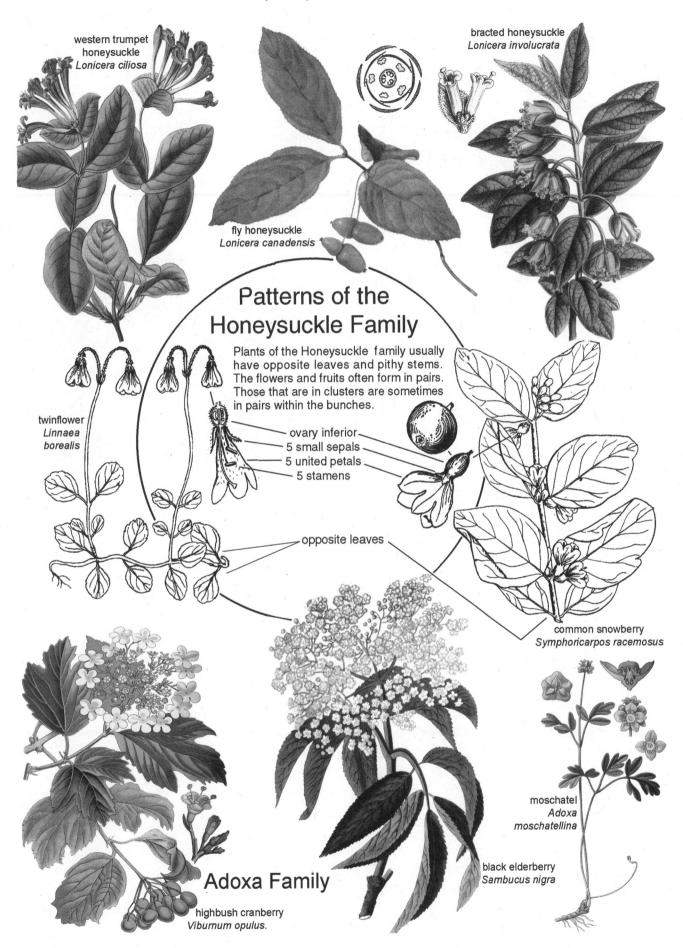

western trumpet
honeysuckle
Lonicera ciliosa

bracted honeysuckle
Lonicera involucrata

fly honeysuckle
Lonicera canadensis

Patterns of the
Honeysuckle Family

Plants of the Honeysuckle family usually
have opposite leaves and pithy stems.
The flowers and fruits often form in pairs.
Those that are in clusters are sometimes
in pairs within the bunches.

ovary inferior
5 small sepals
5 united petals
5 stamens

twinflower
*Linnaea
borealis*

opposite leaves

common snowberry
Symphoricarpos racemosus

Adoxa Family

moschatel
*Adoxa
moschatellina*

black elderberry
Sambucus nigra

highbush cranberry
Viburnum opulus.

177

Ginseng Family—*Araliaceae*

The next time you see a building covered with ivy (*Hedera*), stop and notice the umbels of flowers or berries. Note that they form single umbels, not compound like the closely related Parsley family. The small, greenish-white flowers are regular and may be either unisexual or bisexual. There are 5 small, separate sepals, 5 (sometimes 4 or 10) separate petals and usually 5 (sometimes 3 to numerous) stamens. The stamens are alternate with the petals. The ovary is positioned inferior. It consists of 2 to 5 (up to 15) united carpels with the partition walls present, forming an equal number of chambers. It matures as a red or purple berry with one seed per carpel. The fruit splits apart at the carpels in some species. Note that some species produce flowers and berries in dense heads or elongated spikes. The plants of this family prefer moist environments.

World-wide, there are about 70 genera and 700 species.

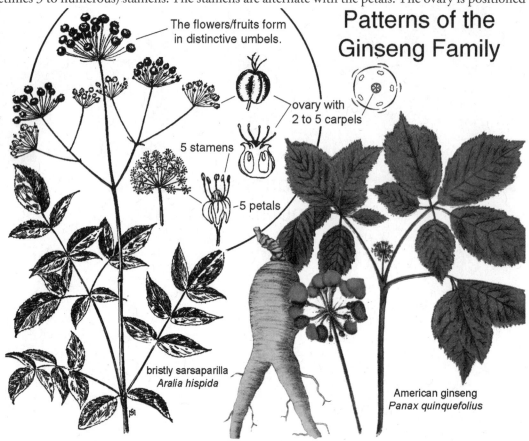

The flowers/fruits form in distinctive umbels.

ovary with 2 to 5 carpels

5 stamens

5 petals

bristly sarsaparilla
Aralia hispida

Patterns of the Ginseng Family

American ginseng
Panax quinquefolius

North American genera are listed below. Volatile oils are common in the Ginseng family; they are useful as diaphoretics to stimulate sweating. English ivy (*Hedera helix*) also contains volatile oils and bitters. It has been used externally to treat dermatitis, inflammations, and burns, or internally to expel parasites and to treat gout, rheumatism, and bronchitis. Caution is advised since the plant is mildly toxic, probably due to the triterpene saponins. *Schefflera* is a common houseplant. Note that ginger (*Zingiber*) belongs to an unrelated family, *Zingiberaceae*.

Key Words: Plants of moist forests with umbels (not compound) and berries.

Aralia—wild sarsaparilla, spikenard (30/4/1) • Found in moist forests throughout North America. It is considered a substitute for the true sarsaparilla (*Smilax* of the Greenbrier family) and either may be used for flavoring root beer. Medicinally, wild sarsaparilla contains an acrid resin (Densmore). It is diaphoretic and stimulant. It also has demulcent properties (Willard). A tea of the root is commonly used for colds and coughing, even pneumonia. This plant can also stimulate menstruation, if it has been delayed by health stress (Moore). A poultice of the root is used on burns, sores, ringworm and skin eruptions. It is also used for intestinal gas, and is reportedly a strong antidote for deadly poisons (Willard).

Oplopanax—devil's club (3/1/1) • *O. horridus*. Native to the Pacific northwest. Devil's club is used similarly to *Aralia*, as a respiratory stimulant and expectorant for chest colds. It also has a history of use as a hypoglycemic agent to lower blood sugar and reduce or eliminate the need for injected insulin in cases of adult-onset diabetes. A poultice of the root has analgesic properties. A tea and bath of the root is used for rheumatism and arthritis (Willard). Herbalist Keith Hess reported that the cut stalks will often take root and grow when inserted into moist ground.

Panax—ginseng (6/2/0) Native from the Midwest to the Atlantic. Ginseng is rich in volatile oils, used especially as a diaphoretic, but also to counteract nausea and the double vision that can accompany dizziness (Kadans).

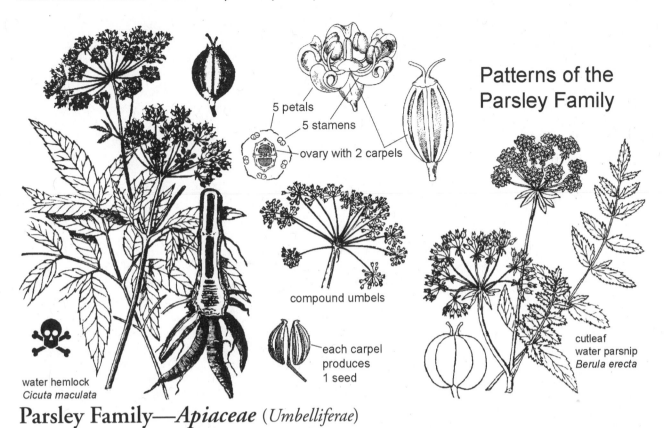

5 petals

5 stamens

ovary with 2 carpels

Patterns of the Parsley Family

compound umbels

each carpel produces 1 seed

water hemlock
Cicuta maculata

cutleaf
water parsnip
Berula erecta

Parsley Family—*Apiaceae* (*Umbelliferae*)

Key Words: Compound umbels. Usually hollow flower stalks.

The Parsley family is as familiar as carrots and parsley. Members of the Parsley family are mostly herbs (rarely shrubs or trees), usually with hollow stems and pinnate leaves. The best pattern for identification is the compound umbels. Notice that all stems of the flower cluster radiate from a single point at the end of the stalk, like an umbrella, or "umbel." At the end of each flower stem there is another umbel of smaller stems, making a compound umbel. Looking closer, the little flowers have 5 sepals (small and underneath), plus 5 petals and 5 stamens. The ovary is positioned inferior. It consists of 2 united carpels, as indicated by the number of styles. Partition walls are present, forming an equal number of chambers. The ovary matures as a schizocarp, a dry fruit that splits into individual one-seeded carpels (mericarps) when dry. Some members of the Buckwheat family also have umbels and compound umbels.

Worldwide, there are about 434 genera and 3,700 species. About 75 genera are native to North America. Most members of the Parsley family are rich with spicy, aromatic volatile oils. Spices from the family include: anise (*Pimpinella*), celery (*Apium*), chervil (*Anthriscus*), coriander or cilantro (*Coriandrum*), caraway (*Carum*), cumin (*Cuminum*), dill (*Anethum*), fennel (*Foeniculum*), and parsley (*Petroselinum*). There are also a number of edible roots in the family, including the carrot (*Daucus*) and parsnip (*Pastinaca*). Caution: the Parsley family also includes some of the most deadly plants in North America, especially hemlock (*Conium*) and water hemlock (*Cicuta*). Many people have died after confusing hemlock with wild carrots. When you see the compound umbel, let it be your warning—you *must* get positive identification of these plants!

Medicinally, the Parsley family is rich in volatile oils. Spicy and stimulating, volatile oils warm the body, open the pores, and encourage sweating. This diaphoretic property is useful to help break a fever. A fever is the body's way of "cooking" the microorganisms that cause infections. Spicy teas and food can help raise a mild fever just high enough to "cook" a virus, thus ending the fever. However, diaphoretics can be dangerous where there is already a high fever; other compounds, such as aspirin, should be used to reduce the fever. Diaphoretics tend to be most effective if used at the very onset of a cold. Volatile oils also have a decongestant effect, as you'll notice when your nose runs after a spicy meal. Intensely diaphoretic plants are often antiviral as well and may even help with venereal diseases.

Aromatic plants are also used as carminatives to expel gas. Some members of this family stimulate menstruation (an emmenagogue) and relieve menstrual cramps. They are sometimes used in conjunction with childbirth, but may be dangerous during a pregnancy. Celery contains furanocoumarins. The juice on the skin can cause dermatitis when exposed to sunlight.

Edible, Medicinal, and Poisonous Plants in the Parsley Family

Angelica—angelica, dong quai (50/21/4) • Widespread in North America, except the Great Plains. The leaves of some species resemble water hemlock leaves. The peeled, boiled roots of Norwegian angelica (*A. archangelica*) are edible (Brown), but most species of *Angelica* are strongly medicinal. The roots and seeds are diaphoretic, diuretic, antispasmodic, and carminative. In traditional Chinese medicine, dong quai (*A. sinensis* and *A. polymorpha*) is recommended for painful menstruation, to relieve cramps, premenstrual syndrome (PMS), irregular menstrual cycles, infrequent periods, and menopausal symptoms. However, *Angelica* is not recommended for people of "weak constitution" (Hobbs).

Berula—creeping water parsnip (1/1/1) *B. erecta*. Native from the Pacific to the Mississippi. It may be poisonous (Pammel).

Bupleurum—thorowax (180/3/1) Several species of *Bupleurum* are used in Chinese medicine. The root is bitter and slightly acrid. It is used to restore normal liver function, especially in patients with hepatitis (Hobbs).

Carum—caraway (25/1/1) • *C. carvi*. Introduced. Caraway is a cultivated herb and spice, often naturalized into the countryside. Medicinally, it is antispasmodic, carminative, and stimulating to digestion, menstruation, lactose production and as an expectorant. The leaves and roots are edible. Some species have bigger roots than others (Sturtevant).

Cicuta—water hemlock (4/4/3) • Water hemlock is the deadliest plant in North America, often mistaken for a wild carrot. The whole plant is toxic, with the highest concentrations in the roots and the base of the stalks (Harrington). It affects the central nervous system, causing convulsions and quick death. Some victims chew their tongues to shreds.

Conium—poison hemlock (2/1/1) • *C. maculatum*. Poison hemlock is less poisonous than *Cicuta*, but not by much. The most toxic parts are in the leaves and stems. A potent infusion of hemlock was used to execute Socrates (Lust). It causes paralysis rather than convulsions (Harrington).

Cymopterus—springparsley (50/35/5) Springparsleys resemble biscuitroots (*Lomatium*). The roots, leaves, and flowers are edible (Sweet). The seeds are used as a digestive aid. The leaves are used to help urinary infections (Moore).

Daucus—carrot, Queen Anne's lace (60/2/1) • Cultivated carrots were bred from the Eurasian wild carrot (*D. carota*), which has a pale, usually stringy taproot. It is now widespread across North America. The American wild carrot (D. *pusillus*) is native to the Pacific coast and southern states. The leaves and seeds of either carrot may be used as a spice. The roots are often woody, but otherwise edible.

Heracleum—cow parsnip (60/2/1) • Cow parsnip contains a potent volatile oil (Densmore) and a furanocoumarin (Schauenberg). The young stalks are minimally edible. The roots and seeds are antispasmodic, carminative, and expectorant (Willard). A tea of the root is good for nausea, gas and indigestion. The fresh root is acrid and should be dried prior to use. A bath, poultice, or tea of the fresh root is used to treat paralysis (Moore, Willard). The mature, green seeds have an analgesic effect on the teeth and gums (Tilford).

Ligusticum—osha, lovage (25/11/5) • The seeds and leaves are dried and used as spice. The root is chewed as a potent diaphoretic, anesthetic, bitter, and expectorant. Osha is a popular and effective herb, particularly favored for viral infections (Moore). The different species vary in form, but memorize the smell of the root as a good aid for identification.

Lomatium—biscuitroot (80/78/11) • Native from the Pacific to the Mississippi. Individual species vary significantly, and may resemble other parsleys. Some biscuitroots are strongly medicinal, while others are tasty and easy to harvest. A one-hour harvest of *L. cous-cous* in the Pryor Mountains of south-central Montana yielded a quart of delicious, starchy roots. Washing and peeling took an additional two hours. Medicinally, *L. dissectum* is valued for its antiviral properties, especially for respiratory infections like the flu or pneumonia, as well as tonsillitis and pharyngitis (Klein).

Orogenia—Indian potato (2/2/1) • The roots are edible raw or cooked (Craighead, Harrington). Author Larry Olsen considers it one of the tastiest foods in the West.

Osmorhiza—sweet cicely (10/8/5) • Sweet cicely root has a powerful anise-like aroma. The intensity varies by species. Most people like the smell, but some find it intensely repelling. I have used a tea of the root to flavor cookies. Medicinally, the root has antiviral, expectorant, and mildly laxative properties (Willard). It is listed as carminative, expectorant and a digestive stimulant (Lust). Sweet cicely may help to balance the blood sugar, while also inhibiting fungal infections of the digestive and reproductive systems (Tilford).

Pastinaca—parsnip (14/1/1) • *P. sativa*. Introduced from Europe. The roots are edible and delicious, either raw or cooked. The green plant contains furanocoumarins and may cause dermatitis on contact with sweaty skin (Pammel).

Perideridia—Yampa (13/13/1) • Yampa is one of my favorite wild edibles. I like to nibble on the flowers or seeds on mountain hikes. The roots are okay raw, but delicious cooked. Read more in *Foraging the Mountain West*. The seeds can be used as seasoning (Willard). Medicinally, eating the seeds is good for indigestion (Sweet).

Sanicula—sanicle (40/17/1) It contains saponins, tannic acid, bitters, and volatile oils (Schauenberg), used as an astringent, expectorant and nervine (Lust). Some species are said to be poisonous (Cook).

Sium—water parsnip (8/2/1) The leaves and stems are reported to be deadly to livestock. The roots may be edible, but the plant resembles *Cicuta* and should be avoided.

Torilis—hedge parsley (5/5/0) Introduced to most of North America, except the Rocky Mountains.

Zizia—zizia (3/3/2) The flowers of *Z. aurea* may be eaten in a salad or cooked like broccoli (Fern).

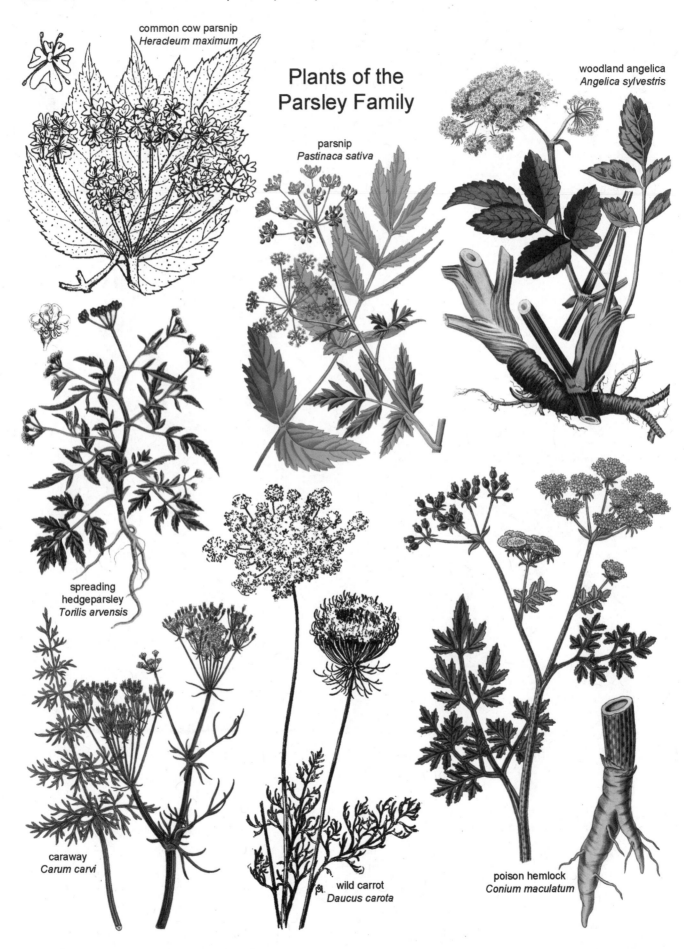

common cow parsnip
Heracleum maximum

Plants of the
Parsley Family

woodland angelica
Angelica sylvestris

parsnip
Pastinaca sativa

spreading
hedgeparsley
Torilis arvensis

caraway
Carum carvi

wild carrot
Daucus carota

poison hemlock
Conium maculatum

Sweet Flag Family—*Acoraceae*

Sweet flag superficially resembles cattails (*Typha*) in appearance and habitat. It is a perennial wetland plant with long, slendar leaves and creeping underground horizontal stems called rhizomes. The rhizomes are highly aromatic. The tightly packed flowerhead greatly resembles those of the Arum family, but without an encompassing spathe.

Sweet flag was classified as part of the Arum family until recent times. Taxonomists still debate whether it belongs in its own order or if should be included in the Water Plantain order. The individual flowers are small and bisexual with 6 tepals (3 sepals and 3 petals that cannot be distinguished from each other), plus 6 stamens. The ovary is positioned superior and consists of 3 united carpels forming a similar number of chambers. It matures as a berry with a leathery skin. Worldwide, there is just the 1 genus and 3 to 6 species.

Acorus—sweet flag (6/2/1) The tender, young roots can be made into candy (Hall). The rhizome can be grated and used as flavoring for spice cake (Lincoff). Our native sweet flag (*A. americanus*) is considered safe, but other species may be carcinogenic. *A. calamus* is banned as a food or food additive in the U.S. (Tyler).

sweet flag
Acorus calamus

Sweet Flag Family

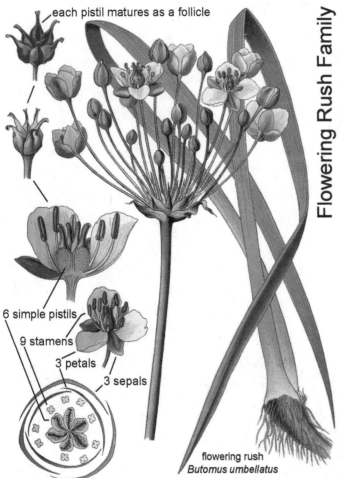

each pistil matures as a follicle

6 simple pistils

9 stamens

3 petals

3 sepals

flowering rush
Butomus umbellatus

Flowering Rush Family

Flowering Rush Family—*Butomaceae*

The flowering rush is in a class by itself—the family is comprised of a single genus with a single species, *Butomus umbellatus*. Flowering rush is native to Eurasia, but introduced in North America as an ornamental plant.

The long, skinny, triangular leaves can grow to more than three feet in length. Flowers form on tall stalks in umbrella-like clusters of twenty to fifty flowers. Individual flowers have 3 pink sepals and 3 larger pink petals, plus 9 stamens. There are 6 simple pistils (apocarpous) or slightly united at the base (syncarpous), positioned superior to the other parts. Each pistil matures as a follicle, a dry fruit that splits open along one side to release its many seeds. Flowering rush is considered a serious invasive species along waterway margins in the Great Lakes region and beyond.

Key Words: Rush-like plants with pink flowers grouped in umbels.

Butomus—flowering rush (1/1/1) The starchy root can be peeled, cooked, and eaten, or dried and ground into powder (Fern).

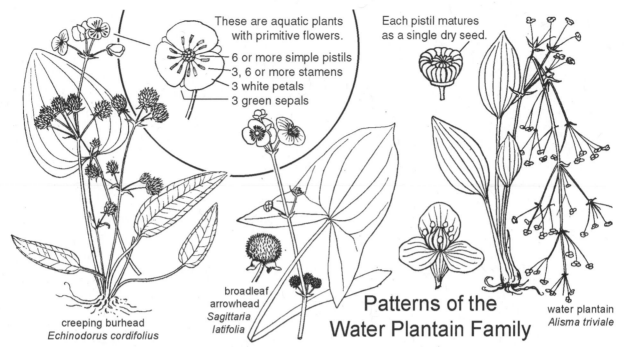

These are aquatic plants with primitive flowers.

6 or more simple pistils
3, 6 or more stamens
3 white petals
3 green sepals

Each pistil matures as a single dry seed.

creeping burhead
Echinodorus cordifolius

broadleaf arrowhead
Sagittaria latifolia

Patterns of the
Water Plantain Family

water plantain
Alisma triviale

Water Plantain Family—*Alismataceae* (a.k.a. *Alismaceae*)

If you compare an arrowhead blossom (*Sagittaria*) to a typical buttercup blossom (*Ranunculus*) you will see some striking similarities, even though the plants are from distantly related families, one a monocot and the other a dicot. Both have numerous pistils clustered together in a ball- or cone-shape in the center of the blossom, surrounded by numerous stamens. Both families have retained many ancestral characteristics, so they look somewhat similar, even though they are taxonomically distant from one another.

Members of the Water Plantain or Arrowhead family are aquatic herbs with basal leaves that are either floating or erect. The flowers have 3 green sepals and 3 white petals. There may be 3, 6, or numerous stamens. These primitive flowers have 6 or more simple pistils, positioned superior to the other parts. Each pistil matures as a single, dry seed, called an achene. Worldwide, there are about 11 genera and 90 species. North America genera are listed below. Many species produce starchy, edible roots.

Key Words: Monocot flowers
with parts in threes and numerous simple pistils.

Alisma—water plantain (10/4/2) • The roots are acrid raw, but edible after thorough cooking or drying (Olsen). The young, cooked plants are also edible and salty tasting. Medicinally, the acrid leaves can be applied as a stimulating poultice for bruises and swellings. The root is reported to lower cholesterol and blood sugar levels and to reduce blood pressure. The powdered seed is astringent and used to stop bleeding. It may cause sterility (Fern).

Baldellia—lesser water plantain (2/1/0) *B. ranunculoides*. Introduced from Europe.

Damasonium—damasonium (5/1/0) Native to the Pacific states.

Echinodorus—burhead (26/4/0) Native to the southern two-thirds of the U.S.

Sagittaria (including *Lophotocarpus*)—arrowhead, wapato (20/16/2) • The slender, long roots form starchy swellings in the fall that can be as large as a small egg. These can be boiled or roasted and eaten. Wapato is rare here in Montana and the swollen roots I found were the size of small marbles. But in Oregon, where wapato grows larger and more abundant, author John Kallas reports harvesting eighty-eight tubers (1.6 lbs) in fifteen minutes, ranging from 3/4 to 2 inches long and 3/4 to 1 1/4 inches wide. He conducted his test in late May, just as the tubers were beginning to sprout new shoots. His technique was to gather the roots in shallow water by stomping around on a small area until the tubers were dislodged and floated to the surface (Kallas).

broadleaf arrowhead
Sagittaria latifolia

Arum Family—*Araceae*

If you have ever seen an *Anthurium*, or "little boy plant," then you have met a member of the Arum family. This is a family of unique plants with mostly basal leaves and minute flowers crowded on a fleshy stalk that is often surrounded by a large, colored bract called a spathe. There are 4 to 6 small, scale-like tepals, a term used when the sepals and petals cannot be distinguished from one another. There are typically 6 (sometimes 1, 2, 4 or 8) stamens. The ovary is positioned superior and consists of 2 or 3 (sometimes 1 to 9) united carpels with the partition walls present, forming an equal number of chambers. It matures as a berry with 1 to numerous seeds.

Worldwide, there are 110 genera and 3,200 species, mostly tropical and subtropical. Note that sweet flag (*Acorus*) has been separated into its own family, *Acoraceae*. Native or common introduced genera are listed below. Several additional genera are cultivated in southern states, and some have established feral populations. Duckweeds were formerly a separate family, but genetic evidence places them within the Arum family.

Common houseplants of the Arum family include *Philodendron*, *Dieffenbachia*, and *Alocasia*. Many members of this family emit foul smells to attract carrion insects; the insects transport pollen from one plant to another. The foliage of a number of species contains needle-like calcium oxalate crystals. These crystals can mechanically injure the mouth and throat when eaten, or can precipitate out in the kidneys, plugging the tubules.

Key Words: Flowers and fruits on a fleshy stalk, often in a spathe.

Orontium—golden club (1/1/0) *O. aquaticum* is native to the southern and eastern states, from Texas to New York.

Arisaema—Jack-in-the-pulpit (150/2/0) The acrid root is pounded and applied as an irritating poultice to stimulate healing for rheumatic joints (Gilmore). It contains calcium oxalate crystals. Much of the acridness can be removed by drying. The dried, powdered root was taken as an expectorant and diaphoretic (Angier).

Arum—arum (12/2/0) Introduced to North America from Europe. The fresh root is extremely acrid, but many species can be utilized as a source of starchy food after cooking or drying (Sturtevant). A tea or syrup of the dried root is used internally as a diaphoretic and expectorant, for asthma, bronchitis, gas and rheumatism (Lust).

Calla—water arum (1/1/0) *C. palustris* is native to Alaska, Canada, and the northeastern states.

Lysichiton—western skunk cabbage (1/1/1) • *L. americanum*. It contains oxalates (Phillips). The root is starchy and edible, but must be thoroughly cooked (Fern). Native Americans roasted, dried and ground the roots for flour (Couplan).

Peltandra—arrow arum (2/2/0) Native to the eastern third of the continent, plus California and Oregon.

Pistia—water cabbage (1/1/0) *P. stratiotes*. Common in waterways in the southern half of North America.

Symplocarpus—eastern skunk cabbage (1/1/0) *S. foetidus*. Found from North Carolina to Iowa, north through Quebec. The young, unfurled leaves are edible after boiling in several changes of water (Lincoff).

greater duckweed
Spirodela polyrhiza

Arum Family
Duckweed Subfamily

Look for small, green aquatic plants with hanging roots floating in ponds.

Duckweed Subfamily—*Lemnoideae*

These are the world's smallest flowering plants. The plants form a thallus (a part not differentiated into leaves and stem), typically no more than a 1/4 inch in diameter. The little plants float in the water with thread-like roots dangling below. While the plants are tiny, the flowers are microscopic. The Duckweeds have separate male and female flowers on the same plant, lacking sepals or petals. Male flowers have 1 or 2 stamens, while female flowers consist of a simple pistil, producing 1 to 7 seeds.

Formerly classified as their own family, *Lemnaceae*, genetic evidence places Duckweeds as a subfamily of the Arum family. North American genera are listed below. Duckweeds are edible, but tend to absorb heavy metals. Only harvest from clean water sources. Also read about the Water Fern family, which may be confused with the Duckweeds.

Key Words: Small, aquatic plants with hanging roots floating in ponds.

Landoltia—duckmeat (1/1/0) *L. punctata*. Also known as *Spirodela punctata*.

Lemna—duckweed (13/9/5) • The plant is edible (Fern), probably when cooked. Duckweed is about 20 percent protein, higher than peanuts or alfalfa, and is cultivated for food in Asia.

Spirodela—greater duckweed (3/1/1) The plant is edible (Fern), probably when cooked.

Wolfiella—bogmat (10/3/0) The plants are rootless, but have feathery leaves that hang down in the water like roots. They have a keel that allows them to maintain their orientation in the water

Wolffia—water meal (12/5/2) The cooked plants are edible and rich in protein and carbohydrates (Fern).

Patterns of the Arum Family

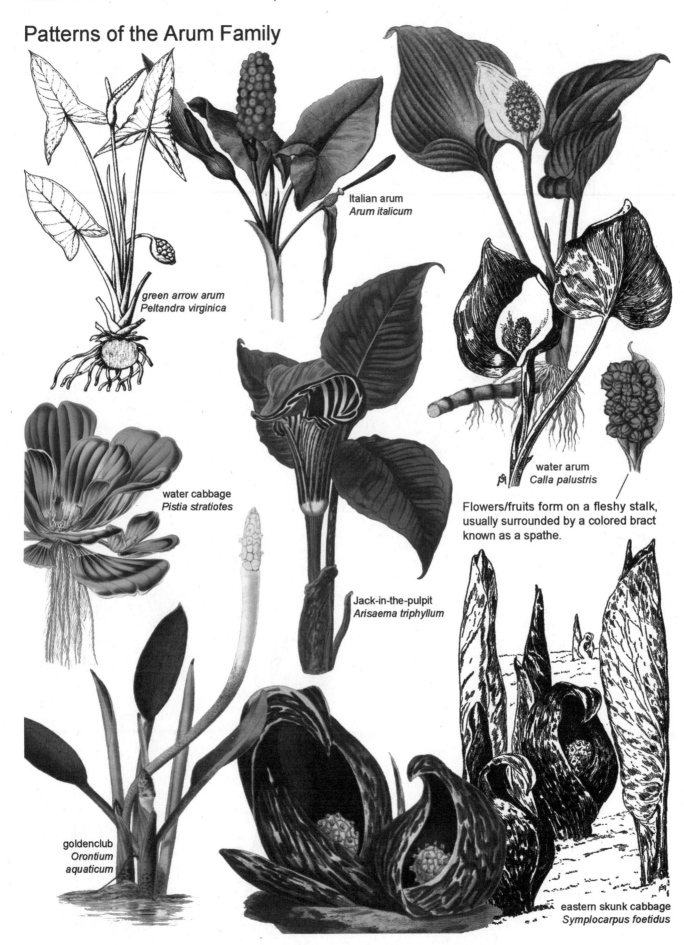

Italian arum
Arum italicum

green arrow arum
Peltandra virginica

water arum
Calla palustris

Flowers/fruits form on a fleshy stalk,
usually surrounded by a colored bract
known as a spathe.

water cabbage
Pistia stratiotes

Jack-in-the-pulpit
Arisaema triphyllum

goldenclub
*Orontium
aquaticum*

eastern skunk cabbage
Symplocarpus foetidus

185

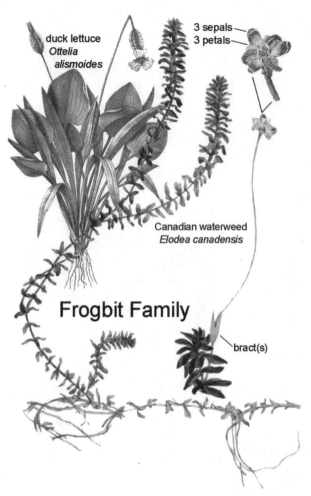

duck lettuce
*Ottelia
alismoides*

3 sepals
3 petals

Canadian waterweed
Elodea canadensis

Frogbit Family

bract(s)

Frogbit Family—*Hydrocharitaceae*

Next time you see an aquarium with live vegetation, take a closer look and see if the Canadian waterweed (*Elodea canadensis*) is included. The plant lives fully submerged, except for the floating flowers. Members of the Frogbit family are highly variable aquatic plants that live submerged, floating, and/or erect with leaves of any shape, size, or arrangement. Flowers emerge from a bract or pair of bracts (modified leaves). These are mostly regular flowers with typically 3 sepals and 3 petals (sometimes 0). Stamens vary from 2 to numerous, and flowers may be bisexual or unisexual. The ovary is positioned inferior with typically 2 to 6 united carpels, forming a single chamber that matures as a typically fleshy capsule with numerous dry or pulpy seeds.

Worldwide, there are about 18 genera and about 140 species. Native or introduced North American genera include: *Blyxa, Egeria, Halophila, Hydrilla, Hydrocharis, Limnobium, Maidenia, Thalassia, Vallisneria*, and the genera listed here. *Najas* is described separately below.

Key Words: Aquatic plants with flower parts in 3s and an inferior ovary.

Elodea—waterweed (12/5/3) Common in silty waters and often utilized in aquariums. Lives fully submerged, except for delicate white flowers.
Ottelia—duck lettuce (1/1/0) *O. alisoides*. Introduced to California and Texas.

Water Nymph Subfamily—*Najadoideae*

The Water Nymphs were formerly treated as a separate family, *Najadaceae*, but genetic evidence places it as a subfamily of the Frogbit family. These are truly aquatic plants that live and even pollinate fully submerged. The leaves are linear and toothed with either stipules or sheathing bases.

The flowers are mostly unisexual, with male and female flowers appearing on the same (monoecious) or separate plants (dioecious). Staminate (male) flowers consist of a single stamen enclosed by a bract. Pistillate (female) flowers consist of a single simple pistil, naked, or sometimes enclosed by a membranous bract, but appear to have 2 or 3 stigma lobes. The pistil matures as a dry seed called an achene. The botanical name is often spelled with an i rather than a j, as in *Naias*.

Key Words: Submerged aquatic plants with toothed, linear leaves.

Najas—water nymph (50/8/2) The plant is thought to be edible. It is valuable as a food source for fish and waterfowl, but may become invasive (Heywood).

holly-leaved
water nymph
Najas marina

solitary pistils

Water Nymph Subfamily

Arrowgrass Family—*Juncaginaceae*

Members of the Arrow-grass family are perennial herbs, typically growing in shallow fresh or salt water or in damp meadows. The flowers can be either bisexual or unisexual. The flowers are small, with 6 tepals (3 sepals + 3 petals that are identical in size and color). There are usually 6 stamens (sometimes 4, and only 1 in *Lilaea*). There are 3 to 6 carpels, either separate as simple pistils (apocarpous) or united as a single compound pistil (syncarpous). The pistil(s) are positioned superior to the other parts, and each carpel matures into a dry fruit, either a follicle (a capsule that opens along a single seam), or an achene (a dry seed). Worldwide, there are 4 genera and about 15 species. North American genera are listed below.

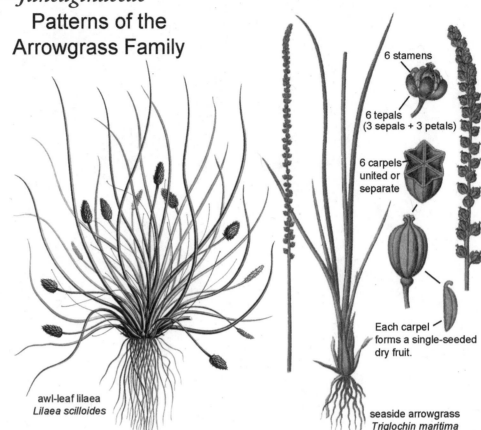

Patterns of the Arrowgrass Family

6 stamens

6 tepals
(3 sepals + 3 petals)

6 carpels united or separate

Each carpel forms a single-seeded dry fruit.

awl-leaf lilaea
Lilaea scilloides

seaside arrowgrass
Triglochin maritima

Key Words: Grassy plants with non-showy flowers and 3 to 6 simple pistils.

Lilaea—flowering quillwort (1/1/1) *L. scilloides*. Native to western North America, from California to Saskatchewan. The plant is sometimes segregated into its own family, *Lilaeaceae*. It is not related to the non-flowering quillwort (*Isoetes*) of the Quillwort family.

Triglochin—arrowgrass (12/3/3) • The leaves and rhizomes (horizontal underground stems) of the Australian water ribbon (*T. procerum*) are used as food by Aborigines (Heywood). Arrowgrass leaves and seeds contain a type of cyanide. They are poisonous raw, but cooking destroys the cyanide (Olsen). The leaves may also be edible with cooking (Harrington). The ashes of the plant are rich in potassium, which is useful for making soap (Fern).

Rannoch-Rush Family—*Scheuchzeriaceae*

Rannoch-rush (*Scheuchzeria palustris*) was formerly included in the Arrowgrass family, but it is unique enough to be a family unto itself. It has narrow, alternating leaves on an erect stem with a basal sheath, often spreading by horizontal rhizomes (underground stems). The flowers are greenish-white or yellow, with 6 tepals (3 sepals and 3 petals that are identical) and 6 stamens. There are 3 simple pistils, positioned superior, each maturing as a dry fruit called a follicle, which splits open along one side to release 1 or 2 seeds per follicle. Also known as "pod grass," the plant grows in *Sphagnum* peat bogs in cool temperate regions across the northern hemsiphere. There is only the 1 species.

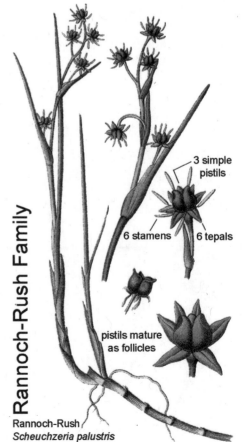

Rannoch-Rush Family

3 simple pistils

6 stamens   6 tepals

pistils mature as follicles

Rannoch-Rush
Scheuchzeria palustris

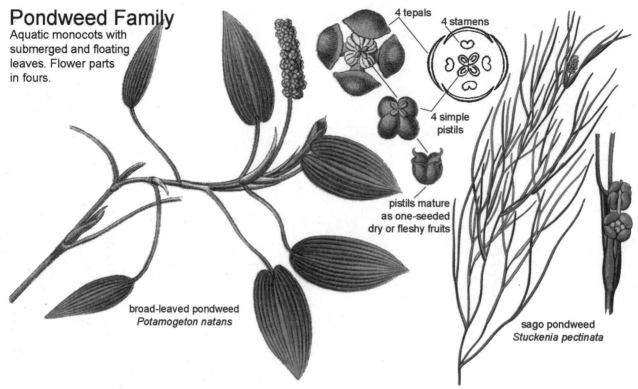

Pondweed Family
Aquatic monocots with submerged and floating leaves. Flower parts in fours.

4 tepals

4 stamens

4 simple pistils

pistils mature as one-seeded dry or fleshy fruits

broad-leaved pondweed
Potamogeton natans

sago pondweed
Stuckenia pectinata

Pondweed Family—*Potamogetonaceae*

    Members of Pondweed family are perennial, aquatic herbs, usually found in fresh or salty water rather than swamps. Plants are submerged or submerged and floating, often with narrow leaves underwater and broad leaves on the surface. Flowers are bisexual or rarely unisexual. There are 4 sepals, 0 petals, 4 stamens, and typically 4 (rarely 1)simple pistils, which are positioned superior, each maturing as a single, dry seed (an achene), or sometimes as a drupe (a berry with a stony seed) or nutlet.

    Worldwide, there are 6 genera and 120 species. The composition of this family has been rototilled numerous times by taxonomists and may be yet again. North American genera are listed below.

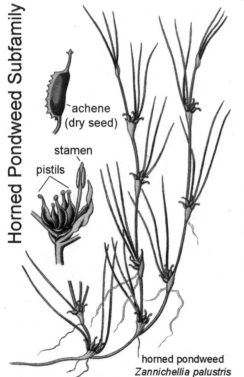

Horned Pondweed Subfamily

achene (dry seed)

stamen

pistils

horned pondweed
Zannichellia palustris

Key Words: Monocots with submerged and floating leaves and flower parts in 4s.

Potamogeton—pondweed (90/30/21) • Root stalks can be cooked in stew (Olsen). They are reported to have a nutty flavor. The rind should be removed (Fern).

Stuckenia—pondweed (6/5/0) Some species have starchy rhizomes or rhizomes with starchy tubers that are edible, especially sago pondweed (*S. pectinata* – formerly *Potamogeton pectinatus*). The starchy tubers are edible raw after separating the hard rind (Harrington).

Horned Pondweed Subfamily—*Zannichelliae*

    These plants were formerly treated as a separate family, *Zannichelliaceae*, but genetic evidence places it as a subfamily of the Pondweed family. These are aquatic plants that live and even pollinate fully submerged. The plants can be recognized by their long, thread-like leaves and stringy appearance. The sepals are absent or reduced to a 3-lobed base under the flowers. North American species have 1 stamen and 1-9 simple pistils, positioned superior, with each pistil maturing as a single dry seed (an achene).

Key Words: Submerged, stringy plants lacking sepals or petals.

Zannichellia—horned pondweed (5/1/1) *Z. palustris*. Found in fresh and brackish waters across the continent.

188

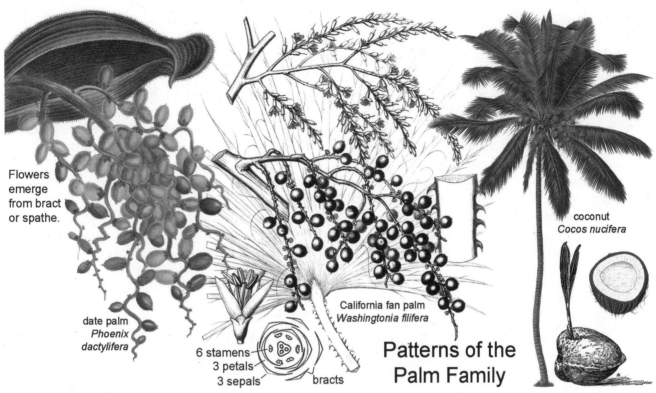

Flowers emerge from bract or spathe.

date palm
Phoenix dactylifera

6 stamens
3 petals
3 sepals
bracts

California fan palm
Washingtonia filifera

Patterns of the Palm Family

coconut
Cocos nucifera

Palm Family—*Arecaceae* (a.k.a. *Palmae* or *Palmaceae*)

If you have ever gone south to avoid Old Man Winter, then you have likely encountered members of the Palm family lining city streets. In North America, the Palm family includes trees and tree-like shrubs with slender, unbranching trunks, and large pinnately or palmately divided leaves. The flowers form in clusters, typically surrounded by or emerging from one or more bracts (modified leaves), which may become woody with age. The flowers are regular, bisexual, and usually small and white. There are typically 3 sepals and 3 petals, plus usually 6 (sometimes 3, 9, or numerous) stamens. The ovary consists of usually 3 carpels (up to 10), either as 3 separate pistils (apocarpous), or united as one pistil (syncarpous), typically maturing as a berry or drupe (a fleshy fruit with a stony seed). World-wide, there are about 200 genera and 2,600 species. North American genera are listed below. Other monocot trees are included in the Banana family (*Musaceae*) and the Bird-of-Paradise family (*Strelitziaceae*).

Key Words: Unbranching monocot trees in southern climates.

Cocos—coconut (1/1/0) *C. nucifera*. Introduced for cultivation. I think every survivalist dreams of becoming stranded on a deserted tropical island, surrounded by coconut trees. The fibrous coconut husk is excellent tinder for fire-starting. Inside the coconut is rich "milk" and nutmeat to sustain a person.

Phoenix—date palm (14/3/0) • Introduced from the Old World and widely cultivated in California, Arizona, and Florida. As a compulsive hunter-gatherer, I am always on the lookout for date palms with ripe dates when I travel south. Sometimes I see ripe dates high in the trees and cannot get to them, but sometimes I get lucky and find a nice crop scattered across the ground.

Pseudophoenix—cherry palm (4/1/0) *P. sargentii*. Red fruits. Native to Florida. Cherry palms resemble date palms (*Phoenix*), hence the botanical name, *Pseudophoenix*.

Rhapidophyllum—needle palm (1/1/0) *R. hystrix*. Tolerates colder temperatures. Native from Mississippi to South Carolina.

Sabal—palmetto (15/5/0) Native from Texas to North Carolina.

Serenoa—saw palmetto (1/1/0) *S. repens*. Native from Texas to South Carolina.

Thrinax—thatch palm (4/2/0) Native to Florida.

Washingtonia—fan palm (2/2/0) Native to Mexico and southern California. Widely cultivated in the desert southwest and Florida. The fruits are edible raw, cooked, or dried for later use. The dried fruit is hard, but can be ground into meal and eaten as porridge (Fern).

Spiderwort Family—*Commelinaceae*

If you have a succulent, creeping houseplant with purple leaves and parallel veins, then you have met the Spiderwort family. Members of this family have alternate, usually sharply folded leaves, and the base of each leaf wraps around the stem. Spiderworts have nearly regular, bisexual flowers with 3 sepals and 3 petals, usually with 2 broad petals and the third reduced in size. The petals range from blue to violet, pink, white or rose-colored, but not yellow in native North American species. The petals sometimes have a sparkly appearance, almost as if they were coated with sugar crystals. There are usually 6 stamens, and the filaments (stamen stems) are often covered with bright hairs. Some stamens may be sterile and different in appearance. The ovary is positioned superior and typically consists of 3 united carpels with the partition walls present, forming an equal number of chambers. It matures as a capsule with a few or many seeds per chamber. Spiderworts could be mistaken for lilies, but most lilies have sepals and petals of approximately equal size and color, while the Spiderworts have smaller, usually greenish sepals.

Worldwide, there are about 40 genera and about 650 species, mostly in the tropics. Six genera are native to North America, as featured below. Several others are cultivated. A number of plants in this family are called "wandering Jew" and are grown as houseplants. The African marble berry (*Pollia condensata*) has shiny, metallic-looking blue berries that are brighter than any other living organism, due to a unique cellular structure that reflects light.

Key Words: Succulent, mucilaginous monocot plants with three nearly equal-sized petals.

Aneilema—(4/1/0) *Aneilema* is introduced and sometimes invasive, found in wetlands from Texas to Georgia. The sepals are the same size and color as the petals.

Callisia—roselings (20/7/0) Native and introduced species are found from Texas to Maryland.

Commelina—day flower, wandering jew (150/8/0) • *Commelina* grows wild across the eastern and southern states. The tender shoots are edible as a salad green or potherb (Duke). The roots of many species are known to be starchy and edible (Sturtevant). Medicinally, a tea of the mucilaginous leaves is used as a gargle for sore throats. The plant has antibacterial properties (Fern).

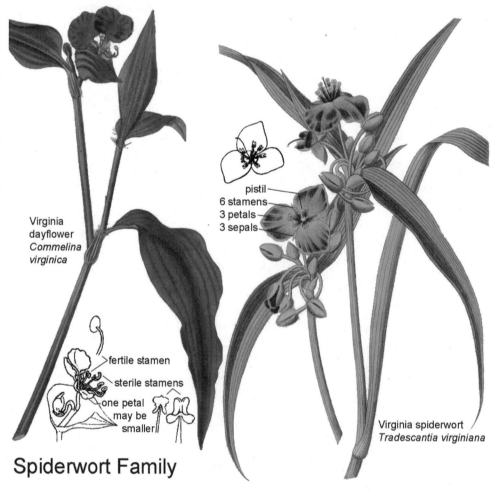

Virginia dayflower
Commelina virginica

pistil
6 stamens
3 petals
3 sepals

fertile stamen
sterile stamens
one petal may be smaller

Virginia spiderwort
Tradescantia virginiana

Spiderwort Family

Murdannia—marsh dewflower (50/3/0) Includes some speices formerly classified as *Aneilema*. These introduced plants are often found in freshwater marshes or along the edges of ponds and streams.

Tinantia—false day flower (14/1/0) *T. anomala* grows in central Texas. (Formerly classified as *Commelinantia*.)

Tradescantia—spiderwort, wandering Jew (71/31/2) • The plant is edible in salads. The stem has a white, mucilaginous sap (Bigfoot). Medicinally, a poultice of the leaves is used on insect bites and cancers. The roots are considered laxative and are used in tea for stomachaches (Fern).

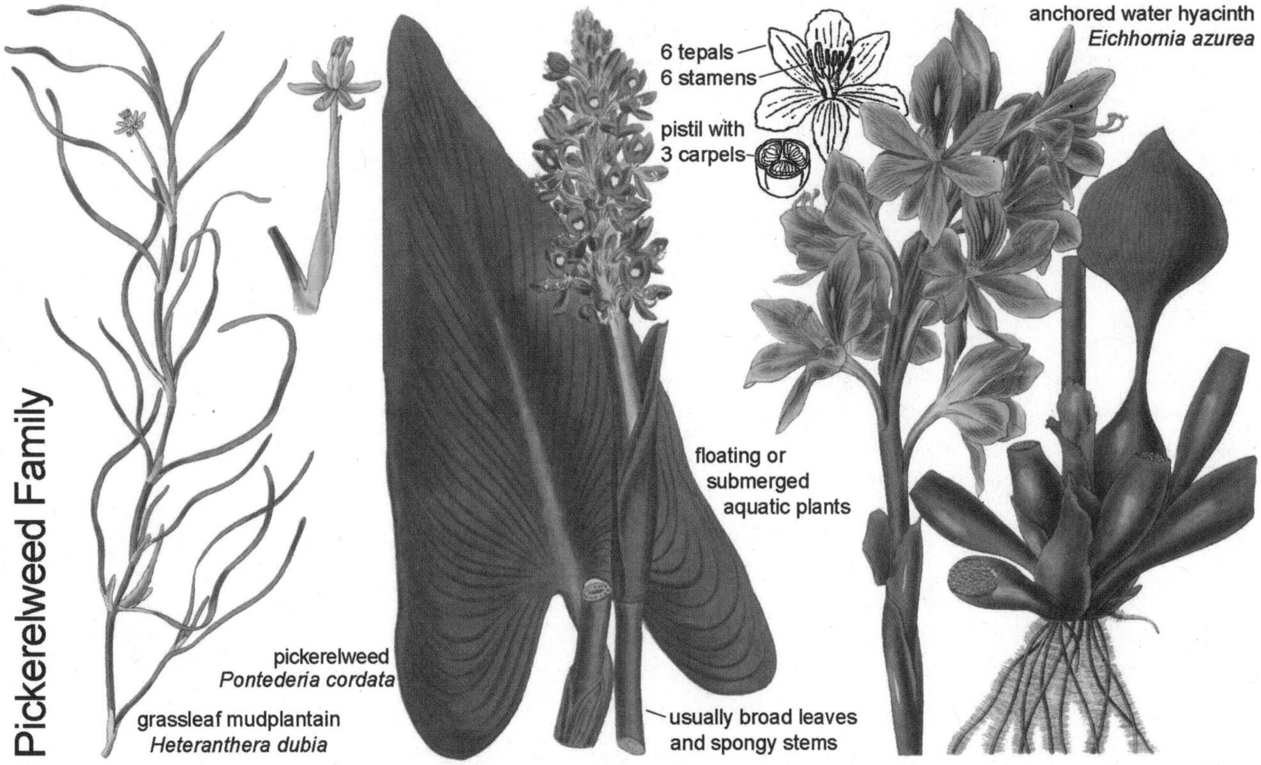
Pickerelweed Family
anchored water hyacinth
Eichhornia azurea
6 tepals
6 stamens
pistil with
3 carpels
floating or
submerged
aquatic plants
pickerelweed
Pontederia cordata
grassleaf mudplantain
Heteranthera dubia
usually broad leaves
and spongy stems

Pickerelweed Family—*Pontederiaceae*

If you've been around warm waterways choked with purple-flowered, floating plants, then you have probably met one member of the Pickerelweed family, the invasive water hyacinth (*Eichhornia*). The Pickerelweed family includes floating or submerged aquatic plants with usually broad, alternating or whorled leaves and spongy stems. The flowers are lily-like, often emerging from a spathe-like bract, with 6 separate or united tepals (3 sepals and 3 petals that are similar in size and color), and 6 stamens (3 in *Heteranthera*) attached to the petals. The ovary is positioned superior and consists of 3 united carpels, but may abort some, forming one to three chambers. It matures as a capsule with numerous seeds per chamber. Worldwide there are about 6 genera and 30 species. North American genera are listed below.

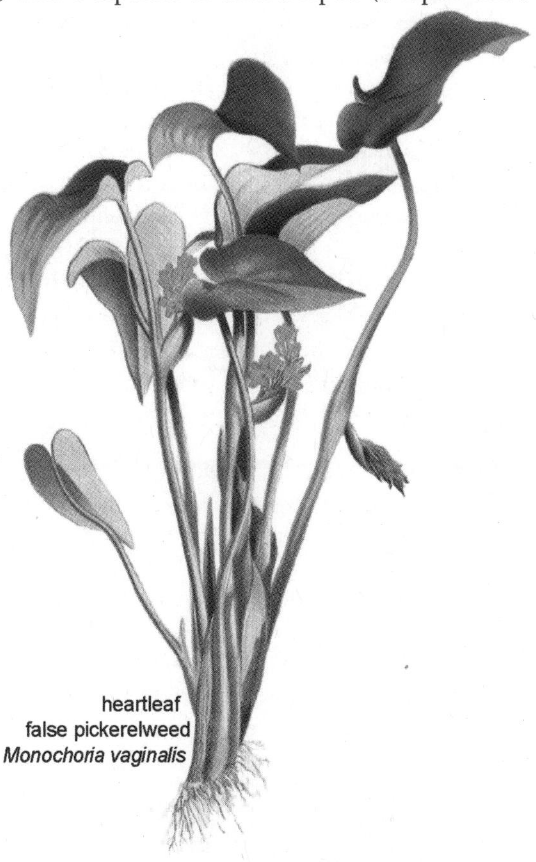
heartleaf
false pickerelweed
Monochoria vaginalis

Key Words:
Aquatic plants with spongy stems and lily-like flowers.

Eichhornia—water hyacinth (7/3/0) Native to South America. Invasive in warm waters of southern states. Water hyacinth thrives in nutrient-rich waters and can be useful for cleansing wastewater, but can also reduce oxygen levels in the water, killing fish.

Heteranthera—mud plantain (12/7/1) Native to North America, and found in most states and provinces.

Monochoria—false pickerelweed (12/1/0) *M. hastata*. Introduced to California.

Pontederia—pickerelweed (6/1/0) *P. cordata* is native to the eastern half of the continent.

Lily Family—*Liliaceae*

Most showy monocot flowers with parts in threes belong to the Lily family or one of its allies. Lilies have 3 sepals and 3 petals, which are identical in size and color (often referred to as 6 tepals). There are 6 stamens, but some species lack anthers on some of the stamens. The overy is positioned superior and consists of 3 united carpels, as indicated by the same number of stigmas. Partition walls are present, forming an equal number of chambers. The ovary matures as a capsule or a berry with 3 to numerous seeds.

Taxonomists have struggled with lily-like flowers, originally lumping them together as a conglomerate Lily family encompassing about 250 genera and 3,700 species. Numerous attempts were made to split the family into proper families and subfamilies based on actual relationships, resulting in many different classification schemes and up to 70 different proposed families. Blue camas (*Camassia*), for example, is listed in different sources as a member of the Lily family, Hyacinth family, Agave family, and now the Agave subfamily of the Asparagus family. The families and subfamilies used here presumeably follow genetic lines and should be reasonably stable in the future. Be sure to read about each of the lily-like families and their subfamiles for clues as to which group your specimen belongs. The redefined Lily family has been reduced to about 16 genera and 640 species.

Key Words: Monocot flowers with parts in threes. Sepals and petals *usually* identical.

Lily Subfamily—*Lilioideae*

Plants of the Lily subfamily usually have larger, more showy blossoms than other lilies, and they grow from starchy bulbs or corms. These bulbs and corms are often edible, but be extremely cautious—plants of the Bunchflower family also have bulbs, and some of them are highly poisonous.

Erythronium—glacier lily, fawn lily, dog-tooth violet (20/18/1) • The starchy corm of the glacier lily is crisp and sweet, but be careful to avoid overharvesting them since plants take years to grow to maturity. The leaves are edible as a salad green or potherb, however, there is a lingering bite to them, which can be emetic in excess. Read more about harvesting glacier lilies in *Participating in Nature*.

Fritillaria—yellowbell, leopard lily, brown lily (130/19/2) • The whole plant is edible, both raw or cooked. The starchy corm is delicious and almost melts in your mouth like butter, but seldom grow in enough abundance to justify collecting a significant quantity of them. The leopard lily is even more rare. A European species contains highly toxic alkaloids (Schauenberg); a species in China is also poisonous (Klein).

Lilium—lily, wood lily (150/25/2) • The pulverized flower was applied by the Dakota Indians to a certain brown spider bite (Gilmore). The bulbs of many *Liliums* are known to be edible (Sturtevant). The Easter lily (*L. longiflorum*) and several other mostly oriental species of lily are toxic to cats, but apparently only to cats.

Lloydia—alpine lily (12/1/1) *L. serotina*. Grows at high elevations from New Mexico to Alaska.

Tulipa—tulip (150/3/0) • Introduced. Tulip bulbs are edible cooked, but most store-bought bulbs are coated with a fungicide to prevent rotting. Only experiment with bulbs that have been planted for a year or more. The petals are also edible.

Sego Lily Subfamily—*Calochortoideae*

This subfamily is not a very intuitive grouping, since there are two distinct patterns here. Both *Calochortus* and *Scoliopus* have basal leaves and large, showy flowers, but unlike true lilies, they have distinct sepals and petals. Both genera produce seed-filled capsules. *Streptopus* and *Prosartes*, on the other hand, have alternating leaves along a kinked stem and smaller flowers with 6 lily-type tepals. Both genera produce berries, rather than capsules.

Calochortus—sego lily, mariposa lily (65/46/7) • The bulb is delicious roasted or boiled, but watch out for death camas (see the Bunchflower family for more information).

Scoliopus—adderstongue (2/2/0) The common name may be confused with the Adder's Tongue family.

Streptopus—twisted stalk (10/4/1) • The young leaves and stalks are edible. The berries are edible but lack flavor.

Prosartes—fairy bells (5/5/2) American species were split out from the Asian *Disporum* as too unrelated.

Indian Cucumber Subfamily—*Medeoloideae*

These are forest plants with basal leaves (*Clintonia*) or whorled leaves (*Medeola*) and 6 lily-like tepals. The fruit is a purple berry.

Clintonia—queen's cup (5/4/1) • The plants are edible: the very young leaves in salad, older leaves cooked (Fern).

Medeola—Indian cucumber (1/1/0) *M. virginiana*. Grows in eastern North America. The crisp roots are edible raw or cooked and reportedly taste like cucumber. The plant may be endangered in some states.

Patterns of the Lily Family

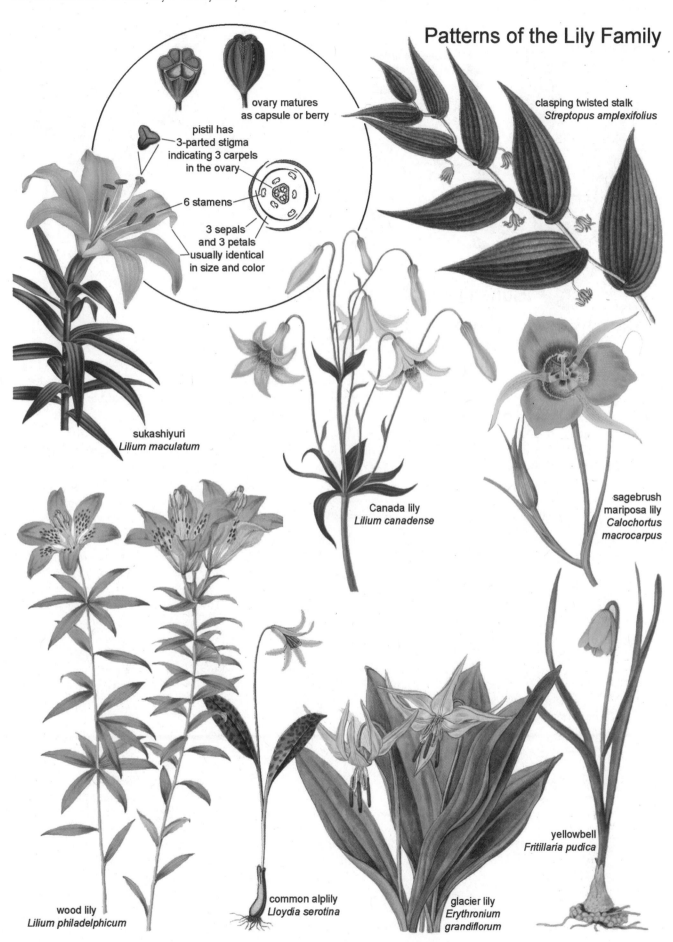

ovary matures
as capsule or berry

pistil has
3-parted stigma
indicating 3 carpels
in the ovary

6 stamens

3 sepals
and 3 petals
usually identical
in size and color

clasping twisted stalk
Streptopus amplexifolius

sukashiyuri
Lilium maculatum

Canada lily
Lilium canadense

sagebrush
mariposa lily
*Calochortus
macrocarpus*

wood lily
Lilium philadelphicum

common alplily
Lloydia serotina

glacier lily
*Erythronium
grandiflorum*

yellowbell
Fritillaria pudica

193

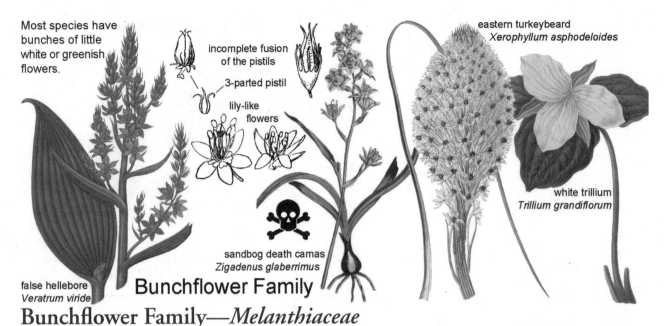

Most species have bunches of little white or greenish flowers.

incomplete fusion of the pistils

3-parted pistil

lily-like flowers

eastern turkeybeard
Xerophyllum asphodeloides

white trillium
Trillium grandiflorum

sandbog death camas
Zigadenus glaberrimus

Bunchflower Family

false hellebore
Veratrum viride

Bunchflower Family—*Melanthiaceae*

Most plants in the Bunchflower family have bunches of little white or greenish, lily-like flowers with 3 sepals and 3 petals that are identical in size and color, plus 6 stamens, and a 3-parted pistil. In most species the pistil has 3 styles which have not completely fused together as they have in the Lily family. The ovary is positioned superior or nearly so, and consists of 3 united carpels with the partition walls present, forming an equal number of chambers. It matures as a capsule with 2 or more seeds per chamber. Note that *Trillium* typically has a single, large flower that does not fit the bunch flower pattern, but is apparently related anyway.

Worldwide, the Bunchflower family includes about 25 genera and 140 species. It is important to learn this family right away because many of them, particularly death camas, are quite poisonous. Unfortunately, taxonomic reshuffling has greatly confused what is and is not a death camas.

Key Words: Bunches of Lily-like flowers with incompletely fused pistils.

Amianthium—fly poison (1/1/0) *A. muscitoxicum*. American colonists mashed the bulb and mixed it with sugar to kill flies.

Anticlea—death camas (11/11/2) This genus consists of species shuffled in from *Zigadenus* and *Stenanthium*, including mountain death camas (*A. elegans*, formerly *Z. elegans*). Death camas contains a toxic alkaloid that may be twice as potent as strychnine (Harrington). Ingestion can cause vomiting, diarrhea and death (Hall). The toxicity of death camas varies according to the species and subspecies and probably varies from place to place and year to year. The lethal dose could be as little as part of one bulb or as many as fifty bulbs. Medicinally, the raw roots have been used externally as a poultice for inflamed joints (Murphey). Do not use without expert supervision.

Melanthium—bunchflower (4/4/0) Species of this genera are sometimes included with *Veratrum* and contain similar alkaloids.

Stenanthium—featherbells (3/3/0) Three species of *Stenanthium* were exported to *Anticlea*, and two species of *Zigadenus* were imported to *Stenanthium*, including the Pine Barrens death camas (*S. leimanthoides*, formerely *Z. leimanthoides*).

Tofieldia—asphodel (3/3/1) *Tofieldia* and the closely related *Triantha* have been segregated into *Tofieldiaceae*.

Toxicoscordion—death camas (9/9/1) Formerly included within *Zigadenus*.

Trillium—birthroot, wake robin (30/26/1) • *Trillium* is listed as astringent, diaphoretic and expectorant. The tea is used internally for asthma, bronchitis, hemorrhaging from the lungs and as menstrual stimulant. The poultice is used externally for insect bites and stings (Lust). It contains some saponin. Sometimes segregated into *Trilliaceae*.

Veratrum—false hellebore (48/7/2) • *Veratrum* contains dangerous alkaloids that depress the nervous system, resulting in a slower heart rate and lower blood pressure (Hall). It is very powerful and considered too dangerous for amateurs to work with (Lust). Native Americans inhaled the dried, powdered root to induce sneezing to clear the sinuses (Klein).

Xerophyllum—beargrass, turkeybeard (2/2/1) The baked root is edible (Fern). The leaves may be used for cordage.

Zigadenus—sandbog death camas (1/1/0) • *Z. glaberrimus*. A native of the southeastern states, the bulb and leaves contain toxic alkaloids. At one time there were about twenty species of death camas within *Zigadenus*. However, based on new evidence, all but *Z. glaberrimus* have been shuffled to other genera, spread out across *Amianthium*, *Anticlea*, *Stenanthium*, and *Toxicoscordion*. At the same time, other plants in these genera were shuffled around as well, rototilling the genera so thoroughly that it can be nearly impossible to sort it all out when researching a particular plant. In cross-referencing with other sources, expect to see death camas listed as various species of *Zigadenus*.

Greenbrier Family—*Smilacaceae*

If you find a monocot vine with flowers or fruits in umbels, it is almost certainly a member of the Greenbrier family. The challenge, however, is recognizing the plant as a monocot, since it has some dicot-like features. These are somewhat woody vines, often with spines, with simple, alternate leaves. The leaves may have either palmate or net-veined leaves, much like dicots plants. Many species have a pair of tendrils at the base of the leaf stem.

In some species of *Smilax*, the flowers emit a foul odor to attract flies and beetles to assist with pollination. Flowers form in an umbel (like an umbrella), superficially resembling some plants from the Ginseng family. The flowers are unisexual, and dioecious (male and female flowers are borne on separate plants). The flowers have 6 tepals (3 sepals and 3 petals of similar size and color). Male flowers have 6 stamens. The female flower has a 3-parted pistil with 3 stigmas. The ovary is positioned superior, and consists of 3 united carpels with the partition walls present, forming an equal number of chambers. It matures as a red or purple berry with 1 or 2 seeds per chamber. Worldwide, the Greenbrier family includes 1 or 2 genera and about 300 species.

Key Words: Monocot vines with umbels.

Smilax—greenbrier, sarsaparilla, carrion flower (300/26/1) • The roots contain a gelatin-like substance that can be extracted by crushing and washing them. The young leaves and shoots are edible as a salad green or potherb (Hall).
The tender young shoots somehwat resemble asapargus in appearance, and can be used similarly, particularly those species without any thorns or spines (Thayer). Be sure to read *The Forager's Harvest* for more information. The root of some species was formerely used in the production of root beer. Medicinally, a tea of the root is listed as diaphoretic, carminative, diuretic and as a blood purifier (Lust).

Greenbrier Family

smooth
carrionflower
*Smilax
herbacea*

Autumn Crocus Family—*Colchicaceae*

If you have rambled through eastern woodlands in springtime, then you have likely encountered the drooping yellow blossoms of a bellwort (*Uvularia*), the North American representative of the Autumn Crocus family. Like other plants that were once included in the Lily family, members of the Autumn Crocus family typically have 3 sepals and 3 petals that are identical in size and color, plus 6 stamens and a 3-parted pistil. The ovary is positioned superior and matures as a capsule with 5 to 50 seeds per chamber. Our bellworts are superficially similar to twisted stalk (*Streptopus*) of the Lily family, since both genera have a main stem that zig-zags between alternating leaves. But bellworts have yellow or creamy flowers and produces seed capsules, while twisted stalk has white or purplish flowers and produces a berry.

Worldwide there are about 20 genera and 200 species. The family name comes from the autumn crocus (*Colchicum*), an Old World native with flowers that bloom in fall, long after the leaves have withered away. The flowers superficially resemble the true *Crocus* of the Iris family, but in *Colchium*, the "stem" is actually an elongated floral tube, with the ovary of flower buried underground.

Key Words (*Uvularia*): Zig-zaggy stalks with droopy yellow flowers.

Disporum—fairy bells (20/0/0) North American species were reclassified as *Prosartes* of the Lily family. Other species of *Disporum* are primarily found in Asia.
Uvularia—bellwort (5/5/0) There are five species of bellwort in North America, ranging from Manitoba to Texas, east to the Atlantic coast.

Autumn Crocus Family

perfoliate bellwort
Uvularia perfoliata

Resembles
twisted stalk
of the Lily family.

195

Amaryllis Family—*Amaryllidaceae*

If you have enjoyed a potted Amaryllis blooming in mid-winter, than you have met the Amaryllis family. Members of this family are typically perennial plants that resprout each year from underground bulbs. The leaves are usually somewhat juicy and tender, rather than fibrous.

The flowers are often grouped in an umbel (like an umbrella), or sometimes solitary, and typially emerge from a spathe-like bract (a modified leaf wrapped around the flowerhead). Otherwise, individual flowers are typical lily-like blossoms with 3 sepals and 3 petals that are identical in size and color. The daffodil (*Narcissus*) has an extra inner whorl called the corona. Most species have 6 stamens. The ovary is positioned either inferior or superior and matures as a capsule with numerous seeds per chamber. The dried petals are often found clinging to the tip of the fruit.

As currently defined, the Amaryllis family encompasses an estimated 60 genera and 850 species, only a handful of which are found in North America. The potted flowers we know as "amaryllis" were segregated from *Amaryllis* into a closely related new genus, *Hippeastrum*, but the old name reamains as the common name. Edibility varies significantly across the family. Onions (*Allium*) and their kin have sometimes been segregated into their own family, and may be yet again.

Key Words:
Monocots with onion-like bulbs and juicy leaves. Flowerheads wrapped in a bract.

Amaryllis Subfamily—*Amaryllidoideae*

Flowers are either solitary or grouped in an umbel, with the flowerhead wrapped in a spathe-like bract.

Crinum—swamp lily (130/4/0) Texas to North Carolina.
Galanthus—snowdrop (15/2/0) European native. Feral.
Leucojum—snowflake (10/2/0) European native. Feral.
Lycoris—red spider lily (13/2/0) Asian native. Feral in the East.
Narcissus—daffodil (30/10/0) Native to the Old World, but feral in North America. The leaves and particularly the bulb contain a toxic alkaloid called lycorine.
Zephyranthes— zephyrlily (60/10/0) Native and introduced species are found from Arizona to Virginia.

wild chives
Allium schoenoprasum

lily-like flowers

flowers often grouped in umbels

autumn zephyrlily
Zephyranthes candida

nodding onion
Allium cernum

cultivated onion
Allium cepa

Amaryllis Family

Onion Subfamily—*Allioideae*

Small flowers are grouped in an umbel, typially emerging from a spathe-like bract. Ovary is positioned superior. Compare to the Asparagus Family / Brodiaea subfamily.

Allium—onion, garlic, chives, leeks (550/80/11) • Various species grow in many different environments from semi-swampy mountain meadows to very dry, south-facing foothill slopes. Be careful to avoid confusing wild onions with death camas from the Bunchflower family. Crush the plant and smell it. If it smells like an onion then it is one. Wild onions make a great addition to almost any wilderness meal. Medicinally, the *Allium* species contain volatile oils and sulfur glycosides. They act as a digestive stimulant, expectorant, anthelmintic and carminative (Lust). Garlic is especially recommended for colds; it has also been shown to lower cholesterol and blood pressure.

Nothoscordum—false garlic (90/3/0) These plants look similar to wild onions and garlic, but lack the odor. It is not known if the plant or bulb is edible, and some sources list them as poisonous, but seemingly without any mention of the specific toxins, symptoms, or reports of illness or fatalities.

Asparagus Family—*Asparagaceae*

In splitting up the old Lily family into smaller families of more closely related plants, taxonomists defined the Asparagus, Brodiaea, Nolina, and Agave families, listing them as distinct families *sensu stricto* ("in the strict sense"), or lumping them together as subfamilies within a conglomerate Asparagus family, *sensu lato* ("in the wider sense"). Taxonomists currently favor the latter, but unfortunately, the conglomerate family lacks any obvious patterns for intuitive identification. Separate descriptions are provided for each of the subfamilies here to clarify identification. Similar to other lily-like families, members of the Asparagus family typically have 3 sepals and 3 petals that are similar in size and color, plus 6 stamens and a 3-parted pistil.

Asparagus Subfamily—*Asparagoideae*

Instead of true leaves, Asparagus has leaf-like branches for photosynthesis. This subfamily includes only two genera, *Asparagus*, from the Old World, and *Hemiphylacus* from Mexico.

Key Words: Fern-like feathery leaves. Fruit is a berry.

Asparagus— (300/4/1) • *A. officinalis* is the cultivated asparagus. It has escaped from gardens and now grows wild in some areas, particularly along roads and fence lines. It is always a delight to find a patch in the spring. Medicinally, asparagus is diuretic, acting to increase cellular activity in the kidneys; it is not recommended for inflamed kidneys. Asparagus is also a bulk fiber laxative. The powdered seeds are used as a diaphoretic and to calm the stomach (Lust).

asparagus
Asparagus officinalis

Brodiaea Subfamily—*Brodiaeoideae*

The Brodiaea have lily-like flowers with 3 sepals and 3 petals that are similar in size and color, plus 6 stamens and a 3-parted pistil. In many species the petals are united, at least at the base, forming tubular flowers. Flowers range from white to blue and purple, rarely red or yellow. They are typically grouped in umbels which emerge from a spathe-like bract (a modified leaf). Brodiaea leaves and flowers are somewhat similar to onions (*Allium*) from the Amaryllis family, but onions produce a bulb, while Brodiaeas produce a starchy corm instead.

Key Words: Tubular flowers in umbels, emerging from a spathe-like bract.

Brodiaea Subfamily

largeflower triteleia
Triteleia grandiflora

firecracker flower
Dichelostemma ida-maia

Bloomeria—golden stars (2/2/0) Grows along the Pacific Coast.

Brevoortia—fire-cracker flower (2/2/0) Both species grow along the Pacific Coast. These plants were formerly included in the *Brodiaea*.

Brodiaea—brodiaea, blue dicks (10/10/0) The *Triteleia* genus was split out of the *Brodiaea*. Many of the plants still appear under either name. For example, *Brodiaea grandiflora* is also listed as *Triteleia grandiflora*.

Muilla—muilla (4/4/0) California, Nevada. The name *Muilla* comes from *Allium* spelled backwards, due to the plant's superficial resemblance to onions.

Triteleia—wild hyacinth, brodiaea (14/14/1) • The cooked bulb is edible and delicious; it has a buttery texture and flavor similar to the starchy corm of the yellowbell. The plants in my area are small and rare, but I had the opportunity to dig up several cups full in eastern Oregon... a real treat.

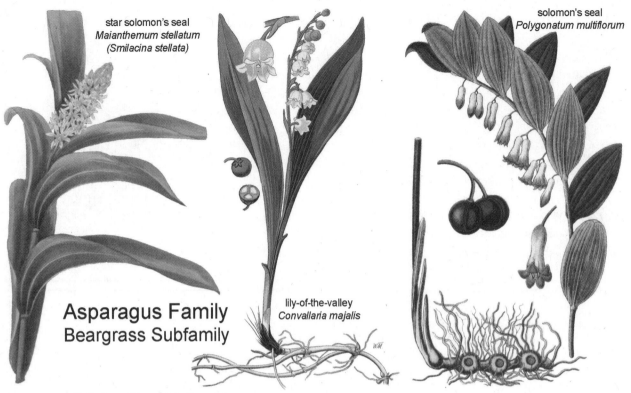

star solomon's seal
Maianthemum stellatum
(*Smilacina stellata*)

solomon's seal
Polygonatum multiflorum

Asparagus Family
Beargrass Subfamily

lily-of-the-valley
Convallaria majalis

Beargrass Subfamily—*Nolinoideae*

The Beargrass subfamily of the Asparagus family was cobbled together from a number of closely related groups of plants that were previously proposed as independent families themselves, including *Ruscaceae*, *Dracaenaceae*, *Convallariaceae*, *Eriospermaceae*, and *Nolinaceae*. And of course, all of these little families were historically lumped together into one big Lily family.

Similar to other lily-like flowers, these plants have 3 sepals and 3 petals that are similar in size and color, plus 6 stamens and a 3-parted pistil. In some species the petals are united and bell-shaped or tubular. The ovary is positioned superior and matures into a berry in *Convallaria* and its closest relatives (pictured above). In *Nolina* and *Dasylirion* the ovary matures as a 3-sided capsule that superficially resembles fruits of the Buckwheat family, while the vegetation confused with *Yucca* and *Agave* from the Agave subfamily. The bottom line is that there isn't a particularly good pattern to summarize this group. Also keep in mind that there is another plant called beargrass (*Xerophyllum*) in the Bunchflower family.

Texas beargrass
Nolina texana

Convallaria—lily-of-the-valley (2/2/0) *Convallaria's* cardiac glycosides can cause an irregular heartbeat (Lust).

Dasylirion—sotol (25/3/0) • The young flower stalk of the plant is rich in sugar, sometimes used to make alcohol. It can be cooked and eaten (Bigfoot, Fern).

Maianthemum—Canada mayflower, false lily-of-the-valley (3/2/1)

Nolina—beargrass (30/14/0) • See also beargrass (*Xerophyllum*) in the Bunchflower family.

Polygonatum—solomon's seal (30/4/0) The young shoots and starchy, mucilaginous roots are edible as potherb s (Sturtevant). The tea is used as a demulcent, expectorant and cough suppressant. A poultice of the root is used as an emollient, possibly with mildly astringent properties.

Smilacina—false solomon seal, solomon's plume (25/5/2) • This genus has recently been folded into *Maianthemum*, but continues to appear in many books as *Smilacina*.

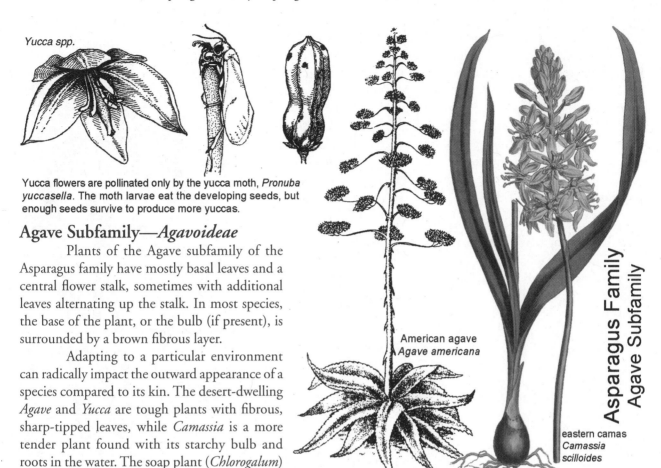

Yucca spp.

Yucca flowers are pollinated only by the yucca moth, *Pronuba yuccasella*. The moth larvae eat the developing seeds, but enough seeds survive to produce more yuccas.

American agave
Agave americana

Asparagus Family
Agave Subfamily

eastern camas
Camassia scilloides

Agave Subfamily—*Agavoideae*

Plants of the Agave subfamily of the Asparagus family have mostly basal leaves and a central flower stalk, sometimes with additional leaves alternating up the stalk. In most species, the base of the plant, or the bulb (if present), is surrounded by a brown fibrous layer.

Adapting to a particular environment can radically impact the outward appearance of a species compared to its kin. The desert-dwelling *Agave* and *Yucca* are tough plants with fibrous, sharp-tipped leaves, while *Camassia* is a more tender plant found with its starchy bulb and roots in the water. The soap plant (*Chlorogalum*) enjoys an intermediate environment and has intermediate characteristics, while the sand lily (*Leucocrinum*) is adapted to shady, moist forests like the Lily family plants it greatly resembles. Some plants in the Agave and Beargrass subfamilies share superficial similarities.

Key Words: Monocots with basal leaves, a central flower stalk, and brown, fibrous basal wrappings.

Agave—agave (300/26/0) • Juice from the leaves can be acrid. The young flower stalk is edible raw or cooked. It is commonly cooked in a steam pit for two to three days to convert the starches to sugar (Bigfoot). Due to its high sugar content, mostly fructose, blue agave (*A. tequilana*) is cultivated and used for making tequila. Sisal fiber comes from *A. sisalana*.

Camassia—blue camas (5/5/1) • Caution is advised: blue camas resembles death camas (*Anticlea /Zigadenus*) before it blooms. Blue camas bulbs are starchy and nearly tasteless, but often golf-ball sized and larger. Camas was a major food source for some Native Americans. The bulbs are rich in inulin, a carbohydrate, as well as a dietary fiber called hemi-cellulose. Neither are digestible raw, but the inulin can be converted to fructose through extended cooking. Native Americans cooked camas bulbs in a steam pit for 10 to 72 hours. In kitchen experiments John Kallas found that pressure-cooking the roots at 257°F for nine hours produced the sweetest tasting roots (Kallas). Read more about blue camas in *Foraging the Mountain West*.

Chlorogalum—soap plant, amole (5/5/0) • Soap plants are native to western North America, from Oregon south to Baja. The starchy root is rich with saponins. California natives crushed the roots and mixed them into slow moving waters to stupefy the fish. (Read more about saponins in the Medicinal Properties section of this book.) The bulbs can be slowly pit-baked to remove the soapy taste.

Hesperaloe—false yucca (5/2/0) Native to Texas.

Hesperocallis—desert lily (1/1/0) *H. undulata*. Native to California, Nevada, and Arizona. The bulbs are edible.

Leucocrinum—sand lily (1/1/1) • *L. montanum*. Native to western North America. It has fleshy roots instead of a bulb.

Manfreda—tuberose (20/4/0) Native from Texas to Maryland.

Schoenolirion—sunnybell (3/3/0) Native from Texas to North Carolina.

Yucca (including *Hesperoyucca*)—yucca, joshua tree (40/38/1) • The flower stem and flowers and especially the root, contain saponin, which is used as a soap substitute. The flowers and pods of some species of yucca are edible (Sturtevant), but many are too bitter to be palatable. The leaves contain some salicin (Pamell).

Grass Tree Family—*Xanthorrhoeaceae*

The Grass Tree family is not native to North America. However, the subfamilies and genera below are widely cultivated here and may be feral in some regions. Formerly considered part of the Lily family, the flowers consist of 3 sepals and 3 petals that are nearly identical in size and color, plus 6 stamens and a 3-parted pistil. The ovary is positioned superior and consists of 3 united carpels with the partition walls usually present, forming an equal number of chambers. It matures as a capsule with 3 or more seeds per cell. See the subfamilies for distinguishing characteristics.

3-parted pistil
6 stamens

yellow day lily
Hemerocallis
lilioasphodelus

ovary with 3 carpels

Lily-like flowers
with 3 sepals and 3 petals
similar in size and color.

Day Lily Subfamily

Day Lily Subfamily—*Hemerocallidoideae*

Many plants of the Day Lily subfamily have fleshy, tuberous roots, which helps distinguish them from other lily-like flowers. Worldwide, there are about 7 or 8 genera and 40 species in the Day Lily Subfamily.

Key Words: Lily-like flowers, but with tuberous roots.

Hemerocallis—day lily (16/2/0) • Day lily is native to Eurasia, but has escaped cultivation in this country. The flowers and buds are edible as a cooked vegetable. The tubers can be harvested any time and eaten raw or cooked (Hall). There have been isolated cases of adverse reactions (nausea, vomiting, diarrhea), possibly do to environmental factors or genetic variants. People who successfully consumed the plant for many years still became ill (Kallas).

Asphodel Subfamily—*Asphodeloideae*

Aloe vera and other species of *Aloe* are widely cultivated, both indoors as house plants, and outdoors in tropical climates. Native to Africa, *Aloe* now grows wild in parts of Texas, Florida, and California. Many plants of this subfamily have thickened, spongy roots with multiple layers to help prevent water loss. *Aloe* looks superficially like *Agave* of the Asparagus family / Agave subfamily but its thick leaves are full of mucilaginous (slimy) juice, useful for treating sunburns. *Agave* has dense, fibrous leaves. Worldwide there are about 15 genera and 750 species in the Asphodel Subfamily.

Asphodel Subfamily

Aloe vera

Key Words: Agave-like plants with tubular flowers and slimy juice.

Aloe—aloe (380/2/0) • My grandmother always treated my sunburns with *Aloe vera*. She split the leaf down the middle and rubbed the slimy, mucilaginous gel over any burns. Often my burns tanned over without peeling after this treatment. It is a family tradition to keep an *Aloe vera* around for such occasions. The treatment should be repeated several times a day for maximum effect. My daughter Cassie perfected this treatment with her sensitive skin, turning horrific sunburns into non-peeling tans, by applying coat-after-coat of Aloe vera gel, as much as her skin could absorb. Read more about mucilaginous substances in the Medicinal Properties section of this book.

The beneficial properties of *Aloe vera* may break down in storage, so that many commercial products have little therapeutic value. Some may even retard healing (Tyler). Taken internally, *Aloe vera* also has cathartic properties (strongly laxative) due to anthraquinone glycosides (Geller) in the bitter yellow latex found immediately beneath the surface of the leaf (Tyler).

Iris Family—*Iridaceae*

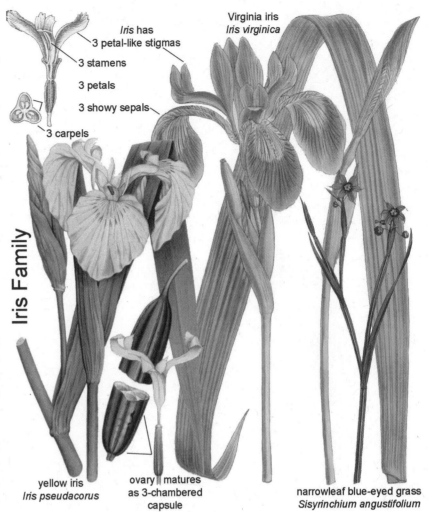

Iris has
3 petal-like stigmas
3 stamens
3 petals
3 showy sepals
3 carpels

Virginia iris
Iris virginica

yellow iris
Iris pseudacorus

ovary matures
as 3-chambered
capsule

narrowleaf blue-eyed grass
Sisyrinchium angustifolium

Iris Family

Stop and look closely at an iris or gladiolus the next time you come across one in a yard, a bouquet, or at the florist. Members of this family produce regular, bisexual flowers with parts in multiples of three. There are 3 sepals, colored to look like petals, and 3 true petals, plus 3 stamens. The ovary is positioned inferior and consists of 3 united carpels, as indicated by the same number of stigmas. Partition walls are usually present, forming an equal number of chambers. It matures as a capsule containing many seeds.

The stigmas of the pistil are often distinctive; in the *Iris* they look like a third set of petals and the stamens are hidden underneath—this is well worth looking at! Overall, the flowers of the Iris family look much like the Lilies. One key difference is that Iris leaves usually lay in a flat plane at the base of the plant. Also note that the Lilies have 6 stamens, while the Irises only have 3.

Worldwide, there are about 70 genera and about 1,800 species. The *Gladiolus* and *Crocus* are commonly cultivated flowers of this family. Saffron is made from the stigmas of *Crocus sativus*. Other cultivated genera include *Tigridia, Freesia, Ixia, Romulea, Neomarica, Moraea, and Trimezia.*

Key Words: "Lily-like flowers with leaves in a flat plane."

Alophia—propeller flower (5/1/0) *A. drummondii*. Found from Texas to Mississippi.

Belamcanda—blackberry lily (1/1/0) *B. chinensis*. Introduced from Asia, and naturalized from Connecticut to Texas. Pods open to reveal cluster of black seeds that resembles blackberry. Now reclassified as *Iris domestica*.

Calydorea—Bartram's ixia (20/1/0) *C. coelestina*. Native to Florida and Georgia.

Iris—iris (225/36/2) • Irises have starchy, but usually acrid roots. Several species are edible, but a few may be potentially dangerous, including the common blue iris (*I. versicolor*) (Pammel). Iris roots were boiled by some Native Americans and applied as a poultice on wounds (Weiner). Irises with acrid qualities are listed as cathartic, emetic, diuretic and as a saliva stimulant. A tea of the root is used for chronic digestive disorders, including heartburn and vomiting, and for migraine headaches caused by indigestion (Lust). The iris is used as a liver and lymph stimulant (Bigfoot). For additional information, be sure to read about acrid substances in the *Medicinal Properties* section of this book. *Iris germanica, I. florentina,* and *I. pallida* are the source of orris root, used in perfume and potpourri. Iris leaves can be used for cordage. Some irises were preferred by Native Americans for making deer snares (Moerman).

Nemastylis—celestial lily (5/4/0) Grows from Arizona to Florida, and north as far as Missouri.

Olsynium—grass widow (17/1/0) *O. douglasii*. Grows from California to British Columbia, as far east as Utah. Previously included in *Sisyrinchium*.

Sisyrinchium—blue-eyed grass (80/44/2) • North American species have mostly blue flowers, but also white and yellow.

snakemouth orchid
Pogonia ophioglossoides

Orchid Family—*Orchidaceae*

The orchids are the only monocot plants in the northern latitudes with distinctive, *irregular* blossoms. It is worth a trip to the floral store to see the unique flowers, but far more exciting to find them in the wild. The flowers have 3 sepals and 3 petals. The sepals can be green or colored like the petals. The lower petal is often modified into a sort of "sack" or "spur." The flowers are bisexual with 1 or 2 stamens combined with the pistil into a column. The ovary is positioned inferior and consists of 3 united carpels, forming a single chamber. It matures as a 3-valved capsule with numerous seeds. The inferior ovary is one of the more distinctive patterns for identifying members of this family. It elongates into a seed capsule while the flowers are still present. The seeds are almost microscopic, consisting of a minute embryo enclosed in a few cells. Orchids associate with fungi, and must find the proper host to successfully germinate.

The Orchid family is the biggest family of flowering plants, most of which inhabit the tropics. Worldwide, there are about 800 genera representing more than 20,000 species, possibly as many as 35,000. Vanilla flavoring is extracted from the immature pods of *Vanilla planifolia*. Many genera are cultivated. There are about 88 genera and at least 140 species of Orchids in North America, mostly in the South. Many orchids are rare and should not be harvested.

Key Words: Irregular monocot flowers with a distinctly inferior ovary.

Amerorchis—round-leaf orchid (1/1/1) *A. rotundifolia*. Found throughout Canada and some northern states.

Aplectrum—Adam and Eve (1/1/0) *A. hyemale*. Native from Oklahoma to Georgia, north to Quebec.

Calopogon—grasspink (5/5/0) Native from Texas to Manitoba, east to the Atlantic.

Calypso—fairy slipper (1/1/1) • *C. bulbosa*. The plant and root are edible raw or cooked (Willard).

Corallorhiza—coral root (15/6/5) • Symbiotic with fungi; most species do not produce chlorophyll. A tea of the root is used as a sedative and nervine (Moore).

Cypripedium—lady slipper (50/10/4) • Lady slipper is considered a non-narcotic sedative (Weiner). A tea of the root is used as a tranquilizer for nervousness or spasms. Overdosing may cause hallucinations. The fresh root may irritate the skin (Lust). It contains a volatile oil and a glucosidal resinoid (Densmore). Hairs on the stems of some species can cause a dermatitis reaction (Pammel).

Epipactis—helleborine, stream orchid (20/2/2) *Epipactis* contains resins, volatile oils and bitter glycosides. It is antispasmodic and sedative, and uplifting rather than depressant (Moore).

Goodyera—rattlesnake plantain (100/4/2) The plant is mucilaginous and astringent; the fresh plant or dry powder is used as a drawing poultice (Moore). The leaves or roots have emollient properties for use on skin conditions (Lust).

Habenaria—bog orchid (600/35/7) • This species is common in my area. The cooked roots are edible, but please do not overharvest the plants.

Neottia—twayblade (30/7/4) Includes species formerly classifed as *Listera*.

Liparis—false twayblade, widelip orchid (350/3/0) Found from British Columbia to Florida, north to Quebec.

Pogonia—snakemouth orchid (7/1/0) *P. ophioglossoides*. Native from Texas to Manitoba, east to the Atlantic.

Spiranthes—ladies' tresses (35/25/2) Various species are found throughout North America. Most have been segregated as other genera, later merged back with *Spiranthes*, with some re-segregated again into other genera.

Tipularia—cranefly (3/1/0) *T. discolor*. Native from Texas to New York.

Triphora—nodding caps (25/5/0) Native from Texas to Ontario, east to the Atlantic.

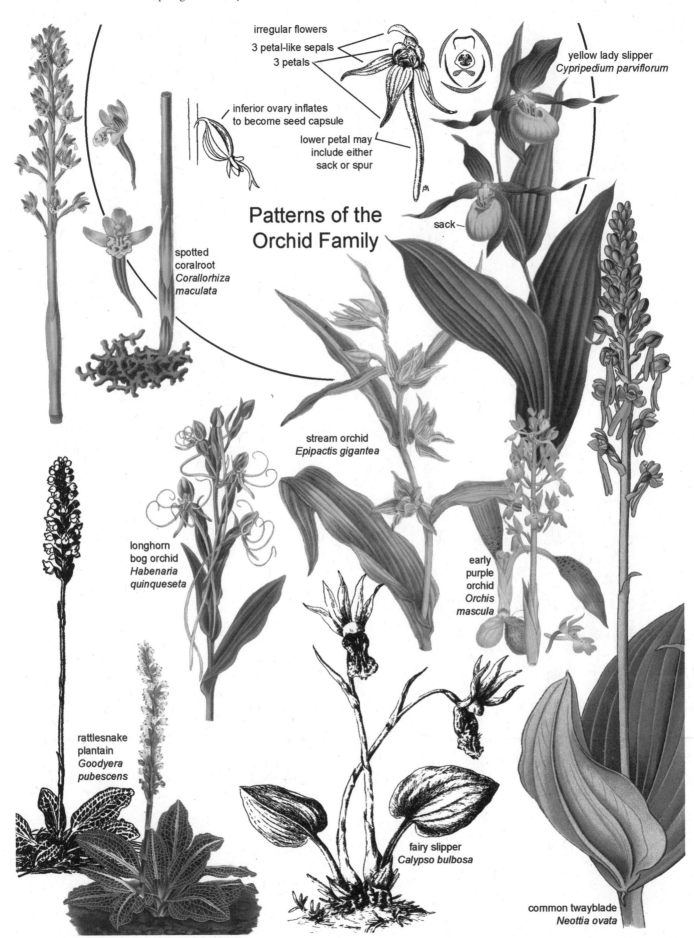

irregular flowers
3 petal-like sepals
3 petals

inferior ovary inflates
to become seed capsule

lower petal may
include either
sack or spur

yellow lady slipper
Cypripedium parviflorum

sack

Patterns of the Orchid Family

spotted
coralroot
*Corallorhiza
maculata*

stream orchid
Epipactis gigantea

longhorn
bog orchid
*Habenaria
quinqueseta*

early
purple
orchid
*Orchis
mascula*

rattlesnake
plantain
*Goodyera
pubescens*

fairy slipper
Calypso bulbosa

common twayblade
Neottia ovata

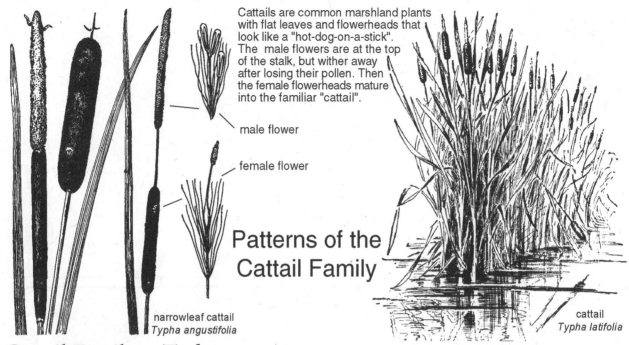

Cattails are common marshland plants with flat leaves and flowerheads that look like a "hot-dog-on-a-stick". The male flowers are at the top of the stalk, but wither away after losing their pollen. Then the female flowerheads mature into the familiar "cattail".

male flower

female flower

Patterns of the Cattail Family

narrowleaf cattail
Typha angustifolia

cattail
Typha latifolia

Cattail Family—*Typhaceae* (Including the Bur-reed Family—*Sparganiaceae*)

The cattail is a distinctive swamp plant with its long, slender, flat leaves and a seedhead that looks like a hot dog on a stick. The seedhead starts developing early in the season; at first it looks like two hot dogs on a stick. The top portion is comprised of thousands of minute male flowers. It produces pollen for about two weeks early in the summer. Cattails are cross-pollinated by the wind, so the sepals and petals have been reduced to minute threads, bristles, and scales around each of the tiny flowers. There are 2 to 5 stamens in each flower. This upper hot-dog-on-a-stick withers away through the summer and eventually drops off. The female part of the stalk is also comprised of thousands of minute flowers. The ovary is positioned superior and consists of a single carpel, producing one tiny seed. There are a great many such flowers, often producing 200,000+ seeds from a single head. They are carried away in the wind by the fluffy cattail down when the seed heads are broken apart.

Genetic evidence places bur-reed (*Sparganium*) within the Cattail family, rather than as an independent family. The flowerheads are round, but develop with male and female flowers in separate heads like cattails, with male flowers above the female flowers. The flowers of either sex have 3 to 6 membranous "tepals" (meaning sepals or petals). Male flowers have 3 or more stamens. Each female flower produces a single seed. Worldwide, there are 2 genera in the Cattail family, listed here, and about 28 species.

Key Words:
Aquatic plants with "hot-dog-on-a-stick" flower heads.

Sparganium—bur-reed (15/10/5) • The roots and bulbous stem bases are edible like cattails (Olsen), as are the male flowers and pollen (Judd).
Typha—cattail (13/3/2) • In addition to seeds, cattails spread by starchy horizontal underground stems called rhizomes. The rhizomes grow a foot or more from the parent plant, then send up an aerial shoot that looks like a separate plant. One cattail seed planted in a tank spread to a diameter of ten feet in a single season, forming ninety-eight aerial shoots, ranging from a few inches to a few feet in height (Yeo). See *Foraging the Mountain West* or *The Forager's Harvest* for details on harvesting and preparing this wondrous edible plant.

simplestem bur-reed
Sparganium erectum

204

Rush Family—*Juncaceae*

The plants of the Rush family might best be described as "lilies turned to grass." These are grassy-looking plants with non-showy flowers, found growing in damp soils or around the perimeter of ponds and lakes. But look close and you will see that the flowers are lily-like, with 3 sepals, 3 petals and 6 (sometimes 3) stamens surrounding a pistil with a 3-chambered ovary and a 3-parted stigma. The ovary is positioned superior and matures as a capsule.

Worldwide, there are about 8 genera and 400 species, mostly of *Juncus*. Two genera are found in North America, as listed below. Be sure to read about the Sedge and Grass families as well.

Members of the Rush family are well represented in the fossil record as far back as the Cretaceous period, mostly because the plants grow in wet habitats where fossils are made. The vegetation is tough enough to fossilize well, and it leaves recognizable imprints in the mud.

Key Words:
"Lilies turned to grass."

Juncus—rush (220/120/28) • The seeds of at least some species were used as food. An edible sugar may be found on top of some plants as well. Medicinally, a tea of the plant may have emetic qualities (Moerman). Some species are used for weaving baskets and chair bottoms.

Luzula—woodrush (80/29/6) The seeds of at least some species may be cooked and eaten (Fern).

common rush
Juncus effusus

3-chambered ovary
with 3-parted stigma
6 stamens
3 petals
3 sepals
Rush Family

Rushes are grass-like plants, but look close and you will see small lily-like flowers with 3 green sepals, 3 green petals, 6 stamens, and a pistil with a 3-parted stigrma.

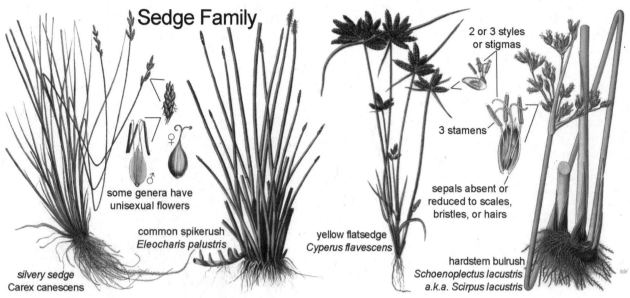

Sedge Family

2 or 3 styles or stigmas

3 stamens

sepals absent or reduced to scales, bristles, or hairs

some genera have unisexual flowers

common spikerush
Eleocharis palustris

yellow flatsedge
Cyperus flavescens

silvery sedge
Carex canescens

hardstem bulrush
Schoenoplectus lacustris
a.k.a. *Scirpus lacustris*

Sedge Family—*Cyperaceae*

"Sedges have edges. Rushes are round. Grasses are hollow. What have you found?" This common rhyme can help you remember the key differences between the Sedge, Rush, and Grass families. Most sedges have triangular stems ("edges"), except for *Scirpus*, which has round stems. Sedges tend to grow in damp ground, often bordering swamps and streams.

Sedges typically have small flowers with the sepals and petals completely absent, or reduced to scales, bristles, or hairs. There are typically 3 stamens (sometimes 6 or 1). The ovary is positioned superior and consists of 2 or 3 united carpels, aborting all but one to form a single chamber. It matures as an achene (a dry seed) or a nutlet. The fruit is either lens-shaped or three-sided, the shape dependent on the number of carpels. Worldwide, there are about 100 genera and 4,500 species. Twenty-four genera are found in North America. Members of the Sedge family generally have edible roots and seeds, although few are worth harvesting.

Key Words: "Sedges have edges."

Carex—sedge (1500/580/121) • Medicinally, a tea of sedge roots is diuretic and diaphoretic. It contains silica, and could irritate the kidneys, especially if they are already inflamed (Lust). I've experimented with harvesting the seeds of various species of sedge. I gathered useable quantities from a couple species, but the seeds seemed so small and flat that they did not seem digestible, even after extensive cooking. Sprouting may help.

Cyperus—flatsedge, chufa (600/100/4) Egyptians cultivated chufa (*C. esculentus*) for its starchy tubers. They can be eaten fresh or cooked, or dried and made into flour (Hall). The tubers can also be roasted and used as a coffee substitute (Angier). The invasive purple nutsedge (*C. rotundus*) is more bitter but also edible. Papyrus (*C. papyrus*) was manufactured by stripping off the outer rind of the stems to expose the sticky, fibrous pith, which was cut into long strips. Strips were placed with overlapping edges on a hard surface and covered by another layer placed at right angles, then pounded together, mashing them into a single sheet, which was dried under pressure and later polished with a rounded object.

Eleocharis—spike rush, spike sedge (200/75/7) The seeds (Olsen) and tubers (Sturtevant) of at least some species are edible. The Chinese water chestnut is *E. dulcis*.

Eriophorum—cotton grass (25/19/5) The roots of at least some species are edible raw or cooked (Moerman).

Scirpus—bulrush (300/22/6) • Some members of this genus are being shuffled into *Schoenoplectus* and other genera. Bulrush roots are somewhat similar to cattail roots, and used similarly. Flour can be obtained from the roots by drying, pounding, and sifting out the fibers. Another method is to cook the roots into mush and then separate out the fibers. The younger roots are rich in sugar; these can be bruised and boiled down to produce a syrup. The pollen can be collected in season and used as flour. The seeds are reported to be edible (Hall), but I have found that they are not very digestible, even after grinding through a flour mill and boiling as mush. Probably they just needed to mature a couple more weeks on the plants. Sprouting the seeds before cooking may help too.

Medicinally, the starchy roots may be used as a drawing poultice, especially if first soaked in a tannic acid solution (Brown). Bulrushes can also be made into a sort of candle. First, carefully strip away the outer layer, revealing the pith. Leave a narrow strip of the outside intact for structural support. Saturate the pith in some type of fat or oil, such as lard, and the "rush light" is ready for use (Mabey).

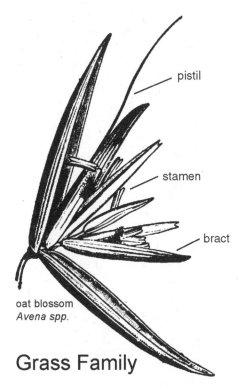

pistil

stamen

bract

oat blossom
Avena spp.

Grass Family

Grass Family—*Poaceae* (*Gramineae*)

Members of the Grass family have hollow flower stems with knee-like nodes or joints, distinguishing them from the Sedge and Rush families, as noted in this little ditty: "Sedges have edges. Rushes are round. Grasses have nodes where the leaves are found." (See the Sedge family an alternative version.)

Grasses are wind pollinated and lack the showy petals and sepals of other flowers because they are do not need to attract insects. The flowers typically have 3 (rarely 2 or 6) stamens. The ovary consists of 3 united carpels forming a single chamber. Two carpels are aborted. The ovary matures as a single seed called a caryopsis (grain) or rarely an achene (a dry seed) or a berry. The flower is contained by modified leaves called bracts. These are the chaff that is later winnowed out of harvested grain.

node

Worldwide, there are about 650 genera and nearly 10,000 species of grass. About 230 genera and 1,000+ species appear in North America. Cereal grains belong to this family, including wheat (*Triticum*), rice (*Oryza*), wild rice (*Zizania*), corn (*Zea*), oats (*Avena*), barley (*Hordeum*), and rye (*Secale*). Millet is a generalized term for grains from several genera including *Echinochloa, Pennisetum, Eleusine, Panicum,* and *Setaria.* The seeds of virtually all other grasses are also considered edible, if they are not infected by the ergot fungus. A notable exception is rye grass (*Lolium*), which is used as a sedative and vasodilator. It is considered poisonous in excess (Lust).

Some grasses are also a source of sugar. Sugar cane (*Saccharum*), corn (*Zea*) and *Sorghum* are processed commercially for sugar. The concentrations of sugar are usually found in the roots or the base of the stalks. Grasses can also be eaten as greens, except that the cellulose isn't digestible. Chew up the grass, swallow the juice, and spit out the fibers. Chewing on the immature seed heads, in particular, is an excellent way to get a healthful and dose of vitamins and minerals. Note, however, that some grasses produce cyanide compounds as they wilt.

Key Words: Grassy plants with knee-like nodes on hollow flower stems.

Ergot Fungus: Be sure to inspect the seeds of all grasses for the presence of ergot fungus (*Claviceps purpurea* or *C. paspali*) before harvesting for food. Ergot consumes the grass seeds, forming a black or purplish powder. Ergot can stimulate uterine contractions and abortions. A derivative of ergot is used as a medicine for migraine and cluster headaches. Ergot is also a source of LSD.

Ergot contamination in cereal grains can be extremely dangerous. *C. paspali* affects the nervous system, causing trembling, staggering, and paranoia. The witch hunts of Salem, Massachusetts in the 1600s are believed to have been connected with ergot contamination in stored grains. Many people were burned at the stake by the Puritans running around on LSD. *C. purpurea*, on the other hand, restricts the blood flow to the extremities, slowly killing the flesh on the fingers, toes, and ears, with long-term consumption. Gangrene bacteria, similar to botulism, rots away the dead tissues, often forming a foul gas.

ergot fungus

A group of religious medics torched the rotting flesh off the victims and prayed they lived. This group adopted St. Anthony as their patron saint, and the disease came to be known as St. Anthony's fire. In 1916 federal government regulations restricted the use of ergot-infested grain to .3% of weight for making flour. This virtually ended the disease of ergotism in this country.

Harvesting and Winnowing Wild Grains

Most grass seeds are edible, but often too small to harvest or process efficiently. Small seeds do not grind well on a metate or swell and turn to mush when cooked as hot cereal, so they tend to pass through the digestive tract intact. The ideal grasses have big seeds, much heavier than the surrounding chaff. This makes it easier to blow the chaff away, while keeping the seeds.

There are three main techniques for harvesting cereal grains with crude implements. One method is to simply strip the whole seed heads by hand, collecting the material in a container. Another method is to beat the seed heads with a stick, catching the seeds in a pan or tarp. The third method is to cut the whole stalks, place them on a tarp, then beat the seeds out. The plants can be dried on the tarp to make the seeds drop more easily.

Next, break the seeds free from the chaff. Rubbing the rough material between the palms is sufficient for most grains. But some seeds are encased in a husk that is impossible to rub free of the grain. These seeds are ground up, husk and all, for a high-fiber cereal. Also, a few kinds of grass seeds can be parched and then rubbed to remove the husk. Grasses that are hairy or sharp should be avoided, as they could cause irritation or injury to the throat.

Winnowing removes the chaff after it has been broken free from the seeds. Winnowing is a bit like gold-panning, where you catch the weighty metal and wash the lighter debris away. In fact, I recommend a gold-pan for this process. Swirling the pan and occasionally tossing the grain lightly into the air brings the light chaff to the surface, so it can be blown away.

Optionally, wait for a breezy day, then toss the rubbed material into the air, so that the seeds fall straight down on a tarp, but a light breeze carries the chaff away. Any remaining bits of chaff are good roughage for digestion.

American sloughgrass
Beckmannia syzigachne

Harvested grains can be cooked whole as a hot cereal, or ground into flour and used for bread or mush. Cooking them whole may reduce the labor involved, but the grains must be cooked almost to mush or they will pass through your system undigested. Very small seeds may not ever soften enough to become digestible. Another alternative is to sprout the seeds. This makes the material digestible, but converts much of the starch and oil content into proteins. Some wild grasses that have a known history of use as cereal grains include:

Achnatherum—rice grass, needle grass (75/32/10) Indian rice grass (*A. hymenoides*, formerly *Oryzopsis hymenoides*) is common in the arid West. The grains are large and easy to process.

Agropyron—crested wheatgrass (23/3/1) • The seeds are harvested with a seed beater and ground on a metate for use as mush or flour (Olsen). Quackgrass (*A. repens*) is now *Elymus repens* or *Elytrigia repens*.

Agrostis—bentgrass, redtop (220/35/12) The seeds are harvested with a seed beater and ground on a metate for use as mush or flour (Olsen).

Beckmannia—sloughgrass (2/1/1) The seeds were eaten by Native Americans in Utah (Sturtevant).

Bromus—bromegrass, cheat grass (150/70/11) • The seeds of many species of bromegrass were eaten by Native Americans (Duke). Cheat grass (*B. tectorum*) was introduced from Europe.

cheatgrass
bromus tectorum

Deschampsia—hairgrass (30/10/3) Harvest seeds with a seed beater and grind on a metate for use as mush or flour (Olsen).

Digitaria—crabgrass (300/27/2) • The seeds are a substitute for rice in Poland. One plant can produce 150,000 seeds (Duke).

Echinochloa—barnyard grass, millet (20/12/2) • The seeds are harvested with a seed beater and ground on a metate for use as mush or flour (Olsen). *E. frumentacea* and *E. esculenta* are known as Japanese millet, grown as a cereal crop.

Elymus—wild rye, wheat grass, quackgrass (150/43/19) • The seeds are harvested with a seed beater or stripped by hand. They are winnowed and ground on a metate for use as mush or flour (Olsen).

Festuca—fescue (450/41/8) • The seeds are parched to remove the husk, ground into flour, or cooked as mush (Olsen).

Glyceria—mannagrass (35/18/4) The is reported to be one of the better-tasting grains found in the West. The seeds are gathered with a seed beater and winnowed to remove the chaff. They are used as a thickening for stews or ground into flour (Olsen).

Hordeum—barley, foxtail barley (25/10/6) Cooking hulled (pearled) barley produces a mucilaginous substance, useful as a demulcent for a sore throat. It is mixed with milk to soothe the stomach and intestines (Lust). Some wild species are known to have been used by Native Americans (Duke).

Oryzopsis—rice grass (40/1/1) Many species formerly in this genus were moved to *Achnatherum* (see above).

Panicum—switch grass (450/34/4) Several species of *Panicum* have been cultivated for grain (Sturtevant).

Phalaris—canary grass (15/11/2) • Preliminary tests indicate that reed canary grass has excellent potential as a cereal crop. The season is very short, near the end of July, and I have not yet been able to do a timed study.

Phleum—timothy grass (15/5/2) • Strip the seeds off by hand, or collect the whole stalks and rub or beat the seeds out. They are easy to winnow, and are really quite a beautiful seed. I hand-stripped the seed heads for my studies and came up with about one quart of rough yield per hour. Twenty minutes of winnowing left me with over a cup of pure seed.

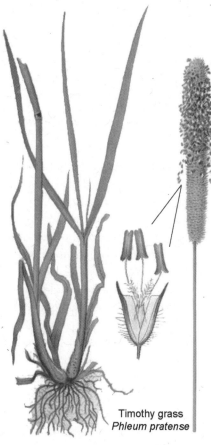

Timothy grass
Phleum pratense

Poa—bluegrass (500/95/30) • Mature seeds can be harvested with a seed beater for a short time before they drop (Olsen).

Setaria—bristlegrass, foxtail (100/25/4) The seeds are edible (Duke).

Sporobolus—dropseed (160/30/6) Sand dropseed (*S. cryptandrus*) was used to make bread and porridge by the Apache, Hopi, and Navajo tribes.

Zizania—wild rice (4/3/1) Wild rice is native to northeastern states with cold climates. The grain is collected by beating the seed heads over a boat. The collected seeds are dried, then parched, rubbed and winnowed to remove the husks. There are only a few days to collect the seeds upon maturity, before they drop (Hall).

Other selected genera from the Grass family

Cymbopogon—lemon grass (55/2/0) Lemon grass (*C. citratus*) is native to India and tropical Asia, but has been introduced to Florida and Hawaii. It is often used as an ingredient in herbal teas.

Hierochloe—sweetgrass (30/4/1) Often burned as incense by Native Americans.

Phragmites—common reed (2/1/1) • The young stalks or roots can sometimes be processed for sugar by drying and beating it into a flour. This sugary flour can be moistened and heated over the fire as a substitute marshmallow. The seeds can be processed by searing off the fluff. Then grind the seeds with the hull, for a high-fiber meal (Duke).

Sorghum—johnson grass (20/3/2) Introduced and highly invasive. The seeds are edible. Some species were once widely grown for sugar. Plants that are stressed from heat, drought, or frost are prone to producing cyanide (Duke).

Puccinellia—alkali grass (50/30/3) Alkali Grass grows in moist, but alkaline environments, especially in cooler climates.

common reed
Phragmites australis

The Medicinal Properties of Plants

Knowledge and Knowing

A number of natural, unflavored foods were placed before a group of infants in a study. Over time, the infants demonstrated the ability to select a nutritionally balanced diet for themselves from the selections at hand. If an infant initially binged on starchy foods, he would later seek out foods high in protein. If at first he ate foods lacking a particular vitamin, he would later eat what was needed to make up the deficit. Without any logical knowledge of diet or nutrition, the infants demonstrated an innate ability to make healthy choices.

Similarly, my son Donald instinctively treated himself with herbs as a toddler. He was covered in mosquito bites after we left a window open overnight. At breakfast, he wiped his oatmeal all over his face to soothe the bites. The slimy or "mucilaginous" property of the oatmeal was ideal to take away the itch.

Unfortunately, we lose our instincts very quickly as we grow up. Our parents teach us which foods are good for us, and if we choke them down we are rewarded with foods that are bad for us. Even without this perverse sense of dietary rewards, we learn language and logic, and ultimately lose our innate abilities. We eat from the fruit of Knowledge and leave the Garden. We acquire Knowledge, but we lose our Knowing.

If we attempt to return to the Garden, it is often with notebook in hand. Scientists, for example, have observed chimpanzees instinctively seeking out medicinal plants when ill. Researchers follow chimps around in the jungle and take note when one significantly alters its behavior, stops eating, and starts consuming different herbs. Those herbs are sent to a lab for analysis in the hopes of finding new and beneficial drugs for people.

The study of edible and medicinal herbs and Stone Age skills (which I also teach) is an attempt, in part, to get back into the Garden. It is an effort to tune into nature, to harvest from the abundance, to live healthy, and to be "one with nature." Those of us who pursue this goal are on a path of Knowledge, picking up pieces of information that will allow us to again reconnect with the whole of nature. Unfortunately, it is impossible to reassemble the whole by picking up its pieces. Through Knowledge we can achieve a relatively balanced life in harmony with nature, but it is very different from the experience of our ancestors. It is still the path of fragmented Knowledge.

We might guess at the nutritional needs of an infant and provide a carefully balanced meal based on reason, but it can never be as good as what the infant innately knows. We might come close on the obvious, major nutrients, vitamins, and minerals, but there are nearly infinite micronutrients and minerals that we can never fully comprehend. Even if we could plan out a perfectly balanced diet in theory, the reality is that every individual is different with needs that are completely unique to him- or herself.

Nearly forty percent of our pharmaceuticals contain constituents originally found in herbs.

Fragmented knowledge is not all bad. There are life-threatening ailments that neither infants nor apes are able to treat, and our ancestors often lost patients to ailments as simple as dysentery (severe, bloody diarrhea). Science has developed heroic procedures to save people from serious injuries and illness. It makes the difference between life and death for people all over the world. Science has also given us the ability to isolate and often synthesize certain compounds from medicinal plants. Nearly forty percent of our pharmaceuticals today contain constituents originally found in herbs.

Those of us with an interest in herbalism are often drawn to it because it is less fragmented than conventional medical science. Herbalists point out that there is a difference between using a whole herb versus using a single active constituent isolated from it. Some plants have a remarkable record of successful use, yet modern science cannot isolate any single constituent to account for the effects. Herbalists claim that it is the action of multiple constituents working together, sometimes from multiple herbs.

Similarly, herbalists can treat certain conditions that medical doctors are unable to even diagnose—because the doctors cannot isolate any specific ailment. People may go to the doctor feeling lousy, but the M.D. might not find anything wrong with them. These "subclinical" conditions are the realm where herbalists excel. Herbalists can use whole plants and life-style changes to promote more efficient functioning of the body's systems, so that the body is better able to help itself.

Herbalism has its place, just as Western medicine or acupuncture have theirs. All are ultimately fragments belonging to the whole. Each can achieve independent results that are beyond reach of the others, and none is complete in itself. An individual must shop around and find what seems to work best for a particular situation. More importantly, an individual must learn to feel and intuit a direction. It is not enough to merely seek treatment after becoming ill. The path of good health is to intuitively select what the body needs at each moment to maintain well-being.

In pursuit of good health, many people have also turned to Eastern philosophies or other sources to find a "natural diet." But it seems like every health guru has their own formula for a true "natural diet." Each guru promotes their own strict diet of what you can and cannot eat to be healthy and live naturally. But these diets are not natural at all, as they are products of fragmented thinking. These diets teach you to eat from the outside, with Knowledge, instead of from the inside, with Knowing.

> *Herbalism has its place, just as Western medicine or acupuncture have theirs. All are fragments belonging to the whole. Each can achieve independent results that are beyond reach of the others, and none is complete in itself.*

It is my hope that this book will help you build on your inner Knowing. The process is quite logical, but the results can be surprisingly intuitive. For instance, as you study plants, you will learn to recognize patterns in appearance, smell, taste, and chemistry. With practice, however, the process of recognition becomes more and more automatic. You will discover that you often *know* a plant, even if you have never seen it before in your life. You will often know the edible and medicinal uses of a plant even before you know its name.

Keep in mind, however, that this guide is intended to identify plants and their properties only. There is a big difference between learning the properties of a plant and knowing how and when to apply them to the human body. Diagnosing an ailment and prescribing medicine requires, in essence, a "Field Guide to the Body," and no guide to plants can provide an adequate substitute. But for starters, I recommend Christopher Hobbs' book, *Foundations of Health: Healing with Herbs & Foods* (ISBN: 0-9618470-8-5). The book rings true to the herbalists' axiom that a healthy digestive system makes for a healthy body. The book is an excellent resource for understanding and facilitating the digestive processes.

About Edible, Medicinal and Poisonous Plants

Botany in a Day covers edible, medicinal, and poisonous plants. Given my interest in wilderness survival skills, I tend to think from the belly and emphasize edible properties when applicable. I often leave out the medicinal properties of a plant to leave room for its edible uses. But overall, there are far more medicinal plants than edible ones, so the majority of the text focuses on medicinal properties.

In fact, *all* plants are medicinal in some context, regardless of whether or not they are otherwise considered edible or poisonous. For example, oatmeal, potato soup, or chicken soup are all foods, but are sometimes used as mild medicines. On the other end of the spectrum, water hemlock (*Cicuta*)—the most poisonous plant in North America—was also once used medicinally. A piece of the root the size of a small marble is enough to kill a person. Some people say that just the juice on the knife after cutting through the root is enough to kill a person. And yet, in very minute doses, water hemlock has been used medicinally. Not all of the patients survived.

Fortunately, there are surprisingly few truly poisonous plants to threaten the novice forager. There are only a few plants in North America that are potent enough to kill a normal, healthy adult. People do die from eating wild plants sometimes, but it always the same half-dozen plants—out of tens of thousands of different species. Learn these few poisonous plants well, and it is relatively difficult to seriously hurt yourself with the others. Fortunately, most poisonous plants taste bad, so you are unlikely to eat enough of one to cause harm.

From the perspective of a person looking for medicinal plants, however, there are many more potentially poisonous plants. If you are looking for that magic herb to cure what ails you, then you are likely to ingest plants that you would not otherwise touch as food. In addition, many herbal concoctions are concentrated, potent extracts of otherwise relatively benign herbs, and we Americans are prone to overdosing. As herbalist Robyn Klein puts it, we tend to think, "If a little is good, more is better!" We pour all kinds of toxins down the hatch in the name of good health. Most herbs are quite safe when used properly, but people can die from overdosing on concentrated herbal extracts.

When it comes to learning about the edible and medicinal uses of plants, it is often assumed that our ancestors figured it out entirely through trial-and-error. There are hundreds of thousands of plant species in the world, and we assume our ancestors approached each specimen without prior insight, eventually discovering by pure chance what was edible or not, and what medicinal effects every plant has. But in reality, there are only a few basic constituents common throughout the plant kingdom, and most of them are recognizable with the five senses. You can learn to determine the uses of many plants without ever knowing their names.

There are only a few basic constituents common throughout the plant kingdom, and most of them are recognizable with the five senses. You can learn to determine the uses of many plants without ever knowing their names.

For instance, suppose you chew up a leaf and get the sensation of "cotton mouth." Your mouth seems to run out of saliva, a good indicator for tannic acid, one of the most prevalent plant constituents. Once you learn to recognize this constituent and know what it is used for, then you know the approximate use of thousands of similar plants around the world. But don't go around randomly sampling the greenery. For safety, it is important to know what every plant is before you put it in your mouth. At the very least, be sure about what a plant *isn't*. If you can rule out every lethal plant in your area, then you may be able to experiment more liberally with other plants. The goal is to become your own teacher.

In many herbal classes, the students often follow the instructor around copying down precise recipes and uses for each plant along the way, but the instructors often gained their knowledge through direct experimentation. When ill, they might try many different plants to see what works. The result is that each herbalist has a unique recipe and different uses for any given plant. This is one of the reasons that herbalism has not been accepted by the medical establishment; to the outsider, the prescriptions and dosage seem completely arbitrary and inconsistent.

Most herbalism is simple and straightforward. Tannic acid, for example, has an astringent effect. The acid binds with proteins, drawing water out of the cells, and causing tissues to constrict. This is a quantifiable effect, and it can be used medicinally for hundreds of different situations, from drawing closed an open wound to helping dry out the bowels in cases of diarrhea. As you learn this broad picture you will develop a much more flexible knowledge of herbalism.

Most herbalists prepare herbs as alcohol tinctures and other herbal extracts. Tinctures are useful because the alcohol dissolves out medicinal constituents that are not water-soluble, significantly increasing the potency of the herbal preparations.

Personally, I prefer using herbs without tincturing, and I have often had better results when I just chewed on raw hunks of root, or drank medicinal teas, than when I have used tinctures. For these reasons, I have intentionally avoided including formulas, recipes, or dosage for using medicinal herbs.

I would rather help you gain the ability to think and intuit for yourself. You will not be limited to any set of recipes or uses, but you will be able to experiment for yourself and see what works. This is the essence of true herbalism.

peppermint
Mentha piperita
Mint Family

Plant Properties

The allure of Western science is great, and modern herbalists have become increasingly focused on fragmented knowledge—the specific constituents of the plants. Everyone wants to know what the active constituents are in the plants they are using. Some plants may have pages worth of constituents, and we want to know what they are and what they do in the body. Sometimes it is helpful to know what is happening at the molecular level to better understand and communicate why a certain herb is used in a certain way. But there are so many variables to deal with when you break a plant apart into its constituents that the information gained is often inaccurate. For example, in earlier editions of this book I wrote that the immunostimulating properties of *Echinacea* and several other herbs were due to their polysaccharide content. It was hypothesized that these complex sugars looked similar to cell walls of bacteria, thereby stimulating the immune system into action. That hypothesis has since been rejected, but the concept is still referenced in the herbal literature.

The greatest danger in pursuing plant constituents is that some herbal products on the market are no longer representative of the whole plants they were derived from. Partly there is a problem with adulteration, where companies either knowingly or unknowingly substitute other herbs for those on the package label. In addition, certain constituents may be highly concentrated through the extraction process. The whole plant may be harmless, but a strong dose of one of its chemicals can be dangerous.

Pennyroyal (*Mentha pulegium*), for instance, is a benign plant as a whole, but individuals have died from overdosing on pure pennyroyal oil, used to cause abortions. These kind of extracts are hardly herbal medicine. They are pharmaceutical concoctions derived from plants fragmented into their constituents. They can be used with remarkable results by expert hands, but are sometimes dangerous for amateurs to utilize. A few words on the label can not begin to accurately prescribe proper conditions for use.

false
pennyroyal
Hedeoma
pulegioides
Mint Family

pennyroyal
Mentha pulegium
Mint Family

Even seemingly benign herbal supplements can have side effects. They might initially energize you, only to cause withdrawals when you stop taking them. Some supplements are more like pharmaceuticals than herbs.

For the purposes of traditional herbalism, there is rarely a need to know all the individual constituents of a plant. Herbalism is rooted in the basic properties, such as *astringent*, *mucilaginous*, or *aromatic*. You can often learn all you need about the active ingredients of a plant with your senses. For instance, plants with white, milky sap contain some type of *latex*. Plants that form suds when beaten in water usually contain *saponin*. Aromatic plants contain *volatile oils*. Plants with a clear, slimy juice are considered *mucilaginous*. It is pretty basic stuff!

Nevertheless, I have included explanations for more specific plant properties. For instance, there are some thirty thousand known volatile oils, which can be consolidated into a dozen or so main groups based on their chemical structure. Any one plant may be chemically dissected into hundreds, even thousands of distinct volatile oils and other constituents. Fortunately, you do not need to learn every individual volatile oil, or even their chemical groups, because they tend to have roughly similar effects on the body. It is helpful to understand that not all volatile oils are equal, yet learning each of these constituents may ultimately teach you less about the plant, not more.

Keep the big picture in mind and stick to the basics as much as possible. Do not focus too much on any one chemical property, or you will begin to open a Pandora's box of new questions and fragments. Each individual substance may have different uses on its own than when combined with the whole of the plant. It is the overall pattern of constituents within a plant that is most important. The specific definitions presented on the following pages are like a crutch to help you get around. Accept the broader definitions without trying to understand their intricacies. You must eventually throw away the crutch of Knowledge and use your Knowing.

Carbohydrates

The basis of all sugars are the elements carbon, hydrogen, and oxygen. The word carbohydrate is derived from these three words, and is used for any type of sugar. Plants make sugars from air, water, and sunlight. They use the sun's energy to break apart H_2O (water) and CO_2 (carbon dioxide), and to recombine these elements into CH_2O (sugar) and O_2 (the oxygen we breathe). These carbohydrates are a means of storing energy. We eat the carbohydrates and release the energy, allowing the molecules to revert to H_2O and CO_2. Enzymes in our saliva break the carbohydrates down into simple sugars. Thus, chewing food longer can bring out the true sweetness. Complex sugars that are improperly digested can ferment in the gut and cause gas.

Starch: Plants like potatoes and cattails store energy in their roots in the form of starchy carbohydrates. This energy reserve is built up over the course of the summer, then used to accelerate growth in the spring. Most seeds also include a starch reserve called the endosperm. Most starchy roots and seeds are edible, but some species contain dangerous alkaloids or acrid substances. Starchy roots can be used medicinally as drawing poultices to absorb toxins or to draw down an inflammation. The effectiveness of these poultices can often be increased by soaking the starchy roots in tannic acid first.

Monosaccharides: Monosaccharides are simple sugars, including glucose, fructose, and galactose. These sugars are metabolized through digestion for energy. They have no known medicinal functions.

Disaccharides: When two simple sugars are combined they are called a disaccharide. Sucrose, for example, is made of a unit of glucose and a unit of fructose. Maltose is a combination of two units of glucose. Lactose is made of glucose and galactose. Most disaccharides are easily broken down through digestion into monosaccharides, and then used for energy. Some disaccharides are indigestible and become "roughage" in our systems. An **oligosaccharide** is a combination of two to ten sugar molecules.

Polysaccharides: Polysaccharides are complex carbohydrates made of many sugar units. Wood is made of one form of polysaccharide called **cellulose**.

Inulin: The word "inulin" is often confused with the unrelated word "insulin." Inulin is a nondigestible carbohydrate that can be converted to fructose through extended exposure to heat and moisture. Undercooked inulin can produce copious gas in the gut. Diabetics are able to eat fructose, and therefore inulin-rich foods. Inulin is usually found in roots and is especially abundant in the Aster family. Dandelion roots are roasted to break the inulin down into sweet-tasting fructose. Jerusalem artichoke tubers (*Helianthus tuberosus*) are sweetest the day after they are cooked. The onion (*Allium*), blue camas (*Camassia*), and many other bulbs are also rich in inulin.

Mucilage: Mucilage is a slimy, moist polysaccharide found in *Aloe vera* and many other herbs. It is especially useful for mild burns and sunburns. The fluid between your body cells is a mucopolysaccharide hydrogel.

narrowleaf plantain
Plantago lanceolata
Plantain Family

Polysaccharides help strengthen this hydrogel after damage. Mucilaginous plants are typically described as emollient when it is used externally on irritated skin, and as demulcent when used internally, as for soothing a sore throat. Mucilage has a mildly expectorant quality, probably by increasing the sliminess of the phlegm enough to release it. Mucilage is sometimes used as a bulk laxative. Mucilage also coats the intestinal tract, reducing irritation and sensitivity to chemicals, acids, and bitters. The Cactus, Mallow, Flax, Purslane, and Borage families are all high in mucilage. Mucilage is also found in members of the Plantain, Violet, and Rose families.

Pectin: Pectins are complex polysaccharides used medicinally for ulcers, wounds, and intestinal problems, such as diarrhea. Kaopectate is a commercial remedy for diarrhea that includes pectin. Pectin also contains calcium and phosphorus, bound with a strong electrical charge that attracts toxic chemicals, heavy metals, and radioactive compounds. The toxins are then eliminated through the bowels. Apples and some other fruits theoretically contain enough pectin to jell without adding commercial pectin. Pectin is especially found in fruits of the Rose family, but also in citrus fruits (*Rutaceae*), and in the Barberry, Mallow, and Aster families.

Gum: Gums are similar to mucilage, but thicker and more sticky. Gums are commonly used as stabilizers in the cosmetic, pharmaceutical, and food-processing industries. Gums prevent other ingredients from separating out of a mixture. Agar gum appears on the labels of many products. It is extracted from a seaweed of the same name. Gums are present in the Pea family and especially common in the Aster family.

Glycosides

A glycoside is a sugar combined with a non-sugar (a-glycone) compound. Herbalists are most interested in the aglycone part; the sugar itself has little therapeutic value. In fact, other than saponins, most glycosides are inactive until separated from the sugar component. Crushing a plant and soaking it in warm water is usually sufficient for the plant's own enzymes to break apart the glycoside and release the active constituents into the water, known as hydrolyzation. Cold water may not activate the enzyme activity, while hot water can alter the chemistry, and in rare cases, may produce toxic substances (Schauenberg).

Sulfur Glycosides: Sulfur glycosides, like glucosinolate and thiocyanate, contain nitrogen in combination with sulfur. They are mostly found in the Mustard, Caper, Nasturtium, and Mignonette families, as well as in onions (*Allium*). Sulfur glycosides are acrid and irritating. In small amounts they stimulate digestion; in larger amounts they can cause heartburn. These plants are often used as a rubifacient poultice; the glycosides irritate the area of application, stimulating circulation and healing. Sulfur from these food sources is also useful for metabolizing and excreting acetaminophen (found in drugs like Tylenol®), which can otherwise build up to toxic levels in the body.

In moderation, sulphur-rich plants can help prevent goiter, a swelling of the thyroid gland often caused by iodine deficiency. Along with iodized salt, the popularization of mustard may have contributed to the virtual disappearance of goiter in the modern world. However, excessive consumption of these plants can block the body's ability to absorb iodine, and *cause* goiter.

Cyanide Glycosides: Cyanide appears in many forms with many names, including cyanophore, cyanogen, hydrocyanic acid and prussic acid. Cyanide glycosides contain nitrogen in combination with hydrogen and carbon. Cyanide occurs widely in nature, especially in the Rose, Honeysuckle, and Flax families. Cherry pits, for example, contain cyanide in the form of a glycoside, known variously as amygdalin, laetrile, or vitamin B17 (see page 94). Laetrile has been promoted as an anti-cancer agent, but with inconclusive results. An overdose of laetrile can cause death. The cyanide reacts with an enzyme in the body called cytochrome oxidase, which normally links oxygen to the individual cells. Cyanide interrupts this process and causes the individual cells to asphyxiate. Plants containing cyanide are sometimes listed as sedative, because they literally choke off the metabolic processes.

The body handles trace amounts of cyanide by adding a molecule of sulfur to create thiocyanate (see *Sulfur Glycosides* above). But excess dosage overwhelms and poisons the body. Chronic consumption of trace amounts will rob the body of sulfur and iodide, leading to thyroid disorders (Klein).

Phenol Glycosides: Phenols come in different forms, but all are carbon-based. Phenols are a component in the other glycosides to follow, including flavonoids, coumarins, anthraquinone, cardiac glycosides and saponins.

Simple phenols: Simple phenols like salicylin (e.g.; salicylic acid, willow, aspirin) are an important class of their own. Salicylic acid affects the thermoregulatory centers and peripheral blood vessels to relieve fevers, pain, and inflammation. Simple phenols are especially useful for treating urinary tract infections, arthritis, rheumatism, and other inflammations. Some forms pass through the digestive tract before they are hydrolyzed (that is, separating the active component from the sugar) in the presence of alkaline urine in the bladder. Hydrolyzation forms potent disinfectants, especially useful for urinary tract infections. If the urine is acid, then sodium bicarbonate must be taken with the herbs for hydrolyzation to occur. Simple phenols are found in the Willow, Birch, and Heath families, plus *Spiraea* and pear (*Pyrus*) of the Rose family.

Flavonoids: Flavonoid glycosides include flavones, flavonals, flavonones, isoflavones, chalcones, and aurones. Plants that are rich in flavonoids have been used as dyes. The word "flavonoid" comes from the Latin "flavus," meaning yellow. Red and yellow fall colors are flavonoids, which are always present in the leaves, but hidden by chlorophyll until fall. Flavonoids are safe for people and animals, but toxic to microorganisms. Plants produce them to protect against disease. Many flavonoids are known to have antiviral and anti-inflammatory properties, but they are especially valued as antioxidants to help prevent free radicals.

In biology, free radicals are otherwise healthy cells that lose electrons at the molecular level. The cells become highly reactive and bind with anything that will balance out their charge, including damaging oxygen molecules.

Antioxidants are foods or supplements, often rich in flavonoids, that provide a source of electrons to stabilize cells before they are injured.

Flavonoids are generally diuretic and relieve cramping. They also affect the heart and circulatory system and strengthen the capillaries. There are about 500 known flavonoids, including vitamins C, E, and P. Flavonoids are found throughout the plant kingdom, but are especially concentrated in fruits, and particularly in wild berries.

Coumarins: There are more than 100 varieties of coumarins grouped into several general types: hydroxycoumarins, methoxycoumarins, furanocoumarins, pyranocoumarins, and dicoumarols. Coumarins have a sweet smell. Medicinally they have anti-inflammatory and antibacterial properties. The Indian breadroot (*Psoralea*) and sweet clover (*Melilotus*) of the Pea family contain coumarins, as do many plants of the Parsley family.

Dicoumarols act as anticoagulants by destroying vitamin K, which is normally produced by bacteria in the small intestine and used by the liver in the manufacture of prothrombin, a blood-clotting protein. Dicoumarol is used to reduce blood clots in heart patients. Excess consumption can prevent the scabbing of clots, or lead to spontaneous internal bleeding. Concentrated doses of dicoumarols are used in rat poison. Dicoumarols are formed when sweet clover (*Melilotus*) is fermented.

Furanocoumarins can have a phytotoxic effect, causing a rash when the skin is exposed to ultraviolet light. Juice from celery leaves, and other Parsley family plants, can make the skin sensitive to sunlight. Furanocoumarins are often toxic to fish.

Anthraquinone Glycosides: Anthraquinone glycosides have purgative (strongly laxative) properties. The glycosides are digested by bile, absorbed by the small intestine, and passed on to the large intestine hours later as purgatives. These glycosides are found in diverse, mostly unrelated plants.

Anthraquinone glycosides are violent purgatives, especially those found in senna *(Cassia)* and *Aloe vera*. They can cause blood to be released with the stools. However, buckthorn (*Rhamnus*) also contains a form of cyanide that gives the laxative a calming effect, so it can be used for several days without irritation. Rhubarb root (*Rheum*), which also contains anthraquinone glycosides, is considered relatively gentle. *Cuscuta* and *Hypericum* contain this purgative glycoside, but the latter is fat-soluble, not digestible by the bile, so it has no effect. Anthraquinones are sometimes associated with churning or gripping pain in the bowels, so spicy herbs like ginger (see *Volatile or Essential Oils*) are often taken with the laxatives for their antispasmodic property. Note that excess use of laxatives can weaken the bowels and result in laxative dependency.

Cardiac Glycosides: Cardiac glycosides stimulate heart contractions. This property can be useful in cases such as water retention caused by a weak heart and kidneys. Anything that helps remove excess fluids from the body is known as a diurectic, in this case achieved through increased heart function. Foxglove (*Digitalis*), lily-of-the-valley (*Convallaria*), and many plants in the Dogbane/Milkweed family are especially rich in cardiac glycosides. Other plants with cardiac glycosides include hellebore (*Helleborus*), pheasant's eye (*Adonis*), water lily (*Nymphaea*), and hedge hyssop (*Gratiola*). However, cardiac glycosides are potentially very dangerous and should not be used internally by amateurs.

Saponin: Saponin is a glycoside poison. It destroys the membranes of red blood cells and releases the hemoglobin. Fortunately, saponin is not easily absorbed by the digestive system, and most of what we eat passes straight through the body. Saponin is widely found in plants, including many vegetables like beans, spinach, and tomatoes. There are many forms of saponin, all with varying potency. Saponin breaks down with prolonged cooking.

Plants that contain saponin can usually be worked into a lather, and are often used as soap substitutes. Saponins are effective at removing dirt but not oils. They are sometimes used as cleansers in cosmetics. Specific plants that are rich in saponins include: yucca root (*Yucca*), buckbrush flowers and berries (*Ceanothus*), snowberry (*Symphoricarpos*), bouncing bet (*Saponaria*), white cockle (*Lychnis*), horse chestnut (*Aesculus*), and *Cyclamen*.

Medicinally, saponins are sometimes used as irritants in the form of sneezing powders or emetics, but more often to stimulate digestion. Saponin may be valuable in certain cases of arthritis where the pain is combined with indigestion or headaches. Saponins clean the intestinal walls and facilitate the body's use of certain substances like calcium and silicon. Saponins also have a diuretic effect.

Saponin-rich plants are often used as fish poison. Fish assimilate saponin directly into the blood stream through their gills, destroying their red blood cells. Adding a significant quantity of a saponin-rich herb into a small, still pond may effectively stun or kill the fish, without harming the fisherman who eats them.

Acids

Natural plant acids come in many different forms. A few common acids are described here.

Tannic Acid: An astringent is any acid substance that causes tissues to constrict. The most common natural astringent is tannic acid. Gallic and malic acids are also astringents. The act of constricting tissues is medicinally useful in a number of ways.

Internally, astringents close off secretions, especially of the digestive system, which is useful for "drying up" diarrhea or dysentery (a severe, often bloody type of diarrhea). Astringents also tighten up ulcerated tissues, facilitating healing in cases of stomach ulcers and bloody urine.

Astringents tone and strengthen mucous membranes, such as in the urinary tract. Many plants with astringent properties are also diuretic in nature, meaning they make you urinate more. The diuretic effect may be due in part to the tannins drawing water out of the cells, but also to simple phenol glycosides (see *Glycosides*) that are often found with tannic acid. Since acids are generally harmful to bacteria, astringent plants are often also listed as antiseptic or antibiotic.

Externally, astringent plants are useful as a poultice or wash to heal cuts, eczema, and eruptions on the skin. Astringent herbs are often listed as anti-inflammatory, useful for tightening up tissues in cases of swellings, sunburns, pimples, blisters, sore throats, inflamed or tired eyes, or as a sitz bath after childbirth to speed the healing of inflamed tissues. Through the act of tightening tissues, astringents act as a sort of toner or strengthener, useful as a facial toner to reduce wrinkles or as a poultice to diminish varicose veins. Similarly, the leaves of astringent plants can be put in shoes to tighten the skin and protect against blistering. Given that astringents cause wounds to tighten up and stop bleeding, they are sometimes listed as hemostatics or coagulants.

Tannic acid is also used for tanning hides. That drying, puckering sensation you get when you taste an astringent is the same action that works on a hide, drawing out the binders to make the hide more flexible. Overconsumption of these tannins is potentially dangerous, and countries where black tea is popular tend to have high rates of stomach cancer. Adding milk to tea reduces the tannin effect, since the tannins binds with milk proteins, instead of proteins in the stomach lining.

Oxalic Acid: The lemony-sour taste in rhubarb and many other plants comes from oxalic acid, also called oxalate, while the true lemon taste comes from citronellal, the potent volatile oil found in lemons. Like other acids, oxalate acts as an astringent when used as a wash for skin problems. But oxalic acid is much harsher than other acids. Internally, it acts as an irritating stimulant to the digestive system. It irritates the system to increase, rather than decrease, digestive secretions, which is helpful as a digestive aid for heartburn or constipation. Intermittent consumption of oxalic acid is okay, but too much can excessively irritate the system, leading to diarrhea and potentially hemorrhaging.

Most plants with oxalic acid are edible, with caution that long-term consumption may block the body's ability to absorb calcium. However, wild plant researcher John Kallas suggests that concern over oxalates arose from a study involving sheep and cows eating very large quantities of oxalate-rich plants. Human metabolism is very different, and most oxalates are excreted with the feces. Oxalates bind with calcium in the digestive tract, making both unavailable for absorption, but this may be a naturally protective effect of the calcium to further reduce the absorption of oxalates. Interestingly, most plants that are rich in oxalic acid are also rich in calcium. The oxalate content of rhubarb stems is actually higher than in the leaves. Kallas has not yet found a verified case of humans ingesting toxic doses of oxalates. In addition, the human body converts excess quantities of vitamin C into oxalates that are filtered through the kidneys and end up in the urine. The body's own production of oxalates is greater than would ever be consumed eating normal quantities of oxalate-rich plants.

There is also little evidence to link dietary oxalates with kidney stones. Kallas suggests that most people should be able to consume as much oxalate-rich food as they want, although it is always prudent to be cautious, especially if you are chronically undernourished in calcium, vitamin D, and phosphorus, or if you have an existing abnormal tendency to produce kidney stones. The Buckwheat, Woodsorrel, Purslane, and Amaranth/Goosefoot families include plants that are rich in oxalic acid. Note that calcium oxalate crystals, such as those in the Arum family, can cause physical damage if ingested.

Citric and Tartaric Acid: Citric and tartaric acids cleanse the mouth, stimulate saliva flow, and reduce the number of cavity-causing bacteria. The acids are considered laxative because they are absorbed very slowly through the intestines, so stools remain soft. Citric and tartaric acids are useful after surgery or in cases of hemorrhoids, to reduce muscle action of the lower abdomen. Citric and other plant acids can also bind with and remove heavy metals and other toxins in the body. Citric acid is primarily found in the Citrus family (*Rutaceae*), but also in raspberries and other fruits of the Rose family, plus members of the Grape family.

Formic Acid: Formic acid is a defensive mechanism used by biting ants and several members of the Stinging Nettle family. Both ants and nettles inject the acid under the skin, causing temporary inflammation. Try applying an astringent herb to take away the itch.

Formic acid is readily digestible, such that both the nettles and most ant species are edible raw or cooked. Some people carefully fold or crush nettle leaves to avoid the stinging hairs and eat them raw, but it is far safer to cook them as a delicious green. Medicinally, formic acid has been used as an irritant to stimulate healing in cases of arthritis. The arthritic joints are whipped with stinging nettles. The resulting irritation improves circulation and facilitates healing. This is a cure for the desperate!

Acrids

Acrid substances cause a hot, biting sensation on the tongue, much like horseradish. Taken internally in moderate amounts, acrid herbs warm the body, dilate the blood vessels, decrease blood pressure, and equalize blood flow to the extremities. For this reason, acrid plants are often listed as emmenagogues (menstrual stimulants), diaphoretics (which cause sweating), diuretics (which cause increased urination), and galactagogues (which increase milk flow). The hot, acrid quality opens you up from the inside out.

horseradish
Armoracia rusticana
Mustard Family

Acrid herbs are sometimes used as expectorants to irritate the mucous membranes and loosen phlegm. Larger doses can cause vomiting (emetic). Caution is advised. Highly acrid herbs could harm the delicate tissues.

Externally, herbs with acrid properties are often used as irritating poultices to stimulate healing under the skin, good for such ailments as bruises, aches, or arthritis. An acrid mustard plaster on the chest can help warm and stimulate congested lungs. Acrid poultices can even stimulate activity in cases of mild paralysis, but be careful, because a strong poultice can cause blistering if left in place too long.

Acrid plants are also used for warts. The plant juice is smeared on the wart a few times each day until the wart disappears. Likewise, acrid plants can be used as a hair rinse to get rid of lice.

Acrid poultices can even be used on external cancerous tumors. A strongly acrid poultice is placed over the cancer to burn out the growth. The body often encases cancerous cells to separate them from healthy ones, and the acrid substances supposedly burns out everything within that casing, leaving a hole that later heals over. This treatment is said to be extremely painful.

The acrid substance in mustard, radish and horseradish (Mustard family), garlic (Amaryllis family), and cow parsnip (Parsley family) comes from a thiocyanate glycoside (*see Glycosides*). The Buttercup, Arum, and Iris families also include many acrid plants.

Latex

Many plants have white, milky sap, which is typically a form of latex. Natural latex was originally the source of rubber for making tires, until the industry switched to synthetic oil products. Plants with milky sap vary from bitter to acrid, and deliciously edible to highly toxic. The Chicory or Dandelion subfamily of the Aster family includes many mildly bitter herbs, excellent in salads for stimulating digestive secretions just prior to eating a big meal.

Plants with an acrid latex sap are used like other acrid substances (above), to irritate and thus stimulate the body. Herbs with acrid latex sap can be taken to stimulate secretions of digestive acids to promote digestion or to assist as a laxative. Latex-rich plants are sometimes used to irritate and stimulate (dilate) the bronchioles to aid in fighting lung infections. Latex-rich plants are also used by women to stimulate lactose production (a galactagogue) and menstruation (an emmenagogue). But caution is advised, since latex sap often contains dangerous alkaloids.

Acrid latex plants are also useful for removing warts. Put the milky sap of a plant on a wart, and the acridness will eat away the growth. Do this multiple times a day until the wart disappears.

Alkaloids

There are approximately 5,000 known alkaloids. Alkaloids contain nitrogen and have a very basic (alkaline) pH. Alkaloidal plants do not fully utilize all the available nitrogen for protein production, so the nitrogen circulates in the sap or accumulates in parts of the plants in the form of alkaloids. Alkaloids are especially produced during periods of rapid plant growth. Somehow the accelerated metabolism apparently uses the nitrogen less efficiently. Overall, alkaloidal plants are more common—and more potent—in hot climates than cold ones.

Alkaloids mixed with acids form salts. Alkaloids usually end in a suffix such as -in, -ine, or -ane. They are named after the plant they are discovered in. For example, the toxic alkaloid in water hemlock (*Cicuta*) is "cicutine."

Alkaloids are often bitter to taste, and some are used to stimulate digestion, but many alkaloids also produce a strong reaction in the nervous system. Alkaloids rarely affect the heart directly, but they may depress or excite the central nervous system, affecting circulation, respiration, and blood pressure. Most alkaloids are water-soluble.

A *narcotic* is any alkaloid that depresses the central nervous system; they are toxic in excess. Narcotics are especially used for their analgesic properties. An analgesic numbs the body's sense of pain, like opium or morphine of the Poppy family. Herbs that depress the central nervous system are often utilized as sedatives. Some depressants can cause hallucinations, including *Datura* and *Hyoscyamus* from the Nightshade family, but the toxicity varies from one area to another, and a slight overdose causes death. Symptoms include an unquenchable thirst, dilation of the pupils, delirium, hallucinations, convulsions, and coma.

Glycoside Alkaloids: Also known as "glycoalkaloids," these alkaloids are most common in the Nightshade family. Green potatoes and nightshade berries contain toxic solanine and chaconine. These alkaloids are harmless in small amounts. A bitter or burning taste signifies higher concentrations. Poisoning can cause stomach pains, ulcers, constipation or diarrhea, drowsiness, apathy, labored breathing, trembling, and ultimately paralysis, loss of consciousness, and death.

Indole Alkaloids: There are over 1,200 indole alkaloids, with diverse medicinal applications. Ergotomine, from the ergot fungus (see the Grass family) has been used as a vasoconstrictor for migraine headaches. Lysergic acid diethylamide (LSD), a hallucinogenic drug, was also originally derived from ergot fungus. Serotonin, tryptamine (like tryptophan), and adrenaline are all indole alkaloids. Most indole alkaloids are found in the Dogbane, Madder, and Logania (not covered in this text) families.

Quinoline Alkaloids: Quinine is an anti-malarial alkaloid of this group.

Isoquinoline Alkaloids: Morphine and several other narcotic, analgesic isoquinoline alkaloids are derived from members of the Poppy family. Mescaline is the hallucinogenic alkaloid in peyote (*Lophophora*) of the Cactus family.

An isoquinoline alkaloid that is non-narcotic is berberine from the Barberry family, also found in goldenseal (*Hydrastis*) and gold thread (*Coptis*) of the Buttercup family. Berberine is extremely bitter, used especially to stimulate liver function. It is strongly antiviral. It may also be effective against the parasite *Giardia*. Ipecac is another non-narcotic alkaloid of this group, derived from *Carapichea* of the Madder family.

Purine Alkaloids: Purine alkaloids can stimulate production of many hormones, particularly adrenaline. Caffeine is a purine-type alkaloid. In large amounts caffeine can lead to nervousness, insomnia, a rapid and irregular heartbeat, elevated blood sugar and cholesterol levels, and heartburn (Tyler).

Pyrrolidine and Tropane Alkaloids: These alkaloids act on the central nervous system, blocking parasympathetic nerve activity. Atropine, hyoscine, hyoscyamine, and scopolamine come from the Nightshade family. Cocaine also belongs to this group; it is derived from coca leaves (*Erythroxylum coca*) of the Coca family. It is unrelated to the source of our chocolate, cocoa (*Theobroma cacao*), from the Sterculia subfamily of the Mallow family.

Pyridine and Piperidine Alkaloids: These alkaloids tend to act first as an irritating stimulant, then as a nerve paralyzer. Cicutine and coniine, from water hemlock and hemlock of the Parsley family, are extremely toxic, fast-acting alkaloids of this group. They cause progressive paralysis of the nervous system and eventually death. Nicotine from the Nightshade family is a similar alkaloid, but not as potent; smokers reduce their life spans by about eight minutes per cigarette. Lobeline from the Harebell family also belongs to this group.

Pyrrolizidine and Quinolizidine Alkaloids: Many of these alkaloids are toxic to people and livestock. Groundsel (*Senecio*) from the Aster family contains a pyrrolizidine-type alkaloid. Comfrey, houndstongue, and borage from the Borage family contain lesser amounts of this alkaloid type. Apparently, the unsaturated forms are more toxic than the saturated forms. Quinolizidine alkaloids are prevalent in the Pea family.

Terpenoid Alkaloids: Some members of the Buttercup family, including *Aconitum* and *Delphinium,* contain highly poisonous terpenoid alkaloids. The popular sedative valerian, from the Valerian family, also contains a terpenoid alkaloid.

Volatile or Essential Oils

Volatile oils are unstable, as the name implies. Plants with a strongly aromatic odor contain significant quantities of these oils. Brush against them or crush a leaf, and the volatile oils vaporize into the air. Our culinary spices are inherently rich in volatile oils.

Medicinally, volatile oils are spicy, stimulating, and warming, causing the body to open up and sweat (diaphoretic or sudorific). This property can help you break a fever. A fever is the body's way of "cooking" the microorganisms that cause infections. Using a diaphoretic herb can help raise a mild fever just high enough to "cook" a virus, ending the fever. However, diaphoretics can be dangerous where there is already a high fever. Diaphoretics tend to be most effective if used at the very onset of a cold. Volatile oils also have a decongestant effect, as you'll notice when your nose runs after a spicy meal.

Warming the body also opens up the blood vessels, allowing blood to flow more freely. This means they have a vasodilator effect, useful for relaxing the blood vessels in cases of hypertension or for stimulating delayed menstruation, called an emmenagogue. Intensely diaphoretic plants may even affect venereal diseases.

Diaphoretics can warm you up and make you sweat, but sweating is also the body's way of cooling itself. Heat is carried away from the body as the sweat evaporates off the skin. Thus a diaphoretic herb can act as a refrigerant or febrifuge. It is no coincidence that hot, spicy food (like Mexican cuisine) originates in hot climates. Chili peppers and jalapeno peppers contain volatile oils that really make you sweat, and that helps to cool you off even when it is extremely hot out. Conversely, in cold climates we eat fatty foods like ice cream to give us calories to burn for warmth.

A hot tea of a spicy herb has a diaphoretic effect as the volatile oils are expelled through the pores of the skin. The same tea served cold may have a diuretic effect, as the volatile oils are expelled through the urine.

Herbs with volatile oils are often listed as being anthelmintic, that is, they kill or expel worms (also called a vermifuge). Similarly, aromatic herbs are often antibiotic or antimicrobial in character. They are also used externally to kill lice and ringworm fungus.

Volatile oils are frequently listed as being carminative (dispels gas). Apparently, the volatile oils function similar to bitters, stimulating secretions from the salivary, stomach, and intestinal glands to improve digestion. The volatile oils also vaporize easily and may directly interact with and break down digestive gas.

Plants with volatile oils are sometimes listed as antidotal for eliminating poisons, such as from snakebite. Apparently the increased sweating eliminates toxins through the skin. The effectiveness of this treatment is questionable for serious poisons, and I have not listed specific antidotal plants in this text. Seek professional medical assistance for such cases if in any way possible. Sweating is, however, a reliable means of cleansing and detoxing from ordinary body pollutants.

Finally, some plants with volatile oils have mildly sedative and nerve-calming properties and may be described as nervine and antispasmodic. The Aster, Dutchman's Pipe, Birch, Cypress, Heath, Ginseng, Parsley and Mint families all contain significant quantities of volatile oils. Many of these herbs may be dangerous during pregnancies, due to their anthelmintic (worm killing) and emmenagogue (menstrual stimulating) properties. The most dangerous ones are those that are also bitter (irritating). Note that medicinal plants rich in volatile oils often have a short shelf life because the desired properties vaporize. Volatile oils and resins are best extracted in alcohol.

In greater detail, volatile oils are combinations of *aromatic molecules*. There are approximately 30,000 different aromatic molecules found in plants, mostly comprised of carbon, hydrogen, and oxygen. They can be separated into a number of subgroups according to their chemical make-up and their effects on the body. A plant might contain just a few aromatic molecules belonging to one subgroup, or hundreds of aromatic molecules belonging to multiple subgroups. Plants are usually grouped in whichever chemical category they contain the most of. Individual aromatic molecules are typically named after the plant they predominately occur in. The suffix often indicates the chemical subgroup an aromatic molecule belongs to. For example, peppermint plants (*Mentha piperita*), contain an alcohol volatile oil named menthol. The name menthol comes from the root word of the mint genus combined with the -ol suffix from alcohol. Menthol is a common ingredient in many cough drops. Listed below are a few of the common chemical groups to which aromatic volatile oils belong.

Alcohols: Alcohol volatile oils are generally considered energizing and non-toxic. These are non-irritating and safe to use. The suffix -ol generally indicates a member of this group or the phenol group.

Aldehydes: Aldehyde volatile oils are anti-inflammatory, antiseptic, sedative and may be irritating to the skin. Citronellal is an aldehyde found in lemons, lemongrass, and other lemon-scented herbs. Cinnamon contains significant concentrations of cinnamic aldehyde.

Coumarins: Coumarin volatile oils can damage the liver, and may lead to photosensitivity. They also thin the blood and act as anticoagulants. (Read more about coumarins under *Glycosides*).

Esters: Ester volatile oils are typically very fragrant. They are considered antispasmodic, antifungal, and relaxing. Esters are the product of a reaction between an alcohol and an acid, forming an acetate.

Ethers: Ether volatile oils have antispasmodic, carminative, stimulant, expectorant, and antiseptic properties.

Ketones: Ketone volatile oils dissolve fats and mucus. Some are quite safe, but others can be toxic in excess. The toxins seem to affect the nervous system, leading to convulsions, stupefaction, seizures or abortion. Junipers (*Thuja*) of the Cypress family contain a toxic ketone volatile oil called thujone. Thujone is also found in wormwood (*Artemisia absinthium*) and tansy (*Tanacetum vulgare*) of the Aster family. Pulegone is a similarly toxic ketone found in pennyroyal *(Mentha pulegium)*. Hyssop (*Hyssopus*) also contains ketone volatile oils. Some plants with nontoxic ketones include jasmine (*Jasminum*) and fennel (*Foeniculum*). The suffix -one often indicates a member of this chemical group.

Oxides: Eucalyptol is an oxide volatile oil found in the *Eucalyptus* tree.

Phenols: Phenol volatile oils can be irritating to the skin and toxic to the liver in excess. They should be used only in moderation. Some plants that contain phenol volatile oils in varying quantities include cloves, thyme, oregano, and savory. The suffix -ol generally indicates a member of this or the alcohol group.

Sulfurs: Volatile oils containing sulfur are typically acrid, like onions and radishes. (See *Acrids* and *Sulfur Glycosides*.)

Terpenes: Terpene volatile oils can be irritating to the skin. They are sub-grouped according to the number of carbon atoms they contain. Monoterpenes, including menthol, camphor, and thujone, contain 10 carbon atoms. Sesquiterpenes such as azulenes and bisabolol, contain 15 carbon atoms. Terpenes with 20, 30, and 40 molecules are rare in plants, with the 30- and 40-molecule terpenes being plant steroids and hormones. The suffix -ene generally indicates a member of this group.

jasmine
Jasminum officinale
Olive Family

Resins

Plant resins are sticky, gummy substances like pine pitch. Resins are formed from oxidized volatile oils; they are complex compounds that form solids at room temperature. Resins do not contain nitrogen. They are insoluble in water, so organic solvents like alcohol are often needed to extract them from the plants. The digestive system produces some such solvents.

Resins are especially useful for their expectorant qualities to help expel phlegm during a cold. Drink a warm tea of a resinous plant and your throat becomes coated with the sticky substance. It protects tissues from irritation when coughing. Moreover, the stickiness seems to slick up the passageways in the body, so phlegm can be more readily coughed up.

Resins typically contain potent volatile oils, such as the turpentine in fir trees. Resins thus have a warming or stimulating property, useful when applied to arthritic joints. Internally, resins often have expectorant, diaphoretic, and diuretic properties. However, plants with resins may lead to kidney troubles with excessive use. The resins do not break down easily in the body, and they can irritate and plug tubules in the kidneys. The Pine, Cypress, and Aster families are especially rich in resins.

Bitters

Herbs with a bitter taste stimulate the body's systems and are most commonly used as digestive aids. You must taste the bitterness in your mouth for these to take effect. The bitter taste signals the nervous system to release digestive fluids all the way down, from saliva to gastric acid and bile. Sampling bitter herbs shortly before a meal will help prepare your digestive system for the main course, which is good to help prevent indigestion. Consuming bitter herbs after the fact, when you already have indigestion, can help your system catch up. It may seem odd to use bitter herbs to increase acidity when already experiencing hyperacidity, but the bitters also stimulate the release of bicarbonate from the liver, pancreas, and Brunner's glands. Bitter herbs influence and balance the whole digestive system, whereas most commercial remedies just neutralize the acid and impair the natural processes. Because bitter herbs help stomach problems, they are often listed as stomachic.

Note that many astringent herbs seem to taste bitter, but they are not true bitters. We are accustomed to such bland and sweet foods in our culture that many people cannot distinguish between bitter and astringent tastes. If an herb dries out your mouth so that you are lacking saliva, then you are sampling an astringent, not a bitter.

Pine Barrens gentian
Gentiana autumnalis
Gentian Family

M.E.Eaton

Bitters are also used as laxatives. Digestive fluids help loosen up the bowels and relieve constipation. Stimulating digestion like this also stimulates muscle contractions to help move matter through the bowels. A mild laxative is sometimes called an aperient. A strong laxative or purgative literally "purges" your system, while a cathartic intensely stimulates bowel movement. Purgative and cathartic herbs can be dangerous.

A third use of bitter herbs is to increase the flow of bile from the liver to the gall bladder and thence into the small intestine. This stimulated flow enhances the liver's ability to evacuate toxins from the body. Herbs that help the liver are often listed as hepatic.

Increasing the flow of bile also helps to break down fats. Consuming bitter herbs as a regular part of the diet can help maintain a healthy system. Bitters are especially helpful to revitalize the body after exhaustion, chronic disease, or lack of appetite, and weakness of the digestive system. But also note that bitter herbs can cool and contract the digestive system in some people, so spicy herbs (rich in volatile oils) are often taken to counteract the effect.

Increasing the flow of bile also dilutes it, which is important to prevent the formation of gallstones. Gallstones are formed when bile becomes concentrated in the gall bladder, and then essentially dries and precipitates into salts, forming a salt crystal in the gall bladder.

Bitter principles are very common in herbs. The Gentian and Buckbean families are especially rich in bitter principles. The Chicory or Dandelion and Thistle subfamilies of the Aster family include many bitter herbs. The Barberry family and a few members of the Buttercup family contain a potent bitter alkaloid known as berberine.

Gelatin

Gelatin is a type of protein. It is the substance that makes Jell-O® set. Gelatin is usually derived from animal hooves and hides, but it is also found in a few plants, such as *Smilax* of the Greenbrier family. Some lichens also contain gelatin. Powdered gelatin can be dusted over an open wound to stop the hemorrhaging.

Bibliography

Books listed with a "•" were utilized as public domain sources of line art printed in the first five editions of *Botany in a Day*. This sixth edition features additional line art as well as a great many color illustrations, also from public domain sources. The artwork was accessed primarily through **www.plantillustrations.org** and **www.delta-intkey.com**. These illustrations were painstakingly edited, rearranged, and labeled by the author for *Botany in a Day* and subject to copyright. Additional illustrations were drawn by the author and also subject to copyright.

I am extremely grateful for the work of all the talented artists who did these illustrations in the 1700s, 1800s, and early 1900s, and I am glad to resurrect their work in this book. I am also grateful for the monumental work of the people who scanned old books and journals and made these works available to the public. If you are looking for quality artwork for your projects, please go to the above sources and download the original, high-quality scans.

_____. "*Hot Stuff: Chili pepper can ease lingering pain after surgery.*" Bozeman Daily Chronicle. May 21, 1996. Pg. 13.

• _____. Text-Book of Western Botany. Ivison, Blakeman & Co.: New York. 1885.

Amrion, Inc. "*Grape Seed Extract.*" Promotional Pamphlet. 1995.

• Andrews, E. F. A Practical Course in Botany. American Book Company. New York. 1911.

Angier, Bradford. Survival with Style. Stackpole Books: Harrisburg, PA. 1972.

Angier, Bradford. Living off the Country. Stackpole Books: Harrisburg, PA. 1956, 1971.

Angier, Bradford. Field Guide to Medicinal Wild Plants. Stackpole Books: Harrisburg, PA. 1978.

Asch, John. The Story of Plants. G. P. Putnam's Sons: USA 1948.

• Bailey, L. H. Standard Cyclopedia of Horticulture. Macmillan Co: New York. Vol. I, 1900, 1914. Vol. 2, 1900, 1914.

Bastin, Harold. Plants Without Flowers. Philosophical Library, Inc.: New York. 1955.

Baumgardt, John Philip. How to Identify Flowering Plant Families. Timber Press: Portland, OR. 1982, 1994.

Bell, Peter R. Green Plants: Their Origin and Diversity. Dioscorides Press: Portland, OR. 1992.

Benson, Lyman. Plant Classification, 2nd Edition. D.C. Heath & Co.: Lexington, MA. 1957, 1979.

Bigfoot, Peter. Useful Wild Western Plants. Reevis Mountain School: Roosevelt, AZ.

• Booth, W. E. & J. C. Wright. Flora of Montana—Part II. Montana State University: Bozeman, MT. 1959, 1962, 1966.

• Britton, Nathaniel Lord, Ph.D. & Hon. Addison Brown. An Illustrated Flora of the Northern United States, Canada, and the British Possessions. Charles Scribner's Sons: New York. Volume I, 1896. Volume II, 1897. Volume III, 1898.

Brown, Annora. Old Man's Garden. J. M. Dent & Sons (Canada) Limited: Toronto. 1954.

Brown, Tom Jr. Tom Brown's Guide to Wild Edible and Medicinal Plants. Berkeley Books. New York. 1985.

Campbell, Douglas H. The Evolution of the Land Plants. Stanford University Press: Stanford University, CA. 1940.

Cobb, B., Lowe, C., & Farnsworth, E. Ferns: Of Northeastern and Central North America, 2nd Edition. Houghton Mifflin Harcourt. 2005.

Corner, E. J. H. The Life of Plants. University of Chicago Press: Chicago. 1964.

Cook, Frank. Personal correspondence. November 2003.

Coon, Nelson. Using Plants for Healing. Hearthside Press: New York. 1963.

• Coulter, John M., A.M. Ph.D. Plant Relations. D. Appleton & Co. New York. 1899.

• Coulter, John M., A.M. Ph.D. A Text-Book of Botany. D. Appleton & Co: New York. 1910.

• Coulter, John M., A.M. Ph.D., Charles R. Barnes Ph.D., Henry C. Cowles Ph.D. A Textbook of Botany, Volume II: Ecology. American Book Company. New York. 1911.

Couplan, Francois Ph.D. The Encyclopedia of Edible Plant of North America. Keats Publishing: New Canaan, CT. 1998.

Craighead, John J., Frank C. Craighead, & Ray J. Davis. A Field Guide to Rocky Mountain Wildflowers. Houghton Mifflin Co: Boston. 1963.

Crellin, John K. and Jane Philpott. Herbal Medicine Past and Present: A Reference Guide to Medicinal Plants. Duke University Press: Durham and London. 1989.

Culpeper, Nicholas. Culpeper's Complete Herbal. W. Foulsham & Co., Ltd.: London.

Cummings, Elsie, J. & Wavie J. Charlton. Survival: Pioneer, Indian and Wilderness Lore. Self-published. Missoula, Montana. 1971, 1972.

• Dana, Mrs. William Starr. How to Know the Wild Flowers. Charles Scribner's Sons. New York. 1909.

• Dayton, William A. Important Western Browse Plants. USDA Handbook No. 101. July 1931.

Densmore, Frances. How Indians Use Wild Plants for Food, Medicine, & Crafts. Dover Publications, Inc.: New York. 1974.

Dorn, Robert L. Vascular Plants of Montana. Mountain West Publishing: Cheyenne, WY. 1984.

Duke, James A. Handbook of Edible Weeds. CRC Press: Boca Raton. 1992.

Duncan, Ursula K., M.A. A Guide to the Study of Lichens. Scholar's Library: Gracie Station, NY. 1959

Elpel, Thomas J. Participating in Nature: Wilderness Survival and Primitive Living Skills, 6th Edition. HOPS Press: Pony, MT. 2009.

Emboden, William A. Jr. Narcotic Plants. The Macmillan Company: New York. 1972.

Fern, Ken. Plants for a Future Database. http://www.axis-net.com/pfaf/plants.html. Jan.-Feb. 1997.

Fukuoka, Masanobu. The Natural Way of Farming. Japan Publications, Inc.: New York. 1985 and 1986.

Geller, Cascade Anderson. *"Pharmacognosy Basics: Predominate Constituent Groups in Common Plant Families"*, 1995 Gaia Symposium Proceedings—Naturopathic Herbal Wisdom. Gaia Herbal Research Institute: Harvard, MA. 1995.

Gibbons, Euell. Stalking the Wild Asparagus. David McKay Company, Inc.: New York. 1962-1973.

Gillaspy, James, Ph.D. *"Purslane: A Personal Perspective."* Bulletin of Primitive Technology. Vol. 1. No. 7. Spring 1994. Pgs. 54-55.

Gilmore, Melvin R. Uses of Plants by the Indians of the Missouri River Region. University of Nebraska Press: Lincoln & London. 1991.

Glimn-Lacy, Janice and Peter B. Kaufman. Botany Illustrated: Introduction to Plants, Major Groups, Flowering Plant Families. Van Nostrand Reinhold Company: New York. 1984.

Green, James. The Herbal Medicine-Maker's Handbook. Simplers Botanical Co.: Forestville, CA. 1990.

Hale, Mason E. How to Know the Lichens. Wm. C. Brown Co. Publishers: Dubuque, IA. 1969, 1979.

Hall, Alan. The Wild Food Trailguide. Holt, Rinehart, & Winston: New York. 1973, 1976.

Hart, Jeff. Montana: Native Plants and Early Peoples. Montana Historical Society Press: Helena, MT. 1976, 1992.

Harrington, H. D. Edible Native Plants of the Rocky Mountains. University of New Mexico Press: Albuquerque, NM. 1967.

• Hayes, Doris W. and George A. Garrison. Key to Important Woody Plants of Eastern Oregon and Washington. Agriculture Handbook No. 148. USDA. December 1960.

Healthy Cell News. *"Flaxseed As Food and Medicine."* Healthy Cell News. Spring/Summer 1997. Page 1.

Healthy Cell News. *"Oil-Protein Combination."* Healthy Cell News. Spring/Summer 1997. Page 2.

Heywood, V. H., Brummitt, R. K., Culham, A., & Seberg, O. Flowering Plant Families of the World (Revised). Firefly Books: Buffalo, NY; Richmond Hill, Ont.: . 2007.

Hobbs, Christopher. Foundations of Health. Botanica Press: Capitola, CA. 1992.

Holmes, Sandra. Outline of Plant Classification. Longman Group Ltd.: New York. 1983.

Hutchins, Alma R. Indian Herbology of North America. Shambala Press: Boston. 1973.

Jaeger, Ellsworth. Wildwood Wisdom.

Judd, W. S., Campbell, C. S., Kellog, E. A., Stevens, P. F., & Donahue, M. J. Plant Systematics: A Phylogenetic Approach (Third Edition). Sunderland, MA: Sinauer Associates. 2008.

Kadans, Joseph M., N.D. Ph.D. Modern Encyclopedia of Herbs. Parker Publishing Company, Inc.: West Nyack, NY. 1970.

Kallas, John. Edible Wild Plants: From Dirt to Plate. Gibbs Smith. Layton, UT. 2010

Kallas, John. *"Amaranth—Staple Food Source for Modern Foragers."* The Wild Food Adventurer. Vol. 3, No. 2. July 1, 1998.

Kallas, John. *"Bull Thistle."* The Wild Food Adventurer. Vol. 2, No. 4. November 15, 1997.

Kallas, John. *"Edible Blue Camas—Preparation Old & New."* The Wild Food Adventurer. Vol. 3, No. 2. July 1, 1998.

Kallas, John. *"Groundnut—Pearls on a String."* The Wild Food Adventurer. Vol. 5, No. 2. June 15, 2000.

Kallas, John. *"Infant—Nitrate Caution."* The Wild Food Adventurer. Vol. 6, No. 1. April 1, 2001.

Kallas, John. *"Oregon Grape: Not for the Faint of Taste."* The Wild Food Adventurer. Vol. 2, No. 2. June 15, 1997.

Kallas, John. *"Oxalates Schmokulates."* The Wild Food Adventurer. Vol. 6, No. 3. August 28, 2001.

Kallas, John. *"Tawny Day Lily—Unpredictably Tainted Fare."* The Wild Food Adventurer. Vol. 5, No. 2. June15, 2000.

Kallas, John. *"Wapato, Indian Potato."* The Wild Food Adventurer. Volume 1, No 4. Dec. 10, 1996.

Kallas, John. *"Wild Spinach: Delicious, Nutritious and Abundant"* The Wild Food Adventurer. Vol. 1, No 2. June 30, 1996.

Kinucan, Edith S. and Penny R. Brons. Wild Wildflowers of the West. Kinucan & Brons: Ketchum, ID. 1979.

Kirk, Donald R. Wild Edible Plants of the Western United States. Naturegraph Publishers: Healdsburg, CA. 1970.

• Kirtikar, K. R. and B. D. Basu. Indian Medicinal Plants. India. 1918.

Klein, Robyn. "The Mountain Herbalist" Montana Pioneer. Livingston, Montana. Articles 1992-1994.

Klein, Robyn. *"The Simple Wort... and the Rest of the Story."* Community Food News: Bozeman, MT. Summer 2000. Page 18.

Kloss, Jethro. Back to Eden. Woodbridge Press Publishing Co.: Santa Barbara, CA. 1981-1983. Kloss 1939.

Krakauer, Jon. Into the Wild. Anchor Books (Doubleday): New York. 1996.

Kramer, Miriam Darnall and John Goude. Dining on the Wilds. Videos. JEG Development. Yucaipa, CA.

Lincoff, Gary. The Joy of Foraging. Quarry Books: Beverly, MA. 2012.

Lust, John, N.D., D.B.M. The Herb Book. Bantam Books: New York. 1974, 1983.

Mabey, Richard. Plantcraft: A guide to the everyday use of wild plants. Universe Books: New York. 1977.

• Mathews, F. Schuyler. Familiar Trees and Their Leaves. D. Appleton & Co.: New York. 1898.

• Mathews, F. Schuyler. The Book of Wildflowers for Young People. Knickerbocker Press. G.P. Putnam's Sons. New York. 1923.

McMenamin, Mark A. and Dianna L. S. Hypersea: Life on Land. Columbia University Press: New York. 1994.

Merwood, Anne. *"Plants of the Apes."* Wildlife Conservation. March-April 1991. Pgs.54-59.

Moerman, Dan. American Indian Ethnobotany Database. http://www.umd.umich.edu/cgi-bin/herb. Jan-Feb. 1997.

Moore, Michael. Medicinal Plants of the Mountain West. Museum of New Mexico Press: Sante Fe, NM. 1979.

Moore, Michael. Medicinal Plants of the Desert and Canyon West. Museum of New Mexico Press: Santa Fe, NM. 1989.

Moore, Michael. Medicinal Plants of the Pacific West. Red Crane Books: Sante Fe, NM. 1993.

Morton, Julia F. *"Cattails (Typha spp.) – Weed Problem or Potential Crop."* Economic Botany. Vol. 29. January - March, 1975. Pages 7-29.

Murphey, Edith Van Allen. Indian Uses of Native Plants. Mendocino County Historical Society: Ukiah, CA. 1959, 1987.

Nyerges, Christopher. *"Plants Which Stun Fish."* Wilderness Way. Vol. 3, Issue 4. 1997. Pgs. 49-54.

Olsen, Larry Dean. Outdoor Survival Skills. Brigham Young University: Provo, UT. 1967, 1972.

Orr, Robert T. and Margaret C. Wildflowers of Western America. Galahad Books: New York. 1974, 1981.

• Pammel, L. H., Ph.D. A Manual of Poisonous Plants. The Torch Press: Cedar Rapids, Iowa. 1911.

• Parsons, Mary Elizabeth. Illustrated by Margaret Warriner Buck. The Wildflowers of California. Philopolis Press. San Francisco. 1921.

Pendell, Dale. Pharmako/poeia: Plant Powers, Poisons, and Herbcraft. Mercury House: San Francisco. 1995.

Phillips, Wayne. "*Poisonous and Medicinal Plants.*" (class hand-out.) HOPS Primitive Fair. 1995.

Platt, Rutherford. Our Flowering World. Dodd, Mead & Co.: New York. 1947.

Platt, Rutherford. This Green World. Dodd, Mead & Co.: New York. 1942, 1988.

Raven, P.H., Evert, R.F., & Eichorn, S.E. Biology of Plants (Seventh Edition). W.H. Freeman: New York. 2004.

Rothschild, Michael. Bionomics. John Macrae / Henry Holt and Company: New York, NY. 1990.

Rogers, Robert D., AHG. Sundew Moonwort: Medicinal Plants of the Prairies. Volumes I, II, III. Jan 1997.

Schauenberg, Paul. Guide to Medicinal Plants. Keats Publishing, Inc.: New Canaan, CT. 1990.

Sheff, Elaine. "Nature's First Aid Kit." Community Food News. Bozeman, MT. Sept/October 1997. Pg. 4.

Smith, James Payne, Jr. Vascular Plant Families. Mad River Press, Inc.: Eureka, CA. 1977.

Spears, P. A Tour of the Flowering Plants. Missouri Botanical Garden Press: St. Louis, MO. 2006.

Spellenberg, Richard. The Audubon Society Field Guide to North American Wildflowers. Alfred A. Knopf: New York. 1979.

Storl, Wolf D. Healing Lyme Disease Naturally. North Atlantic Books: Berkeley, CA. 2010.

Sturtevant, Dr. E. Lewis. Sturtevant's Edible Plants of the World. Dover Publications: New York. 1972.

Sweet, Muriel. Common Edible and Useful Plants of the West. Naturegraph Publishers: Happy Camp, CA. 1976.

Thoreau, Henry David. Faith in a Seed. Island Press / Shearwater Books: Washington, D. C. & Covelo, CA. 1993.

Thayer, Sam. Nature's Garden. Forager's Harvest: Ogema, WI. 2010.

Thayer, Sam. "*Nettles: The Good, The Better, and the Ouch.*" The Forager. Vol. 2, No. 1. Spring 2002. Pages 9-11.

Thayer, Sam. The Forager's Harvest. Forager's Harvest: Ogema, WI. 2006.

Tilford, Gregory L. The EcoHerbalist's Fieldbook. Mountain Weed Publishing: Conner, Montana. 1993.

Tilford, Gregory L. Edible and Medicinal Plants of the West. Mountain Press Publishing Co.: Missoula, MT. 1997.

Tompkins, Peter & Christopher Bird. The Secret Life of Plants. Harper & Row, Publishers: New York. 1973.

Tull, Delena. Edible and Useful Plants of Texas and the Southwest: A Practical Guide. University of Texas Press: Austin, Texas. 1999.

Turner, Nancy J. Plant Technology of First Peoples in British Columbia. UBC Press: Vancouver. 1998, 2000.

Tyler, Varro E., Ph.D. The Honest Herbal. 3rd Ed. Pharmaceutical Products Press (Haworth Press): NY. 1993.

Uphof, J. C. TH. Dictionary of Economic Plants. H. R. Engelmann: New York. 1959.

Treben, Maria. Maria Treben Herbs. http://mariatrebenherbs.com. Accessed April 9, 2013.

Venning, Frank. Wildflowers of North America. Golden Press, Western Publishing Co.: New York. 1984.

Verrill, A. Hyatt. Wonder Plants and Plant Wonders. D. Appleton-Century Company: New York. 1939.

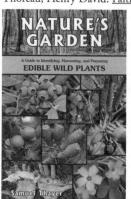

Vitt, Dale H., Janet E. Marsh, and Robin B. Bovey. Mosses, Lichens, & Ferns of Northwest North America. Lone Pine Publishing: Edmonton, Alberta. 1988.

Vogel, Virgil J. American Indian Medicine. University of Oklahoma Press: Norman, OK. 1970.

Weiner, Michael. Earth Medicine-Earth Food. Fawcett Columbine: New York. 1972, 1980.

Willard, Terry, Ph.D. Edible and Medicinal Plants of the Rocky Mountains and Neighboring Territories. Wild Rose College of Natural Healing, Ltd.: Calgary, Alberta. 1992.

Williams, Kim. Eating Wild Plants. Mountain Press Publishing Co.: Missoula, MT. 1977.

Williams, Marc. Personal correspondence. Winter 2012 - 2013. http://www.botanyeveryday.com.

Wilson, Jacque. "Highs and lows of using marijuana." CNN News. http://www.cnn.com/2012/11/07/health/marijuana-research-roundup/index.html. Accessed November 7, 2012.

Wohlberg, Beth. "*Barberry bush beats bacteria.*" High Country News. July 31, 2000. Pg. 8.

Yeo, R. R. "*Life History of Common Cattail.*" WEEDS. Vol 12, No. 4. October 1964.

Zimmer, Carl. "*Hypersea Invasion.*" Discover. October 1995. Pgs. 76-87.

Zomlefer, Wendy B. Guide to Flowering Plant Families. University of North Carolina Press: Chapel Hill, NC. 1994.

A

Abies 46
Abronia 122
Abutilon 105
Acacia 80
Acalypha 77
Acanthus 156
Acer 103
Achillea 169
Achlys 58
Achnatherum 208
Achyranthes 117
Achyronychia 114
Aconitum 56
Acorus 182
Acourtia 167
Acrostichum 44
Actaea 55, 56
Adenocaulon 167
Adenophyllum 170
Adiantum 44
Adlumia 61
Adonis 56, 216
Adoxa 176
Aeonium 64
Aesculus 102, 216
Agalinis 154
Agastache 158
Agave 199
Agoseris 164
Agrimonia 92
Agropyron 208
Agrostemma 114
Agrostis 208
Alcea 105
Alchemilla 92
Aldrovanda 116
Alisma 183
Allenrolfea 119
Allionia 122
Allium 196, 214
Allotropa 137
Alnus 101
Alocasia 184
Aloe 200, 216
Alophia 201
Alternanthera 117
Alyssum 110
Amaranthus 117
Ambrosia 172
Amelanchier 95
Amerorchis 202
Amianthium 22, 194
Ammannia 69
Amorpha 83
Ampelopsis 67
Amphicarpaea 85
Amsinckia 142
Amsonia 140
Anacardium 104
Anagallis 130
Anaphalis 168
Anchusa 142
Andromeda 134
Androsace 130
Aneilema 190
Anemone 56
Anethum 179
Angelica 180
Anisocoma 164

Anoda 105
Antennaria 168
Anthemis 169
Anthriscus 179
Anthurium 184
Antiaris 88
Anticlea 22, 194
Antirrhinum 152
Aphananthe 87
Apios 85
Apium 179
Aplectrum 202
Apocynum 140
Aquilegia 55, 56
Arabidopsis 110
Arabis 110
Arachniodes 45
Aralia 178
Arbutus 134
Arceuthobium 112
Arctium 166
Arctostaphylos 134
Arenaria 114
Argemone 60
Argentina 92
Argyrochosma 44
Arisaema 184
Aristolochia 51
Armoracia 109
Arnica 171
Aronia 95
Artemisia 163, 169, 221
Artocarpus 88
Arum 184
Aruncus 93
Asarum 51
Asclepias 141
Ascyrum 74
Asparagus 197
Asperugo 142
Aspidotis 44
Asplenium 45
Aster 174
Astilbe 66
Astragalus 79, 83
Astrolepis 44
Astronium 104
Athyrium 45
Atrichoseris 164
Atriplex 118
Atropa 146
Avena 207
Averrhoa 73
Axyris 118
Ayenia 107
Azolla 42

B

Baccharis 174
Bacopa 152
Baldellia 183
Balsamorhiza 171
Baptisia 82
Barbarea 110
Bartonia 139
Bassia 119
Beckmannia 208
Bejaria 133
Belamcanda 201
Bellis 174

Berberis 58
Berchemia 96
Berteroa 110
Berula 180
Besseya 152
Beta 118
Betula 101
Bidens 173
Biovularia 153
Bloomeria 197
Blutaparon 117
Blyxa 186
Boehmeria 90
Boerhavia 122
Boisduvalia 70
Borago 142
Boschniakia 154
Botrychium 40
Bouchea 160
Bouchetia 146
Bougainvillea 122
Boykinia 66
Brasenia 50
Brassica 109, 110
Brevoortia 197
Brickellia 167
Brodiaea 197
Bromus 208
Brosimum 88
Broussonetia 88
Browallia 146
Bryonia 98
Buckleya 112
Buddleja 150
Bupleurum 180
Butomus 182

C

Cabomba 50
Caesalpinia 81
Calandrinia 120
Calibrachoa 146
Calla 184
Calliandra 80
Callicarpa 160
Callirhoe 105
Callisia 190
Callitriche 152
Calluna 133
Calocedrus 48
Calochortus 192
Calopogon 202
Caltha 56
Calycoseris 164
Calydorea 201
Calylophus 70
Calypso 202
Calystegia 145
Camassia 192, 199, 214
Camelina 110
Camissonia 70
Campanula 161
Campyloneurum 43
Cannabis 89
Capraria 152
Capsella 110
Capsicum 146
Caragana 83
Carapichea 219
Cardamine 110

Cardaria 110
Cardionema 114
Carduus 166
Carex 206
Carlowrightia 156
Carnegiea 123
Carpenteria 125
Carpinus 101
Carum 179, 180
Carya 99
Cassia 81, 216
Cassiope 132
Castanea 100
Castilleja 154
Catharanthus 140
Caulophyllum 58
Ceanothus 96, 216
Celosia 117
Celtis 87, 89
Centaurea 166
Centaurium 139
Cephalanthus 138
Cerastium 114
Ceratiola 133
Ceratophyllum 54
Ceratopteris 44
Cercidium 81
Cercis 81
Cercocarpus 93
Cereus 123
Cevallia 126
Chaenactis 172
Chaetadelpha 164
Chamaebatia 93
Chamaebatiaria 93
Chamaecrista 81
Chamaecyparis 48
Chamaedaphne 134
Chamaerhodes 92
Chamaesaracha 148
Chamerion 70
Chaptalia 167
Cheilanthes 44
Chelidonium 60
Chelone 152
Chenopodium 118
Chimaphila 136
Chionanthus 149
Chlorogalum 199
Chlorophora 88
Chorispora 110
Chrysanthemum 169
Chrysolepis 100
Chrysopsis 174
Chrysosplenium 66
Chrysothamnus 174
Cicer 85
Cichorium 164
Cicuta 179, 180
Cimicifuga 56
Cinnamomum 53
Circaea 70
Cirsium 166
Cissus 67
Cistanthe 120
Citharexylum 160
Citrullus 98
Clarkia 70
Claviceps 207
Claytonia 120

Clematis 56
Cleome 108
Cleomella 108
Clerodendrum 160
Clintonia 192
Cocos 189
Codiaeum 77
Coffea 138
Colchicum 195
Coleus 157
Collinsia 152
Collomia 128
Colubrina 96
Comandra 112
Comarostaphylis 134
Commelina 190
Condalia 96
Conium 179, 180
Conopholis 154
Conringia 110
Convallaria 198, 216
Convolvulus 145
Coptis 56, 219
Corallorhiza 202
Cordylanthus 154
Corema 133
Coreopsis 173
Coriandrum 179
Corispermum 119
Cornus 124
Coronilla 82
Corydalis 61
Corylus 101
Coryphantha 123
Cosmos 173
Cotinus 104
Cotoneaster 95
Cotyledon 64
Cudrania 88
Coussapoa 88
Cowania 93
Crassula 64
Crataegus 95
Crepis 164
Cressa 145
Crinum 196
Crocus 201
Crookea 74
Crotalaria 82
Croton 77
Cryptantha 142
Cryptogramma 44
Ctenitis 45
Cucumis 98
Cucurbita 98
Cuminum 179
Cuphea 69
Cupressus 48
Cuscuta 145, 216
Cyclamen 130, 216
Cycloloma 119
Cydonia 95
Cymbopogon 209
Cymopterus 180
Cynanchum 141
Cynoglossum 142
Cyperus 206
Cypripedium 202
Cyrtomium 45
Cystopteris 45
Cytisus 82

D

Dalea 83
Damasonium 183
Darlingtonia 129
Darmera 66
Dasylirion 198
Datura 146, 148, 219
Daucus 179, 180
Decodon 69
Decumaria 125
Delphinium 55, 56
Dendrocnide 90
Dennstaedtia 43
Deparia 45
Deschampsia 209
Descurainia 110
Desmanthus 80
Desmodium 82
Deutzia 125
Diamorpha 64
Dianthus 114
Dicentra 61
Dichondra 145
Dicliptera 156
Dieffenbachia 184
Digitalis 152, 216
Digitaria 209
Dionaea 116
Diphasiastrum 38
Diphylleia 58
Diplazium 45
Dipsacus 175
Disporum 195
Dodecatheon 130
Dorstenia 88
Douglasia 130
Downingia 161
Draba 110
Dracocephalum 158
Draperia 144
Drosera 116
Drosophyllum 116
Dryas 93
Drymaria 114
Dryopteris 45
Dudleya 64
Duranta 160
Dyschoriste 156

E

Echeveria 64
Echinacea 172, 212
Echinocereus 123
Echinochloa 207, 209
Echinocystis 98
Echinodorus 183
Egeria 186
Eichhornia 191
Elaeagnus 97
Eleocharis 206
Elephantopus 167
Eleusine 207
Elliottia 133
Ellisia 144
Elodea 186
Elymus 208, 209
Elytrigia 208
Emmenanthe 144
Empetrum 133
Enemion 56

Ephedra 49
Epifagus 154
Epigaea 133
Epilobium 70
Epipactis 202
Equisetum 41
Eriastrum 128
Erica 133
Erigeron 174
Eriobotrya 95
Eriodictyon 144
Eriogonum 113
Eriophorum 206
Eriophyllum 173
Eritrichium 142
Erodium 68
Eruca 110
Erysimum 110
Erythrina 85
Erythronium 192
Erythroxylum 219
Eschscholzia 60
Eucalyptus 221
Eucnide 126
Eucrypta 144
Eupatorium 167
Euphorbia 77
Euphrasia 154
Eustoma 139
Evolvulus 145

F

Fagonia 72
Fagopyrum 113
Fagus 100
Fallugia 92
Fatoua 88
Fendlera 125
Fendlerella 125
Ferocactus 123
Festuca 209
Filago 168
Foeniculum 179, 221
Forestiera 149
Forsythia 149
Fothergilla 62
Fragaria 92
Franseria 172
Frasera 139
Fraxinus 149
Freesia 201
Fremontodendron 107
Fritillaria 192
Froelichia 117
Fuchsia 70
Fumaria 61

G

Gaillardia 173
Galactia 85
Galanthus 196
Galeopsis 158
Galinsoga 172
Galium 138
Gambelia 152
Gaultheria 134
Gaura 70
Gaylussacia 134
Gayophytum 70
Genista 82

Genlisea 153
Gentiana 139
Gentianella 139
Geocarpon 114
Geocaulon 112
Geranium 68
Gerbera 167
Geum 92
Gilia 128
Gillenia 93
Glabraria 53
Gladiolus 201
Glaucium 60
Glaux 130
Glechoma 158
Gleditsia 81
Glyceria 209
Glycine 85
Glycyrrhiza 83
Glyptopleura 164
Gnaphalium 168
Gomphrena 117
Gonolobus 141
Goodyera 202
Gossypianthus 117
Gossypium 105
Gouania 96
Graptopetalum 64
Gratiola 152, 216
Grayia 119
Grindelia 174
Grossularia 65
Guaiacum 72
Guilleminea 117
Gutierrezia 174
Gymnocarpium 45
Gymnocladus 81
Gypsophila 114

H

Habenaria 202
Hackelia 142
Halenia 139
Halogeton 119
Halophila 186
Hamamelis 62
Haplophyton 140
Hedeoma 157, 158
Hedera 178
Hedysarum 79, 82
Heimia 69
Helenium 173
Heliamphora 129
Helianthus 163, 172, 214
Heliotropium 142
Helleborus 216
Hemerocallis 200
Hemiptelea 87
Hemitomes 137
Hepatica 56
Heracleum 180
Herissantia 106
Hesperaloe 199
Hesperis 110
Hesperocallis 199
Hesperochiron 144
Hesperocnide 90
Hesperolinon 78
Hesperoyucca 199
Heteranthera 191
Heterocodon 161

Heuchera 66
Hexastylis 51
Hibiscus 106
Hieracium 164
Hierochloe 209
Hippophae 97
Hippuris 152
Holodiscus 93
Holosteum 114
Hordeum 207, 209
Horkelia 92
Horsfordia 106
Hottonia 130
Houstonia 138
Howellia 161
Hoya 141
Hulsea 173
Humulus 89
Hunzikeria 148
Hybanthus 75
Hydrangea 125
Hydrastis 56, 219
Hydrilla 186
Hydrocera 127
Hydrocharis 186
Hydrophyllum 144
Hygrophila 156
Hylotelephium 64
Hymenopappus 173
Hymenoxys 173
Hyoscyamus 146, 148
Hyosyamus 219
Hypericum 74, 216
Hypolepis 43
Hyssopus 158, 221

I

Iliamna 106
Impatiens 127
Inula 168
Ipomoea 145
Ipomopsis 128
Iresine 117
Iris 201
Isatis 110
Isoetes 39
Isomeris 108
Itea 125
Iva 172
Ixia 201

J

Jacquemontia 145
Jaltomata 148
Jamesia 125
Jasione 161
Jasminum 149, 221
Jeffersonia 58
Juglans 99
Juncus 205
Juniperus 48
Jussiaea 70
Justicia 156

K

Kalanchoe 64
Kallstroemia 72
Kalmia 133
Kalmiopsis 133

Keckiella 152
Kelseya 92
Knautia 175
Krascheninnikovia 118
Krugiodendron 96

L

Lactuca 164
Lagerstroemia 69
Lamium 158
Landoltia 184
Langloisia 128
Lantana 160
Laportea 90
Lapsana 164
Larix 46
Larrea 72
Lathyrus 85
Laurentia 161
Laurus 53
Lavandula 157
Lavatera 106
Lawsonia 69
Ledum 133
Leiophyllum 133
Lemmonia 144
Lemna 184
Lenophyllum 64
Lens 85
Leonurus 158
Lepidium 110
Leptarrhena 66
Leptopteris 42
Leptosiphon 128
Lesquerella 110
Leucaena 80
Leucanthemum 169
Leucocrinum 199
Leucojum 196
Lewisia 120
Liatris 167
Libocedrus 48
Ligusticum 180
Ligustrum 149
Lilaea 187
Lilium 192
Limnobium 186
Limnophila 152
Limosella 150
Linanthus 128
Linaria 152
Lindera 53
Linnaea 176
Linum 78
Liparis 202
Liparophyllum 162
Lippia 160
Liquidambar 62
Liriodendron 52
Lithocarpus 100
Lithophragma 66
Lithospermum 142
Littorella 150
Lloydia 192
Lobelia 161
Lobularia 110
Loiseleuria 133
Lolium 207
Lomariopsis 45
Lomatium 180
Lomatogonium 139

Lonicera 176
Lopezia 70
Lophophora 123, 219
Lophotocarpus 183
Lotus 84
Ludwigia 70
Luetkea 92
Luffa 98
Lupinus 82
Luzula 205
Lychnis 114, 216
Lycium 148
Lycopodiella 38
Lycopodium 38
Lycopus 158
Lycoris 196
Lygodesmia 164
Lyonia 134
Lyonothamnus 93
Lysichiton 184
Lysiloma 80
Lysimachia 130
Lythrum 69

M

Maclura 88
Macrosiphonia 140
Madia 172
Magnolia 52
Mahonia 58
Maianthemum 198
Maidenia 186
Malacothrix 164
Malosma 104
Malus 95
Malva 106
Malvastrum 106
Mandevilla 140
Mandragora 146
Manfreda 199
Mangifera 104
Manihot 77
Marah 98
Margaranthus 148
Marrubium 157, 158
Matelea 141
Matricaria 169
Matteuccia 45
Medeola 192
Medicago 84
Melampyrum 154
Melanthium 194
Melilotus 84, 216
Melochia 107
Melothria 98
Menodora 149
Mentha 157, 158,
    213, 221
Mentzelia 126
Menyanthes 162
Menziesia 133
Merremia 145
Mertensia 142
Metopium 104
Michelia 52
Microgramma 43
Microseris 164
Microsteris 128
Mimosa 80
Mimulus 150

Minuartia 114
Mirabilis 122
Misanteca 53
Mitchella 138
Mitella 66
Modiola 106
Mohavea 152
Moldavica 158
Monarda 158
Monardella 157, 158
Moneses 136
Monnina 86
Monochoria 191
Monolepis 119
Monotropa 137
Monotropsis 137
Monsonia 68
Montia 120
Moraea 201
Morus 88
Muilla 197
Murdannia 190
Musanga 88
Myosotis 142
Myosurus 56
Myriophyllum 63

N

Najas 186
Nama 144
Nandina 58
Napaea 106
Narcissus 196
Nasturtium 109, 110
Navarretia 128
Nectandra 53
Nectouxia 148
Nelumbo 50
Nemastylis 201
Nemophila 144
Neomarica 201
Neottia 202
Nepeta 158
Nephrolepis 45
Nephrophyllidium
    139, 162
Nerium 140
Nestronia 112
Neurodium 43
Nicandra 148
Nicolletia 170
Nicotiana 148
Nolina 198
Nothochelone 152
Notholaena 44
Nothoscordum 196
Nuphar 50
Nuttallanthus 152
Nymphaea 50, 216
Nymphoides 139, 162
Nyssa 124

O

Obolaria 139
Ocimum 157
Ocotea 53
Odontosoria 43
Oemleria 94
Oenothera 70
Olea 149

Olsynium 201
Onobrychis 82
Onoclea 45
Onopordum 166
Ophioglossum 40
Oplopanax 178
Opuntia 123
Origanum 157
Ornithostaphylos 134
Orobanche 154
Orogenia 180
Orontium 184
Orthilia 136
Orthocarpus 154
Oryctes 148
Oryza 207
Oryzopsis 208, 209
Osmanthus 149
Osmaronia 94
Osmorhiza 180
Osmunda 42
Osmundastrum 42
Ostrya 101
Ottelia 186
Oxalis 73
Oxydendrum 134
Oxyria 113
Oxystylis 108
Oxytropis 83

P

Paeonia 63
Panax 178
Panicum 207, 209
Papaver 60
Parietaria 90
Parkinsonia 81
Parnassia 66
Paronychia 114
Parthenocissus 67
Pastinaca 180
Pecluma 43
Pectis 170
Pedicularis 154
Pediocactus 123
Peganum 72
Pelargonium 68
Pellaea 44
Peltandra 184
Pennisetum 207
Penstemon 152
Perideridia 180
Persea 53
Petalonyx 126
Petalostemon 83
Petasites 170
Petrophyton 93
Petroselinum 179
Petunia 146, 148
Phacelia 144
Phalaris 209
Phanerophlebia 45
Phaseolus 85
Phemeranthus 120
Philadelphus 125
Philodendron 184
Phlebodium 184
Phlegmariurus 38
Phleum 209
Phlox 128

Phoenix 189
Pholistoma 144
Phoradendron 112
Photinia 95
Phragmites 209
Phryma 150
Phyla 160
Phyllodoce 133
Physalis 146, 148
Physaria 110
Physocarpus 93
Picea 46
Pieris 134
Pilea 90
Pimpinella 179
Pinguicula 153
Pinus 46
Pistacia 104
Pistia 184
Pisum 85
Pityopus 137
Pityrogramma 44
Planera 87
Plantago 15, 150
Platycarya 99
Plectritis 175
Pleopeltis 43
Pleuricospora 137
Poa 209
Podophyllum 58
Pogonia 202
Polanisia 108
Polemonium 128
Pollia 190
Polygala 86
Polygonatum 198
Polygonum 113
Polypodium 43
Polypompholyx 153
Polystichum 45
Pontederia 191
Populus 76
Porophyllum 170
Porterella 161
Portulaca 120
Potamogeton 188
Potentilla 92
Prenanthella 164
Prenanthes 164
Primula 130
Priva 160
Prosartes 192
Proserpinaca 63
Prosopis 80
Prunella 158
Prunus 94
Pseudolycopodiella 38
Pseudophoenix 189
Pseudostellaria 114
Pseudotsuga 46
Psoralea 83
Pteridium 43
Pteris 44
Pterocarya 99
Pteroceltis 87
Pterospora 137
Puccinellia 209
Pueraria 85
Pulsatilla 56
Punica 69

Purshia 93
Pyracantha 95
Pyrola 136
Pyrularia 112
Pyrus 95

Q

Quercus 100
Quincula 148

R

Rafinesquia 164
Ranunculus 17, 56
Raphanus 109
Ratibida 172
Reynosia 96
Rhamnus 96, 216
Rhapidophyllum 189
Rheum 113, 216
Rhinanthus 154
Rhodiola 64
Rhododendron 133
Rhus 104
Rhynchosia 85
Ribes 65
Ricinus 77
Robinia 83
Romanzoffia 144
Romulea 201
Rorippa 110
Rosa 3, 92
Rosmarinus 157
Rotala 69
Rubus 92
Rudbeckia 172
Ruellia 156
Rumex 113

S

Sabal 189
Sabbatia 139
Saccharum 207
Sageretia 96
Sagina 114
Sagittaria 17, 183
Saintpaulia 75
Salicornia 119
Salix 76
Salsola 119
Salvia 157, 158
Salvinia 42
Sambucus 176
Samolus 130
Sanguinaria 60
Sanguisorba 92
Sanicula 180
Sapindus 102
Saponaria 114, 216
Sarcobatus 118, 119
Sarcodes 137
Sarcostemma 141
Sarracenia 129
Sassafras 53
Satureja 157
Saxifraga 66
Scabiosa 175
Schefflera 178
Scheuchzeria 187
Schinus 104

Schoenolirion 199
Scirpus 206
Scleranthus 114
Sclerolinon 78
Scoliopus 192
Scoparia 152
Scrophularia 150
Scutellaria 158
Sebastiana 77
Secale 207
Sechium 98
Sedum 64
Selaginella 39
Sempervivum 64
Senecio 170
Senna 81
Sequoia 48
Sequoiadendron 48
Serenoa 189
Setaria 207, 209
Shepherdia 97
Sibbaldia 92
Sidalcea 106
Silene 114
Silybum 166
Sisymbrium 110
Sisyrinchium 201
Sium 180
Smilacina 198
Smilax 195, 222
Solanum 146, 148
Solidago 174
Sonchus 164
Sorbus 95
Sorghum 207, 209
Sparganium 204
Spartium 82
Specularia 161
Spergula 114
Spergularia 114
Sphaeralcea 106
Sphagnum 8
Spinacia 118
Spiraea 93
Spiranthes 202
Spirodela 184
Spondias 104
Sporobolus 209
Stachys 158
Stachytarpheta 160
Stanleya 110
Steironema 130
Stellaria 114
Stenandrium 156
Stenanthium 22, 194
Stenosiphon 70
Stephanomeria 164
Stokesia 167
Streptopus 192
Strophostyles 85
Stuckenia 188
Stylisma 145
Suaeda 119
Suckleya 119
Swertia 139
Symphoricarpos 176
Symphoricarpus 216
Symphytum 142
Symplocarpus 184
Synthyris 152
Syringa 149

T

Tagetes 170
Talinopsis 120
Talinum 120
Tamarindus 81
Tanacetum 169, 221
Taraxacum 164
Taxodium 48
Taxus 49
Tectaria 45
Telesonix 66
Tetramerium 156
Teucrium 157
Thalassia 186
Thalictrum 56
Thelesperma 173
Theobroma 107, 219
Thermopsis 82
Thesium 112
Thlaspi 110
Thrinax 189
Thuja 48, 221
Thymus 157
Tiarella 66
Tidestromia 117
Tigridia 201
Tilia 107
Tinantia 190
Tipularia 202
Todea 42
Tofieldia 194
Torilis 180
Torreya 49
Townsendia 174
Toxicodendron 104
Toxicoscordion 22
Trapa 69
Trachelospermum 140
Tradescantia 190
Tragopogon 164
Trautvetteria 56
Treculia 88
Tribulus 72
Tricardia 144
Trientalis 130
Trifolium 84
Triglochin 187
Trigonella 84
Trillium 194
Trimezia 201
Triodanis 161
Triosteum 176
Triphora 202
Triphysaria 154
Tripleurospermum 169
Triteleia 197
Triticum 207
Trixis 167
Trollius 56
Tsuga 46
Tulipa 192
Turbina 145
Turricula 144
Tussilago 170
Typha 204

U

Ulex 82
Ulmus 87

Umbellularia 53
Urera 90
Urtica 90
Utricularia 153
Uvularia 195

V

Vaccaria 114
Vaccinium 2, 134
Valeriana 175
Valerianella 175
Vallisneria 186
Vancouveria 58
Vanilla 202
Vauquelinia 93
Veratrum 194
Verbascum 150
Verbena 160
Vernonia 167
Veronica 152
Veronicastrum 152
Viburnum 176
Vicia 85
Vigna 85
Viguiera 172
Villarsia 162
Vinca 140
Viola 75
Viscum 112
Vitex 160
Vitis 67
Vittaria 44

W

Waltheria 107
Washingtonia 189
Whipplea 125
Wislizenia 108
Wolffia 184
Wolfiella 184
Wyethia 172

X

Xanthium 172
Xanthorhiza 56
Xerophyllum 194
Xylococcus 134

Y

Yeatesia 156
Yucca 199, 216

Z

Zannichellia 188
Zauschneria 70
Zea 207
Zelkova 87
Zephyranthes 196
Zigadenus 22, 194
Zingiber 178
Zizania 209
Zizia 180
Ziziphus 96
Zygocactus 123
Zygophyllum 72

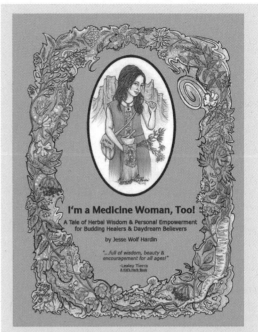

A

acacia 80
acanthus 156
Adam and Eve 202
adder's tongue 40
adderstongue (lily) 192
African rue 72
African violet 75
agave 199
agrimony 92
alder 101
alfalfa 84
algae 8
algerita 58
alkali grass 209
alkaliweed 145
Allegheny vine 61
alligatorweed 117
almond 94
aloe 200
alpine forget-me-not 142
alpinegold 173
alpine lily 192
alumroot 66
alyssum 110
amaranth 117
amaryllis 196
American hornbeam 101
American mistletoe 112
amole 199
andromeda 134
anemone 56
angelica 180
anise 179
anoda 105
Apache plume 92
apple 95
apple of Peru 148
apricot 94
arbor-vitae 48
Arizona poppy 72
Arizona rosewood 93
arnica 171
arrow arum 184
arrowgrass 187
arrowhead 17, 183
arrowleaf balsamroot 171
arroyo fameflower 120
artichoke 163, 166
arum 184
ash 149
asparagus 197
aspen 76
asphodel 194
aster 174
astilbe 66
Aunt Lucy 144
autumn olive 97
avens 92
avocado 53
ayenia 107
azalea 133

B

baby blue eyes 144
baby's breath 114
babystars 128
bachelor's buttons 166
Baja birdbush 134
bald cypress 48

ball cactus 123
baneberry 56
barberry 58
barley 207, 209
barnyard grass 209
barrel cactus 123
Bartram's ixia 201
basil 157
basswood 107
bastard toadflax 112
bay laurel 53
bay tree 53
bean 15, 85
bean caper 72
bearberry 134
bear breeches 156
beargrass 194
bedstraw 138
bee balm 158
beeblossom 70
beech 100
beechdrops 154
beehive cactus 123
beeplant 108
beggarstick 142, 173
belladonna 146
bell pepper 146
bellwort 195
bentgrass 208
bergamot 158
betony 158
bilberry 134
bindweed 145
birch 101
bird-of-paradise tree 81
bird's beak 154
bird's foot trefoil 84
birthroot 194
birthwort 51
biscuitroot 180
bistort 113
bitterbrush 93
bittercress 110
bitternut 99
bitterroot 120
bittersweet 148
blackberry 92
blackberry lily 201
black cohosh 56
black-eyed peas 85
black haw 176
black locust 83
black medic 84
bladder fern 45
bladdermallow 106
bladderpod 110
bladderwort 153
blanket flower 173
blazing star 126, 167
bleeding heart 61
bloodleaf 117
bloodroot 60
blue beech 101
bluebell 142
blueberry 2, 134
blueberry climber 67
blue buttons 175
blue camas 199, 214
blue cohosh 58
blue dicks 197
blue-eyed grass 201

blue-eyed Mary 152
bluegrass 209
blue star 140
bluets 138
bogmat 184
bog orchid 202
bog rosemary 134
boneset 167
borage 142, 219
bouchea 160
bouncing bet 114
box elder 103
boxthorn 148
bracken fern 43
bractspike 156
brake fern 44
bramble fern 43
breadfruit 88
breadroot 83
bride's feathers 93
brightwhite 164
bristlegrass 209
bristlemallow 106
broccoli 109
brodiaea 197
bromegrass 208
brookfoam 66
brooklime 152
brookweed 130
broom 82
broom crowberry 133
broomrape 154
brown-eyed Susan 173
brown lily 192
Brussel sprouts 109
bryony 98
buckbean 162
buckbrush 96, 216
buckeye 102
buckthorn 96, 216
buckwheat 113
buffaloberry 97
buffalobur 148
buffalo nut 112
bugbane 56
bugleweed 158
bugseed 119
bulrush 206
bunchberry 124
bunchflower 194
bundleflower 80
burdock 166
burhead 183
burnet 92
bur-reed 204
bush anenome 125
bush violet 146
butterbur 170
buttercup 12, 17, 56
butterfly bush 150
butternut 99
butterwort 153
button bush 138
buzzy lizzy 127

C

cabbage 109
cacao 107
cactus 123
calicoflower 161
California bay tree 53

California bee plant 150
California bladderpod 108
California nutmeg 49
California pitcher plant 129
California poppy 60
camphor tree 53
campion 114
Canada mayflower 198
canaigre 113
canary grass 209
cancer root 154
candystick 137
canker root 56
canola 109
cantaloupe 98
caragana 83
caraway 179, 180
cardinal flower 161
carnation 114
carrion flower 195
carrot 179, 180
carveseed 164
cascara sagrada 96
cashew 104
castor bean 77
Catalina ironwood 93
catchweed 142
catnip 158
catstongue 160
cattail 204
cauliflower 109
cayenne 146
ceanothus 96
celandine 60
celery 179
celestial lily 201
centaury 139
chaff flower 117
chamomile 169
chaparral 72
chayote 98
cheat grass 208
checkermallow 106
cheeseweed 106
cherry 94, 215
cherry palm 189
chervil 179
chestnut 100
chia 158
chick pea 85
chickweed 114
chicory 164, 218
chili pepper 146
chinchweed 170
Chinese lantern 148
chinquapin 100
chives 196
chocolate 107
chokeberry 95
Christmasberry 95
Christmas cactus 123
chrysanthemum 169
chufa 206
cigar flower 69
cilantro 179
cinnamon 53
cinnamon fern 42
cinquefoil 92
clammy weed 108
clarkia 70

clearweed 90
cleavers 138
clematis 56
cliff brake 44
cliffbush 125
cliff fern 45
climbing dogbane 140
cloak fern 44
clover 84
clubmoss 9, 38
clustervine 145
coastal stonecrop 64
cobra lily 129
cocklebur 172
cockroach plant 140
cockscomb 117
coconut 189
coffee bean tree 81
coltsfoot 170
columbine 56
comfrey 142, 219
common reed 209
coneflower 172
coneplant 137
copper bush 133
copper leaf 77
coralbean 85
coral root 202
coriander 179
cork oak 100
corkscrew plant 153
corn 15, 207
corncockle 114
cornelian cherry 124
cornflower 166
cornsalad 175
corydalis 61
cosmos 173
cota 173
cotoneaster 95
cotton 105
cotton flower 117
cotton grass 206
cottonrose 168
cotton thistle 166
cottonwood 76
cow cockle 114
cow parsnip 180, 218
cow peas 85
cowwheat 154
coyote mint 157, 158
crabgrass 209
crabweed 88
cranberry 134
cranefly 202
creasy greens 110
creeping cucumber 98
creeping water parsnip 180
creosote bush 72
crepe myrtle 69
crested wheatgrass 208
crossflower 110
croton 77
crowberry 133
crown-of-thorns 77
crown vetch 82
cucumber 98
cudweed 168
Culver's root 152
cumin 179
cupflower 148

currant 65
cycad 10
cypress 48

D

daffodil 196
daisy 169, 174
damasonium 183
dandelion 12, 164, 214, 218
date palm 189
day flower 190
day lily 200
dead nettle 158
death camas 194
deathcamas 22
deercabbage 162
deer's foot 58
deer's tongue 139
delphinium 56
desert dandelion 164
desert lily 199
desertpeony 167
desert savior 64
desert snapdragon 152
desert sweet 93
devil's club 178
devilwood 149
dewdrops 160
dill 179
dock 113
dodder 145
dogbane 140
dog-tooth violet 192
dogweed 170
dogwood 124
dong quai 180
Douglas fir 46
draperia 144
dropseed 209
dryad 93
drymary 114
duck lettuce 186
duckmeat 184
duckweed 184
Dudleya 64
dusty maiden 172
Dutchman's breeches 61
Dutchman's pipe 51
dwarf flax 78
dwarf gentian 139
dwarf mistletoe 112
dyer's woad 110

E

eggplant 146, 148
elderberry 176
elecampane 168
elephant head 154
elephant's foot 167
elf orpine 64
elm 87
enchanter's nightshade 70
endive 163, 164
epazote 118
ergot fungus 207
European bay laurel 53
evening primrose 70
everlasting 168
eyebright 154

F

fagonbushes 72
fairy bells 192, 195
fairy duster 80
fairy slipper 202
false alyssum 110
false bindweed 145
false bugbane 56
false cloak fern 44
false dandelion 164
false day flower 190
false dragonhead 158
false flax 110
false foxglove 154
false garlic 196
false hellebore 194
false holly 148
false horsemint 158
false huckleberry 133
false indigo 83
false lily-of-the-valley 198
false mallow 106
false miterwort 66
false nettle 90
false pennyroyal 158
false pickerelweed 191
false ragweed 172
false rue anemone 56
false solomon seal 198
false spirea 66
false spleenwort 45
false toadflax 112
false twayblade 202
false yucca 199
fameflower 120
fanwort 50
fawn lily 192
featherbells 194
featherfoil 130
felwort 139
fendlerbush 125
fennel 179, 221
fenugreek 84
fern 9
fescue 209
fetterbush 134
feverwort 176
fiddleleaf 144
fiddleneck 142
fiddlewood 160
field chickweed 114
fiestaflower 144
figwort 150
filbert 101
fir 46
fire-cracker flower 197
fireweed 70
firmoss 38
five eyes 148
flame flower 120
flannelbush 107
flatsedge 206
flax 78
fleabane daisy 174
floating heart 162
flowering ferns 42
flowering quillwort 187
flowering rush 182
fly poison 194
flyweed 133

fogfruit 160
foldwing 156
forget-me-not 142
forsythia 149
fournwort 156
four o'clock 122
foxglove 152, 216
foxtail 209
fringed fern 45
fringetree 149
frogbit 186
fumitory 61
fuzzybean 85

G

garbanzo bean 85
garden pea 85
garlic 196, 218
gayfeather 167
gentian 139
geranium 68
germander 157
German madwort 142
giant hyssop 158
giant pigweed 172
giant sequoia 48
gilia 128
ginger 51, 178
ginkgo 10
ginseng 178
glacier lily 192
glademallow 106
glasswort 119
globe amaranth 117
globe flower 56
globemallow 106
goatsbeard 164
goatweed 152
goji berry 148
goldenaster 174
golden club 184
goldeneye 172
golden pea 82
golden polypody 43
goldenrod 174
goldenseal 56
golden stars 197
gold fern 44
gold thread 56
gooseberry 65
goosefoot 118
gorse 82
grape 67
grape fern 40
grass of Parnassus 66
grasspink 202
grass widow 201
gravel ghost 164
greenbrier 195
greenbright 152
greenthread 173
green violet 75
gromwell 142
ground cherry 148
groundcone 154
ground ivy 158
ground nut 85
ground plum 83
groundsel 170, 219
ground smoke 70

grouse whortleberry 2
gumweed 174

H

hackberry 87, 89
hairgrass 209
Halberd fern 45
harebell 161
hare's ear mustard 110
hawksbeard 164
hawkweed 164
hawthorn 95
hay-scented fern 43
hazelnut 101
heartleaf wild ginger 51
heath 133
heather 133
hedgehog cactus 123
hedge hyssop 152, 216
hedge nettle 158
hedge parsley 180
heliotrope 142, 144
helleborine 202
hemlock 179
hemlock tree 46
hemp 89
hempnettle 158
henbane 148
henbit 158
henna tree 69
hesperochiron 144
hibiscus 106
hickory 99
hideseed 144
highbush cranberry 176
hog peanut 85
hog plum 104
hole-in-the-sand plant 170
holly fern 45
hollyhock 105
honeydew 98
honey locust 81
honeysuckle 176
honeysweet 117
hop-hornbeam 101
hop sage 119
hopniss 85
hops vine 89
horehound 157, 158
hornbeam 101
horned pondweed 188
hornpoppy 60
hornwort 8, 54
horse chestnut 102, 216
horsemint 158
horseradish 109, 218
horsetail 9, 41
houndstongue 142, 219
huckleberry 2, 134
husk tomato 148
hydrangea 125
hyssop 158

I

incense cedar 48
Indian breadroot 216
Indian cucumber 192
Indian mallow 105
Indian paintbrush 154
Indian physic 93

Indian pink 114
Indian pipe 137
Indian plum 94
Indian potato 180
Indian rhubarb 66
indigo bush 83
insideout flower 58
iodine bush 119
iris 201
ironweed 167
ironwood 101
ivy 178

J

jackfruit 88
Jack-in-the-pulpit 184
Jacob's ladder 128
jade plant 64
jagged chickweed 114
jalapeno 146
jasmine 149, 221
Jerusalem artichoke 172, 214
jewelweed 127
Jimsonweed 148
Joe Pye weed 167
Johnson grass 209
joint fir 49
joint grass 41
Joshua tree 199
Judas tree 81
juniper 48

K

kale 109
kalmiopsis 133
keckiella 152
kelseya 92
Kentucky coffee bean 81
kinnikinnick 134
kittentail 152
knapweed 166
knotgrass 114
knotweed 113
kochia 119
kohlrabi 109
kudzu vine 85

L

Labrador tea 133
lace fern 44, 45
ladies' tresses 202
lady fern 45
lady slipper 202
lady's mantle 92
lamb's quarters 118
lancewood 53
langloisia 128
lantana 160
larch 46
larkspur 56
laurel 133
laurel sumac 104
lavender 157
lead plant 83
lead tree 80
leather fern 44
leatherleaf 134
leatherpetal 64
leechbush 112

leeks 196
lemonade berry 104
lemon grass 209
lentil 85
leopard lily 192
leptarrhena 66
lesser water plantain 183
lettuce 163, 164
lichens 8
licorice weed 152
lignonberry 134
lignum vitae 72
lilac 149
lily 192
lily-of-the-valley 198, 216
linanthus 128
linden 107
lip fern 44
lippia 160
little rose 92
liveforever 64
liverleaf 56
liverwort 8
lobelia 161
locoweed 79, 83
locust tree 83
loosestrife 69, 130
lopseed 150
loquat 95
lotus 50
lousewort 154
lovage 180
lupine 82

M

madrone 134
magnolia 12, 52
ma huang 49
maidenhair 44
mallow 106
mango 104
mannagrass 209
man of the earth 145
manroot 98
manzanita 134
maple 103
marble berry 190
mare's tail 152
marigold 170
marijuana 89
mariposa lily 192
marjoram 157
marsh dewflower 190
marsh felwort 139
marshmallow 105
marsh marigold 56
marshweed 152
matweed 117
mayapple 58
mayweed 169
meadow rue 56
meadowsweet 93
menodora 149
mermaid weed 63
mesquite 80
Mexican jumping bean 77
milkpea 85
milk thistle 166
milk vetch 83
milkweed 141
milkwort 86

millet 207, 209
miner's candle 142
miner's lettuce 120
mint 157, 158
mission manzanita 134
mistletoe 112
mist maiden 144
miterwort 66
mock orange 125
mombin 104
monkey flower 150
monkshood 56
moonwort 40
Mormon tea 49
morning glory 145
moschatel 176
mosquito fern 42
moss 8
moss campion 114
moss rose 120
motherwort 158
mountain ash 95
mountain avens 93
mountain balm 144
mountain heath 133
mountain mahogany 93
mountain misery 93
mountain sorrel 113
mouse ear 164
mouse-ear cress 110
mousetail 56
mud plantain 191
mudwort 150
muilla 197
mulberry 88
mule's ears 172
mullein 150
mums 169
musclewood 101
muskmelon 98
mustard 109, 110, 218

N

nailwort 114
nannyberry 176
Navajo tea 173
nectarine 94
needle grass 208
needle palm 189
netvein hollyfern 45
nightshade 148
ninebark 93
nipplewort 164
nodding caps 202
nutmeg 49

O

oak 100
oak fern 45
oats 207
okra 105
oleander 140
oleaster 97
one-flowered wintergreen
    136
onion 196, 214, 215
onyxflower 114
orache 118
orchid 202
Oregon grape 58

Oregon myrtle 53
oryctes 148
osage orange 88
osha 180
osoberry 94
ostrich fern 45
owl clover 154
oxeye daisy 169

P

painted tongue 146
palm 189
palmetto 189
palo verde 81
pansy 75
paper mulberry 88
parsley 179
parsnip 179, 180
partridge berry 138
partridge foot 92
pasque flower 56
peach 94
pear 95, 215
pearlflower 161
pearlwort 114
pearly everlasting 168
pecan 99
pellitory 90
pennycress 110
pennyroyal 158, 213
penstemon 152
peony 63
peppermint 157, 158
pepperweed 110
pequin 146
periwinkle 140
Peruvian pepper tree 104
petunia 146, 148
peyote 123
phacelia 144
pheasant's eye 56, 216
phlox 128
pickerelweed 191
pickleweed 119
pigmy pipes 137
pigmy weed 64
pignut 99
pigweed 117
pimento 146
pimpernel 130
pincushion flower 175
pincushion plant 128
pine 46
pineapple weed 169
pinedrops 137
pinefoot 137
pinesap 137
pink 114
pink root 92
pipsissewa 136
piratebush 112
pistachio 104
pitcher plant 129
plantain 15, 150
plum 94
plumeseed 164
plums 94
poinsettia 77
pointloco 83
poison hemlock 180
poison ivy 104

poison oak 104
poison sumac 104
poisontree 104
polypody 43
pomegranate 69
pond lily 50
pond spice 53
pondweed 188
ponysfoot 145
poodle-dog bush 144
poplar 76
poppy 60
poppymallow 105
poreleaf 170
porterella 161
potato 146, 148
poverty weed 119
prairie clover 83
prairie coneflower 172
prickly lettuce 164
prickly pear 123
prickly poppy 60
Pride of Rochester 125
primrose 130
primrose-willow 70
prince's pine 136
prince's plume 110
privet 149
propeller flower 201
pumpkin 98
pumpkins 98
puncture vine 72
purple coneflower 172
purslane 120
pussypaws 120
pussytoes 168
pygmyflower 86
pyramidflower 107
pyrola 136

Q

quackgrass 209
Queen Anne's lace 180
queen's cup 192
quillwort 39
quince 95
quinoa 118

R

rabbitbrush 174
radish 109, 218
ragweed 172
ragwort 170
rannoch-rush 187
raspberry 92
rattle box 82
rattlesnake plantain 202
rattlesnakeroot 164
rattleweed 154
red bay 53
redbud 81
red cedar 48
red maids 120
red root 96
red spider lily 196
redstem 69
redtop 208
redwood 48
resurrection fern 43
resurrection plant 39

rhododendron 133
rhubarb 113, 216, 217
ribbon fern 43
rice 207
rice grass 208, 209
rock brake 44
rockcap fern 43
rock cress 110
rocket 110
rocket salad 110
rock jasmine 130
rock mat 93
rock trumpet 140
rose 3, 92
roselings 190
rosemallow 106
rosemary 157
rosewood 93
rotala 69
rubberweed 173
rush 205
Russian olive 97
Russian pigweed 118
Russian thistle 119
rye 207
rye grass 207

S

sacred bamboo 58
saffron 201
sage 157, 158
sagebrush 163, 169
saguaro 123
sainfoin 82
salal 134
salmonberry 92
salsify 164
saltbush 118
saltlover 119
sandcarpet 114
sand heath 133
sand lily 199
sandpaper plant 126
sand spurry 114
sand verbena 122
sandwort 114
sanicle 180
sarsaparilla 195
saskatoon 95
sassafras 53
savine 48
savory 157
saw palmetto 189
saxifrage 66
scalebud 164
scarlet gilia 128
scarlet trumpet 128
scorpionweed 144
Scotch broom 82
Scotch thistle 166
scouring rush 41
screw bean 80
scurf pea 83
seaberry 97
seablush 175
sea-buckthorn 97
sea milkwort 130
seaside petunia 146
sedge 206
seepweed 119
seepwillow 174

sego lily 192
self heal 158
senna 81, 216
sensitive fern 45
sensitive pea 81
serviceberry 95
shaggytuft 156
shamrock 73
sheep's bit 161
shepherd's purse 110
shield fern 45
shoestring fern 44
shooting star 130
shoreweed 150
shrubby yellowcrest 69
shrub verbena 160
sibbaldia 92
silkplant 90
silverberry 97
silverpuffs 164
silverweed 92, 117
skeletonweed 164
skullcap 158
skunk cabbage 184
slender phlox 128
slippery elm 87
sloughgrass 208
smartweed 113
smoketree 104
smotherweed 119
snake cotton 117
snake fern 43
snakeherb 156
snakeroot 86
snakeweed 174
snapdragon 152
sneezeweed 173
snoutbean 85
snowball tree 176
snowberry 176, 216
snowdrop 196
snowflake 196
snow plant 137
soapberry 102
soap plant 199
soapwort 114, 216
soldierweed 172
Solomon's plume 198
Solomon's seal 198
sorrel 113
sorrelvine 67
sotol 198
sourwood 134
sowthistle 164
soybean 85
Spanish broom 82
spearmint 157, 158
spectacle fruit 108
speedwell 152
Sphagnum 8
spice bush 53
spiderling 122
spiderwort 190
spike moss 39
spikenard 178
spike rush 206
spike sedge 206
spiny caper 108
spiraea 93
spleenwort 45
spring beauty 120

springparsley 180
spruce 46
spurge 77
spurred gentian 139
spurry 114
squash 98
staggerbush 134
St. Andrew's cross 74
starflower 130
star fruit 73
starthistle 166
starwort 114
stingbush 126
stinging nettle 90
stinging serpent 126
stinking yew 49
stinkleaf 148
stinkweed 108
stitchwort 114
St. John's wort 74
Stoke's aster 167
stonecrop 64
stoneseed 142
stork's bill 68
St. Peterswort 74
strap fern 43
strawberry 92
stream orchid 202
suckleya 119
sugarbowl 56
sugar cane 207
sumac 104
summer holly 134
sunbonnets 167
suncups 70
sundew 116
sundrops 70
sunflower 163, 172
sunnybell 199
sun tubers 172
swamp bay 53
swamp lily 196
swamp loosestrife 69
swampprivet 149
swampweed 156
sweet cicely 180
sweet clover 84, 216
sweet flag 182
sweetgrass 209
sweetgum 62
sweet pea 85
sweet pinesap 137
sweet potato 145
sweet spire 125
sweetvetch 82
sweet William 114
switch grass 209
sword fern 45
Syrian rue 72
syringa 125

T

tabasco 146
tackstem 164
tamarack 46
tamarind 81
tanbark oak 100
tansy 169
tansy mustard 110
tapioca 77

tarragon 169
tarweed 172
teaberry 2
teasel 175
thatch palm 189
thesium 112
thimbleberry 92
thistle 166
thorn-apple 148
thoroughwort 167
thorowax 180
threefold 167
threehearts 144
thyme 157
tickseed 173
tick trefoil 82
Timothy grass 209
tinytim 114
toadflax 152
tobacco 148
tobacco root 175
tomatillo 146
tomato 146, 148
touch-me-not 127
Townsend's daisies 174
trailing arbutus 133
trailplant 167
transvaal daisy 167
tree mallow 106
trumpet 128
tuberose 199
tulip 192
tulip tree 52
tumble mustard 110
tupelo 124
turkeybeard 194
turkey mullein 77
turnip 109
turtlehead 152
twayblade 202
twinflower 176
twinleaf 58
twinpod 110
twinsorus fern 45
twisted stalk 192

U

uhaloa 107
umbrellaleaf 58
Utah fendlerbush 125

V

valerian 175
vanilla 202
vein fern 45
velvetmallow 106
Venus fly trap 116
Venus' looking glass 161
verbena 160
vervain 160
vetch 83, 85
violet 75
Virginia creeper 67
virgin's bower 56

W

wake robin 194
wallflower 110
walnut 99

wandering jew 190
wapato 183
water arum 184
water cabbage 184
water caltrop 69
water carpet 66
watercress 109, 110
water elm 87
water fern 42, 44
water hemlock
        179, 180, 211
water horehound 158
water howellia 161
water hyacinth 191
waterhyssop 152
waterleaf 144
water lily 50, 216
water meal 184
watermelon 98
water milfoil 63
water nymph 186
water parsnip 180
water plantain 183
water shield 50
water starwort 152
waterweed 186
waterwheel plant 116
waterwillow 156
wedgelet fern 43
western nettle 90
wheat 207
wheat grass 209
whispering bells 144
white cedar 48
white cockle 216
white heather 132
whitetop 110
whitlow grass 110
widelip orchid 202
wild buckwheat 113
wild cucumber 98
wild geranium 68
wild ginger 51
wild gourd 98
wild hollyhock 106
wild hyacinth 197
wild indigo 82
wild licorice 83
wild olive 149
wild petunia 156
wild rice 207, 209
wild rye 209
wild sarsaparilla 178
willow 76, 215
willowherb 70
windmills 122
winged pigweed 119
winterfat 118
wintergreen 134, 136
wirelettuce 164
witchalder 62
witch hazel 62
wolfberry 148
woodbine 67
woodland beardtongue 152
woodland star 66
wood lily 192
wood nettle 90
woodrose 145
woodrush 205
woodsorrel 73

woodvamp 125
woollystar 128
woolly sunflower 173
woollywhite 173
wormwood 169, 221
wormseed 118
wrightwort 156

Y

yampa 180
yarrow 163, 169
yellowbell 192
yellowcress 110
yellowcrest 69
yellowflax 78
yellow pond lily 50
yellowroot 56
yerba de selva 125
yerba santa 144
yew 49
yucca 199, 216

Z

zebrawood 104
zephyrlily 196
zizia 180

Index to Plant Families and Subfamilies by Botanical Names

Plant families (*-aceae*) and subfamilies (*-oideae*) are often reclassified as one or the other, so try either suffix in this index.

A

Acanthaceae 156
Aceraceae 102
Acoraceae 182
Adiantaceae 44
Adoxaceae 176
Agavoideae 199
Alismaceae 183
Alismataceae 183
Allioideae 196
Altingiaceae 62
Amaranthaceae 117
Amaryllidaceae 196
Amygdaloideae 93
Anacardiaceae 104
Apiaceae 179
Apocynaceae 140
Araceae 184
Araliaceae 178
Arbutoideae 134
Arecaceae 189
Aristolochiaceae 51
Asclepiadoideae 141
Asparagaceae 197
Asphodeloideae 200
Aspleniaceae 45
Asteraceae 163
Asteroideae 167
Averrhoaceae 73
Azollaceae 42

B

Balsaminaceae 127
Berberidaceae 58
Betulaceae 101
Boraginaceae 142
Brassicaceae 109
Brodiaeoideae 197
Butomaceae 182

C

Cabombaceae 50
Cactaceae 123
Caesalpinioideae 81
Calochortoideae 192
Campanulaceae 161
Camphorosmoideae 119
Cannabaceae 89
Capparaceae 108
Caprifoliaceae 176
Carduoideae 166
Caryophyllaceae 114

Cassiopoideae 132
Celastraceae 66
Cephalotaxaceae 49
Ceratophyllaceae 54
Chenopodioideae 118
Cichorioideae 164
Cleomaceae 108
Clusiaceae 74
Colchicaceae 195
Commelinaceae 190
Compositae 163
Convallariaceae 198
Convolvulaceae 145
Corispermoideae 119
Cornaceae 124
Coryloideae 101
Crassulaceae 64
Cruciferae 109
Cucurbitaceae 98
Cupressaceae 48
Cuscutaceae 145
Cyperaceae 206

D

Dennstaedtiaceae 43
Dioscoreaceae 145
Dipsacaceae 175
Dracaenaceae 198
Droseraceae 116
Drosophyllaceae 116
Dryadoideae 93
Dryopteridaceae 45

E

Elaeagnaceae 97
Empetraceae 133
Ephedraceae 49
Equisetaceae 41
Ericaceae 132
Ericoideae 133
Eriospermaceae 198
Euphorbiaceae 77

F

Fabaceae 79
Faboideae 82
Fagaceae 100
Flacourtiaceae 76
Fumarioideae 61

G

Gentianaceae 139

Geraniaceae 68
Gesneriaceae 75
Gomphrenoideae 117
Gramineae 207
Grossulariaceae 65
Guttiferae 74

H

Haloragaceae 63
Hamamelidaceae 62
Hemerocallidoideae 200
Hippocastanaceae 102
Hippuridaceae 152
Huperziaceae 38
Hydrangeaceae 125
Hydrocharitaceae 186
Hydrophylloideae 144
Hypericaceae 74

I

Iridaceae 201
Isoetaceae 39

J

Juglandaceae 99
Juncaceae 205
Juncaginaceae 187

L

Labiatae 157
Lamiaceae 157
Lauraceae 53
Leguminosae 79
Lemnoideae 184
Lentibulariaceae 153
Liliaceae 192
Linaceae 78
Loasaceae 126
Lobelioideae 161
Lycopodiaceae 38
Lythraceae 69

M

Magnoliaceae 52
Malvaceae 105
Medeoloideae 192
Melanthiaceae 194
Menyanthaceae 162
Mimosoideae 80
Monotropoideae 137
Montiaceae 120

Moraceae 88
Musaceae 189
Mutisioideae 167

N

Najadoideae 186
Nelumbonaceae 50
Nitrariaceae 72
Nolinoideae 198
Nyctaginaceae 122
Nymphaeaceae 50
Nyssoideae 124

O

Oleaceae 149
Onagraceae 70
Ophioglossaceae 40
Orchidaceae 202
Orobanchaceae 154
Osmundaceae 42
Oxalidaceae 73

P

Paeoniaceae 63
Palmaceae 189
Palmae 189
Papaveraceae 60
Papilionaceae 79
Philadelphaceae 125
Phrymaceae 150
Pinaceae 46
Plantaginaceae 150
Poaceae 207
Podophyllaceae 58
Polemoniaceae 128
Polygalaceae 86
Polygonaceae 113
Polypodiaceae 43
Pontederiaceae 191
Portulacaceae 120
Potamogetonaceae 188
Primulaceae 130
Pteridaceae 44
Pyroloideae 136

R

Ranunculaceae 55
Rhamnaceae 96
Rosaceae 91
Rosoideae 92
Rubiaceae 138
Ruscaceae 198

S

Salicaceae 76
Salicornioideae 119
Salviniaceae 42
Santalaceae 112
Sapindaceae 102
Sarcobataceae 118
Sarraceniaceae 129
Saxifragaceae 66
Scheuchzeriaceae 187
Scrophulariaceae 150
Selaginellaceae 39
Smilacaceae 195
Solanaceae 146
Sparganiaceae 204
Sterculioideae 107
Strelitziaceae 189
Suaedoideae 119

T

Taxaceae 49
Taxodiaceae 48
Tilioideae 107
Tofieldiaceae 194
Typhaceae 204

U

Ulmaceae 87
Umbelliferae 179
Urticaceae 90

V

Vaccinioideae 134
Valerianaceae 175
Verbenaceae 160
Violaceae 75
Viscaceae 112
Vitaceae 67

W

Woodsiaceae 45

X

Xanthorrhoeaceae 200

Z

Zannichelliae 188
Zingiberaceae 51, 178
Zygophyllaceae 72

Highlighted names indicate good **primary** and **secondary** families for beginning botanists.

A

Acanthus 156
Adder's Tongue 40
Adoxa 176
Agave 199
Almond 93
Amaranth 117
Amaryllis 196
Apple 95
Arrowgrass 187
Arrowhead 183
Arum 184
Asparagus 197
Asphodel 200
Aster 163
Autumn Crocus 195

B

Bald Cypress 48
Barberry 58
Basswood 107
Beargrass 198
Beech 100
Beeplant 108
Birch 101
Bird-of-
  Paradise Tree 81
Birthwort 51
Bladderwort 153
Bleeding Heart 61
Blueberry 134
Borage 142
Bracken Fern 43
Brodiaea 197
Broomrape 154
Buckbean 162
Buckthorn 96
Buckwheat 113
Bugseed 119
Bunchflower 194
Bur-reed 204
Buttercup 55

C

Cacao 107
Cactus 123
Caesalpinia 81
Caltrop 72

Camphorosma 119
Cashew 104
Cattail 204
Cedar 48
Chicory 164
Clubmoss 38
Crowberry 133
Cypress 48

D

Dandelion 164
Day Lily 200
Dogbane 140
Dogwood 124
Dryad 93
Duckweed 184
Dutchman's Pipe 51

E

Elm 87
Evening Primrose 70

F

Fanwort 50
Figwort 150
Flax 78
Flowering Rush 182
Four O'Clock 122
Frogbit 186
Fumitory 61

G

Gentian 139
Geranium 68
Ginseng 178
Globe Amaranth 117
Gooseberry 65
Goosefoot 117
Gourd 98
Grape 67
Grapefern 40
Grass 207
Grass Tree 200
Greenbrier 195

H

Harebell 161
Hazelnut 101
Heath 132

Hemp 89
Honeysuckle 176
Horned Pondweed 188
Hornwort 54
Horse Chestnut 102
Horsetail 41
Hydrangea 125

I

Indian Cucumber 192
Indian Pipe 137
Iris 201

L

Laurel 53
Lily 192
Loasa 126
Lobelia 161
Loosestrife 69
Lopseed 150
Lotus 50

M

Madder 138
Madrone 134
Magnolia 52
Maidenhair Fern 44
Mallow 105
Maple 103
Mayapple 58
Milkweed 141
Milkwort 86
Mimosa 80
Miner's Lettuce 120
Mint 157
Mistletoe 112
Mormon Tea 49
Morning Glory 145
Mulberry 88
Mustard 109
Mutisia 167

N

Nightshade 146
Nitre Bush 72

O

Oleaster 97
Olive 149

Onion 196
Orchid 202

P

Palm 189
Parsley 179
Pea 79
Peony 63
Phlox 128
Pickerelweed 191
Pickleweed 119
Pine 46
Pink 114
Pitcher Plant 129
Plantain 150
Plum 94
Polypod 43
Pondweed 188
Poppy 60
Primrose 130
Purslane 120
Pyrola 136

Q

Quillwort 39

R

Rannoch-Rush 187
Rose 91
Royal Fern 42
Rush 205

S

Saint John's Wort 74
Sandalwood 112
Saxifrage 66
Sedge 206
Seepweed 119
Sego 192
Senna 81
Soapberry 102
Sphagnum 8
Spiderwort 190
Spike Moss 39
Spleenwort 45
Spurge 77
Staff Tree 66
Star Fruit 73
Stinging Nettle 90

Stonecrop 64
Sumac 104
Sundew 116
Sunflower 163
Sweet Flag 182

T

Teasel 175
Thistle 166
Touch-Me-Not 127
Tupelo 124

V

Valerian 175
Verbena 160
Violet 75

W

Walnut 99
Water Fern 42
Waterleaf 144
Water Lily 50
Water Milfoil 63
Water Nymph 186
Water Plantain 183
White Heather 132
Willow 76
Witch Hazel 62
Wood Fern 45
Woodsorrel 73

Y

Yew 49

Shanleya's Quest
A Botany Adventure for Kids Ages 9 to 99
By Thomas J. Elpel Illustrated by Gloria Brown

In a world where time is a liquid that falls as rain upon the land, young Shanleya paddles her canoe out to the Tree Islands to learn plant traditions of her people. Each island is home to a separate family of plants and an unforgettable Guardian with lessons to teach about the identification and uses of those plants. *Shanleya's Quest* is a truly unique educational book that presents botanical concepts and plant identification skills in an easy and fun metaphorical format for children, as well as for adults who are young at heart.

Read the book. Play the game!
Both are available from **www.hopspress.com**.

"I own both Shanleya's Quest *and* Botany in a Day *and I can't say enough great things about them. I teach mostly 3rd to 8th graders, and my goal is primarily to help my students establish a relationship with plants. Your materials are incredibly supportive of that, not to mention engaging, effective and fun."*

—Katharine K.
Minneapolis, Minnisota

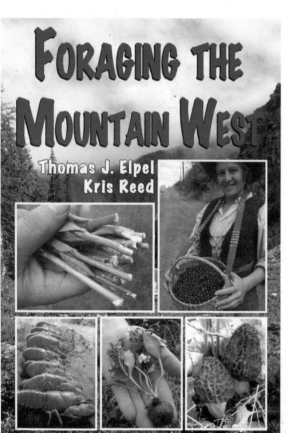

Foraging the Mountain West
Gourmet Edible Plants, Mushrooms, and Meats
By Thomas J. Elpel and Kris Reed

There's food in them thar hills! There is also food in the valleys, meadows, swamps, and all around town, too... maybe even in your own backyard. *Foraging the Mountain West* is a guide to harvesting and celebrating nature's abundance. Reach out and explore the world with your taste buds. Discover new delights you will never find at the store. Connect with nature on a deeper level by meeting, greeting, and eating plants, fungi, and creatures that share your neighborhood. Become a little more self-sufficient, and a lot more aware.

Foraging the Mountain West is a hands-on manual for identifying, harvesting, and preparing real food. It is written for the backpacker who would rather bring more knowledge and fewer provisions into the wilderness. It is intended for the happy homemaker who wants to eat well and spend less. It is ideal for the creative chef who wants to explore new ingredients and impress diners with novel dishes.

The authors brought together years of experience and fun to show you, a prospective forager, what, when, where, why, and how to gather wild and feral plants, mushrooms, and neglected wayside crops. Beyond plants, this is a guide for successful fishing without a pole, hunting without weapons, and even shopping without money. This book will help you fill your freezer and satiate your appetite.

Foraging the Mountain West will help you dream in winter, cleanse in spring, forage in summer, and gorge in fall. The book includes hundreds of vivid color photos detailing every essential aspect of foraging. This guide is not meant to sit on your coffee table. It is meant to start a revolution! **Available Spring 2014 from www.hopspress.com.**